STRONG OPINIONS

Books by Vladimir Nabokov

Ada, a novel

Bend Sinister, a novel

The Defense, a novel

Despair, a novel

Eugene Onegin, by Alexander Pushkin,
    translated from the Russian, with a Commentary

The Eye, a novel

The Gift, a novel

Glory, a novel

Invitation to a Beheading, a novel

King, Queen, Knave, a novel

Laughter in the Dark or Camera Obscura, a novel

Lolita, a novel

Mary, a novel

Nabokov's Dozen, a collection of short stories

Nabokov's Quartet, a collection of short stories

Nikolai Gogol, a critical biography

Pale Fire, a novel

Pnin, a novel

Poems and Problems

The Real Life of Sebastian Knight, a novel

A Russian Beauty and Other Stories, a collection
    of short stories

The Song of Igor's Campaign, Anon.,
    translated from Old Russian

Speak, Memory or Conclusive Evidence, a memoir

Strong Opinions, a collection of articles,
    letters, and interviews

Three Russian Poets, verse translation from the Russian

Transparent Things, a novel

The Waltz Invention, a drama

VLADIMIR NABOKOV

STRONG OPINIONS

McGraw-Hill Book Company

New York • St. Louis • San Francisco • Toronto

Book design by Marcy J. Katz
Art Director: Robert L. Mitchell

1 2 3 4 5 6 7 8 9 B P B P 7 9 8 7 6 5 4 3

Library of Congress Cataloging in Publication Data

Nabokov, Vladimir Vladimirovich, 1899–
    Strong opinions.

    I. Title.
PS3527.A15S7   809   73-6604
ISBN 0-07-045737-9

(Additional copyright notices
appear under Acknowledgments.)

ACKNOWLEDGMENTS

The interview with Alvin Toffler originally appeared in *Playboy* Magazine. Copyright © 1963 by *Playboy*. Reprinted by permission of Playboy Enterprises, Inc.

The interview with Herbert Gold and George A. Plimpton originally appeared in *The Paris Review*. Copyright © 1967 by *The Paris Review*. It is reprinted by permission of The Viking Press, Inc., and will be included in the new fourth volume of *Writers at Work* to be published by The Viking Press, Inc.

Interview with Martin Esslin copyright © 1968 by The New York Times Company. Reprinted by permission.

Interview with Nicholas Garnham copyright © 1968 by Nicholas Garnham. Reprinted by permission.

Interviews with Alden Whitman copyright © 1969, 1971 by The New York Times Company. Reprinted by permission.

Interview with James Mossman copyright © 1969 by James Mossman. Reprinted by permission of John V. Mossman.

The interview with Allene Talmey was first published in *Vogue*. Copyright © 1969 by The Condé Nast Publications Inc. Reprinted by permission.

Interview with Israel Shenker copyright © 1972 by The New York Times Company. Reprinted by permission.

The interview with Simona Morini was first published in *Vogue*. Copyright © 1972 by the Condé Nast Publications Inc. Reprinted by permission.

Interview with Peter Duval-Smith and Christopher Burstall copyright © 1962 by Peter Duval-Smith. Reprinted by permission.

Portions of the interview with Martha Duffy first appeared in *Time*. Reprinted by permission of *Time*, The Weekly Newsmagazine; copyright © 1969 Time Inc.

Interview with Jane Howard copyright © 1964 Time Inc. Reprinted with permission.

to Véra

CONTENTS

FOREWORD

I think like a genius, I write like a distinguished author, and I speak like a child. Throughout my academic ascent in America, from lean lecturer to Full Professor, I have never delivered to my audience one scrap of information not prepared in typescript beforehand and not held under my eyes on the bright-lit lectern. My hemmings and hawings over the telephone cause long-distance callers to switch from their native English to pathetic French. At parties, if I attempt to entertain people with a good story, I have to go back to every other sentence for oral erasures and inserts. Even the dream I describe to my wife across the breakfast table is only a first draft.

In these circumstances nobody should ask me to submit to an interview if by "interview" a chat between two normal human beings is implied. It has been tried at least twice in the old days, and once a recording machine was present, and when the tape was rerun and I had finished laughing, I knew that never in my life would I repeat that sort of performance. Nowadays I take every precaution to ensure a dignified beat of the mandarin's fan. The interviewer's questions have to be sent to me in writing, answered by me in writing, and reproduced verbatim. Such are the three absolute conditions.

But the interviewer wishes to visit me. He wishes to see my pencil poised above the page, my painted lampshade, my bookshelves, my old white borzoi asleep at my feet. He feels he needs the background music of bogus informality, and as many colorful details as can be memorized, if not actually jotted down ("N. gulped down his vodka and quipped with a grin—"). Have I the heart to cancel the cosiness? I have.

A certain excellent lotion for thinning hair is by nature of an unattractive, emulsive tint. Its makers try to correct this by adding some green color—green being meant to suggest, by cosmetological tradition, the freshness of spring, pine-woods, jade, tree frogs, and so forth. The bottle, however, has to be vigorously shaken in order to have its contents viridate; otherwise, in repose, all that shows is an inchwide green border topping the unchanged, genuine, opalescent pillar of liquid. *Not* shaking the bottle before use is with me a matter of principle.

Similarily, in dealing with the results of interviews as they appear on the printed page, I ignore the floating decor and keep only the basic substance. My files contain the results of some forty interviews in several languages. Only some of the American and British ones have been included here. A few of those have had to be skipped because, by a kind of awful alchemy, and not merely by a good shake, my authentic response got so hopelessly mixed with the ar-tificial color of human interest, added by the manufacturer, as to defy separation. In other cases I have had no trouble in leaving out the well-meant little touches (as well as the gaudiest journalistic inventions), thus gradually eliminating every element of spontaneity, all semblance of actual talk. The thing is transmuted finally into a more or less neatly paragraphed essay, and that is the ideal form a written interview should take.

My fiction allows me so seldom the occasion to air my private views that I rather welcome, now and then, the questions put to me in sudden spates by charming, courte-ous, intelligent visitors. In this volume, the question-and-answer section is followed by a few Letters to Editors, which are "self-explanatory," as lawyers put it in their precise way. Finally, there is a batch of essays, all but one of which were written in America or Switzerland.

Swinburne has a shrewd comment on "the rancorous and reptile crew of poeticules who decompose into criticasters." This curious phenomenon was typical of the situation in the small literary world of the Russian emigration in Paris around 1930 when the aesthetics of Bunin, Hodasevich and one or two other outstanding authors underwent particularly nasty attacks from variously "committed" criticules. In those years I methodically derided the detracters of art and enjoyed tremendously the exasperation my writings caused in that clique; but translating today my numerous old essays from my difficult Russian into pedantic English and explaining nice points of former dislocation and strategy is a task of little interest either to me or the reader. The only exception I have allowed myself is the piece on Hodasevich.

In result, the present body of my occasional English prose, shorn of its long Russian shadow, seems to reflect an altogether more agreeable person than the "V. Sirin," evoked with mixed feelings by émigré memoirists, politicians, poets, and mystics, who still remember our skirmishes of the nineteen-thirties in Paris. A milder, easier temper permeates today the expression of my opinions, however strong; and this is as it should be.

Vladimir Nabokov
Montreux, 1973

Interviews

1

On the morning of June 5, 1962, the *Queen Elizabeth* brought my wife and me from Cherbourg to New York for the film première of *Lolita*. On the day of our arrival three or four journalists interviewed me at the St. Regis hotel. I have a little cluster of names jotted down in my pocket diary but am not sure which, if any, refers to that group. The questions and answers were typed from my notes immediately after the interview.

Interviewers do not find you a particularly stimulating person. Why is that so?

I pride myself on being a person with no public appeal. I have never been drunk in my life. I never use schoolboy words of four letters. I have never worked in an office or in a coal mine. I have never belonged to any club or group. No creed or school has had any influence on me whatsoever. Nothing bores me more than political novels and the literature of social intent.

Still there must be things that move you—likes and dislikes.

My loathings are simple: stupidity, oppression, crime, cruelty, soft music. My pleasures are the most intense known to man: writing and butterfly hunting.

[3]

You write everything in longhand, don't you?
   Yes. I cannot type.

Would you agree to show us a sample of your rough drafts?
   I'm afraid I must refuse. Only ambitious nonentities and hearty mediocrities exhibit their rough drafts. It is like passing around samples of one's sputum.

Do you read many new novels? Why do you laugh?
   I laugh because well-meaning publishers keep sending me—with "hope-you-will-like-it-as-much-as-we-do" letters —only one kind of fiction: novels truffled with obscenities, fancy words, and would-be weird incidents. They seem to be all by one and the same writer—who is not even the shadow of my shadow.

What is your opinion of the so-called "anti-novel" in France?
   I am not interested in groups, movements, schools of writing and so forth. I am interested only in the individual artist. This "anti-novel" does not really exist; but there does exist one great French writer, Robbe-Grillet; his work is grotesquely imitated by a number of banal scribblers whom a phony label assists commercially.

I notice you "haw" and "er" a great deal. Is it a sign of approaching senility?
   Not at all. I have always been a wretched speaker. My vocabulary dwells deep in my mind and needs paper to wriggle out into the physical zone. Spontaneous eloquence seems to me a miracle. I have rewritten—often several times—every word I have ever published. My pencils outlast their erasers.

What about TV appearances?
   Well (you always begin with "well" on TV), after one

such appearance in London a couple of years ago I was accused by a naive critic of squirming and avoiding the camera. The interview, of course, had been carefully rehearsed. I had carefully written out all my answers (and most of the questions), and because I am such a helpless speaker, I had my notes (mislaid since) on index cards arranged before me—ambushed behind various innocent props; hence I could neither stare at the camera nor leer at the questioner.

Yet you have lectured extensively——
In 1940, before launching on my academic career in America, I fortunately took the trouble of writing one hundred lectures—about 2,000 pages—on Russian literature, and later another hundred lectures on great novelists from Jane Austen to James Joyce. This kept me happy at Wellesley and Cornell for twenty academic years. Although, at the lectern, I evolved a subtle up and down movement of my eyes, there was never any doubt in the minds of alert students that I was reading, not speaking.

When did you start writing in English?
I was bilingual as a baby (Russian and English) and added French at five years of age. In my early boyhood all the notes I made on the butterflies I collected were in English, with various terms borrowed from that most delightful magazine *The Entomologist.* It published my first paper (on Crimean butterflies) in 1920. The same year I contributed a poem in English to the Trinity Magazine, Cambridge, while I was a student there (1919–1922). After that in Berlin and in Paris I wrote my Russian books— poems, stories, eight novels. They were read by a reasonable percentage of the three million Russian émigrés, and were of course absolutely banned and ignored in Soviet Russia. In the middle thirties I translated for publication in English two of my Russian novels, *Despair* and *Camera*

Obscura (retitled *Laughter in the Dark* in America). The first novel that I wrote directly in English was *The Real Life of Sebastian Knight*, in 1939 in Paris. After moving to America in 1940, I contributed poems and stories to *The Atlantic* and *The New Yorker* and wrote four novels, *Bend Sinister* (1947), *Lolita* (1955), *Pnin* (1957) and *Pale Fire* (1962). I have also published an autobiography, *Speak, Memory* (1951), and several scientific papers on the taxonomy of butterflies.

Would you like to talk about Lolita?
Well, no. I said everything I wanted to say about the book in the Afterword appended to its American and British editions.

Did you find it hard to write the script of Lolita?
The hardest part was taking the plunge—deciding to undertake the task. In 1959 I was invited to Hollywood by Harris and Kubrick, but after several consultations with them I decided I did not want to do it. A year later, in Lugano, I received a telegram from them urging me to reconsider my decision. In the meantime a kind of script had somehow taken shape in my imagination so that actually I was glad they had repeated their offer. I traveled once more to Hollywood and there, under the jacarandas, worked for six months on the thing. Turning one's novel into a movie script is rather like making a series of sketches for a painting that has long ago been finished and framed. I composed new scenes and speeches in an effort to safeguard a *Lolita* acceptable to me. I knew that if I did not write the script somebody else would, and I also knew that at best the end product in such cases is less of a blend than a collision of interpretations. I have not yet seen the picture. It may turn out to be a lovely morning mist as perceived through mosquito netting, or it may turn out to be the swerves of a scenic drive as felt by the horizontal passenger of an

ambulance. From my seven or eight sessions with Kubrick during the writing of the script I derived the impression that he was an artist, and it is on this impression that I base my hopes of seeing a plausible *Lolita* on June 13th in New York.

What are you working at now?

I am reading the proofs of my translation of Pushkin's *Eugene Onegin*, a novel in verse which, with a huge commentary, will be brought out by the Bollingen Foundation in four handsome volumes of more than five hundred pages each.

Could you describe this work?

During my years of teaching literature at Cornell and elsewhere I demanded of my students the passion of science and the patience of poetry. As an artist and scholar I prefer the specific detail to the generalization, images to ideas, obscure facts to clear symbols, and the discovered wild fruit to the synthetic jam.

And so you preserved the fruit?

Yes. My tastes and disgusts have influenced my ten-year-long work on *Eugene Onegin*. In translating its 5500 lines into English I had to decide between rhyme and reason—and I chose reason. My only ambition has been to provide a crib, a pony, an absolutely literal translation of the thing, with copious and pedantic notes whose bulk far exceeds the text of the poem. Only a paraphrase "reads well"; my translation does not; it is honest and clumsy, ponderous and slavishly faithful. I have several notes to every stanza (of which there are more than 400, counting the variants). This commentary contains a discussion of the original melody and a complete explication of the text.

Do you like being interviewed?

Well, the luxury of speaking on one theme—oneself—is a sensation not to be despised. But the result is sometimes puzzling. Recently the Paris paper *Candide* had me spout wild nonsense in an idiotic setting. But I have also often met with considerable fair play. Thus *Esquire* printed all my corrections to the account of an interview that I found full of errors. Gossip writers are harder to keep track of, and they are apt to be very careless. Leonard Lyons made me explain why I let my wife handle motion picture transactions by the absurd and tasteless remark: "Anyone who can handle a butcher can handle a producer."

2

In mid-July, 1962, Peter Duval-Smith and Christopher Burstall came for a BBC television interview to Zermatt where I happened to be collecting that summer. The lepidoptera lived up to the occasion, so did the weather. My visitors and their crew had never paid much attention to those insects and I was touched and flattered by the childish wonderment with which they viewed the crowds of butterflies imbibing moisture on brookside mud at various spots of the mountain trail. Pictures were taken of the swarms that arose at my passage, and other hours of the day were devoted to the reproduction of the interview proper. It eventually appeared on the *Bookstand* program and was published in *The Listener* (November 22, 1962). I have mislaid the cards on which I had written my answers. I suspect that the published text was taken straight from the tape for it teems with inaccuracies. These I have tried to weed out ten years later but was forced to strike out a few sentences here and there when memory refused to restore the sense flawed by defective or improperly mended speech.

The poem I quote (with metrical accents added) will be found translated into English in Chapter Two of *The Gift*, G. P. Putnam's Sons, New York, 1963.

Would you ever go back to Russia?
I will never go back, for the simple reason that all the

Russia I need is always with me: literature, language, and my own Russian childhood. I will never return. I will never surrender. And anyway, the grotesque shadow of a police state will not be dispelled in my lifetime. I don't think they know my works there—oh, perhaps a number of readers exist there in my special secret service, but let us not forget that Russia has grown tremendously provincial during these forty years, apart from the fact that people there are told what to read, what to think. In America I'm happier than in any other country. It is in America that I found my best readers, minds that are closest to mine. I feel intellectually at home in America. It is a second home in the true sense of the word.

You're a professional lepidopterist?
Yes, I'm interested in the classification, variation, evolution, structure, distribution, habits, of lepidoptera: this sounds very grand, but actually I'm an expert in only a very small group of butterflies. I have contributed several works on butterflies to the various scientific journals—but I want to repeat that my interest in butterflies is exclusively scientific.

Is there any connection with your writing?
There is in a general way, because I think that in a work of art there is a kind of merging between the two things, between the precision of poetry and the excitement of pure science.

In your new novel, Pale Fire, *one of the characters says that reality is neither the subject nor the object of real art, which creates its own reality. What is that reality?*
Reality is a very subjective affair. I can only define it as a kind of gradual accumulation of information; and as specialization. If we take a lily, for instance, or any other kind of

natural object, a lily is more real to a naturalist than it is to an ordinary person. But it is still more real to a botanist. And yet another stage of reality is reached with that botanist who is a specialist in lilies. You can get nearer and nearer, so to speak, to reality; but you never get near enough because reality is an infinite succession of steps, levels of perception, false bottoms, and hence unquenchable, unattainable. You can know more and more about one thing but you can never know everything about one thing: it's hopeless. So that we live surrounded by more or less ghostly objects—that machine, there, for instance. It's a complete ghost to me—I don't understand a thing about it and, well, it's a mystery to me, as much of a mystery as it would be to Lord Byron.

You say that reality is an intensely subjective matter, but in your books it seems to me that you seem to take an almost perverse delight in literary deception.

The fake move in a chess problem, the illusion of a solution or the conjuror's magic: I used to be a little conjuror when I was a boy. I loved doing simple tricks—turning water into wine, that kind of thing; but I think I'm in good company because all art is deception and so is nature; all is deception in that good cheat, from the insect that mimics a leaf to the popular enticements of procreation. Do you know how poetry started? I always think that it started when a cave boy came running back to the cave, through the tall grass, shouting as he ran, "Wolf, wolf," and there was no wolf. His baboon-like parents, great sticklers for the truth, gave him a hiding, no doubt, but poetry had been born—the tall story had been born in the tall grass.

You talk about games of deception, like chess and conjuring. Are you, in fact, fond of them yourself?

I am fond of chess but deception in chess, as in art, is only part of the game; it's part of the combination, part of

[11]

the delightful possibilities, illusions, vistas of thought, which can be false vistas, perhaps. I think a good combination should always contain a certain element of deception.

You spoke about conjuring in Russia, as a child, and one remembers that some of the most intense passages in a number of your books are concerned with the memories of your lost childhood. What is the importance of memory to you?

Memory is, really, in itself, a tool, one of the many tools that an artist uses; and some recollections, perhaps intellectual rather than emotional, are very brittle and sometimes apt to lose the flavor of reality when they are immersed by the novelist in his book, when they are given away to characters.

Do you mean that you lose the sense of a memory once you have written it down?

Sometimes, but that only refers to a certain type of intellectual memory. But, for instance—oh, I don't know, the freshness of the flowers being arranged by the under-gardener in the cool drawing-room of our country house, as I was running downstairs with my butterfly net on a summer day half a century ago: that kind of thing is absolutely permanent, immortal, it can never change, no matter how many times I farm it out to my characters, it is always there with me; there's the red sand, the white garden bench, the black fir trees, everything, a permanent possession. I think it is all a matter of love: the more you love a memory, the stronger and stranger it is. I think it's natural that I have a more passionate affection for my old memories, the memories of my childhood, than I have for later ones, so that Cambridge in England or Cambridge in New England is less vivid in my mind and in my self than some kind of nook in the park on our country estate in Russia.

Do you think that such an intense power of memory as yours has inhibited your desire to invent in your books?
No, I don't think so.

The same sort of incident turns up again and again, sometimes in slightly different forms.
That depends on my characters.

Do you still feel Russian, in spite of so many years in America?
I do feel Russian and I think that my Russian works, the various novels and poems and short stories that I have written during these years, are a kind of tribute to Russia. And I might define them as the waves and ripples of the shock caused by the disappearance of the Russia of my childhood. And recently I have paid tribute to her in an English work on Pushkin.

Why are you so passionately concerned with Pushkin?
It started with a translation, a literal translation. I thought it was very difficult and the more difficult it was, the more exciting it seemed. So it's not so much caring about Pushkin—I love him dearly of course, he is the greatest Russian poet, there is no doubt about that—but it was again the combination of the excitement of finding the right way of doing things and a certain approach to reality, to the reality of Pushkin, through my own translations. As a matter of fact I am very much concerned with things Russian and I have just finished revising a good translation of my novel, *The Gift*, which I wrote about thirty years ago. It is the longest, I think the best, and the most nostalgic of my Russian novels. It portrays the adventures, literary and romantic, of a young Russian expatriate in Berlin, in the twenties; but he's not myself. I am very careful to keep my characters beyond the limits of my own identity. Only the background of the novel can be said to

contain some biographical touches. And there is another thing about it that pleases me: probably my favorite Russian poem is one that I happened to give to my main character in that novel.

Written by yourself?
  Which I wrote myself, of course; and now I'm wondering whether I might be able to recite it in Russian. Let me explain it: there are two persons involved, a boy and a girl, standing on a bridge above the reflected sunset, and there are swallows skimming by, and the boy turns to the girl and says to her, "Tell me, will you always remember *that* swallow?—not any kind of swallow, not those swallows, there, but that particular swallow that skimmed by?" And she says, "Of course I will," and they both burst into tears.

Odnázhdy my pód-vecher óba
Stoyáli na stárom mostú.
Skazhí mne, sprosíl ya, do gróba
Zapómnish' von lástochku tú?
I tý otvechála: eshchyó by!

I kák my zaplákali óba,
Kak vskríknula zhízn' na letú!
Do závtra, navéki, do gróba,
Odnázhdy na stárom mostú . . .

What language do you think in?
  I don't think in any language. I think in images. I don't believe that people think in languages. They don't move their lips when they think. It is only a certain type of illiterate person who moves his lips as he reads or ruminates. No, I think in images, and now and then a Russian phrase or an English phrase will form with the foam of the brainwave, but that's about all.

[14]

You started writing in Russian and then you switched to English, didn't you?

Yes, that was a very difficult kind of switch. My private tragedy, which cannot, indeed should not, be anybody's concern, is that I had to abandon my natural language, my natural idiom, my rich, infinitely rich and docile Russian tongue, for a second-rate brand of English.

You have written a shelf of books in English as well as your books in Russian. And of them only Lolita *is well known. Does it annoy you to be the* Lolita *man?*

No, I wouldn't say that, because *Lolita* is a special favorite of mine. It was my most difficult book—the book that treated of a theme which was so distant, so remote, from my own emotional life that it gave me a special pleasure to use my combinational talent to make it real.

Were you surprised at the wild success when it came?

I was surprised that the book was published at all.

Did you, in fact, have any doubts about whether Lolita *ought to be printed, considering its subject matter?*

No; after all, when you write a book you generally envisage its publication, in some far future. But I was pleased that the book was published.

What was the genesis of Lolita?

She was born a long time ago, it must have been in 1939, in Paris; the first little throb of *Lolita* went through me in Paris in '39, or perhaps early in '40, at a time when I was laid up with a fierce attack of intercostal neuralgia which is a very painful complaint—rather like the fabulous stitch in Adam's side. As far as I can recall the first shiver of inspiration was somehow prompted in a rather mysterious way by a newspaper story, I think it was in *Paris Soir*,

[15]

about an ape in the Paris Zoo, who after months of coaxing by scientists produced finally the first drawing ever charcoaled by an animal, and this sketch, reproduced in the paper, showed the bars of the poor creature's cage.

Did Humbert Humbert, the middle-aged seducer, have any original?

No. He's a man I devised, a man with an obsession, and I think many of my characters have sudden obsessions, different kinds of obsessions; but he never existed. He did exist after I had written the book. While I was writing the book, here and there in a newspaper I would read all sorts of accounts about elderly gentlemen who pursued little girls: a kind of interesting coincidence but that's about all.

Did Lolita herself have an original?

No, Lolita didn't have any original. She was born in my own mind. She never existed. As a matter of fact, I don't know little girls very well. When I consider this subject, I don't think I know a single little girl. I've met them socially now and then, but Lolita is a figment of my imagination.

Why did you write Lolita?

It was an interesting thing to do. Why did I write any of my books, after all? For the sake of the pleasure, for the sake of the difficulty. I have no social purpose, no moral message; I've no general ideas to exploit, I just like composing riddles with elegant solutions.

How do you write? What are your methods?

I find now that index cards are really the best kind of paper that I can use for the purpose. I don't write consecutively from the beginning to the next chapter and so on to the end. I just fill in the gaps of the picture, of this jigsaw puzzle which is quite clear in my mind, picking out a piece here and a piece there and filling out part of the sky and part of the landscape and part of the—I don't know, the carousing hunters.

Another aspect of your not entirely usual consciousness is the extraordinary importance you attach to color.

Color. I think I was born a painter—really!—and up to my fourteenth year, perhaps, I used to spend most of the day drawing and painting and I was supposed to become a painter in due time. But I don't think I had any real talent there. However, the sense of color, the love of color, I've had all my life: and also I have this rather freakish gift of seeing letters in color. It's called color hearing. Perhaps one in a thousand has that. But I'm told by psychologists that most children have it, that later they lose that aptitude when they are told by stupid parents that it's all nonsense, an A isn't black, a B isn't brown—now don't be absurd.

What colors are your own initials, VN?

V is a kind of pale, transparent pink: I think it's called, technically, quartz pink: this is one of the closest colors that I can connect with the V. And the N, on the other hand, is a greyish-yellowish oatmeal color. But a funny thing happens: my wife has this gift of seeing letters in color, too, but her colors are completely different. There are, perhaps, two or three letters where we coincide, but otherwise the colors are quite different. It turned out, we discovered one day, that my son, who was a little boy at the time—I think he was ten or eleven—sees letters in colors, too. Quite naturally he would say, "Oh, this isn't that color, this is this color," and so on. Then we asked him to list his colors and we discovered that in one case, one letter which he sees as purple, or perhaps mauve, is pink to me and blue to my wife. This is the letter M. So the combination of pink and blue makes lilac in his case. Which is as if genes were painting in aquarelle.

Whom do you write for? What audience?

I don't think that an artist should bother about his audience. His best audience is the person he sees in his shaving mirror every morning. I think that the audience an artist imagines, when he imagines that kind of a thing, is a room filled with people wearing his own mask.

In your books there is an almost extravagant concern with masks and disguises: almost as if you were trying to hide yourself behind something, as if you'd lost yourself.

Oh, no. I think I'm always there; there's no difficulty about that. Of course there is a certain type of critic who when reviewing a work of fiction keeps dotting all the i's with the author's head. Recently one anonymous clown, writing on *Pale Fire* in a New York book review, mistook all the declarations of my invented commentator in the book for my own. It is also true that some of my more responsible characters are given some of my own ideas. There is John Shade in *Pale Fire*, the poet. He does borrow some of my own opinions. There is one passage in his poem, which is part of the book, where he says something I think I can endorse. He says—let me quote it, if I can remember; yes, I think I can do it: "I loathe such things as jazz, the white-hosed moron torturing a black bull, rayed with red, abstractist bric-a-brac, primitivist folk masks, progressive schools, music in supermarkets, swimming pools, brutes, bores, class-conscious philistines, Freud, Marx, fake thinkers, puffed-up poets, frauds and sharks." That's how it goes.

It is obvious that neither John Shade nor his creator are very clubbable men.

I don't belong to any club or group. I don't fish, cook, dance, endorse books, sign books, co-sign declarations, eat oysters, get drunk, go to church, go to analysts, or take part in demonstrations.

[18]

It sometimes seems to me that in your novels—in Laughter in the Dark *for instance—there is a strain of perversity amounting to cruelty.*

I don't know. Maybe. Some of my characters are, no doubt, pretty beastly, but I really don't care, they are outside my inner self like the mournful monsters of a cathedral façade—demons placed there merely to show that they have been booted out. Actually, I'm a mild old gentleman who loathes cruelty.

3

This exchange with Alvin Toffler appeared in *Playboy* for January, 1964. Great trouble was taken on both sides to achieve the illusion of a spontaneous conversation. Actually, my contribution as printed conforms meticulously to the answers, every word of which I had written in longhand before having them typed for submission to Toffler when he came to Montreux in mid-March, 1963. The present text takes into account the order of my interviewer's questions as well as the fact that a couple of consecutive pages of my typescript were apparently lost in transit. *Egreto perambis doribus!*

With the American publication of Lolita *in 1958, your fame and fortune mushroomed almost overnight from high repute among the literary* cognoscenti—*which you had enjoyed for more than 30 years—to both acclaim and abuse as the world-renowned author of a sensational best seller. In the aftermath of this* cause célèbre, *do you ever regret having written* Lolita?

On the contrary, I shudder retrospectively when I recall that there was a moment, in 1950, and again in 1951, when I was on the point of burning Humbert Humbert's little black diary. No, I shall never regret *Lolita*. She was like the composition of a beautiful puzzle—its composition and its solution at the same time, since one is a mirror view of the other, depending on the way you look. Of course she completely eclipsed my other works—at least those I wrote in English: *The Real Life of Sebastian Knight, Bend Sinister,* my short stories, my book of recollections; but I cannot grudge her this. There is a queer, tender charm about that mythical nymphet.

Though many readers and reviewers would disagree that her charm is tender, few would deny that it is queer—so much so that when director Stanley Kubrick proposed his plan to make a movie of Lolita, *you were quoted as saying, "Of course they'll have to change the plot. Perhaps they will make Lolita a dwarfess. Or they will make her 16 and Humbert 26." Though you finally wrote the screenplay yourself, several reviewers took the film to task for watering down the central relationship. Were you satisfied with the final product?*

I thought the movie was absolutely first-rate. The four main actors deserve the very highest praise. Sue Lyon bringing that breakfast tray or childishly pulling on her sweater in the car—these are moments of unforgettable acting and directing. The killing of Quilty is a masterpiece, and so is the death of Mrs. Haze. I must point out, though, that I had nothing to do with the actual production. If I had, I might have insisted on stressing certain things that were not stressed—for example, the different motels at which they stayed. All I did was write the screenplay, a preponderating portion of which was used by Kubrick. The "watering down," if any, did not come from my aspergillum.

Do you feel that Lolita's *twofold success has affected your life for the better or for the worse?*

I gave up teaching—that's about all in the way of change. Mind you, I loved teaching, I loved Cornell, I loved composing and delivering my lectures on Russian writers and European great books. But around 60, and especially in winter, one begins to find hard the physical process of teaching, the getting up at a fixed hour every other morning, the struggle with the snow in the driveway, the march through long corridors to the classroom, the effort of drawing on the blackboard a map of James Joyce's Dublin or the arrangement of the semi-sleeping car of the St. Petersburg–Moscow express in the early 1870s—without an understanding of which neither *Ulysses* nor *Anna Karenin*, respectively, makes sense. For some reason my most vivid memories concern examinations. Big amphitheater in Goldwin Smith. Exam from 8 A.M. to 10:30. About 150 students—unwashed, unshaven young males and reasonably well-groomed young females. A general sense of tedium and disaster. Half-past eight. Little coughs, the clearing of nervous throats, coming in clusters of sound, rustling of pages. Some of the martyrs plunged in meditation, their arms locked behind their heads. I meet a dull gaze directed at me, seeing in me with hope and hate the source of forbidden knowledge. Girl in glasses comes up to my desk to ask: "Professor Kafka, do you want us to say that . . . ? Or do you want us to answer only the first part of the question?" The great fraternity of C-minus, backbone of the nation, steadily scribbling on. A rustle arising simultaneously, the majority turning a page in their bluebooks, good teamwork. The shaking of a cramped wrist, the failing ink, the deodorant that breaks down. When I catch eyes directed at me, they are forthwith raised to the ceiling in pious meditation. Windowpanes getting misty. Boys peeling off sweaters. Girls chewing gum in rapid cadence. Ten minutes, five, three, time's up.

Citing in Lolita *the same kind of acid-etched scene you've just described, many critics have called the book a masterful satiric social commentary on America. Are they right?*

   Well, I can only repeat that I have neither the intent nor the temperament of a moral or social satirist. Whether or not critics think that in *Lolita* I am ridiculing human folly

[22]

leaves me supremely indifferent. But I am annoyed when the glad news is spread that I am ridiculing America.

But haven't you written yourself that there is "nothing more exhilarating than American Philistine vulgarity"?
No, I did not say that. That phrase has been lifted out of context, and, like a round, deep-sea fish, has burst in the process. If you look up my little after-piece, "On a Book Entitled Lolita," which I appended to the novel, you will see that what I really said was that in regard to Philistine vulgarity—which I do feel is most exhilarating—no difference exists between American and European manners. I go on to say that a proletarian from Chicago can be just as Philistine as an English duke.

Many readers have concluded that the Philistinism you seem to find the most exhilarating is that of America's sexual mores.
Sex as an institution, sex as a general notion, sex as a problem, sex as a platitude—all this is something I find too tedious for words. Let us skip sex.

Have you ever been psychoanalyzed?
Have I been *what?*

Subjected to psychoanalytical examination.
Why, good God?

In order to see how it is done. Some critics have felt that your barbed comments about the fashionability of Freudianism, as practiced by American analysts, suggest a contempt based upon familiarity.
Bookish familiarity only. The ordeal itself is much too silly and disgusting to be contemplated even as a joke. Freudism and all it has tainted with its grotesque implications and methods appears to me to be one of the vilest

[23]

deceits practiced by people on themselves and on others. I reject it utterly, along with a few other medieval items still adored by the ignorant, the conventional, or the very sick.

Speaking of the very sick, you suggested in Lolita *that Humbert Humbert's appetite for nymphets is the result of an unrequited childhood love affair; in* Invitation to a Beheading *you wrote about a 12-year-old girl, Emmie, who is erotically interested in a man twice her age; and in* Bend Sinister *your protagonist dreams that he is "surreptitiously enjoying Mariette (his maid) while she sat, wincing a little, in his lap during the rehearsal of a play in which she was supposed to be his daughter." Some critics, in poring over your works for clues to your personality, have pointed to this recurrent theme as evidence of an unwholesome preoccupation on your part with the subject of sexual attraction between pubescent girls and middle-aged men. Do you feel that there may be some truth in this charge?*

I think it would be more correct to say that had I not written *Lolita*, readers would not have started finding nymphets in my other works and in their own households. I find it very amusing when a friendly, polite person says to me—probably just in order to be friendly and polite—"Mr. Nabórkov," or "Mr. Nabáhkov," or "Mr. Nabkov" or "Mr. Nabóhkov," depending on his linguistic abilities, "I have a little daughter who is a regular Lolita." People tend to underestimate the power of my imagination and my capacity of evolving serial selves in my writings. And then, of course, there is that special type of critic, the ferrety, human-interest fiend, the jolly vulgarian. Someone, for instance, discovered telltale affinities between Humbert's boyhood romance on the Riviera and my own recollections about little Colette, with whom I built damp sand castles in Biarritz when I was ten. Somber Humbert was, of course, thirteen and in the throes of a pretty extravagant sexual excitement, whereas my own romance with Colette had no trace of erotic desire and indeed was perfectly commonplace and normal. And, of course, at nine and ten years of age, in that set, in those times, we knew nothing whatsoever about the false facts of life that are imparted nowadays to infants by progressive parents.

Why false?

Because the imagination of a small child—especially a town child—at once distorts, stylizes, or otherwise alters the bizarre things he is told about the busy bee, which neither he nor his parents can distinguish from a bumblebee, anyway.

What one critic has termed your "almost obsessive attention to the phrasing, rhythm, cadence and connotation of words" is evident even in the selection of names for your own celebrated bee and bumblebee—Lolita and Humbert Humbert. How did they occur to you?

For my nymphet I needed a diminutive with a lyrical lilt to it. One of the most limpid and luminous letters is "L". The suffix "-ita" has a lot of Latin tenderness, and this I required too. Hence: Lolita. However, it should not be pronounced as you and most Americans pronounce it: Low-lee-ta, with a heavy, clammy "L" and a long "o". No, the first syllable should be as in "lollipop", the "L" liquid and delicate, the "lee" not too sharp. Spaniards and Italians pronounce it, of course, with exactly the necessary note of archness and caress. Another consideration was the welcome murmur of its source name, the fountain name: those roses and tears in "Dolores." My little girl's heartrending fate had to be taken into account together with the cuteness and limpidity. Dolores also provided her with another, plainer, more familiar and infantile diminutive: Dolly, which went nicely with the surname "Haze," where Irish mists blend with a German bunny—I mean, a small German hare.

You're making a word-playful reference, of course, to the German term for rabbit—Hase. But what inspired you to dub Lolita's aging inamorato with such engaging redundancy?

That, too, was easy. The double rumble is, I think, very nasty, very suggestive. It is a hateful name for a hateful person. It is also a kingly name, and I did need a royal vibration for Humbert the Fierce and Humbert the Humble. Lends itself also to a number of puns. And the execrable diminutive "Hum" is on a par, socially and emotionally, with "Lo," as her mother calls her.

Another critic has written of you that "the task of sifting and selecting just the right succession of words from that multilingual memory, and of arranging their many-mirrored nuances into the proper juxtapositions, must be psychically exhausting work." Which of all your books, in this sense, would you say was the most difficult to write?

Oh, *Lolita*, naturally. I lacked the necessary information—that was the initial difficulty. I did not know any American 12-year-old girls, and I did not know America; I had to invent America and Lolita. It had taken me some forty years to invent Russia and Western Europe, and now I was faced by a similar task, with a lesser amount of time at my disposal. The obtaining of such local ingredients as would allow me to inject average "reality" into the brew of individual fancy proved, at fifty, a much more difficult process than it had been in the Europe of my youth.

Though born in Russia, you have lived and worked for many years in America as well as in Europe. Do you feel any strong sense of national identity?

I am an American writer, born in Russia and educated in England where I studied French literature, before spending fifteen years in Germany. I came to America in 1940 and decided to become an American citizen, and make America my home. It so happened that I was immediately exposed

[26]

to the very best in America, to its rich intellectual life and to its easygoing, good-natured atmosphere. I immersed myself in its great libraries and its Grand Canyon. I worked in the laboratories of its zoological museums. I acquired more friends than I ever had in Europe. My books—old books and new ones—found some admirable readers. I became as stout as Cortez—mainly because I quit smoking and started to munch molasses candy instead, with the result that my weight went up from my usual 140 to a monumental and cheerful 200. In consequence, I am one-third American—good American flesh keeping me warm and safe.

You spent 20 years in America, and yet you never owned a home or had a really settled establishment there. Your friends report that you camped impermanently in motels, cabins, furnished apartments and the rented homes of professors away on leave. Did you feel so restless or so alien that the idea of settling down anywhere disturbed you?

The main reason, the background reason, is, I suppose, that nothing short of a replica of my childhood surroundings would have satisfied me. I would never manage to match my memories correctly—so why trouble with hopeless approximations? Then there are some special considerations: for instance, the question of impetus, the habit of impetus. I propelled myself out of Russia so vigorously, with such indignant force, that I have been rolling on and on ever since. True, I have rolled and lived to become that appetizing thing, a "full professor," but at heart I have always remained a lean "visiting lecturer." The few times I said to myself anywhere: "Now, that's a nice spot for a permanent home," I would immediately hear in my mind the thunder of an avalanche carrying away the hundreds of far places which I would destroy by the very act of settling in one particular nook of the earth. And finally, I don't much care for furniture, for tables and chairs and lamps and rugs and things—perhaps because in my opulent childhood

I was taught to regard with amused contempt any too-earnest attachment to material wealth, which is why I felt no regret and no bitterness when the Revolution abolished that wealth.

You lived in Russia for twenty years, in West Europe for 20 years, and in America for twenty years. But in 1960, after the success of Lolita, *you moved to France and Switzerland and have not returned to the U.S. since. Does this mean, despite your self-identification as an American writer, that you consider your American period over?*

I am living in Switzerland for purely private reasons—family reasons and certain professional ones too, such as some special research for a special book. I hope to return very soon to America—back to its library stacks and mountain passes. An ideal arrangement would be an absolutely soundproofed flat in New York, on a top floor—no feet walking above, no soft music anywhere—and a bungalow in the Southwest. Sometimes I think it might be fun to adorn a university again, residing and writing there, not teaching, or at least not teaching regularly.

Meanwhile you remain secluded—and somewhat sedentary, from all reports—in your hotel suite. How do you spend your time?

I awake around seven in winter: my alarm clock is an Alpine chough—big, glossy, black thing with big yellow beak—which visits the balcony and emits a most melodious chuckle. For a while I lie in bed mentally revising and planning things. Around eight: shave, breakfast, enthroned meditation, and bath—in that order. Then I work till lunch in my study, taking time out for a short stroll with my wife along the lake. Practically all the famous Russian writers of the nineteenth century have rambled here at one time or another. Zhukovski, Gogol, Dostoevski, Tolstoy—who courted the hotel chambermaids to the detriment of his health—and many Russian poets. But then, as much could

[28]

be said of Nice or Rome. We lunch around one P.M., and I am back at my desk by half-past one and work steadily till half-past six. Then a stroll to a newsstand for the English papers, and dinner at seven. No work after dinner. And bed around nine. I read till half-past eleven, and then tussle with insomnia till one A.M. About twice a week I have a good, long nightmare with unpleasant characters imported from earlier dreams, appearing in more or less iterative surroundings—kaleidoscopic arrangements of broken impressions, fragments of day thoughts, and irresponsible mechanical images, utterly lacking any possible Freudian implication or explication, but singularly akin to the procession of changing figures that one usually sees on the inner palpebral screen when closing one's weary eyes.

Funny that witch doctors and their patients have never hit on that simple and absolutely satisfying explanation of dreaming. Is it true that you write standing up, and that you write in longhand rather than on a typewriter?

Yes. I never learned to type. I generally start the day at a lovely old-fashioned lectern I have in my study. Later on, when I feel gravity nibbling at my calves, I settle down in a comfortable armchair alongside an ordinary writing desk; and finally, when gravity begins climbing up my spine, I lie down on a couch in a corner of my small study. It is a pleasant solar routine. But when I was young, in my twenties and early thirties, I would often stay all day in bed, smoking and writing. Now things have changed. Horizontal prose, vertical verse, and sedent scholia keep swapping qualifiers and spoiling the alliteration.

Can you tell us something more about the actual creative process involved in the germination of a book—perhaps by reading a few random notes for or excerpts from a work in progress?

Certainly not. No fetus should undergo an exploratory operation. But I can do something else. This box contains

[29]

index cards with some notes I made at various times more or less recently and discarded when writing *Pale Fire*. It's a little batch of rejects. Help yourself. "Selene, the moon. Selenginsk, an old town in Siberia: moon-rocket town" . . . "Berry: the black knob on the bill of the mute swan" . . . "Dropworm: a small caterpillar hanging on a thread" . . . "In *The New Bon Ton Magazine*, volume five, 1820, page 312, prostitutes are termed 'girls of the town'" . . . "Youth dreams: forgot pants; old man dreams: forgot dentures" . . . "Student explains that when reading a novel he likes to skip passages 'so as to get his own idea about the book and not be influenced by the author'" . . . "Naprapathy: the ugliest word in the language."

"And after rain, on beaded wires, one bird, two birds, three birds, and none. Muddy tires, sun" . . . "Time without consciousness—lower animal world; time with consciousness—man; consciousness without time—some still higher state" . . . "We think not in words but in shadows of words. James Joyce's mistake in those otherwise marvelous mental soliloquies of his consists in that he gives too much verbal body to thoughts" . . . "Parody of politeness: That inimitable 'Please' —'Please send me your beautiful——' which firms idiotically address to themselves in printed forms meant for people ordering their product." . . .

"Naive, nonstop, peep-peep twitter of chicks in dismal crates late, late at night, on a desolate frost-bedimmed station platform" . . . "The tabloid headline TORSO KILLER MAY BEAT CHAIR might be translated: '*Celui qui tue un buste peut bien battre une chaise*'" . . . "Newspaper vendor, handing me a magazine with my story: 'I see you made the slicks.' " "Snow falling, young father out with tiny child, nose like a pink cherry. Why does a parent immediately say something to his or her child if a stranger smiles at the latter? 'Sure,' said the father to the infant's interrogatory gurgle, which had been going on for some time, and would have been left to go on in the quiet falling snow, had I not smiled in passing" . . . "Inter-columniation: dark-blue sky between two white col-umns." . . . "Place-name in the Orkneys: Papilio" . . . "Not 'I, too, lived in Arcadia,' but 'I,' says Death, even am in Arcadia'—legend on a shepherd's tomb (*Notes and Queries,* June 13, 1868, p. 561)" . . . "Marat collected butterflies" . . . "From the aesthetic point of view, the tapeworm is certainly an undesirable boarder. The gravid segments frequently crawl out of a person's anal canal, sometimes in chains, and have been reported a source of social embarrassment." (*Ann. N. Y. Acad. Sci.* 48:558).

What inspires you to record and collect such disconnected impressions and quotations?

All I know is that at a very early stage of the novel's development I get this urge to garner bits of straw and fluff, and eat pebbles. Nobody will ever discover how clearly a bird visualizes, or if it visualizes at all, the future nest and the eggs in it. When I remember afterwards the force that made me jot down the correct names of things, or the inches and tints of things, even before I actually needed the information, I am inclined to assume that what I call, for want of a better term, inspiration, had been already at work, mutely pointing at this or that, having me accumu-late the known materials for an unknown structure. After the first shock of recognition—a sudden sense of "*this* is what I'm going to write"—the novel starts to breed by itself; the process goes on solely in the mind, not on paper; and to be aware of the stage it has reached at any given moment, I do not have to be conscious of every exact phrase. I feel a kind of gentle development, an uncurling inside, and I know that the details are there already, that in fact I would see them plainly if I looked closer, if I stopped the machine and opened its inner compartment; but I prefer to wait until what is loosely called inspiration has com-pleted the task for me. There comes a moment when I am informed from within that the entire structure is finished. All I have to do now is take it down in pencil or pen. Since this entire structure, dimly illumined in one's mind, can be compared to a painting, and since you do not have to work gradually from left to right for its proper perception, I may direct my flashlight at any part or particle of the picture when setting it down in writing. I do not begin my novel at the beginning. I do not reach chapter three before I reach chapter four, I do not go dutifully from one page to the next, in consecutive order; no, I pick out a bit here and a bit there, till I have filled all the gaps on paper. This is why I like writing my stories and novels on index cards, numbering them later when the whole set is complete. Every card is rewritten many times. About three cards make one typewritten page, and when finally I feel that the conceived picture has been copied by me as faithfully as physically possible—a few vacant lots always remain, alas—then I dictate the novel to my wife who types it out in triplicate.

In what sense do you copy "the conceived picture" of a novel?

A creative writer must study carefully the works of his rivals, including the Almighty. He must possess the inborn capacity not only of recombining but of re-creating the given world. In order to do this adequately, avoiding duplication of labor, the artist should *know* the given world. Imagination without knowledge leads no farther than the back yard of primitive art, the child's scrawl on the fence, and the crank's message in the market place. Art is never simple. To return to my lecturing days: I automatically gave low marks when a student used the dreadful phrase "sincere and simple"—"Flaubert writes with a style which is always simple and sincere"—under the impression that this was the greatest compliment payable to prose or poetry. When I struck the phrase out, which I did with such rage in my pencil that it ripped the paper, the student complained that this was what teachers had always taught him: "Art is simple, art is sincere." Someday I must trace this vulgar absurdity to its source. A schoolmarm in Ohio? A progressive ass in New York? Because, of course, art at its greatest is fantastically deceitful and complex.

In terms of modern art, critical opinion is divided about the sincerity or deceitfulness, simplicity or complexity, of contemporary abstract painting. What is your own opinion?

I do not see any essential difference between abstract and primitive art. Both are simple and sincere. Naturally, we should not generalize in these matters: it is the individual artist that counts. But if we accept for a moment the general notion of "modern art," then we must admit that the trouble with it is that it is so commonplace, imitative, and academic. Blurs and blotches have merely replaced the mass prettiness of a hundred years ago, pictures of Italian girls, handsome beggars, romantic ruins, and so forth. But just as among those corny oils there might occur the work of a true artist with a richer play of light and shade, with some original streak of violence or tenderness, so among the corn of primitive and abstract art one may come across a flash of great talent. Only talent interests me in paintings and books. Not general ideas, but the individual contribution.

A contribution to society?

A work of art has no importance whatever to society. It is only important to the individual, and only the individual reader is important to me. I don't give a damn for the group, the community, the masses, and so forth. Although I do not care for the slogan "art for art's sake"—because unfortunately such promoters of it as, for instance, Oscar Wilde and various dainty poets, were in reality rank moralists and didacticists—there can be no question that what makes a work of fiction safe from larvae and rust is not its social importance but its art, only its art.

[33]

What do you want to accomplish or leave behind—or should this be of no concern to the writer?

Well, in this matter of accomplishment, of course, I don't have a 35-year plan or program, but I have a fair inkling of my literary afterlife. I have sensed certain hints, I have felt the breeze of certain promises. No doubt there will be ups and downs, long periods of slump. With the Devil's connivance, I open a newspaper of 2063 and in some article on the books page I find: "Nobody reads Nabokov or Fulmerford today." Awful question: Who is this unfortunate Fulmerford?

While we're on the subject of self-appraisal, what do you regard as your principal failing as a writer—apart from forgetability?

Lack of spontaneity; the nuisance of parallel thoughts, second thoughts, third thoughts; inability to express myself properly in any language unless I compose every damned sentence in my bath, in my mind, at my desk.

You're doing rather well at the moment, if we may say so.

It's an illusion.

Your reply might be taken as confirmation of critical comments that you are "an incorrigible leg puller," "a mystificator," and "a literary agent provocateur." How do you view yourself?

I think my favorite fact about myself is that I have never been dismayed by a critic's bilge or bile, and have never once in my life asked or thanked a reviewer for a review. My second favorite fact—or shall I stop at one?

No, please go on.

The fact that since my youth—I was 19 when I left Russia—my political creed has remained as bleak and changeless as an old gray rock. It is classical to the point of triteness. Freedom of speech, freedom of thought, freedom

[34]

of art. The social or economic structure of the ideal state is of little concern to me. My desires are modest. Portraits of the head of the government should not exceed a postage stamp in size. No torture and no executions. No music, except coming through earphones, or played in theaters.

Why no music?

I have no ear for music, a shortcoming I deplore bitterly. When I attend a concert—which happens about once in five years—I endeavor gamely to follow the sequence and relationship of sounds but cannot keep it up for more than a few minutes. Visual impressions, reflections of hands in lacquered wood, a diligent bald spot over a fiddle, these take over, and soon I am bored beyond measure by the motions of the musicians. My knowledge of music is very slight; and I have a special reason for finding my ignorance and inability so sad, so unjust: There is a wonderful singer in my family—my own son. His great gifts, the rare beauty of his bass, and the promise of a splendid career—all this affects me deeply, and I feel a fool during a technical conversation among musicians. I am perfectly aware of the many parallels between the art forms of music and those of literature, especially in matters of structure, but what can I do if ear and brain refuse to cooperate? I have found a queer substitute for music in chess—more exactly, in the composing of chess problems.

Another substitute, surely, has been your own euphonious prose and poetry. As one of few authors who have written with eloquence in more than one language, how would you characterize the textural differences between Russian and English, in which you are regarded as equally facile?

In sheer number of words, English is far richer than Russian. This is especially noticeable in nouns and adjectives. A very bothersome feature that Russian presents is the dearth, vagueness, and clumsiness of technical terms.

For example, the simple phrase "to park a car" comes out—if translated back from the Russian—as "to leave an automobile standing for a long time." Russian, at least polite Russian, is more formal than polite English. Thus, the Russian word for "sexual"—*polovoy*—is slightly indecent and not to be bandied around. The same applies to Russian terms rendering various anatomical and biological notions that are frequently and familiarly expressed in English conversation. On the other hand, there are words rendering certain nuances of motion and gesture and emotion in which Russian excels. Thus by changing the head of a verb, for which one may have a dozen different prefixes to choose from, one is able to make Russian express extremely fine shades of duration and intensity. English is, syntactically, an extremely flexible medium, but Russian can be given even more subtle twists and turns. Translating Russian into English is a little easier than translating English into Russian, and 10 times easier than translating English into French.

You have said you will never write another novel in Russian. Why?

During the great, and still unsung, era of Russian intellectual expatriation—roughly between 1920 and 1940—books written in Russian by émigré Russians and published by émigré firms abroad were eagerly bought or borrowed by émigré readers but were absolutely banned in Soviet Russia—as they still are (except in the case of a few dead authors such as Kuprin and Bunin, whose heavily censored works have been recently reprinted there), no matter the theme of the story or poem. An émigré novel, published, say, in Paris and sold over all free Europe, might have, in those years, a total sale of 1,000 or 2,000 copies— that would be a best seller—but every copy would also pass from hand to hand and be read by at least 20 persons, and at least 50 annually if stocked by Russian lending libraries, of which there were hundreds in West Europe alone. The era of expatriation can be said to have ended during World War II. Old writers died, Russian publishers also vanished, and worst of all, the general atmosphere of exile culture, with its splendor, and vigor, and purity, and reverberative force, dwindled to a sprinkle of Russian-language periodicals, anemic in talent and provincial in tone. Now to take my own case: It was not the financial side that really mattered; I don't think my Russian writings ever brought me more than a few hundred dollars per year, and I am all for the ivory tower, and for writing to please one reader alone—one's own self. But one also needs some reverberation, if not response, and a moderate multiplication of one's self throughout a country or countries; and if there be nothing but a void around one's desk, one would expect it to be at least a sonorous void, and not circumscribed by the walls of a padded cell. With the passing of years I grew less and less interested in Russia and more and more indifferent to the once-harrowing thought that my books would remain banned there as long as my contempt for the police state and political oppression prevented me from entertaining the vaguest thought of return. No, I will not write another novel in Russian, though I do allow myself a very few short poems now and then. I wrote my last Russian novel a quarter of a century ago. But today, in compensation, in a spirit of justice to my little American muse, I am doing something else. But perhaps I should not talk about it at this early stage.

Please do.

Well, it occurred to me one day—while I was glancing at the varicolored spines of *Lolita* translations into languages I do not read, such as Japanese, Finnish or Arabic—that the list of unavoidable blunders in these fifteen or twenty versions would probably make, if collected, a fatter volume than any of them. I had checked the French translation, which was basically very good yet would have bristled with unavoidable errors had I not corrected them. But what could I do with Portuguese or Hebrew or Danish? Then I imagined something else. I imagined that in some distant future somebody might produce a Russian version of *Lolita*. I trained my inner telescope upon that particular point in the distant future and I saw that every paragraph, pock-marked as it is with pitfalls, could lend itself to hideous mistranslation. In the hands of a harmful drudge, the Russian version of *Lolita* would be entirely degraded and botched by vulgar paraphrases or blunders. So I decided to translate it myself. Up to now I have about sixty pages ready.

Are you presently at work on any new project?
Good question, as they say on the lesser screen. I have just finished correcting the last proofs of my work on Pushkin's *Eugene Onegin*—four fat little volumes which are to appear this year in the Bollingen Series; the actual translation of the poem occupies a small section of volume one. The rest of the volume and volumes two, three and four contain copious notes on the subject. This opus owes its birth to a casual remark my wife made in 1950—in response to my disgust with rhymed paraphrases of *Eugene Onegin*, every line of which I had to revise for my students—"Why don't you translate it yourself?" This is the result. It has taken some ten years of labor. The index alone runs to 5,000 cards in three long shoe boxes; you see them over there on that shelf. My translation is, of course, a literal one, a crib, a pony. And to the fidelity of transposal I have sacrificed everything: elegance, euphony, clarity, good taste, modern usage, and even grammar.

In view of these admitted flaws, are you looking forward to reading the reviews of the book?
I really don't read reviews about myself with any special eagerness or attention unless they are masterpieces of wit and acumen—which does happen now and then. And I

never reread them, though my wife collects the stuff, and though maybe I shall use a spatter of the more hilarious *Lolita* items to write someday a brief history of the nymphet's tribulations. I remember, however, quite vividly, certain attacks by Russian émigré critics who wrote about my first novels 30 years ago; not that I was more vulnerable then, but my memory was certainly more retentive and enterprising, and I was a reviewer myself. In the nineteen-twenties I was clawed at by a certain Mochulski who could never stomach my utter indifference to organized mysticism, to religion, to the church—any church. There were other critics who could not forgive me for keeping aloof from literary "movements," for not airing the "*angoisse*" that they wanted poets to feel, and for not belonging to any of those groups of poets that held sessions of common inspiration in the back rooms of Parisian cafés. There was also the amusing case of Georgiy Ivanov, a good poet but a scurrilous critic. I never met him or his literary wife Irina Odoevtsev; but one day in the late nineteen-twenties or early nineteen-thirties, at a time when I regularly reviewed books for an émigré newspaper in Berlin, she sent me from Paris a copy of a novel of hers with the wily inscription "*Spasibo za* Korolya, *damu, valeta*" (thanks for *King, Queen, Knave*)—which I was free to understand as "Thanks for writing that book," but which might also provide her with the alibi: "Thanks for sending me your book," though I never sent her anything. *Her* book proved to be pitifully trite, and I said so in a brief and nasty review. Ivanov retaliated with a grossly personal article about me and my stuff. The possibility of venting or distilling friendly or unfriendly feelings through the medium of literary criticism is what makes that art such a skewy one.

You have been quoted as saying: My pleasures are the most intense known to man: butterfly hunting and writing. Are they in any way comparable?
   No, they belong essentially to quite different types of

enjoyment. Neither is easy to describe to a person who has not experienced it, and each is so obvious to the one who has that a description would sound crude and redundant. In the case of butterfly hunting I think I can distinguish four main elements. First, the hope of capturing—or the actual capturing—of the first specimen of a species unknown to science: this is the dream at the back of every lepidopterist's mind, whether he be climbing a mountain in New Guinea or crossing a bog in Maine. Secondly, there is the capture of a very rare or very local butterfly—things you have gloated over in books, in obscure scientific reviews, on the splendid plates of famous works, and that you now see on the wing, in their natural surroundings, among plants and minerals that acquire a mysterious magic through the intimate association with the rarities they produce and support, so that a given landscape lives twice: as a delightful wilderness in its own right and as the haunt of a certain butterfly or moth. Thirdly, there is the naturalist's interest in disentangling the life histories of little-known insects, in learning about their habits and structure, and in determining their position in the scheme of classification—a scheme which can be sometimes pleasurably exploded in a dazzling display of polemical fireworks when a new discovery upsets the old scheme and confounds its obtuse champions. And fourthly, one should not ignore the element of sport, of luck, of brisk motion and robust achievement, of an ardent and arduous quest ending in the silky triangle of a folded butterfly lying on the palm of one's hand.

What about the pleasures of writing?

They correspond exactly to the pleasures of reading, the bliss, the felicity of a phrase is shared by writer and reader: by the satisfied writer and the grateful reader, or—which is the same thing—by the artist grateful to the unknown force in his mind that has suggested a combination of images and by the artistic reader whom this combination satisfies.

[40]

Every good reader has enjoyed a few good books in his life so why analyze delights that both sides know? I write mainly for artists, fellow-artists and follow-artists. However, I could never explain adequately to certain students in my literature classes, the aspects of good reading—the fact that you read an artist's book not with your heart (the heart is a remarkably stupid reader), and not with your brain alone, but with your brain and spine. "Ladies and gentlemen, the tingle in the spine really tells you what the author felt and wished you to feel." I wonder if I shall ever measure again with happy hands the breadth of a lectern and plunge into my notes before the sympathetic abyss of a college audience.

What is your reaction to the mixed feelings vented by one critic in a review which characterized you as having a fine and original mind, but "not much trace of a generalizing intellect," and as "the typical artist who distrusts ideas"?

In much the same solemn spirit, certain crusty lepidopterists have criticized my works on the classification of butterflies, accusing me of being more interested in the subspecies and the subgenus than in the genus and the family. This kind of attitude is a matter of mental temperament, I suppose. The middlebrow or the upper Philistine cannot get rid of the furtive feeling that a book, to be great, must deal in great ideas. Oh, I know the type, the dreary type! He likes a good yarn spiced with social comment; he likes to recognize his own thoughts and throes in those of the author; he wants at least one of the characters to be the author's stooge. If American, he has a dash of Marxist blood, and if British, he is acutely and ridiculously class-conscious; he finds it so much easier to write about ideas than about words; he does not realize that perhaps the reason he does not find general ideas in a particular writer is that the particular ideas of that writer have not yet become general.

[41]

Dostoevski, who dealt with themes accepted by most readers as universal in both scope and significance, is considered one of the world's great authors. Yet you have described him as "a cheap sensationalist, clumsy and vulgar." Why?

Non-Russian readers do not realize two things: that not all Russians love Dostoevski as much as Americans do, and that most of those Russians who do, venerate him as a mystic and not as an artist. He was a prophet, a claptrap journalist and a slapdash comedian. I admit that some of his scenes, some of his tremendous, farcical rows are extraordinarily amusing. But his sensitive murderers and soulful prostitutes are not to be endured for one moment— by this reader anyway.

Is it true that you have called Hemingway and Conrad "writers of books for boys"?

That's exactly what they are. Hemingway is certainly the better of the two; he has at least a voice of his own and is responsible for that delightful, highly artistic short story, "The Killers." And the description of the iridescent fish and rhythmic urination in his famous fish story is superb. But I cannot abide Conrad's souvenir-shop style, bottled ships and shell necklaces of romanticist clichés. In neither of those two writers can I find anything that I would care to have written myself. In mentality and emotion, they are hopelessly juvenile, and the same can be said of some other beloved authors, the pets of the common room, the consolation and support of graduate students, such as—but some are still alive, and I hate to hurt living old boys while the dead ones are not yet buried.

What did you read when you were a boy?

Between the ages of ten and fifteen in St. Petersburg, I must have read more fiction and poetry—English, Russian and French—than in any other five-year period of my life. I relished especially the works of Wells, Poe, Browning,

Keats, Flaubert, Verlaine, Rimbaud, Chekhov, Tolstoy, and Alexander Blok. On another level, my heroes were the Scarlet Pimpernel, Phileas Fogg, and Sherlock Holmes. In other words, I was a perfectly normal trilingual child in a family with a large library. At a later period, in Western Europe, between the ages of 20 and 40, my favorites were Housman, Rupert Brooke, Norman Douglas, Bergson, Joyce, Proust, and Pushkin. Of these top favorites, several—Poe, Jules Verne, Emmuska Orczy, Conan Doyle, and Rupert Brooke—have lost the glamour and thrill they held for me. The others remain intact and by now are probably beyond change as far as I am concerned. I was never exposed in the twenties and thirties, as so many of my coevals have been, to the poetry of the not quite first-rate Eliot and of definitely second-rate Pound. I read them late in the season, around 1945, in the guest room of an American friend's house, and not only remained completely indifferent to them, but could not understand why anybody should bother about them. But I suppose that they preserve some sentimental value for such readers as discovered them at an earlier age than I did.

What are your reading habits today?

Usually I read several books at a time—old books, new books, fiction, nonfiction, verse, anything—and when the bedside heap of a dozen volumes or so has dwindled to two or three, which generally happens by the end of one week, I accumulate another pile. There are some varieties of fiction that I never touch—mystery stories, for instance, which I abhor, and historical novels. I also detest the so-called "powerful" novel—full of commonplace obscenities and torrents of dialogue—in fact, when I receive a new novel from a hopeful publisher—"hoping that I like the book as much as he does"—I check first of all how much dialogue there is, and if it looks too abundant or too sustained, I shut the book with a bang and ban it from my bed.

[43]

Are there any contemporary authors you do enjoy reading?

I do have a few favorites—for example, Robbe-Grillet and Borges. How freely and gratefully one breathes in their marvelous labyrinths! I love their lucidity of thought, the purity and poetry, the mirage in the mirror.

Many critics feel that this description applies no less aptly to your own prose. To what extent do you feel that prose and poetry intermingle as art forms?

Except that I started earlier—that's the answer to the first part of your question. As to the second: Well, poetry, of course, includes all creative writing; I have never been able to see any generic difference between poetry and artistic prose. As a matter of fact, I would be inclined to define a good poem of any length as a concentrate of good prose, with or without the addition of recurrent rhythm and rhyme. The magic of prosody may improve upon what we call prose by bringing out the full flavor of meaning, but in plain prose there are also certain rhythmic patterns, the music of precise phrasing, the beat of thought rendered by recurrent peculiarities of idiom and intonation. As in today's scientific classifications, there is a lot of overlapping in our concept of poetry and prose today. The bamboo bridge between them is the metaphor.

You have also written that poetry represents "the mysteries of the irrational perceived through rational words." But many feel that the "irrational" has little place in an age when the exact knowledge of science has begun to plumb the most profound mysteries of existence. Do you agree?

This appearance is very deceptive. It is a journalistic illusion. In point of fact, the greater one's science, the deeper the sense of mystery. Moreover, I don't believe that any science today has pierced any mystery. We, as newspaper readers, are inclined to call "science" the cleverness of an electrician or a psychiatrist's mumbo jumbo. This, at best, is applied science, and one of the characteristics of applied science is that yesterday's neutron or today's truth dies tomorrow. But even in a better sense of "science"—as the study of visible and palpable nature, or the poetry of pure mathematics and pure philosophy—the situation remains as hopeless as ever. We shall never know the origin of life, or the meaning of life, or the nature of space and time, or the nature of nature, or the nature of thought.

Man's understanding of these mysteries is embodied in his concept of a Divine Being. As a final question, do you believe in God?

To be quite candid—and what I am going to say now is something I never said before, and I hope it provokes a salutary little chill—I know more than I can express in words, and the little I can express would not have been expressed, had I not known more.

4

On August 18, 1964, Jane Howard of *Life* magazine sent me eleven questions. I have kept the typescript of my replies. In mid-September she arrived in Montreux with the photographer Henry Grossman. Text and pictures appeared in the November 20 issue of *Life*.

What writers and persons and places have influenced you most?
In my boyhood I was an extraordinarily avid reader. By the age of 14 or 15 I had read or re-read all Tolstoy in Russian, all Shakespeare in English, and all Flaubert in French—besides hundreds of other books. Today I can always tell when a sentence I compose happens to resemble in cut and intonation that of any of the writers I loved or detested half a century ago; but I do not believe that any particular writer has had any definite influence upon me. As to the influence of places and persons, I owe many metaphors and sensuous associations to the North Russian landscape of my boyhood, and I am also aware that my father was responsible for my appreciating very early in life the thrill of a great poem.

Have you ever seriously contemplated a career other than in letters?
Frankly, I never thought of letters as a career. Writing has always been for me a blend of dejection and high spirits, a torture and a pastime—but I never expected it to be a source of income. On the other hand, I have often

dreamt of a long and exciting career as an obscure curator of lepidoptera in a great museum.

Which of your writings has pleased you most?
I would say that of all my books *Lolita* has left me with the most pleasurable afterglow—perhaps because it is the purest of all, the most abstract and carefully contrived. I am probably responsible for the odd fact that people don't seem to name their daughters Lolita any more. I have heard of young female poodles being given that name since 1956, but of no human beings. Well-wishers have tried to translate *Lolita* into Russian, but with such execrable results that I'm now doing a translation myself. The word "jeans," for example, is translated in Russian dictionaries as "wide, short trousers"—a totally unsatisfactory definition.

In the foreword to The Defense *you allude to psychiatry. Do you think the dependence of analyzed on analysts is a great danger?*
I cannot conceive how anybody in his right mind should go to a psychoanalyst, but of course if one's mind is deranged one might try anything; after all, quacks and cranks, shamans and holy men, kings and hypnotists have cured people—especially hysterical people. Our grandsons no doubt will regard today's psychoanalysts with the same amused contempt as we do astrology and phrenology. One of the greatest pieces of charlatanic, and satanic, nonsense imposed on a gullible public is the Freudian interpretation of dreams. I take gleeful pleasure every morning in refuting the Viennese quack by recalling and explaining the details of my dreams without using one single reference to sexual symbols or mythical complexes. I urge my potential patients to do likewise.

How do your views on politics and religion affect what you write?
I have never belonged to any political party but have always loathed and despised dictatorships and police states,

as well as any sort of oppression. This goes for regimentation of thought, governmental censorship, racial or religious persecution, and all the rest of it. Whether or not my simple credo affects my writing does not interest me. I suppose that my indifference to religion is of the same nature as my dislike of group activities in the domain of political or civic commitments. I have allowed some of my creatures in some of my novels to be restless freethinkers but here again I do not care one bit what kind of faith or brand of non-faith my reader may assign to their maker.

Would you have liked to have lived at a time other than this?
My choice of "when" would be influenced by that of "where." As a matter of fact, I would have to construct a mosaic of time and space to suit my desires and demands. It would be too complicated to tabulate all the elements of this combination. But I know pretty well what it should include. It should include a warm climate, daily baths, an absence of radio music and traffic noise, the honey of ancient Persia, a complete microfilm library, and the unique and indescribable rapture of learning more and more about the moon and the planets. In other words, I think I would like my head to be in the United States of the nineteen-sixties, but would not mind distributing some of my other organs and limbs through various centuries and countries.

With what living writers do you feel a particular sympathy?
When Mr. N. learns from an interview that Mr. X., another writer, has named as his favorites Mr. A., Mr. B. and Mr. N., this inclusion may puzzle Mr. N. who considers, say, Mr. A.'s work to be primitive and trite. I would not like to puzzle Mr. C., Mr. D., or Mr. X., all of whom I like.

Do you anticipate that more of your works will be made into films? On the basis of Lolita, *does the prospect please you?*

I greatly admired the film *Lolita* as a film—but was sorry not to have been given an opportunity to collaborate in its actual making. People who liked my novel said the film was too reticent and incomplete. If, however, all the next pictures based on my books are as charming as Kubrick's, I shall not grumble too much.

Which of the languages you speak do you consider the most beautiful?

My head says English, my heart, Russian, my ear, French.

Why do you prefer Montreux as a headquarters? Do you in any way miss the America you parodied so exquisitely in Lolita? *Do you find that Europe and the US are coming to resemble each other to a discouraging degree?*

I think I am trying to develop, in this rosy exile, the same fertile nostalgia in regard to America, my new country, as I evolved for Russia, my old one, in the first post-revolution years of West-European expatriation. Of course, I miss America—even Miss America. If Europe and America are coming to resemble each other more and more—why should I be discouraged? Amusing, perhaps, and, perhaps, not quite true, but certainly not discouraging in any sense I can think of. My wife and I are very fond of Montreux, the scenery of which I needed for *Pale Fire*, and still need for another book. There are also family reasons for our living in this part of Europe. I have a sister in Geneva and a son in Milan. He is a graduate of Harvard who came to Italy to complete his operatic training, which he combines with racing an Italian car in major events and translating the early works of his father from Russian into English.

[49]

What is your prognosis for the health of Russian letters?
There is no plain answer to your question. The trouble is that no government however intelligent or humane is capable of generating great artists, although a bad government certainly can pester, thwart, and suppress them. We must also remember—and this is very important—that the only people who flourish under all types of government are the Philistines. In the aura of mild regimes there is exactly as rare a chance of a great artist's appearing on the scene as there is in the less happy times of despicable dictatorships. Therefore I cannot predict anything though I certainly hope that under the influence of the West, and especially under that of America, the Soviet police state will gradually wither away. Incidentally, I deplore the attitude of foolish or dishonest people who ridiculously equate Stalin with McCarthy, Auschwitz with the atom bomb, and the ruthless imperialism of the USSR with the earnest and unselfish assistance extended by the USA to nations in distress.

P.S.

Dear Miss Howard, allow me to add the following three points:
1) My answers must be published accurately and completely: verbatim, if quoted; in a faithful version, if not.
2) I must see the proofs of the interview—semifinal and final.
3) I have the right to correct therein all factual errors and specific slips ("Mr. Nabokov is a small man with long hair," etc.)

5

In September, 1965, Robert Hughes visited me here to make a filmed interview for the Television 13 Educational Program in New York. At our initial meetings I read from prepared cards, and this part of the interview is given below. The rest, represented by some fifty pages typed from the tape, is too colloquial and rambling to suit the scheme of the present book.

As with Gogol and even James Agee, there is occasionally confusion about the pronunciation of your last name. How does one pronounce it correctly?

It is indeed a tricky name. It is often misspelt, because the eye tends to regard the "a" of the first syllable as a misprint and then tries to restore the symmetrical sequence by triplicating the "o"—filling up the row of circles, so to speak, as in a game of crosses and naughts. No–bow–cough. How ugly, how wrong. Every author whose name is fairly often mentioned in periodicals develops a bird-watcher's or caterpillar-picker's knack when scanning an article. But in my case I always get caught by the word "nobody" when capitalized at the beginning of a sentence. As to pronunciation, Frenchmen of course say Nabo*koff*, with the accent on the last syllable. Englishmen say *Na*bokov, accent on the first, and Italians say Nabokov, accent in the middle, as Russians also do. Na–*bo*–kov. A heavy open "o" as in "Knickerbocker". My New England ear is not offended by the long elegant middle "o" of Nabokov as delivered in American academies. The awful "Na–bah–kov" is a despicable gutterism. Well, you can make your choice now. Incidentally, the first name is pronounced Vladeemer—rhyming with "redeemer"—not Vladimir rhyming with Faddimere (a place in England, I think).

How about the name of your extraordinary creature, Professor P–N–I–N?

The "p" is sounded, that's all. But since the "p" is mute in English words starting with "pn", one is prone to insert a supporting "uh" sound—"Puh–nin"—which is wrong. To get the "pn" right, try the combination "Up North", or still better "Up, Nina!", leaving out the initial "u". Pnorth, Pnina, Pnin. Can you do that? . . . That's fine.

You're responsible for brilliant summaries of the lives and works of Pushkin and Gogol. How would you summarize your own?

It is not so easy to summarize something which is not quite finished yet. However, as I've pointed out elsewhere, the first part of my life is marked by a rather pleasing chronological neatness. I spent my first twenty years in Russia, the next twenty in Western Europe, and the twenty years after that, from 1940 to 1960, in America. I've been living in Europe again for five years now, but I cannot promise to stay around another fifteen so as to retain the rhythm. Nor can I predict what new books I may write. My best Russian novel is a thing called, in English, *The Gift.* My two best American ones are *Lolita* and *Pale Fire.*

I am now in the process of translating *Lolita* into Russian, which is like completing the circle of my creative life. Or rather starting a new spiral. I've lots of difficulties with technical terms, especially with those pertaining to the motor car, which has not really blended with Russian life as it, or rather she, has with American life. I also have trouble with finding the right Russian terms for clothes, varieties of shoes, items of furniture, and so on. On the other hand, descriptions of tender emotions, of my nymphet's grace and of the soft, melting American landscape slip very delicately into lyrical Russian. The book will be published in America or perhaps Paris; traveling poets and diplomats will smuggle it into Russia, I hope. Shall I read three lines of this Russian version? Of course, incredible as it may seem, perhaps not everybody remembers the way *Lolita* starts in English. So perhaps I should do the first lines in English first. Note that for the necessary effect of dreamy tenderness both "l"s and the "t" and indeed the whole word should be iberized and not pronounced the American way with crushed "l"s, a coarse "t", and a long "o": "Lolita, light of my life, fire of my loins. My sin, my soul. Lo-lee-ta: the tip of the tongue taking a trip of three steps down the palate to tap, at three, on the teeth. Lo. Lee. Ta." Now comes the Russian. Here the first syllable of her name sounds more like an "ah" sound than an "o" sound, but the rest is like Spanish: (*Reads in Russian*) "*Lah–lee–ta, svet moey zhizni, ogon' moih chresel. Greh moy, dusha moya.*" And so on.

Beyond what's stated and implied in your various prefaces, have you anything to add about your readers and/or your critics?
Well, when I think about critics in general, I divide the family of critics into three subfamilies. First, professional reviewers, mainly hacks or hicks, regularly filling up their allotted space in the cemeteries of Sunday papers. Secondly, more ambitious critics who every other year collect their magazine articles into volumes with allusive scholarly titles— *The Undiscovered Country*, that kind of thing. And thirdly, my fellow writers, who review a book they like or loathe. Many bright blurbs and dark feuds have been engendered that way. When an author whose work I admire praises my work, I cannot help experiencing, besides a ripple of almost human warmth, a sense of harmony and satisfied logic. But I have also the idiotic feeling that he or

she will very soon cool down and vaguely turn away if I do not do something at once, but I don't know what to do, and I never do anything, and next morning cold clouds conceal the bright mountains. In all other cases, I must confess, I yawn and forget. Of course, every worthwhile author has quite a few clowns and criticules—wonderful word: criticules, or criticasters—around him, demolishing one another rather than him with their slapsticks. Then, also, my various disgusts which I like to voice now and then seem to irritate people. I happen to find second-rate and ephemeral the works of a number of puffed-up writers—such as Camus, Lorca, Kazantzakis, D. H. Lawrence, Thomas Mann, Thomas Wolfe, and literally hundreds of other "great" second-raters. And for this, of course, I'm automatically disliked by their camp-followers, kitsch-followers, fashion-followers, and all kinds of automatons. Generally speaking, I'm supremely indifferent to adverse criticism in regard to my fiction. But on the other hand, I enjoy retaliating when some pompous dunce finds fault with my translations and divulges a farcical ignorance of the Russian language and literature.

Would you describe your first reactions to America? And how you first came to write in English?

I had started rather sporadically to compose in English a few years before migrating to America, where I arrived in the lilac mist of a May morning, May 28, 1940. In the late thirties, when living in Germany and France, I had translated two of my Russian books into English and had written my first straight English novel, the one about Sebastian Knight. Then, in America, I stopped writing in my native tongue altogether except for an occasional poem which, incidentally, caused my Russian poetry to improve rather oddly in urgency and concentration. My complete switch from Russian prose to English prose was exceedingly painful—like learning anew to handle things after losing seven or eight fingers in an explosion. I have described the writing of *Lolita* in the afterpiece appended in '58 to the

American edition. The book was first published in Paris at a time when nobody else wanted it, 10 years ago now—10 years—how time crawls!

As to *Pale Fire*, although I had devised some odds and ends of Zemblan lore in the late fifties in Ithaca, New York, I felt the first real pang of the novel, a rather complete vision of its structure in miniature, and jotted it down—I have it in one of my pocket diaries—while sailing from New York to France in 1959. The American poem discussed in the book by His Majesty, Charles of Zembla, was the hardest stuff I ever had to compose. Most of it I wrote in Nice, in winter, walking along the Promenade des Anglais or rambling in the neighboring hills. A good deal of Kinbote's commentary was written here in the Montreux Palace garden, one of the most enchanting and inspiring gardens I know.* I'm especially fond of its weeping cedar, the arboreal counterpart of a very shaggy dog with hair hanging over its eyes.

What is your approach to the teaching of literature?

I can give you some examples. When studying Kafka's famous story, my students had to know exactly what kind of insect Gregor turned into (it was a domed beetle, not the flat cockroach of sloppy translators) and they had to be able to describe exactly the arrangement of the rooms, with the position of doors and furniture, in the Samsa family's flat. They had to know the map of Dublin for *Ulysses*. I believe in stressing the specific detail; the general ideas can take care of themselves. *Ulysses*, of course, is a divine work of art and will live on despite the academic nonentities who turn it into a collection of symbols or Greek myths. I once gave a student a C-minus, or perhaps a D-plus, just for applying to its chapters the titles borrowed from Homer while not even noticing the comings and goings of the man in the brown mackintosh. He didn't even know who the man in

*Now disfigured by a tennis court and a parking place.

[55]

the brown mackintosh was. Oh, yes, let people compare me to Joyce by all means, but my English is patball to Joyce's champion game.

How did you come to live in Switzerland?
The older I get and the more I weigh, the harder it is for me to get out of this or that comfortable armchair or deckchair into which I have sunk with an exhalation of content. Nowadays I find it as difficult to travel from Montreux to Lausanne as to travel to Paris, London, or New York. On the other hand, I'm ready to walk 10 or 15 miles per day, up and down mountain trails, in search of butterflies, as I do every summer. One of the reasons I live in Montreux is because I find the view from my easy chair wonderfully soothing and exhilarating according to my mood or the mood of the lake. I hasten to add that not only am I not a tax dodger, but that I also have to pay a plump little Swiss tax on top of my massive American taxes which are so high they almost cut off that beautiful view. I feel very nostalgic about America and as soon as I muster the necessary energy I shall return there for good.

Where is the easy chair?
The easy chair is in the other room, in my study. It was a metaphor, after all: the easy chair is the entire hotel, the garden, everything.

Where would you live in America?
I think I would like to live either in California, or in New York, or in Cambridge, Mass. Or in a combination of these three.

Because of your mastery of our language, you are frequently compared with Joseph Conrad.
Well, I'll put it this way. When a boy, I was a voracious reader, as all boy writers seem to be, and between 8 and 14 I used to enjoy tremendously the romantic

productions—romantic in the large sense—of such people as Conan Doyle, Kipling, Joseph Conrad, Chesterton, Oscar Wilde, and other authors who are essentially writers for very young people. But as I have well said somewhere before, I differ from Joseph Conradically. First of all, he had not been writing in his native tongue before he became an English writer, and secondly, I cannot stand today his polished clichés and primitive clashes. He once wrote that he preferred Mrs. Garnett's translation of *Anna Karenin* to the original! This makes one dream—"ça fait rêver" as Flaubert used to say when faced with some abysmal stupidity. Ever since the days when such formidable mediocrities as Galsworthy, Dreiser, a person called Tagore, another called Maxim Gorky, a third called Romain Rolland, used to be accepted as geniuses, I have been perplexed and amused by fabricated notions about so-called "great books". That, for instance, Mann's asinine *Death in Venice* or Pasternak's melodramatic and vilely written *Zhivago* or Faulkner's corncobby chronicles can be considered "masterpieces," or at least what journalists call "great books," is to me an absurd delusion, as when a hypnotized person makes love to a chair. *My* greatest masterpieces of twentieth century prose are, in this order: Joyce's *Ulysses*; Kafka's *Transformation*; Biely's *Petersburg*; and the first half of Proust's fairy tale *In Search of Lost Time*.

What do you think of American writing? I noticed there are no American masterpieces on your list. What do you think of American writing since 1945?

Well, seldom more than two or three really first-rate writers exist simultaneously in a given generation. I think that Salinger and Updike are by far the finest artists in recent years. The sexy, phony type of best seller, the violent, vulgar novel, the novelistic treatment of social or political problems, and, in general, novels consisting mainly of dialogue or social comment—these are absolutely banned from my bedside. And the popular mixture of

pornography and idealistic humbuggery makes me positively vomit.

What do you think of Russian writing since 1945?
    Soviet literature . . . Well, in the first years after the
Bolshevik revolution, in the twenties and early thirties, one
could still distinguish through the dreadful platitudes of
Soviet propaganda the dying voice of an earlier culture.
The primitive and banal mentality of enforced politics—
any politics—can only produce primitive and banal art.
This is especially true of the so-called "social realist" and
"proletarian" literature sponsored by the Soviet police
state. Its jackbooted baboons have gradually exterminated
the really talented authors, the special individual, the fragile
genius. One of the saddest cases is perhaps that of Osip
Mandelshtam—a wonderful poet, the greatest poet among
those trying to survive in Russia under the Soviets—whom
that brutal and imbecile administration persecuted and
finally drove to death in a remote concentration camp. The
poems he heroically kept composing until madness eclipsed
his limpid gifts are admirable specimens of a human mind
at its deepest and highest. Reading them enhances one's
healthy contempt for Soviet ferocity. Tyrants and torturers
will never manage to hide their comic stumbles behind their
cosmic acrobatics. Contemptuous laughter is all right, but
it is not enough in the way of moral relief. And when I read
Mandelshtam's poems composed under the accursed rule of
those beasts, I feel a kind of helpless shame, being so free to
live and think and write and speak in the free part of the
world.——That's the only time when liberty is bitter.

WALKING IN MONTREUX
WITH INTERVIEWER

This is a ginkgo—the sacred tree of China, now rare in the

wild state. The curiously veined leaf resembles a butter-fly—which reminds me of a little poem:

> The ginkgo leaf, in golden hue, when shed,
> A muscat grape,
> Is an old-fashioned butterfly, ill-spread,
> In shape.

This, in my novel *Pale Fire*, is a short poem by John Shade—by far the greatest of *invented* poets.

PASSING A SWIMMING POOL

I don't mind sharing the sun with sunbathers but I dislike immersing myself in a swimming pool. It is after all only a big tub where other people join you—makes one think of those horrible Japanese communal bathtubs, full of a floating family, or a shoal of businessmen.

DOG NEAR TELEPHONE BOOTH

Must remember the life line of that leash from the meek dog to the talkative lady in that telephone booth. "A long wait"—good legend for an oil painting of the naturalistic school.

BOYS KICKING A BALL IN A GARDEN

Many years have passed since I gathered a soccer ball to my breast. I was an erratic but rather spectacular goalkeep-er in my Cambridge University days 45 years ago. After that I played on a German team when I was about 30, and saved my last game in 1936 when I regained consciousness in the pavilion, knocked out by a kick but still clutching the ball which an impatient teammate was trying to pry out of my arms.

DURING A STROLL NEAR VILLENEUVE

Late September in Central Europe is a bad season for collecting butterflies. This is not Arizona, alas.

In this grassy nook near an old vineyard above the Lake of Geneva, a few fairly fresh females of the very common Meadow Brown still flutter about here and there—lazy old widows. There's one.

Here is a little sky-blue butterfly, also a very common thing, once known as the Clifden Blue in England.

The sun is getting hotter. I enjoy hunting in the buff but I doubt anything interesting can be obtained today. This pleasant lane on the banks of Geneva Lake teems with butterflies in summer. Chapman's Blue and Mann's White, two rather local things, occur not far from here. But the white butterflies we see in this particular glade, on this nice but commonplace autumn day, are the ordinary Whites: the Small White and Green-Veined White.

Ah, a caterpillar. Handle with care. Its golden-brown coat can cause a nasty itch. This handsome worm will become next year a fat, ugly, drab-colored moth.

IN ANSWER TO THE QUESTION: WHAT SCENES ONE WOULD LIKE TO HAVE FILMED

Shakespeare in the part of the King's Ghost.
The beheading of Louis the Sixteenth, the drums drown-

ing his speech on the scaffold.

Herman Melville at breakfast, feeding a sardine to his cat.

Poe's wedding. Lewis Carroll's picnics.

The Russians leaving Alaska, delighted with the deal. Shot of a seal applauding.

6

This interview (published in *Wisconsin Studies in Contemporary Literature*, vol. VIII, no. 2, spring 1967) was conducted on September 25, 27, 28, 29, 1966, at Montreux, Switzerland. Mr. Nabokov and his wife have for the last six years lived in an opulent hotel built in 1835, which still retains its nineteenth-century atmosphere. Their suite of rooms is on the sixth floor, overlooking Lake Geneva, and the sounds of the lake are audible through the open doors of their small balcony. Since Mr. Nabokov does not like to talk off the cuff (or "Off the Nabocuff," as he said) no tape recorder was used. Mr. Nabokov either wrote out his answers to the questions or dictated them to the interviewer; in some instances, notes from the conversation were later recast as formal questions-and-answers. The interviewer was Nabokov's student at Cornell University in 1954, and the references are to Literature 311–312 (MWF, 12), a course on the Masterpieces of European Fiction (Jane Austen, Gogol, Dickens, Flaubert, Tolstoy, Stevenson, Kafka, Joyce, and Proust). Its enrollment had reached four hundred by the time of Nabokov's resignation in 1959. The footnotes to the interview, except where indicated, are provided by the interviewer, Alfred Appel, Jr.

For years bibliographers and literary journalists didn't know whether to group you under "Russian" or "American." Now that you're living in Switzerland there seems to be complete agreement that you're American. Do you find this kind of distinction at all important regarding your identity as a writer?

I have always maintained, even as a schoolboy in Russia, that the nationality of a worthwhile writer is of secondary importance. The more distinctive an insect's aspect, the less apt the taxonomist is to glance first of all at the locality label under the pinned specimen in order to decide which of several vaguely described races it should be assigned to. The writer's art is his real passport. His identity should be immediately recognized by a special pattern or unique coloration. His habitat may confirm the correctness of the determination but should not lead to it. Locality labels are known to have been faked by unscrupulous insect dealers. Apart from these considerations I think of myself today as an American writer who has once been a Russian one.

The Russian writers you have translated and written about all precede the so-called "age of realism," which is more celebrated by English and American readers than is the earlier period. Would you say something about your temperamental or artistic affinities with the great writers of the 1830–40 era of masterpieces? Do you see your own work falling under such general rubrics as a tradition of Russian humor?

The question of the affinities I may think I have or not have with nineteenth-century Russian writers is a classificational, not a confessional matter. There is hardly a single Russian major writer of the past whom pigeonholers have not mentioned in connection with me. Pushkin's blood runs through the veins of modern Russian literature as inevitably as Shakespeare's through those of English literature.

Many of the major Russian writers, such as Pushkin, Lermontov, and Bely, have distinguished themselves in both poetry and prose, an uncommon accomplishment in English and American literature. Does this signal fact have anything to do with the special nature of

Russian literary culture, or are there technical or linguistic resources which make this kind of versatility more possible in Russian? And as a writer of both prose and poetry, what distinctions do you make between them?

On the other hand, neither Gogol nor Tolstoy nor Chekhov were distinguished versificators. Moreover, the dividing line between prose and poetry in some of the greatest English or American novels is not easy to draw. I suppose you should have used the term "rhymed poetry" in your question, and then one might answer that Russian rhymes are incomparably more attractive and more abundant than English ones. No wonder a Russian prose writer frequents those beauties, especially in his youth.

Who are the great American writers you most admire?

When I was young I liked ·Poe, and I still love Melville, whom I did not read as a boy. My feelings towards James are rather complicated. I really dislike him intensely but now and then the figure in the phrase, the turn of the epithet, the screw of an absurd adverb, cause me a kind of electric tingle, as if some current of his was also passing through my own blood. Hawthorne is a splendid writer. Emerson's poetry is delightful.

You have often said that you "don't belong to any club or group," and I wonder if the historical examples of the ways Russian writers have allowed ideology to determine if not destroy their art, culminating in the Socialist Realism of our own time, have not gone a long way in shaping your own skepticism and aversion to didacticism of any kind. Which "historical examples" have you been most conscious of?

My aversion to groups is rather a matter of temperament than the fruit of information and thought. I was born that way and have despised ideological coercion instinctively all my life. Those "historical examples" by the way are not as clear-cut and obvious as you seem to imply. The mystical didacticism of Gogol or the utilitarian moralism of Tolstoy, or the reactionary journalism of Dostoevski, are of their own poor making and in the long run nobody really takes them seriously.

Would you say something about the controversy surrounding the Chernyshevski biography in The Gift? *You have commented on this briefly before, but since its suppression in the thirties expresses such a transcendent irony and seems to justify the need for just such a parody, I think your readers would be most interested, especially since so little is known about the émigré communities, their magazines, and the role of intellectuals in these communities. If you would like to describe something of the writer's relationship to this world, please do.*

Everything that can be profitably said about Count Godunov-Cherdyntsev's biography of Chernyshevski has been said by Koncheyev in *The Gift.* I can only add that I devoted as much honest labor to the task of gathering the material for the Chernyshevski chapter as I did to the composing of Shade's poem in *Pale Fire.* As to the suppression of that chapter by the editors of *Sovremennye Zapiski,* it was indeed an unprecedented occurrence, quite out of keeping with their exceptional broad-mindedness, for, generally speaking, in their acceptance or rejection of literary works they were guided exclusively by artistic standards. As to the latter part of your question, the revised Chapter Fourteen in *Speak, Memory* will provide additional information.

Do you have any opinions about the Russian anti-utopian tradition (if it can be called this), from Odoevski's "The Last Suicide" and "A City Without a Name" in Russian Nights *to Bryusov's* The Republic of the Southern Cross *and Zamyatin's* We *(to name only a few)?*

I am indifferent to those works.

Is it fair to say that Invitation to a Beheading *and* Bend Sinister *are cast as mock anti-utopian novels, with their idelogical centers removed—the totalitarian state becoming an extreme and fantastic metaphor for the imprisonment of the mind, thus making consciousness, rather than politics, the subject of these novels?*

Yes, possibly.

Speaking of ideology, you have often expressed your hostility to Freud, most noticeably in the forewords to your translated novels. Some readers have wondered which of Freud's works or theories you were most offended by and why. The parodies of Freud in Lolita *and* Pale Fire *suggest a wider familiarity with the good doctor than you have ever publicly granted. Would you comment on this?*

Oh, I am not up to discussing again that figure of fun. He is not worthy of more attention than I have granted him in my novels and in *Speak, Memory.* Let the credulous and the vulgar continue to believe that all mental woes can be cured by a daily application of old Greek myths to their private parts. I really do not care.

Your contempt for Freud's "standardized symbols" extends to the assumptions of a good many other theorizers. Do you think literary criticism is at all purposeful, and if so, what kind of criticism would you point to? Pale Fire *makes it clear what sort you find gratuitous (at best).*

My advice to a budding literary critic would be as follows. Learn to distinguish banality. Remember that mediocrity thrives on "ideas." Beware of the modish message. Ask yourself if the symbol you have detected is not your own footprint. Ignore allegories. By all means place the "how" above the "what" but do not let it be confused with the "so what." Rely on the sudden erection of your small dorsal hairs. Do not drag in Freud at this point. All the rest depends on personal talent.

As a writer, have you ever found criticism instructive—not so much the reviews of your own books, but any general criticism? From your own experiences do you think that an academic and a literary career nourish one another? Since many writers today know no other alternative than a life on campus I'd be very interested in your feelings about this. Do you think that your own work in America was at all shaped by your being part of an academic community?

I find criticism most instructive when an expert proves to me that my facts or my grammar are wrong. An academic career is especially helpful to writers in two ways: 1) easy access to magnificent libraries and 2) long vacations. There is of course the business of teaching, but old professors have young instructors to correct examination papers for them, and young instructors, authors in their own right, are followed by admiring glances along the corridors of Vanity Hall. Otherwise, our greatest rewards, such as the reverberations of our minds in such minds as vibrate responsively in later years, force novelist-teachers to nurse lucidity and honesty of style in their lectures.

What are the possibilities of literary biography?

They are great fun to write, generally less fun to read. Sometimes the thing becomes a kind of double paper chase: first, the biographer pursues his quarry through letters and diaries, and across the bogs of conjecture, and then a rival authority pursues the muddy biographer.

Some critics may find the use of coincidence in a novel arch or contrived. I recall that you yourself at Cornell called Dostoevski's usage of coincidence crude.

But in "real" life they do happen. Last night you were telling us at dinner a very funny story about the use of the title "Doctor" in Germany, and the very next moment, as my loud laughter was subsiding, I heard a person at the

[67]

next table saying to her neighbor in clear French tones coming through the tinkling and shuffling sounds of a restaurant—"Of course, you never know with the Germans if 'Doctor' means a dentist or a lawyer." Very often you meet with some person or some event in "real" life that would sound pat in a story. It is not the coincidence in the story that bothers us so much as the coincidence of coincidences in several stories by different writers, as, for instance, the recurrent eavesdropping device in nineteenth-century Russian fiction.

Could you tell us something about your work habits as a writer, and the way you compose your novels. Do you use an outline? Do you have a full sense of where a fiction is heading even while you are in the early stages of composition?

In my twenties and early thirties, I used to write, dipping pen in ink and using a new nib every other day, in exercise books, crossing out, inserting, striking out again, crumpling the page, rewriting every page three or four times, then copying out the novel in a different ink and a neater hand, then revising the whole thing once more, re-copying it with new corrections, and finally dictating it to my wife who has typed out all my stuff. Generally speaking, I am a slow writer, a snail carrying its house at the rate of two hundred pages of final copy per year (one spectacular exception was the Russian original of *Invitation to a Beheading*, the first draft of which I wrote in one fortnight of wonderful excitement and sustained inspiration). In those days and nights I generally followed the order of chapters when writing a novel but even so, from the very first, I relied heavily on mental composition, constructing whole paragraphs in my mind as I walked in the streets or sat in my bath, or lay in bed, although often deleting or rewriting them afterward. In the late thirties, beginning with *The Gift*, and perhaps under the influence of the many notes needed, I switched to another, physically more practical, method—that of writing with an eraser-capped pencil on index cards. Since I always have at the very start a curiously clear preview of the entire novel before me or above me, I find cards especially convenient when not following the logical sequence of chapters but preparing instead this or that passage at any point of the novel and filling in the gaps in no special order. I am afraid to get mixed up with Plato, whom I do not care for, but I do think that in my case it is true that the entire book, before it is written, seems to be ready ideally in some other, now transparent, now dimming, dimension, and my job is to take down as much of it as I can make out and as precisely as I am humanly able to. The greatest happiness I experience in composing is when I feel I cannot understand, or rather catch myself not understanding (without the presupposition of an already existing creation) how or why that image or structural move or exact formulation of phrase has just come to me. It is sometimes rather amusing to find my readers trying to elucidate in a matter-of-fact way these wild workings of my not very efficient mind.

One often hears from writers talk of how a character takes hold of them and in a sense dictates the course of the action. Has this ever been your experience?

I have never experienced this. What a preposterous experience! Writers who have had it must be very minor or insane. No, the design of my novel is fixed in my imagination and every character follows the course I imagine for him. I am the perfect dictator in that private world insofar as I alone am responsible for its stability and truth. Whether I reproduce it as fully and faithfully as I would wish, is another question. Some of my old works reveal dismal blurrings and blanks.

Pale Fire *appears to some readers to be in part a gloss of Plato's myth of the cave, and the constant play of Shades and Shadows throughout your work suggests a conscious Platonism. Would you care to comment on this possibility?*

As I have said I am not particularly fond of Plato, nor would I survive very long under his Germanic regime of militarism and music. I do not think that this cave business has anything to do with my Shade and Shadows.

Since we are mentioning philosophy per se, I wonder if we might talk about the philosophy of language that seems to unfold in your works, and whether or not you have consciously seen the similarities, say, between the language of Zemblan and what Ludwig Wittgenstein had to say about a "private language." Your poet's sense of the limitations of language is startlingly similar to Wittgenstein's remark on the referential basis of language. While you were at Cambridge, did you have much contact with the philosophy faculty?

No contact whatsoever. I am completely ignorant of Wittgenstein's works, and the first time I heard his name must have been in the fifties. In Cambridge I played football and wrote Russian verse.

When in Canto Two John Shade describes himself, "I stand before the window and I pare/My fingernails," you are echoing Stephen Dedalus in A Portrait of the Artist as a Young Man, *on the artist who "remains within or behind or beyond or above his handiwork, invisible, refined out of existence, indifferent, paring his fingernails." In almost all of your novels, especially in* Invitation to a Beheading, Bend Sinister, Pale Fire, *and* Pnin—*but even in* Lolita, *in the person of the seventh hunter in Quilty's play, and in several other phosphorescent glimmers which are visible to the careful reader—the creator is indeed behind or above his handiwork, but he is not invisible and surely not indifferent. To what extent are you consciously "answering" Joyce in* Pale Fire, *and what are your feelings about his esthetic stance—or alleged stance, because perhaps you may think that Stephen's remark doesn't apply to* Ulysses?

Neither Kinbote nor Shade, nor their maker, is answering Joyce in *Pale Fire*. Actually, I never liked *A Portrait of the Artist as a Young Man*. I find it a feeble and garrulous book. The phrase you quote is an unpleasant coincidence.

You have granted that Pierre Delalande influenced you, and I would readily admit that influence-mongering can be reductive and deeply offensive if it tries to deny a writer's originality. But in the instance of yourself and Joyce, it seems to me that you've consciously profited from Joyce's example without imitating him—that you've realized the implications in Ulysses *without having had recourse to obviously "Joycean" devices (stream-of-consciousness, the "collage" effects created out of the vast flotsam and jetsam of everyday life). Would you comment on what Joyce has meant to you as a writer, his importance in regard to his liberation and expansion of the novel form?*

My first real contact with *Ulysses*, after a leering glimpse in the early twenties, was in the thirties at a time when I was definitely formed as a writer and immune to any literary influence. I studied *Ulysses* seriously only much later, in the fifties, when preparing my Cornell courses. That was the best part of the education I received at Cornell. *Ulysses* towers over the rest of Joyce's writings, and in comparison to its noble originality and unique lucidity of thought and style the unfortunate *Finnegans Wake* is nothing but a formless and dull mass of phony folklore, a cold pudding of a book, a persistent snore in the next room, most aggravating to the insomniac I am. Moreover, I always detested regional literature full of quaint old-timers and imitated pronunciation. *Finnegans Wake's* façade disguises a very conventional and drab tenement house, and only the infrequent snatches of heavenly intonations redeem it from utter insipidity. I know I am going to be excommunicated for this pronouncement.

Although I cannot recall your mentioning the involuted structure of Ulysses *when you lectured on Joyce, I do remember your insisting*

*that the hallucinations in Nighttown are the author's and not
Stephen's or Bloom's, which is one step away from a discussion of
the involution. This is an aspect of Ulysses almost totally ignored
by the Joyce Industry, and an aspect of Joyce which would seem to be
of great interest to you. If Joyce's somewhat inconsistent involutions
tend to be obscured by the vastness of his structures, it might be said
that the structuring of your novels depends on the strategy of
involution. Could you comment on this, or compare your sense of
Joyce's presence in and above his works with your own intention—
that is, Joyce's covert appearances in Ulysses; the whole Shakes-
peare-paternity theme which ultimately spirals into the idea of the
"parentage" of Ulysses itself; Shakespeare's direct address to
Joyce in Nighttown ("How my Oldfellow chokit his Thurs-
day-momum," that being Bloomsday); and Molly's plea to Joyce,
"O Jamesy let me up out of this"—all this as against the way
the authorial voice—or what you call the "anthropomor-
phic deity impersonated by me"—again and again appears in your
novels, most strikingly at the end.*

One of the reasons Bloom cannot be the active party in
the Nighttown chapter (and if he is not, then the author is
directly dreaming it up for him, and around him, with
some "real" episodes inserted here and there) is that Bloom,
a wilting male anyway, has been drained of his manhood
earlier in the evening and thus would be quite unlikely to
indulge in the violent sexual fancies of Nighttown.

*Ideally, how should a reader experience or react to "the end" of one
of your novels, that moment when the vectors are removed and the
fact of the fiction is underscored, the cast dismissed? What common
assumptions about literature are you assaulting?*

The question is so charmingly phrased that I would love
to answer it with equal elegance and eloquence, but I
cannot say very much. I think that what I would welcome
at the close of a book of mine is a sensation of its world
receding in the distance and stopping somewhere there,

suspended afar like a picture in a picture: *The Artist's Studio* by Van Bock.[1]

It may well be a failure of perception, but I've always been unsure of the very last sentences of Lolita, *perhaps because the shift in voice at the close of your other books is so clear, but is one supposed to "hear" a different voice when the masked narrator says "And do not pity C. Q. One had to choose between him and H. H., and one wanted H. H. . . ." and so forth? The return to the first person in the next sentence makes me think that the mask has not been lifted, but readers trained on* Invitation to a Beheading, *among other books, are always looking for the imprint of that "master thumb," to quote Franklin Lane in* Pale Fire, *"that made the whole involuted, boggling thing one beautiful straight line."*

No, I did not mean to introduce a different voice. I did want, however, to convey a constriction of the narrator's sick heart, a warning spasm causing him to abridge names and hasten to conclude his tale before it was too late. I am glad I managed to achieve this remoteness of tone at the end.

Do Franklin Lane's Letters *exist? I don't wish to appear like Mr. Goodman in* The Real Life of Sebastian Knight, *but I understand that Franklin Lane did exist.*

Frank Lane, his published letters, and the passage cited by Kinbote, certainly exist. Kinbote was rather struck by Lane's handsome melancholy face. And of course "lane" is the last word of Shade's poem. The latter has no significance.

[1] Research has failed to confirm the existence of this alleged "Dutch Master," whose name is only an alphabetical step away from being a significant anagram, a poor relation of Quilty's anagrammatic mistress, "Vivian Darkbloom."

In which of your early works do you think you first begin to face the possibilities that are fully developed in Invitation to a Beheading *and reach an apotheosis in the "involute abode" of* Pale Fire?

Possibly in *The Eye*, but *Invitation to a Beheading* is on the whole a burst of spontaneous generation.

Are there other writers whose involuted effects you admire? Sterne? Pirandello's plays?

I never cared for Pirandello. I love Sterne but had not read him in my Russian period.

The Afterword to Lolita *is significant, obviously, for many reasons. Is it included in all the translations which, I understand, number about twenty-five?*

Yes.

You once told me after a class at Cornell that you'd been unable to read more than one hundred or so pages of Finnegans Wake. *As it happens, on page 104 there begins a section very close in spirit to* Pale Fire, *and I wonder if you've ever read this, or seen the similarity. It is the history of all the editions and interpretations of Anna Livia Plurabelle's Letter (or "Mamafesta," text included). Among the three pages listing the various titles of ALP's letter, Joyce includes* Try our Taal on a Taub *(which we are already doing), and I wondered if you would comment on Swift's contribution to the literature about the corruption of learning and literature. Is it only a coincidence that Kinbote's "Forword" to* Pale Fire *is dated "Oct. 19," which is the date of Swift's death?*

I finished *Finnegans Wake* eventually. It has no inner connection with *Pale Fire*. I think it is so nice that the day on which Kinbote committed suicide (and he certainly did after putting the last touches to his edition of the poem) happens to be both the anniversary of Pushkin's *Lyceum* and that of "poor old man Swift" 's death, which is news to me (but see variant in note to line 231). In common with Pushkin, I am fascinated by fatidic dates. Moreover, when dating some special event in my novels I often choose a more or less familiar one as a *point de repère* (which helps to check a possible misprint in the proofs), as for instance "April 1" in the diary of Hermann in *Despair*.

Mention of Swift moves me to ask about the genre of Pale Fire; *as a "monstrous semblance of a novel," do you see it in terms of some tradition or form?*

The form of *Pale Fire* is specifically, if not generically, new. I would like to take this pleasant opportunity to correct the following misprints in the Putnam edition, 1962, second impression: On page 137, end of note to line 143, "rustic" should be "rusty". On page 151, "Catskin Week" should be "Catkin Week." On page 223, the line number in the reference at the end of the first note should be not "550" but "549". On page 237, top, "For" should be "for". On page 241, the word "lines" after "*disent-prise*" should be "rhymes". And on page 294, the comma after "Arnold" should be replaced by an open parenthesis. Thank you.[2]

Do you make a clear distinction between satire and parody? I ask this because you have so often said you do not wish to be taken as a "moral satirist," and yet parody is so central to your vision.

Satire is a lesson, parody is a game.

[2] Since Mr. Nabokov has opened an Errata Department, the following misprints from the Lancer Books paperback edition of *Pale Fire*, 1963, should be noted: on page 17, fifth line from bottom of middle paragraph, "sad" should be "saw." On page 60, note to lines 47–48, line 21 should be "burst an appendix," not "and." On page 111, fourth line of note to line 172, "inscription" is misspelled. On page 158, last sentence of note to line 493, "filfth" should be "filth." Nabokov's other books are relatively free from misprints, except for the Popular Library paperback edition of *The Gift*, 1963, whose blemishes are too numerous to mention.

[75]

Chapter Ten in The Real Life of Sebastian Knight *contains a wonderful description of how parody functions in your own novels. But your sense of what "parody" means seems to stretch the usual definition, as when Cincinnatus in* Invitation to a Beheading *tells his mother, "You're still only a parody . . . Just like this spider, just like those bars, just like the striking of that clock." All art, then, or at least all attempts at a "realistic" art, would seem to produce a distortion, a "parody." Would you expand on what you mean by "parody" and why, as Fyodor says in* The Gift, *"The spirit of parody always goes along with genuine poetry"?*

When the poet Cincinnatus C., in my dreamiest and most poetical novel, accuses (not quite fairly) his mother of being a parody, he uses the word in its familiar sense of "grotesque imitation." When Fyodor, in *The Gift*, alludes to that "spirit of parody" which plays iridescently around the spray of genuine "serious" poetry, he is referring to parody in the sense of an essentially lighthearted, delicate, mockingbird game, such as Pushkin's parody of Derzhavin in *Exegi Monumentum.*

What is your opinion of Joyce's parodies? Do you see any difference in the artistic effect of scenes such as the maternity hospital and the beach interlude with Gerty Macdowell? Are you familiar with the work of younger American writers who have been influenced by both you and Joyce, such as Thomas Pynchon (a Cornellian, Class of '59, who surely was in Literature 312), and do you have any opinion on the current ascendancy of the so-called parody-novel (John Barth, for instance)?

The literary parodies in the Maternal Hospital chapter are on the whole jejunish. Joyce seems to have been hampered by the general sterilized tone he chose for that chapter, and this somehow dulled and monotonized the inlaid skits. On the other hand, the frilly novelette parodies in the Masturbation scene are highly successful; and the sudden junction of its clichés with the fireworks and tender sky of real poetry is a feat of genius. I am not familiar with the works of the two other writers you mention.[3]

Why, in Pale Fire, *do you call parody the "last resort of wit"?*
It is Kinbote speaking. There are people whom parody upsets.

Are the composition of Lolita *and* Speak, Memory, *two very different books about the spell exerted by the past, at all connected in the way that the translations of* The Song of Igor's Campaign *and* Eugene Onegin *are related to* Pale Fire*? Had you finished all the notes to* Onegin *before you began* Pale Fire*?*
Yes, I had finished all my notes to *Onegin* before I began *Pale Fire.* Flaubert speaks in one of his letters, in relation to a certain scene in *Madame Bovary,* about the difficulty of painting *couleur sur couleur.* This in a way is what I tried to do in retwisting my own experience when inventing Kinbote. *Speak, Memory* is strictly autobiographic. There is nothing autobiographic in *Lolita.*

Although self-parody seems to be a vital part of your work, you are a writer who believes passionately in the primacy of the imagination. Yet your novels are filled with little details that seem to have been purposely pulled from your own life, as a reading of Speak, Memory *makes clear, not to mention the overriding patterns, such as the lepidopteral motif, which extend through so many of your books. They seem to partake of something other than the involuted voice, to suggest some clearly held idea about the interrelationship between self-knowledge and artistic creation, self-parody and identity. Would you comment on this, and the significance of*

[3] Mrs. Nabokov, who graded her husband's examination papers, did remember Pynchon, but only for his "unusual" handwriting: half printing, half script.

[77]

autobiographical hints in works of art that are literally not *autobiographical?*

I would say that imagination is a form of memory. Down, Plato, down, good dog. An image depends on the power of association, and association is supplied and prompted by memory. When we speak of a vivid individual recollection we are paying a compliment not to our capacity of retention but to Mnemosyne's mysterious foresight in having stored up this or that element which creative imagination may want to use when combining it with later recollections and inventions. In this sense, both memory and imagination are a negation of time.

C. P. Snow has complained about the gulf between the "two cultures," the literary and scientific communities. As someone who has bridged this gulf, do you see the sciences and humanities as necessarily opposed? Have your experiences as a scientist influenced your performance as an artist? Is it fanciful to use the vocabulary of physics in describing the structures of some of your novels?

I might have compared myself to a Colossus of Rhodes bestriding the gulf between the thermodynamics of Snow and the Laurentomania of Leavis, had that gulf not been a mere dimple of a ditch that a small frog could straddle. The terms "physics" and "egghead" as used nowadays evoke in me the dreary image of applied science, the knack of an electrician tinkering with bombs and other gadgets. One of those "Two Cultures" is really nothing but utilitarian technology; the other is B-grade novels, ideological fiction, popular art. Who cares if there exists a gap between such "physics" and such "humanities"? Those Eggheads are terrible Philistines. A real good head is not oval but round.

Where, through what window, do lepidoptera come in?

My passion for lepidopterological research, in the field, in the laboratory, in the library, is even more pleasurable than the study and practice of literature, which is saying a good deal. Lepidopterists are obscure scientists. Not one is mentioned in Webster. But never mind. I have re-worked the classification of various groups of butterflies, have described and figured several species and subspecies. My names for the microscopic organs that I have been the first to see and portray have safely found their way into biological dictionaries (compare this to the wretched entry under "nymphet" in Webster's latest edition). The tactile delights of precise delineation, the silent paradise of the camera lucida, and the precision of poetry in taxonomic description represent the artistic side of the thrill which accumulation of new knowledge, absolutely useless to the layman, gives its first begetter. Science means to me above all natural science. Not the ability to repair a radio set; quite stubby fingers can do that. Apart from this basic consideration, I certainly welcome the free interchange of terminology between any branch of science and any raceme of art. There is no science without fancy, and no art without facts. Aphoristicism is a symptom of arteriosclerosis.

In Pale Fire, Kinbote complains that "The coming of summer represented a problem in optics." The Eye is well-titled, since you plumb these problems throughout your fiction; the apprehension of "reality" is a miracle of vision, and consciousness is virtually an optical instrument in your work. Have you studied the science of optics at all, and would you say something about your own visual sense, and how you feel it has served your fiction?

I am afraid you are quoting this out of context. Kinbote was simply annoyed by the spreading foliage of summer interfering with his Tom-peeping. Otherwise you are right in suggesting that I have good eyes. Doubting Tom should have worn spectacles. It is true, however, that even with the best of visions one must touch things to be *quite* sure of "reality."

[79]

You have said that Alain Robbe-Grillet and Jorge Luis Borges are among your favorite contemporary writers. Do you find them to be at all similar? Do you think Robbe-Grillet's novels are as free of "psychology" as he claims?

Robbe-Grillet's claims are preposterous. Those manifestos, those dodoes, die with the dadas. His fiction is magnificently poetical and original, and the shifts of levels, the interpenetration of successive impressions and so forth belong of course to psychology—psychology at its best. Borges is also a man of infinite talent, but his miniature labyrinths and the roomy ones of Robbe-Grillet are quite differently built, and the lighting is not the same.

I recall your humorous remarks at Cornell about two writers experiencing "telepathy" (I believe you were comparing Dickens and Flaubert). You and Borges were both born in 1899 (but so was Ernest Hemingway!). Your Bend Sinister *and Borges' story "The Circular Ruins" are conceptually similar, but you do not read Spanish and that story was first translated into English in 1949, two years after* Bend Sinister's *birth, just as in Borges' "The Secret Miracle," Hladik has created a verse drama uncannily similar to your recently Englished play,* The Waltz Invention, *which precedes Borges' tale, but which he could not have read in Russian. When were you first aware of Borges' fictions, and have you and he had any kind of association or contact, other than telepathic?*

I read a Borges story for the first time three or four years ago. Up till then I had not been aware of his existence, nor do I believe he knew, or indeed knows, anything about me. That is not very grand in the way of telepathy. There are affinities between *Invitation to a Beheading* and *The Castle*, but I had not yet read Kafka when I wrote my novel. As to Hemingway, I read him for the first time in the early forties, something about bells, balls, and bulls, and loathed it. Later I read his admirable "The Killers" and the wonderful fish story which I was asked to translate into Russian but could not for some reason or other.

Your first book was a translation of Lewis Carroll into Russian. Do you see any affinities between Carroll's idea of "nonsense" and your bogus or "mongrel" languages in Bend Sinister *and* Pale Fire?

In common with many other English children (I was an English child) I have been always very fond of Carroll. No, I do not think that his invented language shares any roots with mine. He has a pathetic affinity with H. H. but some odd scruple prevented me from alluding in *Lolita* to his perversion and to those ambiguous photographs he took in dim rooms. He got away with it, as so many other Victorians got away with pederasty and nympholepsy. His were sad scrawny little nymphets, bedraggled and half-undressed, or rather semi-undraped, as if participating in some dusty and dreadful charade.

You have had wide experience as a translator and have made fictive use of translation. What basic problems of existence do you find implicit in the art and act of translation?

There is a certain small Malayan bird of the thrush family which is said to sing only when tormented in an unspeakable way by a specially trained child at the annual Feast of Flowers. There is Casanova making love to a harlot while looking from a window at the nameless tortures inflicted on Damiens. These are the visions that sicken me when I read the "poetical" translations from martyred Russian poets by some of my famous contemporaries. A tortured author and a deceived reader, this is the inevitable outcome of arty paraphrase. The only object and justification of translation is the conveying of the most exact information possible and this can be only achieved by a literal translation, with notes.

Mention of translation brings me to one of the Kinbotian problems faced by critics who comment on your Russian novels in translation, but who themselves have no Russian. It has been said that translations such as The Defense *and* Despair *must contain many stylistic revisions (certainly the puns), and moreover are in general much richer in language than* Laughter in the Dark, *written at about the same time but, unlike the others, translated in the thirties. Would you comment on this? If the style of* Laughter in the Dark *suggests it should have preceded* Despair, *perhaps it actually was written much earlier: in the BBC interview of four years ago,[4] you said that you wrote* Laughter in the Dark *when you were twenty-six, which would have been 1925, thus making it your first novel. Did you actually write it this early, or is the reference to age a slip in memory, no doubt caused by the distracting presence of the BBC machinery.*

I touched up details here and there in those novels and reinstated a scene in *Despair*, as the Foreword explains. That "twenty-six" is certainly wrong. It is either a telescopation or I must have been thinking of *Mashenka*, my first novel written in 1925. The Russian original version (*Kamera Obskura*) of *Laughter in the Dark* was written in 1931, three years before *Otchayanie* (*Despair*), and an English translation by Winifred Roy, insufficiently revised by me, appeared in London in 1936. A year later, on the Riviera, I attempted—not quite successfully—to English the thing anew for Bobbs-Merrill, who published it in New York in 1938.

There is a parenthetical remark in Despair *about a "vulgar, mediocre Herzog." Is that a bit of added fun about a recent best seller?*

Herzog means "Duke" in German and I was speaking of a conventional statue of a German Duke in a city square.

Since the reissued edition of Laughter in the Dark *is not graced by one of your informative forewords, would you tell us something*

4 Peter Duval-Smith, "Vladimir Nabokov on his Life and Work," *Listener*, LXVIII (Nov. 22, 1962), 856–58. Reprinted as "What Vladimir Nabokov Thinks of his Work," *Vogue*, CXLI (March 1, 1963), 152–55.

about the book's inception and the circumstances under which you wrote it? Commentators are quick to suggest similarities between Margot and Lolita, but I'm much more interested in the kinship between Axel Rex and Quilty. Would you comment on this, and perhaps on the other perverters of the imagination one finds throughout your work, all of whom seem to share Rex's evil qualities.

Yes, some affinities between Rex and Quilty exist, as they do between Margot and Lo. Actually, of course, Margot was a common young whore, not an unfortunate little Lolita. Anyway I do not think that those recurrent sexual oddities and morbidities are of much interest or importance. My Lolita has been compared to Emmie in *Invitation*, to Mariette in *Bend Sinister*, and even to Colette in *Speak, Memory*—the last is especially ludicrous. But I think it might have been simply English jollity and leg-pulling.[5]

The Doppelgänger *motif figures prominently throughout your fiction; in* Pale Fire *one is tempted to call it a Tripling (at least). Would you say that* Laughter in the Dark *is your earliest Double fiction?*

I do not see any Doubles in *Laughter in the Dark*. A lover can be viewed as the betrayed party's Double but that is pointless.

Would you care to comment on how the Doppelgänger *motif has been both used and abused from Poe, Hoffmann, Andersen, Dostoevski, Gogol, Stevenson, and Melville, down to Conrad and Mann? Which* Doppelgänger *fictions would you single out for praise?*

The *Doppelgänger* subject is a frightful bore.

[5] A reference to Kingsley Amis' review of *Lolita*, "She was a Child and I was a Child," *Spectator*, CCIII (Nov. 6, 1959), p. 636.

What are your feelings about Dostoevski's celebrated The Double*; after all, Hermann in* Despair *considers it as a possible title for his manuscript.*

Dostoevski's *The Double* is his best work though an obvious and shameless imitation of Gogol's "Nose." Felix in *Despair* is really a *false* double.

Speaking of Doubles brings me to Pnin*, which in my experience has proved to be one of your most popular novels and at the same time one of your most elusive to those readers who fail to see the relationship of the narrator and the characters (or who fail to even notice the narrator until it's too late). Four of its seven chapters were published in* The New Yorker *over a considerable period (1953–57), but the all-important last chapter, in which the narrator takes control, is only in the book. I'd be most interested to know if the design of* Pnin *was complete while the separate sections were being published, or whether your full sense of its possibilities occurred later.*

Yes, the design of *Pnin* was complete in my mind when I composed the first chapter which, I believe, in this case was actually the first of the seven I physically set down on paper. Alas, there was to be an additional chapter, between Four (in which, incidentally, the boy at St. Mark's and Pnin both dream of a passage from my drafts of *Pale Fire*, the revolution in Zembla and the escape of the king—that is telepathy for you!) and Five (where Pnin drives a car). In that still uninked chapter, which was beautifully clear in my mind down to the last curve, Pnin recovering in the hospital from a sprained back teaches himself to drive a car in bed by studying a 1935 manual of automobilism found in the hospital library and by manipulating the levers of his cot. Only one of his colleagues visits him there—Professor Blorenge. The chapter ended with Pnin's taking his driver's examination and pedantically arguing with the instructor who has to admit Pnin is right. A combination of chance circumstances in 1956 prevented me from actually writing that chapter, then other events intervened, and it is only a mummy now.

In a television interview last year, you singled out Bely's St. Petersburg, along with works by Joyce, Kafka, and Proust, as one of the greatest achievements in twentieth-century prose (an endorsement, by the way, which has prompted Grove Press to reissue St. Petersburg, with your statement across the front cover). I greatly admire this novel but, unhappily enough, it is relatively unknown in America. What are its qualities which you most admire? Bely and Joyce are sometimes compared; is the comparison a just one?

Petersburg is a splendid fantasy, but this is a question I plan to answer elsewhere. There does exist some resemblance in manner between *Petersburg* and certain passages in *Ulysses*.

Although I've never seen it discussed as such, the Ableukhov father-son relationship to me constitutes a doubling, making Petersburg *one of the most interesting and fantastic permutations of the* Doppelgänger *theme. Since this kind of doubling (if you would agree it is one) is surely the kind you'd find more congenial, say, than the use Mann makes of the motif in* Death in Venice, *would you comment on its implications?*

Those murky matters have no importance to me as a writer. Philosophically, I am an indivisible monist. Incidentally, your handwriting is very like mine.

Bely lived in Berlin in 1922–23. Did you know him there? You and Joyce lived in Paris at the same time; did you ever meet him?

Once, in 1921 or 1922, at a Berlin restaurant where I was dining with two girls. I happened to be sitting back to back with Andrey Bely who was dining with another writer, Aleksey Tolstoy, at the table behind me. Both writers were at the time frankly pro-Soviet (and on the point of returning

[85]

to Russia), and a White Russian, which I still am in that particular sense, would certainly not wish to speak to a *bolshevizan* (fellow traveler). I was acquainted with Aleksey Tolstoy but of course ignored him. As to Joyce, I saw him a few times in Paris in the late thirties. Paul and Lucy Léon, close friends of his, were also old friends of mine. One night they brought him to a French lecture I had been asked to deliver on Pushkin under the auspices of Gabriel Marcel (it was later published in the *Nouvelle revue française*). I had happened to replace at the very last moment a Hungarian woman writer, very famous that winter, author of a best-selling novel, I remember its title, *La Rue du Chat qui Pêche*, but not the lady's name. A number of personal friends of mine, fearing that the sudden illness of the lady and a sudden discourse on Pushkin might result in a suddenly empty house, had done their best to round up the kind of audience they knew I would like to have. The house had, however, a pied aspect since some confusion had occurred among the lady's fans. The Hungarian consul mistook me for her husband and, as I entered, dashed towards me with the froth of condolence on his lips. Some people left as soon as I started to speak. A source of unforgettable consolation was the sight of Joyce sitting, arms folded and glasses glinting, in the midst of the Hungarian football team. Another time my wife and I had dinner with him at the Léons' followed by a long friendly evening of talk. I do not recall one word of it but my wife remembers that Joyce asked about the exact ingredients of *myod*, the Russian "mead," and everybody gave him a different answer. In this connection, there is a marvelous howler in the standard English version of *The Brothers Karamazov*: a supper table at Zosima's abode is described with the translator hilariously misreading "Médoc" (in Russian transliteration in the original text), a French wine greatly appreciated in Russia, as *medok*, the diminutive of *myod* (mead). It would have been fun to recall that I spoke of this to Joyce but unfortunately I came across this incarnation of *The Karamazovs* some ten years later.

You mentioned Aleksey Tolstoy a moment ago. Would you say something about him?

He was a writer of some talent and has two or three science fiction stories or novels which are memorable. But I wouldn't care to categorize writers, the only category being originality and talent. After all, if we start sticking group labels, we'll have to put *The Tempest* in the SF category, and of course thousands of other valuable works.

Tolstoy was initially an anti-Bolshevik, and his early work precedes the Revolution. Are there any writers totally of the Soviet period whom you admire?

There were a few writers who discovered that if they chose certain plots and certain characters they could get away with it in the political sense, in other words, they wouldn't be told what to write and how to finish the novel. Ilf and Petrov, two wonderfully gifted writers, decided that if they had a rascal adventurer as protagonist, whatever they wrote about his adventures could not be criticized from a political point of view, since a perfect rascal or a madman or a delinquent or any person who was outside Soviet society—in other words, any picaresque character—could not be accused either of being a bad Communist or not being a good Communist. Thus Ilf and Petrov, Zoshchenko, and Olesha managed to publish some absolutely first-rate fiction under that standard of complete independence, since these characters, plots, and themes could not be treated as political ones. Until the early thirties they managed to get away with it. The poets had a parallel system. They thought, and they were right at first, that if they stuck to the garden—to pure poetry, to lyrical imitations, say, of gypsy songs, such as Ilya Selvinski's—that then they were safe. Zabolotski found a third method of writing, as if the "I" of the poem were a perfect imbecile, crooning in a dream, distorting words, playing with words as a half-insane person would. All these people were enormously gifted but the regime finally caught up with them and they disappeared, one by one, in nameless camps.

By my loose approximation, there remain three novels, some fifty stories, and six plays still in Russian. Are there any plans to translate these? What of The Exploit, *written during what seems to have been your most fecund period as a "Russian writer"— would you tell us something, however briefly, about this book?*

Not all of that stuff is as good as I thought it was thirty years ago but some of it will probably be published in English by and by. My son is now working on the translation of *The Exploit.* It is the story of a Russian expatriate, a romantic young man of my set and time, a lover of adventure for adventure's sake, proud flaunter of peril, climber of unnecessary mountains, who merely for the pure thrill of it decides one day to cross illegally into Soviet Russia, and then cross back to exile. Its main theme is the overcoming of fear, the glory and rapture of that victory.

I understand that The Real Life of Sebastian Knight *was written in English in 1938. It is very dramatic to think of you bidding farewell to one language and embarking on a new life in another in this way. Why did you decide to write in English at this time, since you obviously could not have known for certain you would emigrate two years later? How much more writing in Russian did you do between* Sebastian Knight *and your emigration to America in 1940, and once there, did you ever compose in Russian again?*

Oh, I did know I would eventually land in America. I switched to English after convincing myself on the strength of my translation of *Despair* that I could use English as a

[88]

wistful standby for Russian.[6] I still feel the pangs of that substitution, they have not been allayed by the Russian poems (my best) that I wrote in New York, or the 1954 Russian version of *Speak, Memory*, or even my recent two-years-long work on the Russian translation of *Lolita*, which will be published in 1967. I wrote *Sebastian Knight* in Paris, 1938. We had that year a charming flat on rue Saïgon, between the Etoile and the Bois. It consisted of a huge handsome room (which served as parlor, bedroom, and nursery) with a small kitchen on one side and a large sunny bathroom on the other. This apartment had been some bachelor's delight but was not meant to accommodate a family of three. Evening guests had to be entertained in the kitchen so as not to interfere with my future translator's sleep. And the bathroom doubled as my study. Here is the *Doppelgänger* theme for you.

Do you remember any of those "evening guests"?
    I remember Vladislav Hodasevich, the greatest poet of his time, removing his dentures to eat in comfort, just as a grandee would do in the past.

Many people are surprised to learn that you have written seven plays, which is strange, since your novels are filled with "theatrical" effects that are patently unnovelistic. Is it just to say that your frequent allusions to Shakespeare are more than a matter of playful or respectful homage? What do you think of the drama as a form? What are the characteristics of Shakespeare's plays which you find most congenial to your own esthetic?
    The verbal poetical texture of Shakespeare is the greatest the world has known, and is immensely superior to the

----

[6] In 1936, while living in Berlin, Nabokov translated *Despair* for the English firm John Long, who published it in 1937. The most recent and final edition of *Despair* (New York, 1966) is, as Nabokov explains in its Foreword, a revision of both the early translation and of *Otchayanie* itself.

structure of his plays as plays. With Shakespeare it is the metaphor that is the thing, not the play. My most ambitious venture in the domain of drama is a huge screenplay based on *Lolita*. I wrote it for Kubrick who used only bits and shadows of it for his otherwise excellent film.

When I was your student, you never mentioned the Homeric parallels in discussing Joyce's Ulysses. *But you did supply "special information" in introducing many of the masterpieces: a map of Dublin for* Ulysses, *the arrangement of streets and lodgings in* Dr. Jekyll and Mr. Hyde, *a diagram of the interior of a railway coach on the Moscow-Petersburg express in* Anna Karenin, *and a floor plan of the Samsa apartment in* The Metamorphosis *and an entomological drawing of Gregor. Would you be able to suggest some equivalent for your own readers?*

Joyce himself very soon realized with dismay that the harping on those essentially easy and vulgar "Homeric parallelisms" would only distract one's attention from the real beauty of his book. He soon dropped these pretentious chapter titles which already were "explaining" the book to non-readers. In my lectures I tried to give factual data only. A map of three country estates with a winding river and a figure of the butterfly *Parnassius mnemosyne* for a cartographic cherub will be the endpaper in my revised edition of *Speak, Memory*.

Incidentally, one of my colleagues came into my office recently with the breathless news that Gregor is not *a cockroach (he had read an article to that effect). I told him I've known that for 12 years, and took out my notes to show him my drawing from what was for one day only Entomology 312. What kind of beetle, by the way, was Gregor?*

It was a domed beetle, a scarab beetle with wing-sheaths, and neither Gregor nor his maker realized that when the room was being made by the maid, and the window was open, he could have flown out and escaped and joined the other happy dung beetles rolling the dung balls on rural paths.

How are you progressing in your novel, The Texture of Time*? Since the* données *for some of your novels seem to be present, however fleetingly, in earlier novels, would it be fair to suggest that Chapter Fourteen of* Bend Sinister *contains the germ for your latest venture?*

In a way, yes; but my *Texture of Time*, now almost half-ready, is only the central rose-web of a much ampler and richer novel, entitled *Ada*, about passionate, hopeless, rapturous sunset love, with swallows darting beyond the stained window and that radiant shiver . . .

Speaking of données*: At the end of* Pale Fire, *Kinbote says of Shade and his poem, "I even suggested to him a good title—the title of the book in me whose pages he was to cut:* Solus Rex; *instead of which I saw* Pale Fire, *which meant to me nothing." In 1940* Sovremennye Zapiski *published a long section from your "unfinished" novel,* Solus Rex, *under that title. Does* Pale Fire *represent the "cutting" of its pages? What is the relationship between it, the other untranslated fragment from* Solus Rex *("Ultima Thule," published in* Novyy Journal, *New York, 1942) and* Pale Fire*?*

My *Solus Rex* might have disappointed Kinbote less than Shade's poem. The two countries, that of the Lone King and the Zembla land, belong to the same biological zone. Their subarctic bogs have much the same butterflies and berries. A sad and distant kingdom seems to have haunted my poetry and fiction since the twenties. It is not associated with my personal past. Unlike Northern Russia, both Zembla and Ultima Thule are mountainous, and their languages are of a phony Scandinavian type. If a cruel prankster kidnapped Kinbote and placed him, blindfolded, in the Ultima Thule countryside, Kinbote would not know—at least not immediately—by the sap smells and bird calls that he was not back in Zembla, but he would be tolerably sure that he was not on the banks of the Neva.

This may be like asking a father to publicly declare which of his children is most loved, but do you have one novel towards which you feel the most affection, which you esteem over all others?

The most affection, *Lolita*; the greatest esteem, *Priglashenie na Kazn'.*[7]

And as a closing question, sir, may I return to Pale Fire: *where, please, are the crown jewels hidden?*[8]

In the ruins, sir, of some old barracks near Kobaltana (q.v.); but do not tell it to the Russians.

[7] *Invitation to a Beheading*
[8] One hesitates to explain a joke, but readers unfamiliar with *Pale Fire* should be informed that the hiding place of the Zemblan crown jewels is never revealed in the text, and the Index entry under "crown jewels," to which the reader must now refer, is less than helpful. "Kobaltana" is also in the Index.

7

Most of the questions were submitted by Herbert Gold, during a visit to Montreux in September, 1966. The rest (asterisked) were mailed to me by George A. Plimpton. The combined set appeared in *The Paris Review* of October, 1967.

Good morning. Let me ask forty-odd questions.
Good morning. I am ready.

Your sense of the immorality of the relationship between Humbert Humbert and Lolita is very strong. In Hollywood and New York, however, relationships are frequent between men of forty and girls very little older than Lolita. They marry—to no particular public outrage; rather, public cooing.
No, it is not *my* sense of the immorality of the Humbert Humbert–Lolita relationship that is strong; it is Humbert's sense. *He* cares, I do not. *I* do not give a damn for public morals, in America or elsewhere. And, anyway, cases of men in their forties marrying girls in their teens or early twenties have no bearing on Lolita whatever. Humbert was fond of "little girls"—not simply "young girls." Nymphets are girl-children, not starlets and "sex kittens." Lolita was twelve, not eighteen, when Humbert met her. You may remember that by the time she is fourteen, he refers to her as his "aging mistress."

One critic has said about you that "his feelings are like no one else's." Does this make sense to you? Or does it mean that you know your feelings better than others know theirs? Or that you have discovered yourself at other levels? Or simply that your history is unique?

I do not recall that article; but if a critic makes such a statement, it must surely mean that he has explored the feelings of literally millions of people, in at least three countries, before reaching his conclusion. If so, I am a rare fowl indeed. If, on the other hand, he has merely limited himself to quizzing members of his family or club, his statement cannot be discussed seriously.

Another critic has written that your "worlds are static. They may become tense with obsession, but they do not break apart like the worlds of everyday reality." Do you agree? Is there a static quality in your view of things?

Whose "reality"? "Everyday" where? Let me suggest that the very term "everyday reality" is utterly static since it presupposes a situation that is permanently observable, essentially objective, and universally known. I suspect you have invented that expert on "everyday reality." Neither exists.

He does (names him). A third critic has said that you "diminish" your characters "to the point where they become ciphers in a cosmic farce." I disagree; Humbert, while comic, retains a touching and insistent quality—that of the spoiled artist.

I would put it differently: Humbert Humbert is a vain and cruel wretch who manages to appear "touching." That epithet, in its true, tear-iridized sense, can only apply to my poor little girl. Besides, how can I "diminish" to the level of ciphers, et cetera, characters that I have invented myself? One can "diminish" a biographee, but not an eidolon.

**E. M. Forster speaks of his major characters sometimes taking over and dictating the course of his novels. Has this ever been a problem for you, or are you in complete command?*

My knowledge of Mr. Forster's works is limited to one novel which I dislike; and anyway it was not he who fathered that trite little whimsy about characters getting out of hand; it is as old as the quills, although of course one sympathizes with *his* people if they try to wriggle out of that trip to India or whereever he takes them. My characters are galley slaves.

**Clarence Brown of Princeton has pointed out striking similarities in your work. He refers to you as "extremely repetitious" and that in wildly different ways you are in essence saying the same thing. He speaks of fate being the "muse of Nabokov." Are you consciously aware of "repeating yourself," or to put it another way, that you strive for a conscious unity to your shelf of books?*

I do not think I have seen Clarence Brown's essay, but he may have something there. Derivative writers seem versatile because they imitate many others, past and present. Artistic originality has only its own self to copy.

**Do you think literary criticism is at all purposeful? Either in general, or specifically about your own books? Is it ever instructive?*

The purpose of a critique is to say something about a book the critic has or has not read. Criticism can be instructive in the sense that it gives readers, including the author of the book, some information about the critic's intelligence, or honesty, or both.

**And the function of the editor? Has one ever had literary advice to offer?*

By "editor" I suppose you mean proofreader. Among these I have known limpid creatures of limitless tact and tenderness who would discuss with me a semicolon as if it

[95]

were a point of honor—which, indeed, a point of art often is. But I have also come across a few pompous avuncular brutes who would attempt to "make suggestions" which I countered with a thunderous ".stet!"

Are you a lepidopterist, stalking your victims? If so, doesn't your laughter startle them?

On the contrary, it lulls them into the state of torpid security which an insect experiences when mimicking a dead leaf. Though by no means an avid reader of reviews dealing with my own stuff, I happen to remember the essay by a young lady who attempted to find entomological symbols in my fiction. The essay might have been amusing had she known something about Lepidoptera. Alas, she revealed complete ignorance and the muddle of terms she employed proved to be only jarring and absurd.

How would you define your alienation from the so-called "White Russian" refugees?

Well, historically I am a "White Russian" myself, since all Russians who left Russia as my family did in the first years of the Bolshevist tyranny because of their opposition to it were and remained "White Russians" in the large sense. But these refugees were split into as many social fractions and political factions as the entire nation had been before the Bolshevist coup. I do not mix with "black-hundred" White Russians and do not mix with the so-called "bolshevizans," that is "pinks." On the other hand, I have friends among intellectual Constitutional Monarchists as well as among intellectual Social Revolutionaries. My father was an old-fashioned liberal, and I do not mind being labeled an old-fashioned liberal too.

How would you define your alienation from present-day Russia?

As a deep distrust of the phony thaw now advertised. As a constant awareness of unredeemable iniquities. As a complete indifference to all that moves a patriotic Sovetski man of today. As the keen satisfaction of having discerned as early as 1918 (nineteen eighteen) the *meshchantsvo* (petty bourgeois smugness, Philistine essence) of Leninism.

**How do you now regard the poets Blok and Mandelshtam and others who were writing in the days before you left Russia?*
I read them in my boyhood, more than a half-century ago. Ever since that time I have remained passionately fond of Blok's lyrics. His long pieces are weak, and the famous *The Twelve* is dreadful, self-consciously couched in a phony "primitive" tone, with a pink cardboard Jesus Christ glued on at the end. As to Mandelshtam, I also knew him by heart, but he gave me a less fervent pleasure. Today, through the prism of a tragic fate, his poetry seems greater than it actually is. I note incidentally that professors of literature still assign these two poets to different schools. There is only one school: that of talent.

I know your work has been read and is attacked in the Soviet Union. How would you feel about a Soviet edition of your work?
Oh, they are welcome to my work. As a matter of fact, the Editions Victor are bringing out my *Invitation to a Beheading* in a reprint of the original Russian of 1935, and a New York publisher (Phaedra) is printing my Russian translation of *Lolita*. I am sure the Soviet Government will be happy to admit officially a novel that seems to contain a prophecy of Hitler's regime, and a novel that is thought to condemn bitterly the American system of motels.

Have you ever had contact with Soviet citizens? Of what sort?
I have practically no contact with them though I did once agree, in the early thirties or late twenties, to meet—out of sheer curiosity—an agent from Bolshevist Russia who was trying hard to get émigré writers and artists to return to the

fold. He had a double name, Tarasov something, and had written a novelette entitled *Chocolate*, and I thought I might have some sport with him. I asked him would I be permitted to write freely and would I be able to leave Russia if I did not like it there. He said that I would be so busy liking it there that I would have no time to dream of going abroad again. I would, he said, be perfectly free to choose any of the many themes Soviet Russia bountifully allows a writer to use, such as farms, factories, forests in Fakistan—oh, lots of fascinating subjects. I said farms, et cetera, bored me, and my wretched seducer soon gave up. He had better luck with the composer Prokofiev.

Do you consider yourself an American?
  Yes, I do. I am as American as April in Arizona. The flora, the fauna, the air of the Western states are my links with Asiatic and Arctic Russia. Of course, I owe too much to the Russian language and landscape to be emotionally involved in, say, American regional literature, or Indian dances, or pumpkin pie on a spiritual plane; but I do feel a suffusion of warm, lighthearted pride when I show my green USA passport at European frontiers. Crude criticism of American affairs offends and distresses me. In home politics I am strongly anti-segregationist. In foreign policy, I am definitely on the government's side. And when in doubt, I always follow the simple method of choosing that line of conduct which may be the most displeasing to the Reds and the Russells.

Is there a community of which you consider yourself a part?
  Not really. I can mentally collect quite a large number of individuals whom I am fond of but they would form a very disparate and discordant group if gathered in real life, on a real island. Otherwise, I would say that I am fairly comfortable in the company of American intellectuals who have read my books.

**What is your opinion of the academic world as a milieu for the creative writer? Could you speak specifically of the value or detriment of your teaching at Cornell?

A first-rate college library with a comfortable campus around it is a fine milieu for a writer. There is of course the problem of educating the young. I remember how once, between terms, not at Cornell, a student brought a transistor set with him into the reading room. He managed to state that 1) he was playing "classical" music; that 2) he was doing it "softly"; and that 3) "there were not many readers around in summer." I was there, a one-man multitude.

Would you describe your relationship with the contemporary literary community? With Edmund Wilson, Mary McCarthy, your magazine editors and book publishers?

The only time I ever collaborated with any writer was when I translated with Edmund Wilson Pushkin's *Mozart and Salieri* for the *New Republic* twenty-five years ago, a rather paradoxical recollection in view of his making such a fool of himself last year when he had the audacity of questioning my understanding of *Eugene Onegin*. Mary McCarthy, on the other hand, has been very kind to me recently in the same *New Republic*, although I do think she added quite a bit of her own angelica to the pale fire of Kinbote's plum pudding. I prefer not to mention here my relationship with Girodias. I have answered in *Evergreen* his scurvy article in the Olympia anthology. Otherwise, I am on excellent terms with all my publishers. My warm friendship with Catharine White and Bill Maxwell of *The New Yorker* is something the most arrogant author cannot evoke without gratitude and delight.

**Could you say something of your work habits? Do you write to a preplanned chart? Do you jump from one section to another, or do you move from the beginning through to the end?

The pattern of the thing precedes the thing. I fill in the

[99]

gaps of the crossword at any spot I happen to choose. These bits I write on index cards until the novel is done. My schedule is flexible but I am rather particular about my instruments: lined Bristol cards and well-sharpened, not too hard, pencils capped with erasers.

Is there a particular picture of the world which you wish to develop? The past is very present for you, even in a novel of the "future," such as Bend Sinister. *Are you a "nostalgist"? In what time would you prefer to live?*

In the coming days of silent planes and graceful aircycles, and cloudless silvery skies, and a universal system of padded underground roads to which trucks shall be relegated like Morlocks. As to the past, I would not mind retrieving from various corners of spacetime certain lost comforts, such as baggy trousers and long, deep bathtubs.

You know, you do not have to answer all my Kinbote-like questions.

It would never do to start skipping the tricky ones. Let us continue.

Besides writing novels, what do you, or would you, like most to do?

Oh, hunting butterflies, of course, and studying them. The pleasures and rewards of literary inspiration are nothing beside the rapture of discovering a new organ under the microscope or an undescribed species on a mountainside in Iran or Peru. It is not improbable that had there been no revolution in Russia, I would have devoted myself entirely to lepidopterology and never written any novels at all.

What is most characteristic of poshlust *in contemporary writing? Are there temptations for you in the sin of* poshlust? *Have you ever fallen?*

"Poshlust," or in a better transliteration *poshlost*, has

many nuances and evidently I have not described them clearly enough in my little book on Gogol, if you think one can ask anybody if he is tempted by *poshlost*. Corny trash, vulgar clichés, Philistinism in all its phases, imitations of imitations, bogus profundities, crude, moronic and dishonest pseudo-literature—these are obvious examples. Now, if we want to pin down *poshlost* in contemporary writing we must look for it in Freudian symbolism, moth-eaten mythologies, social comment, humanistic messages, political allegories, overconcern with class or race, and the journalistic generalities we all know. *Poshlost* speaks in such concepts as "America is no better than Russia" or "We all share in Germany's guilt." The flowers of *poshlost* bloom in such phrases and terms as "the moment of truth," "charisma," "existential" (used seriously), "dialogue" (as applied to political talks between nations), and "vocabulary" (as applied to a dauber). Listing in one breath Auschwitz, Hiroshima, and Vietnam is seditious *poshlost*. Belonging to a very select club (which sports *one* Jewish name—that of the treasurer) is genteel *poshlost*. Hack reviews are frequently *poshlost*, but it also lurks in certain highbrow essays. *Poshlost* calls Mr. Blank a great poet, and Mr. Bluff a great novelist. One of *poshlost's* favorite breeding places has always been the Art Exhibition; there it is produced by so-called sculptors working with the tools of wreckers, building crankshaft cretins of stainless steel, zen stereos, polystyrene stinkbirds, objects *trouvés* in latrines, cannon balls, canned balls. There we admire the *gabinetti* wallpatterns of so-called abstract artists, Freudian surrealism, roric smudges, and Rorschach blots—all of it as corny in its own right as the academic "September Morns" and "Florentine Flowergirls" of half a century ago. The list is long, and, of course, everybody has his *bête noire*, his black pet, in the series. Mine is that airline ad: the snack served by an obsequious wench to a young couple—she eyeing ecstatically the cucumber canapé, he admiring wistfully the hostess. And, of course, *Death in Venice*. You see the range.

Are there contemporary writers you follow with great pleasure?
There are several such writers, but I shall not name
them. Anonymous pleasure hurts nobody.

Do you follow some with great pain?
No. Many accepted authors simply do not exist for me.
Their names are engraved on empty graves, their books are
dummies, they are complete nonentities insofar as my taste
in reading is concerned. Brecht, Faulkner, Camus, many
others, mean absolutely nothing to me, and I must fight a
suspicion of conspiracy against my brain when I see
blandly accepted as "great literature" by critics and fellow
authors Lady Chatterley's copulations or the pretentious
nonsense of Mr. Pound, that total fake. I note he has
replaced Dr. Schweitzer in some homes.

***As an admirer of Borges and Joyce you seem to share their
pleasure in teasing the reader with tricks and puns and puzzles.
What do you think the relationship should be between reader and
author?*
I do not recollect any puns in Borges but then I read him
only in translation. Anyway, his delicate little tales and
miniature Minotaurs have nothing in common with Joyce's
great machines. Nor do I find many puzzles in that most
lucid of novels, *Ulysses.* On the other hand, I detest
Finnegans Wake in which a cancerous growth of fancy
word-tissue hardly redeems the dreadful joviality of the
folklore and the easy, too easy, allegory.

What have you learned from Joyce?
Nothing.

Oh, come.
James Joyce has not influenced me in any manner
whatsoever. My first brief contact with *Ulysses* was around
1920 at Cambridge University, when a friend, Peter Mro-

zovski, who had brought a copy from Paris, chanced to read to me, as he stomped up and down my digs, one or two spicy passages from Molly's monologue, which, *entre nous soit dit*, is the weakest chapter in the book. Only fifteen years later, when I was already well formed as a writer and reluctant to learn or unlearn anything, I read *Ulysses* and liked it enormously. I am indifferent to *Finnegans Wake* as I am to all regional literature written in dialect—even if it be the dialect of genius.

Aren't you doing a book about James Joyce?
But not only about him. What I intend to do is publish a number of twenty-page essays on several works—*Ulysses*, *Madame Bovary*, Kafka's *Transformation*, *Don Quixote*, and others—all based on my Cornell and Harvard lectures. I remember with delight tearing apart *Don Quixote*, a cruel and crude old book, before six hundred students in Memorial Hall, much to the horror and embarrassment of some of my more conservative colleagues.

What about other influences? Pushkin?
In a way—no more than, say, Tolstoy or Turgenev were influenced by the pride and purity of Pushkin's art.

Gogol?
I was careful *not* to learn anything from him. As a teacher, he is dubious and dangerous. At his worst, as in his Ukrainian stuff, he is a worthless writer; at his best, he is incomparable and inimitable.

Anyone else?
H. G. Wells, a great artist, was my favorite writer when I was a boy. *The Passionate Friends, Ann Veronica, The Time Machine, The Country of the Blind*, all these stories are far better than anything Bennett, or Conrad, or, in fact, any of

Wells' contemporaries would produce. His sociological cogitations can be safely ignored, of course, but his romances and fantasias are superb. There was an awful moment at dinner in our St. Petersburg house one night, when Zinaïda Vengerov, his translator, informed Wells, with a toss of her head: "You know, *my* favorite work of yours is *The Lost World.*" "She means the war the Martians lost," said my father quickly.

Did you learn from your students at Cornell? Was the experience purely a financial one? Did teaching teach you anything valuable?
My method of teaching precluded genuine contact with my students. At best, they regurgitated a few bits of my brain during examinations. Every lecture I delivered had been carefully, lovingly handwritten and typed out, and I leisurely read it out in class, sometimes stopping to rewrite a sentence and sometimes repeating a paragraph—a mnemonic prod which, however, seldom provoked any change in the rhythm of wrists taking it down. I welcomed the few shorthand experts in my audience, hoping they would communicate the information they stored to their less fortunate comrades. Vainly I tried to replace my appearances at the lectern by taped records to be played over the college radio. On the other hand, I deeply enjoyed the chuckle of appreciation in this or that warm spot of the lecture hall at this or that point of my lecture. My best reward comes from those former students of mine who ten or fifteen years later write to me to say that they now understand what I wanted of them when I taught them to visualize Emma Bovary's mistranslated hairdo or the arrangement of rooms in the Samsa household or the two homosexuals in *Anna Karenin.* I do not know if I learned anything from teaching but I know I amassed an invaluable amount of exciting information in analyzing a dozen novels for my students. My salary as you happen to know was not exactly a princely one.

Is there anything you would care to say about the collaboration your wife has given you?

She presided as adviser and judge over the making of my first fiction in the early twenties. I have read to her all my stories and novels at least twice. She has reread them all when typing them and correcting proofs and checking translations into several languages. One day in 1950, at Ithaca, New York, she was responsible for stopping me and urging delay and second thoughts as, beset with technical difficulties and doubts, I was carrying the first chapters of *Lolita* to the garden incinerator.

What is your relation to the translations of your books?

In the case of languages my wife and I know or can read—English, Russian, French, and to a certain extent German and Italian—the system is a strict checking of every sentence. In the case of Japanese or Turkish versions, I try not to imagine the disasters that probably bespatter every page.

What are your plans for future work?

I am writing a new novel but of this I cannot speak. Another project I have been nursing for some time is the publication of the complete screenplay of *Lolita* that I made for Kubrick. Although there are just enough borrowings from it in his version to justify my legal position as author of the script, the film is only a blurred skimpy glimpse of the marvelous picture I imagined and set down scene by scene during the six months I worked in a Los Angeles villa. I do not wish to imply that Kubrick's film is mediocre; in its own right, it is first-rate, but it is not what I wrote. A tinge of *poshlost* is often given by the cinema to the novel it distorts and coarsens in its crooked glass. Kubrick, I think, avoided this fault in his version, but I shall never understand why he did not follow my directions

and dreams. It is a great pity; but at least I shall be able to have people read my *Lolita* play in its original form.

If you had the choice of one and only one book by which you would be remembered, which one would it be?
The one I am writing or rather dreaming of writing. Actually, I shall be remembered by *Lolita* and my work on *Eugene Onegin.*

Do you feel you have any conspicuous or secret flaw as a writer?
The absence of a natural vocabulary. An odd thing to confess, but true. Of the two instruments in my possession, one—my native tongue—I can no longer use, and this not only because I lack a Russian audience, but also because the excitement of verbal adventure in the Russian medium has faded away gradually after I turned to English in 1940. My English, this second instrument I have always had, is however a stiffish, artificial thing, which may be all right for describing a sunset or an insect, but which cannot conceal poverty of syntax and paucity of domestic diction when I need the shortest road between warehouse and shop. An old Rolls-Royce is not always preferable to a plain Jeep.

What do you think about the contemporary competitive ranking of writers?
Yes, I have noticed that in this respect our professional book reviewers are veritable bookmakers. Who's in, who's out, and where are the snows of yesteryear. All very amusing. I am a little sorry to be left out. Nobody can decide if I am a middle-aged American writer or an old Russian writer—or an ageless international freak.

What is your great regret in your career?
That I did not come earlier to America. I would have

liked to have lived in New York in the thirties. Had my Russian novels been translated then, they might have provided a shock and a lesson for pro-Soviet enthusiasts.

Are there significant disadvantages to your present fame?
   Lolita is famous, not I. I am an obscure, doubly obscure, novelist with an unpronounceable name.

8

On February 17, 1968, Martin Esslin came to see me at my hotel in Montreux with the object of conducting an interview for *The New York Times Book Review*. The following letter awaited him downstairs.

"Welcome! I have devoted a lot of pleasurable time to answering in writing the questions sent to me by your London office. I have done so in a concise, stylish, printable form. Could I please ask you to have my answers appear in *The New York Times Book Review* the way they are prepared here? (Except that you may want to interrupt the longer answers by several inserted questions). That convenient method has been used to mutual satisfaction in interviews with *Playboy, The Paris Review, Wisconsin Studies, Le Monde, La Tribune de Genève*, etc. Furthermore, I like to see the proofs for checking last-minute misprints or possible little flaws of fact (dates, places). Being an unusually muddled speaker (a poor relative of the writer) I would like the stuff I prepared in typescript to be presented as direct speech on my part, whilst other statements which I may stammer out in the course of our chats, and the gist of which you might want to incorporate in The Profile, should be used, please, obliquely or paraphrastically, without any quotes. Naturally, it is for you to decide whether the background material should be kept separate in its published form from the question-and-answer section.

I am leaving the attached material with the concierge

because I think you might want to peruse it before we meet. I am very much looking forward to seeing you. Please give me a ring when you are ready."

The text given below is that of the typescript. The interview appeared in *The New York Times Book Review* on May 12, 1968.

How does VN live and relax?

A very old Russian friend of ours, now dwelling in Paris, remarked recently when she was here, that one night, forty years ago, in the course of a little quiz at one of her literary parties in Berlin, I, being asked where I would like to live, answered, "In a large comfortable hotel." That is exactly what my wife and I are doing now. About every other year she and I fly (she) or sail (she and I), back to our country of adoption but I must confess that I am a very sluggish traveler unless butterfly hunting is involved. For that purpose we usually go to Italy where my son and translator (from Russian into English) lives; the knowledge of Italian he has acquired in the course of his main career (opera singing) assists him, incidentally, in checking some of the Italian translations of my stuff. My own Italian is limited to "*avanti*" and "*prego*".

After waking up between six and seven in the morning, I write till ten-thirty, generally at a lectern which faces a bright corner of the room instead of the bright audiences of my professorial days. The first half-hour of relaxation is breakfast with my wife, around eight-thirty, and the creaming of our mail. One kind of letter that goes into the wastepaper basket at once, with its enclosed stamped envelope and my picture, is the one from the person who tells me he has a large collection of autographs (Somerset Maugham, Abu Abdul, Karen Korona, Charles Dodgson, Jr., etc.) and would like to add my name, which he misspells. Around eleven, I soak for twenty minutes in a hot bath, with a sponge on my head and a wordsman's worry in it, encroaching, alas, upon the nirvana. A stroll with my wife along the lake is followed by a frugal lunch and a two-hour nap after which I resume my work until dinner at seven. An American friend gave us a Scrabble set in Cyrillic alphabet, manufactured in Newtown, Conn.; so we play Russian *skrebl* for an hour or two after dinner. Then I read in bed—periodicals or one of the novels that proud publishers optimistically send me. Between eleven and midnight begins my usual fight with insomnia. Such are my habits in the cold season. Summers I spend in the pursuit of lepidoptera on flowery slopes and mountain screes; and, of course, after my daily hike of fifteen miles or more, I sleep even worse than in winter. My last resort in this business of relaxation is the composing of chess problems. The recent publication of two of them (in *The Sunday Times* and *The Evening News* of London) gave me more pleasure, I think, than the printing of my first poems half a century ago in St. Petersburg.

VN's social circle?

The tufted ducks and crested grebes of Geneva Lake. Some of the nice people in my new novel. My sister Elena in Geneva. A few friends in Lausanne and Vevey. A steady stream of brilliant American intellectuals visiting me in the riparian solitude of a beautifully reflected sunset. A Mr. Van Veen who travels down from his mountain chalet every other day to meet a dark lady, whose name I cannot divulge, on a street corner that I glimpse from my mammoth-tusk tower. Who else? A Mr. Vivian Badlook.

VN's feelings about his work?

My feelings about my work are, on the whole, not unfriendly. Boundless modesty and what people call "humility" are virtues scarcely conducive to one's complacently dwelling upon one's own work—particularly when one lacks them. I see it segmented into four stages. First comes meditation (including the accumulation of seemingly haphazard notes, the secret arrowheads of research); then the actual writing, and rewriting, on special index cards that my stationer orders for me: "special" because those you buy here come lined on both sides, and if, in the process of writing, a blast of inspiration sweeps a card onto the floor, and you pick it up without looking, and go on writing, it may happen—it has happened—that you fill in its under-side, numbering it, say, 107, and then cannot find your 103 which hides on the side, used before. When the fair copy on cards is ready, my wife reads it, checking it for legibility and spelling, and has it transferred onto pages by a typist who knows English; the reading of galleys is a further part of that third stage. After the book is out, foreign rights come into play. I am trilingual, in the proper sense of writing, and not only speaking, three languages (in that sense practically all the writers I personally know or knew in America, including a babel of paraphrasts, are strictly monolinguists). *Lolita* I have translated myself in Russian (recently published in New York by Phaedra, Inc.); but otherwise I am able to control and correct only the French translations of my novels. That process entails a good deal of wrestling with booboos and boners, but on the other hand allows me to reach my fourth, and final, stage—that of rereading my own book a few months after the original printing. What judgment do I then pronounce? Am I still satisfied with my work? Does the afterglow of achievement correspond to the foreglow of conception? It should and it does.

VN's opinions: on the modern world; on contemporary politics; on contemporary writers; on drug addicts who might consider Lolita *"square"?*

I doubt if we can postulate the objective existence of a "modern world" on which an artist should have any definite and important opinion. It has been tried, of course, and even carried to extravagant lengths. A hundred years ago, in Russia, the most eloquent and influential reviewers were left-wing, radical, utilitarian, political critics, who demanded that Russian novelists and poets portray and sift the modern scene. In those distant times, in that remote country, a typical critic would insist that a literary artist be a "reporter on the topics of the day," a social commentator, a class-war correspondent. That was half a century before the Bolshevist police not only revived the dismal so-called progressive (really, regressive) trend characteristic of the eighteen sixties and seventies, but, as we all know, enforced it. In the old days, to be sure, great lyrical poets or the incomparable prose artist who composed *Anna Karenin* (which should be transliterated without the closing "a"— she was not a ballerina) could cheerfully ignore the left-wing progressive Philistines who requested Tyutchev or Tolstoy to mirror politico-social soapbox gesticulations instead of dwelling on an aristocratic love affair or the beauties of nature. The dreary principles once voiced in the reign of Alexander the Second and their subsequent sinister transmutation into the decrees of gloomy police states (Kosygin's dour face expresses that gloom far better than Stalin's dashing mustache) come to my mind whenever I hear today retro-progressive book reviewers in America and England plead for a little more social comment, a little less artistic whimsy. The accepted notion of a "modern world" continuously flowing around us belongs to the same type of abstraction as say, the "quaternary period" of paleontology. What I feel to be the real modern world is the world the artist creates, his own mirage, which becomes a new *mir* ("world" in Russian) by the very act of his shedding, as it were, the age he lives in. My mirage is produced in my private desert, an arid but ardent place, with the sign No Caravans Allowed on the trunk of a lone palm. Of course, good minds do exist whose caravans of general ideas lead somewhere—to curious bazaars, to photogenic temples; but an independent novelist cannot derive much true benefit from tagging along.

I would also want to establish first a specific definition of the term politics, and that might mean dipping again in the remote past. Let me simplify matters by saying that in my parlor politics as well as in open-air statements (when subduing, for instance, a glib foreigner who is always glad to join our domestic demonstrators in attacking America), I content myself with remarking that what is bad for the Reds is good for me. I will abstain from details (they might lead to a veritable slalom of qualificatory parentheses), adding merely that I do not have any neatly limited political views or rather that such views as I have shade off into a vague old-fashioned liberalism. Much less vaguely—quite adamantically, or even adamantinely—I am aware of a central core of spirit in me that flashes and jeers at the brutal farce of totalitarian states, such as Russia, and her embarrassing tumors, such as China. A feature of my inner prospect is the absolute abyss yawning between the barbed-wire tangle of police states and the spacious free-dom of thought we enjoy in America and Western Europe.

I am bored by writers who join the social-comment racket. I despise the corny Philistine fad of flaunting four-letter words. I also refuse to find merit in a novel just because it is by a brave Black in Africa or a brave White in Russia—or by any representative of any single group in America. Frankly, a national, folklore, class, masonic, religious, or any other communal aura involuntarily prej-udices me against a novel, making it harder for me to peel the offered fruit so as to get at the nectar of possible talent. I could name, but will not, a number of modern artists whom I read purely for pleasure, and not for edification. I find comic the amalgamation of certain writers under a common label of, say, "Cape Codpiece Peace Resistance" or "Welsh Working-Upperclass Rehabilitation" or "New Hairwave School." Incidentally, I frequently hear the distant whining of people who complain in print that I dislike the writers whom *they* venerate such as Faulkner, Mann, Camus, Dreiser, and of course Dostoevski. But I can assure them that because I detest certain writers I am not impairing the well-being of the plaintiffs in whom the images of my victims happen to form organic galaxies of esteem. I can prove, indeed, that the works of those authors really exist independently and separately from the organs of affection throbbing in the systems of irate strangers.

Drug addicts, especially young ones, are conformists flocking together in sticky groups, and I do not write for groups, nor approve of group therapy (the big scene in the Freudian Farce); as I have said often enough, I write for myself in multiplicate, a not unfamiliar phenomenon on the horizons of shimmering deserts. Young dunces who turn to drugs cannot read *Lolita*, or any of my books; some in fact cannot read at all. Let me also observe that the term "square" already dates as a slang word, for nothing dates quicker than radical youth, nor is there anything more Philistine, more bourgeois, more ovine than this business of drug duncery. Half a century ago, a similar fashion among the smart set of St. Petersburg was cocaine sniffing combined with phony orientalities. The better and brighter minds of my young American readers are far removed from those juvenile fads and faddists. I also used to know in the past a Communist agent who got so involved in trying to wreck anti-Bolshevist groups by distributing drugs among them that he became an addict himself and lapsed into a dreamy state of commendable metempsychic sloth. He must be grazing today on some grassy slope in Tibet if he has not yet lined the coat of the fortunate shepherd.

9

On September 3, 1968, Nicholas Garnham interviewed me at the Montreux Palace for *Release*, BBC–2. The interview was faithfully reproduced in *The Listener*, October 10, of the same year: a neat and quick job. I have used its title for the present collection.

You have said your novels have 'no social purpose, no moral message.' What is the function of your novels in particular and of the novel in general?
One of the functions of all my novels is to prove that the novel in general does not exist. The book I make is a subjective and specific affair. I have no purpose at all when composing my stuff except to compose it. I work hard, I work long, on a body of words until it grants me complete possession and pleasure. If the reader has to work in his turn—so much the better. Art is difficult. Easy art is what you see at modern exhibitions of things and doodles.

In your prefaces you constantly mock Freud, the Viennese witch-doctor.
Why should I tolerate a perfect stranger at the bedside of my mind? I may have aired this before but I'd like to repeat that I detest not one but four doctors: Dr. Freud, Dr. Zhivago, Dr. Schweitzer, and Dr. Castro. Of course, the first takes the fig, as the fellows say in the dissecting-room.

I've no intention to dream the drab middle-class dreams of an Austrian crank with a shabby umbrella. I also suggest that the Freudian faith leads to dangerous ethical consequences, such as when a filthy murderer with the brain of a tapeworm is given a lighter sentence because his mother spanked him too much or too little—it works both ways. The Freudian racket looks to me as much of a farce as the jumbo thingum of polished wood with a polished hole in the middle which doesn't represent anything except the gaping face of the Philistine who is told it is a great sculpture produced by the greatest living caveman.

The novel on which you are working is, I believe, about 'time'? How do you see 'time'?
My new novel (now 800 typed pages long) is a family chronicle, mostly set in a dream America. Of its five parts one is built around my notion of time. I've drawn my scalpel through spacetime, space being the tumor, which I assign to the slops. While not having much physics, I reject Einstein's slick formulae; but then one need not know theology to be an atheist. Both my female creatures have Irish and Russian blood. One girl lasts 700 pages, dying young; her sister stays with me till the happy ending, when 95 candles burn in a birthday cake the size of a manhole lid.

Could you tell me which other writers you admire and have been influenced by?
I'd much prefer to speak of the modern books that I hate at first sight: the earnest case histories of minority groups, the sorrows of homosexuals, the anti-American Sovietnam sermon, the picaresque yarn larded with juvenile obscenities. That's a good example of self-imposed classification— books stuck together in damp lumpy groups, forgotten titles, amalgamated authors. As for influence, well, I've never been influenced by anyone in particular, dead or quick, just as I've never belonged to any club or movement.

In fact, I don't seem to belong to any clear-cut continent. I'm the shuttlecock above the Atlantic, and how bright and blue it is there, in my private sky, far from the pigeonholes and the clay pigeons.

The pattern of games such as chess and poker seems to hold a great fascination for you and to correspond to a fatalistic view of life. Could you explain the role of fate in your novels?

I leave the solution of such riddles to my scholarly commentators, to the nightingale voices in the apple trees of knowledge. Impersonally speaking, I can't find any so-called main ideas, such as that of fate, in my novels, or at least none that would be expressed lucidly in less than the number of words I used for this or that book. Moreover, I'm not interested in games as such. Games mean the participation of other persons; I'm interested in the lone performance—chess problems, for example, which I compose in glacial solitude.

There are constant references in your novels to popular movies and pulp fiction. You seem to delight in the atmosphere of such popular culture. Do you enjoy the originals and how do these relate to your own use of them?

No, I loathe popular pulp, I loathe go-go gangs, I loathe jungle music, I loathe science fiction with its gals and goons, suspense and suspensories. I especially loathe vulgar movies—cripples raping nuns under tables, or naked-girl breasts squeezing against the tanned torsos of repulsive young males. And, really, I don't think I mock popular trash more often than do other authors who believe with me that a good laugh is the best pesticide.

What has the fact of exile from Russia meant to you?

The type of artist who is always in exile even though he may never have left the ancestral hall or the paternal parish is a well-known biographical figure with whom I feel some affinity; but in a straighter sense, exile means to an artist only one thing—the banning of his books. All my books, ever since I wrote my first one 43 years ago on the moth-eaten couch of a German boardinghouse, are suppressed in the country of my birth. It's Russia's loss, not mine.

There is a sense, in all your fiction, of the imagined being so much truer than boring old reality. Do you see the categories of imagination, dream, and reality as distinct and, if so, in what way?

Your use of the word "reality" perplexes me. To be sure, there is an average reality, perceived by all of us, but that is not true reality: it is only the reality of general ideas, conventional forms of humdrummery, current editorials. Now if you mean by "old reality" the so-called "realism" of old novels, the easy platitudes of Balzac or Somerset Maugham or D. H. Lawrence—to take some especially depressing examples—then you are right in suggesting that the reality faked by a mediocre performer is boring, and that imaginary worlds acquire by contrast a dreamy and unreal aspect. Paradoxically, the only real, authentic worlds are, of course, those that seem unusual. When my fancies will have been sufficiently imitated, they, too, will enter the common domain of average reality, which will be false, too, but within a new context which we cannot yet guess. Average reality begins to rot and stink as soon as the act of individual creation ceases to animate a subjectively perceived texture.

Would it be fair to say that you see life as a very funny but cruel joke?

Your term "life" is used in a sense which I cannot apply to a manifold shimmer. Whose life? What life? Life does not exist without a possessive epithet. Lenin's life differs from, say, James Joyce's as much as a handful of gravel does from a blue diamond, although both men were exiles in Switzerland and both wrote a vast number of words. Or take the destinies of Oscar Wilde and Lewis Carroll—one flaunting a flamboyant perversion and getting caught, and the other hiding his humble but much more evil little secret behind the emulsions of the developing-room, and ending up by being the greatest children's story writer of all time. I'm not responsible for those real-life farces. My own life has been incomparably happier and healthier than that of Genghis Khan, who is said to have fathered the first Nabok, a petty Tatar prince in the twelfth century who married a Russian damsel in an era of intensely artistic Russian culture. As to the lives of my characters, not all are grotesque and not all are tragic: Fyodor in *The Gift* is blessed with a faithful love and an early recognition of his genius; John Shade in *Pale Fire* leads an intense inner existence, far removed from what you call a joke. You must be confusing me with Dostoevski.

10

Before coming to Montreux in mid-March, 1969, *Time* reporters Martha Duffy and R. Z. Sheppard sent me a score of questions by telex. The answers, neatly typed out, were awaiting them when they arrived, whereupon they added a dozen more, of which I answered seven. Some of the lot were quoted in the May 23, 1969, issue—the one with my face on the cover.

There seem to be similarities in the rhythm and tone of Speak, Memory *and* Ada, *and in the way you and Van retrieve the past in images. Do you both work along similar lines?*

The more gifted and talkative one's characters are, the greater the chances of their resembling the author in tone or tint of mind. It is a familiar embarrassment that I face with very faint qualms, particularly since I am not really aware of any special similarities—just as one is not aware of sharing mannerisms with a detestable kinsman. I loathe Van Veen.

The following two quotations seem closely related: "I confess I do not believe in time. I like to fold my magic carpet, after use, in such a way as to superimpose one part of the pattern upon another." (Speak, Memory) *and "pure time, perceptual time, tangible time, time free of content, context and running commentary—this is my time and theme. All the rest is numerical symbol or some aspect of*

[120]

space. *(Ada).* *Will you give me a lift on your magic carpet to point out how time is animated in the story of Van and Ada?*

In his study of time my creature distinguishes between text and texture, between the contents of time and its almost tangible essence. I ignored that distinction in my *Speak, Memory* and was mainly concerned with being faithful to the patterns of my past. I suspect that Van Veen, having less control over his imagination than I, novelized in his indulgent old age many images of his youth.

You have spoken in the past of your indifference to music, but in Ada *you describe time as "rhythm, the tender intervals between stresses." Are these rhythms musical, aural, physical, cerebral, what?*

Those "intervals" which seem to reveal the gray gaps of time between the black bars of space are much more similar to the interspaces between a metronome's monotonous beats than to the varied rhythms of music or verse.

If, as you have said, "mediocrity thrives on 'ideas,' " why does Van, who is no mediocrity, start explaining at length near the end of the book his ideas about time? Is this the vanity of Van? Or is the author commenting on or parodying his story?

By "ideas" I meant of course general ideas, the big, sincere ideas which permeate a so-called great novel, and which, in the inevitable long run, amount to bloated topicalities stranded like dead whales. I don't see any connection between this and my short section devoted to a savant's tussle with a recondite riddle.

Van remarks that "we are explorers in a very strange universe," and this reader feels that way about Ada. *You are known for your drawings—is it possible to draw your created universe? You have said that the whole substance of a book is in your head when you start writing on the cards. When did terra, antiterra, demonia,*

Ardis, etc., enter the picture? Why are the annals for terra fifty years behind? Also, various inventions and mechanical contrivances (like Prince Zemski's bugged harem) make seemingly anachronistic appearances. Why?

Antiterra happens to be an anachronistic world in regard to Terra—that's all there is to it.

In the Robert Hughes film about you, you say that in Ada, *metaphors start to live and turn into a story . . . "bleed and then dry up." Will you elaborate, please?*

The reference is to the metaphors in the Texture-of-Time section of *Ada:* gradually and gracefully they form a story—the story of a man traveling by car through Switzerland from east to west; and then the images fade out again.

Was Ada *the most difficult of your books to write? If so, would you discuss the major difficulties?*

Ada was physically harder to compose than my previous novels because of its greater length. In terms of the index cards on which I write and rewrite my stuff in pencil, it made, in the final draft, some 2,500 cards which Mme. Callier, my typist since *Pale Fire*, turned into more than 850 pages. I began working on the Texture-of-Time section some ten years ago, in Ithaca, upstate New York, but only in February, 1966, did the entire novel leap into the kind of existence that can and must be put into words. Its springboard was Ada's telephone call (in what is now the penultimate part of the book).

You call Ada *a family novel. Is your reversal of the sentiment in the opening line of* Anna Karenin *a parody or do you think your version is more often true? Is incest one of the different possible roads to happiness? Are the Veens happy at Ardis—or only in the memory of Ardis?*

If I had used incest for the purpose of representing a possible road to happiness or misfortune, I would have been a best-selling didactician dealing in general ideas. Actually I don't give a damn for incest one way or another. I merely like the "bl" sound in siblings, bloom, blue, bliss, sable. The opening sentences of *Ada* inaugurate a series of blasts directed throughout the book at translators of unprotected masterpieces who betray their authors by "transfigurations" based on ignorance and self-assertiveness.

Do you distinguish between Van the artist and Van the scientist? As his creator, what is your opinion of Van's works? Is Ada in part about an artist's inner life? In the Hughes film, you speak of illusionary moves in novels as in chess. Does Van make some false turnings in his story?

Objective, or at least one-mirror-removed, opinions of Van's efforts are stated quite clearly in the case of his *Letters from Terra* and two or three other compositions of his. I—or whoever impersonates me—is obviously on Van's side in the account of his anti-Vienna lecture on dreams.

Is Ada the artist's muse? How much does Van know about her? She seems to appear and reappear in his story and to dramatize successive stages of his life. When he borrows the first line of 'L'invitation au voyage' in his poem to her, does he suggest so close an identification as Baudelaire's—'aimer et mourir au pays qui te ressemble' ?

A pretty thought but not mine.

The twelve-year-old Ada's precocious sexuality is bound to bring comparison to Lolita. Is there any other connection between the two girls in your mind? Do you have the same affection for her as for Lolita? Is it, as Van says, that "all bright kids are depraved"?

The fact that Ada and Lolita lose their virginity at the same age is about the only peg on which to hang a comparison. Incidentally, Lolita, diminutive of Dolores, a little Spanish gypsy, is mentioned many times throughout *Ada*.

You once remarked that you are an "indivisible monist." Please elaborate.

Monism, which implies a oneness of basic reality, is seen to be divisible when, say, "mind" sneakily splits away from "matter" in the reasoning of a muddled monist or half-hearted materialist.

What are your future writing plans? You have mentioned publishing a book on Joyce and Kafka and your Cornell lectures. Will they appear soon? Are you thinking about another novel? Can you say anything about it now? Any poetry?

I have been working for the last months on an English translation of some of my Russian poems (dating from 1916 to this day) commissioned by McGraw-Hill. In 1968, I finished revising for the Princeton Press a second edition of my *Eugene Onegin* which will be even more gloriously and monstrously literal than the first.

Do you ever consider returning to America? To California, as you mentioned a few years ago? Can you say why you left the US? Do you still feel in some way American?

I am an American, I feel American, and I like that feeling. I live in Europe for family reasons, and I pay a US federal income tax on every cent I earn at home or abroad. Frequently, especially in spring, I dream of going to spend my purple-plumed sunset in California, among the lark-spurs and oaks, and in the serene silence of her university libraries.

Would you ever want to teach or lecture again?

No. Much as I like teaching, the strain of preparing lectures and delivering them would be too fatiguing today, even if I used a tape recorder. In this respect I have long come to the conclusion that the best teaching is done by records which a student can run as many times as he wants, or has to, in his soundproof cell. And at the end of the year he should undergo an old-fashioned, difficult, four-hour-long examination, with monitors walking between the desks.

Are you interested in working on the movie of Ada*? With its tactile, sensual beauty and its overlapping visual images,* Ada *seems a natural for films. There are stories of film executives converging on Montreux to read and bid on the book. Did you meet them? Did they ask many questions or seek your advice?*

Yes, film people did converge on my hotel in Montreux—keen minds, great enchanters. And, yes, I would indeed like very much to write, or help writing, a screenplay that would reflect *Ada*.

Some of your funniest remarks in recent novels have concerned driving and the problems of the road (including the image of the author groping with time as with the contents of a glove compartment). Do you drive? Enjoy motoring? Do you travel much? What means do you prefer? Have you plans to travel in the next year or so?

In the summer of 1915, in northern Russia, I, an adventurous lad of sixteen, noticed one day that our chauffeur had left the family convertible throbbing all alone before its garage (part of the huge stable at our place in the country); next moment I had driven the thing, with a sickly series of bumps, into the nearest ditch. That was the first time I ever drove a car. The second and last time was thirty-five years later, somewhere in the States, when my wife let me take the wheel for a few seconds and I narrowly missed crashing into the only car standing at the far side of a spacious parking lot. Between 1949 and 1959 she has driven me more than 150,000 miles all over North America—mainly on butterfly-hunting trips.

Salinger and Updike seem to be the only US writers you have praised. Have you any additions to the list? Have you read

Norman Mailer's recent political and social reportage (Armies of the Night)? *If so, do you admire it? Do you admire any American poets in particular?*

This reminds me: You know, it sounds preposterous, but I was invited last year to cover that political convention in Chicago in the company of two or three others writers. I did not go, naturally, and still believe it must have been some sort of joke on the part of *Esquire*—inviting *me* who can't tell a Democrat from a Republican and hates crowds and demonstrations.

What is your opinion of Russian writers like Solzhenitzyn, Abram Tertz, Andrey Voznesenski, who have been widely read in the last couple of years in the US?

It is only from a literary point of view that I could discuss fellow artists, and that would entail, in the case of the brave Russians you mention, a professional examination not only of virtues but also of flaws. I do not think that such objectivity would be fair in the livid light of the political persecution which brave Russians endure.

How often do you see your son? How do you and he collaborate on translating your work? Do you work together from the start of a project or do you act as editor or adviser?

We chose the hub of Europe for domicile not to be too far from our son Dmitri who lives near Milan. We see him not as often as we would like, now that his operatic career (he has a magnificent bass voice) requires him to travel to various countries. This defeats somewhat our purpose of residing in Europe. It also means that he cannot devote as much time as before to co-translating my old stuff.

In Ada *Van says that a man who loses his memory will room in heaven with guitarists rather than great or even mediocre writers. What would be your preference in celestial neighbors?*

It would be fun to hear Shakespeare roar with ribald

laughter on being told what Freud (roasting in the other place) made of his plays. It would satisfy one's sense of justice to see H. G. Wells invited to more parties under the cypresses than slightly bogus Conrad. And I would love to find out from Pushkin whether his duel with Ryleev, in May, 1820, was really fought in the park of Batovo (later my grandmother's estate) as I was the first to suggest in 1964.

Will you speak briefly about the émigré life of the twenties and thirties? Where, for instance, were you a tennis instructor? Whom did you teach? Mr. Appel mentioned that he thought you gave lectures to émigré groups. If so, what were your subjects? It seems you must have traveled a good deal. Is that true?

I gave tennis lessons to the same people, or friends of the same people, to whom I gave lessons of English or French since around 1921, when I still shuttled between Cambridge and Berlin, where my father was co-editor of an émigré Russian language daily, and where I more or less settled after his death in 1922. In the thirties I was frequently asked to give public readings of my prose and verse by émigré organizations. In the course of those activities I traveled to Paris, Prague, Brussels and London, and then, one blessed day in 1939, Aldanov, a fellow writer and a dear friend, said to me: "Look, next summer or the one after that, I am invited to lecture at Stanford in California but I cannot go, so would you like to replace me?" That's how the third spiral of my life started to coil.

Where and when did you meet your wife? Where and when did you marry? Can you or she describe her background and girlhood briefly? In what city and/or country did you court her? If I am correct that she is also Russian, did you or any of your brothers and sisters meet her when you were children?

I met my wife, Véra Slonim, at one of the émigré charity balls in Berlin at which it was fashionable for Russian young ladies to sell punch, books, flowers, and toys. Her father was a St. Petersburg jurist and industrialist, ruined by the revolution. We might have met years earlier at some party in St. Petersburg where we had friends in common. We married in 1925, and were at first extremely hard up.

The Appels and others have said that Cornell's student literati were less attracted to your fiction course than sorority sisters, frat brothers, and athletes. Were you aware of that? If the above is true, the reason given was that you were "a flamboyant, funny lecturer." This description seems at variance with your self-drawn picture as a remote lecturer. Can you talk just a little more about your life as a teacher, as this is an inevitable part of the cover story. How did the students seem to you then? They called the big course "Dirty Lit." Do you think it was you or the Masterpieces of European Fiction that shocked them? Or would anything have shocked them? What would you think of teaching on today's more activist, demonstration-struck campuses?

Classes varied from term to term during my seventeen years of teaching. I do remember that my approach and principles irritated or puzzled such students of literature (and their professors) as were accustomed to "serious" courses replete with "trends," and "schools," and "myths," and "symbols," and "social comment," and something unspeakably spooky called "climate of thought." Actually, those "serious" courses were quite easy ones, with the student required to know not the books but about the books. In my classes, readers had to discuss specific details, not general ideas. "Dirty Lit" was an inherited joke: it had been applied to the lectures of my immediate predecessor, a sad, gentle, hard-drinking fellow who was more interested in the sex life of authors than in their books. Activist, demonstration-struck students of the present decade would, I suppose, either drop my course after a couple of lectures or end by getting a fat F if they could not answer such exam questions as: *Discuss the twinned-dream theme in the* case of two teams of dreamers, *Stephen D.–Bloom*, and *Vronski–Anna*. None of my questions ever presupposed the advocacy of a fashionable interpretation or critical view that a teacher might wish to promote. All my questions were impelled by only one purpose: to discover at all cost if the student had thoroughly imbibed and assimilated the novels in my course.

I can now see that if you don't share Van's system of "distressibles," you well might. Are you, like him, insomniac?

I have described the insomnias of my childhood in *Speak, Memory.* They still persecute me every other night. Helpful pills do exist but I am afraid of them. I detest drugs. My habitual hallucinations are quite monstrously sufficient, thank Hades. Looking at it objectively, I have never seen a more lucid, more lonely, better balanced mad mind than mine.

Immediately following the above quote, Van warns against the "assassin pun." You are obviously a brilliant and untiring punner and it would seem particularly appropriate if you would briefly discuss the pun for Time which, God knows, is porous from the bullets of a particularly clumsy but determined assassin.

In a poem about poetry as he understands it, Verlaine warns the poet against using *la pointe assassine*, that is introducing an epigrammatic or moral point at the end of a poem, and thereby murdering the poem. What amused me was to pun on "point," thus making a pun in the very act of prohibiting it.

You have been a Sherlock Holmes buff. When did you lose your taste for mystery fiction. Why?

With a very few exceptions, mystery fiction is a kind of collage combining more or less original riddles with conventional and mediocre artwork.

Why do you so dislike dialogue in fiction?

Dialogue can be delightful if dramatically or comically stylized or artistically blended with descriptive prose; in other words, if it is a feature of style and structure in a given work. If not, then it is nothing but automatic typewriting, formless speeches filling page after page, over which the eye skims like a flying saucer over the Dust Bowl.

11

In April, 1969, Alden Whitman sent me these questions and came to Montreux for a merry interview shortly before my seventieth birthday. His piece appeared in *The New York Times*, April 19, 1969, with only two or three of my answers retained. The rest are to be used, I suppose, as "Special to The New York Times" at some later date by A. W., if he survives, or by his successor. I transcribe some of our exchanges.

You have called yourself "an American writer, born in Russia and educated in England." How does this make you an American writer?

An American writer means, in the present case, a writer who has been an American citizen for a quarter of a century. It means, moreover, that all my works appear first in America. It also means that America is the only country where I feel mentally and emotionally at home. Rightly or wrongly, I am not one of those perfectionists who by dint of hypercriticizing America find themselves wallowing in the same muddy camp with indigenous rascals and envious foreign observers. My admiration for this adopted country of mine can easily survive the jolts and flaws that, indeed, are nothing in comparison to the abyss of evil in the history of Russia, not to speak of other, more exotic, countries.

In the poem "To My Soul," you wrote, possibly of yourself, as "a provincial naturalist, an eccentric lost in paradise." This appears to link your interest in butterflies to other aspects of your life, writing, for instance. Do you feel that you are "an eccentric lost in paradise"?

An eccentric is a person whose mind and senses are excited by things that the average citizen does not even notice. And, per contra, the average eccentric—for there are many of us, of different waters and magnitudes—is utterly baffled and bored by the adjacent tourist who boasts of his business connections. In that sense, I often feel lost; but then, other people feel lost in my presence too. And I also know, as a good eccentric should, that the dreary old fellow who has been telling me all about the rise of mortgage interest rates may suddenly turn out to be the greatest living authority on springtails or tumblebugs.

Dreams of flight or escape recur in many of your poems and stories. Is this a reflection of your own years of wandering?

Yes, in part. The odd fact, however, is that in my early childhood, long before the tremendously dull peripatetics of Revolution and Civil War set in, I suffered from nightmares full of wanderings and escapes, and desolate station platforms.

What did you enjoy (and disenjoy) in your Harvard experience? And what induced you to leave Cambridge?

My Harvard experience consisted of seven blissful years (1941–1948) of entomological research at the wonderful and unforgettable Museum of Comparative Zoology and of one spring term (1952) of lecturing on the European novel to an audience of some 600 young strangers in Memorial Hall. Apart from that experience, I lectured at Wellesley for half-a-dozen years and then, from 1948, was on the faculty of Cornell, ending as full professor of Russian Literature and author of American *Lolita*, after which (in 1959) I decided to devote myself entirely to writing. I greatly enjoyed Cornell.

In the United States you are probably more widely known for Lolita *than for any other single book or poem. If you had your way, what book or poem or story would you like to be known for in the U.S.?*

I am immune to the convulsions of fame; yet, I think that the harmful drudges who define today, in popular dictionaries, the word "nymphet" as "a very young but sexually attractive girl," without any additional comment or reference, should have their knuckles rapped.

Has the sexual kick in literature reached a peak? Will it not now decline?

I am completely indifferent to the social aspect of this or any other group activity. Historically, the pornographic record set by the ancients still remains unbroken. Artistically, the dirtier typewriters try to get, the more conventional and corny their products become, e.g. such novels as *Miller's Thumb* and *Tailor's Spasm.*

What is your attitude toward modern violence?

I abhor the brutality of all brutes, white or black, brown or red. I despise red knaves and pink fools.

Reflecting on your life, what have been its truly significant moments?

Every moment, practically. Yesterday's letter from a reader in Russia, the capture of an undescribed butterfly last year, learning to ride a bicycle in 1909.

How do you rank yourself among writers (living) and of the immediate past?

I often think there should exist a special typographical

sign for a smile—some sort of concave mark, a supine round bracket, which I would now like to trace in reply to your question.

If you were writing your own obituary, what would you stress or emphasize as your contribution to literature, to the climate of opinion (art and esthetics) of the last 50 years?

In my case the afterglow of a recent work (say, *Ada*, finished last Christmas) mingles at once with the hazy aurora of a new task. My next book, dawning as it does in ideal tint and tone, seems for the moment better than anything I wrote before. What I am trying to emphasize is a special thrill of anticipation which by its very nature cannot be treated necrologically.

What books have you enjoyed lately?

I seldom experience nowadays the spinal twinge which is the only valid reaction to a new piece of great poetry—such as, for example, Richard Wilbur's "Complaint," a poem about his marvelous duchess (Phoenix Bookshop edition, 1968).

12

In early June, 1969, Philip Oakes sent me a series of questions on behalf of *The Sunday Times*, London. I happened to be greatly annoyed by the editorial liberties that periodicals in other countries had been taking with material I had supplied. When he arrived on June 15, I gave him my written answers accompanied by the following note.

> When preparing interviews I invariably write out my replies (and sometimes additional questions) taking great care to make them as concise as possible.
>
> My replies represent unpublished material, should be printed verbatim and in toto, and copyrighted in my name.
>
> Answers may be rearranged in whatever order the interviewer or the editor wishes: for example, they may be split, with insertion of the questioner's comments or bits of descriptive matter (but none of the latter material may be ascribed to me).
>
> Unprepared remarks, quips, etc., may come from me during the actual colloquy but may not be published without my approval.
>
> The article will be shown to me before publication so as to avoid factual errors (*e.g.*, in names, dates, etc.).

Mr. Oakes' article appeared in *The Sunday Times* on June 22, 1969.

As a distinguished entomologist and novelist do you find that your two main preoccupations condition, restrict, or refine your view of the world?

What world? Whose world? If we mean the average

world of the average newspaper reader in Liverpool, Livorno, or Vilno, then we are dealing in trivial generalities. If, on the other hand, an artist invents his own world, as I think I do, then how can he be said to influence his own understanding of what he has created himself? As soon as we start defining such terms as "the writer," "the world," "the novel," and so on, we slip into a solipsismal abyss where general ideas dissolve. As to butterflies—well, my taxonomic papers on lepidoptera were published mainly in the nineteen forties, and can be of interest to only a few specialists in certain groups of American butterflies. In itself, an aurelian's passion is not a particularly unusual sickness; but it stands outside the limits of a novelist's world, and I can prove this by the fact that whenever I allude to butterflies in my novels, no matter how diligently I rework the stuff, it remains pale and false and does not really express what I want it to express—what, indeed, it can only express in the special scientific terms of my entomological papers. The butterfly that lives forever on its type-labeled pin and in its O. D. ("original description") in a scientific journal dies a messy death in the fumes of the arty gush. However—not to let your question go completely unanswered—I must admit that in one sense the entomological satellite does impinge upon my novelistic globe. This is when certain place-names are mentioned. Thus if I hear or read the words "Alp Grum, Engadine" the normal observer within me may force me to imagine the belvedere of a tiny hotel on its 2000-meter-tall perch and mowers working along a path that winds down to a toy railway; but what *I* see first of all and above all is the Yellow-banded Ringlet settled with folded wings on the flower that those damned scythes are about to behead.

What was the most amusing item you recently found in the papers?
    That bit about Mr. E. Pound, a venerable fraud, making a "sentimental visit" to his alma mater in Clinton, New

York, and being given a standing ovation by the commencement audience—consisting, apparently, of morons and madmen.

Have you seen the cinema version of your Laughter in the Dark?

I have. Nicol Williamson is, of course, an admirable actor, and some of the sequences are very good. The scene with the water-ski girl, gulping and giggling, is exceptionally successful. But I was appalled by the commonplace quality of the sexual passages. I would like to say something about that. Clichés and conventions breed remarkably fast. They occur as readily in the primitive jollities of the jungle as in the civilized obligatory scenes of our theater. In former times Greek masks must have set many a Greek dentition on edge. In recent films, including *Laughter in the Dark*, the porno grapple has *already* become a cliché though the device is but half-a-dozen years old. I would have been sorry that Tony Richardson should have followed that trite trend, had it not given me the opportunity to form and formulate the following important notion: theatrical acting, in the course of the last centuries, has led to incredible refinements of stylized pantomine in the representation of, say, a person eating, or getting deliciously drunk, or looking for his spectacles, or making a proposal of marriage. Not so in regard to the imitation of the sexual act which on the stage has absolutely no tradition behind it. The Swedes and we have to start from scratch and what I have witnessed up to now on the screen—the blotchy male shoulder, the false howls of bliss, the four or five mingled feet—all of it is primitive, commonplace, conventional, and therefore disgusting. The lack of art and style in these paltry copulations is particularly brought into evidence by their clashing with the marvelously high level of acting in virtually all other imitations of natural gestures on our stage and screen. This is an attractive topic to ponder further, and directors should take notice of it.

[137]

When you are writing your novels, you have a remarkable sense of history and period, although the situations in which your characters are involved reflect perennial dilemmas. Do you feel that any given time creates special problems which interest you as a writer?

We should define, should we not, what we mean by "history." If "history" means a "written account of events" (and that is about all Clio can claim), then let us inquire *who* actually—what scribes, what secretaries—took it down and how qualified they were for the job. I am inclined to guess that a big part of "history" (the unnatural history of man—not the naive testimony of rocks) has been modified by mediocre writers and prejudiced observers. We know that police states (*e.g.*, the Soviets) have actually snipped out and destroyed such past events in old books as did not conform to the falsehoods of the present. But even the most talented and conscientious historian may err. In other words, I do not believe that "history" exists apart from the historian. If I try to select a keeper of records, I think it safer (for my comfort, at least) to choose my own self. But nothing recorded or thought up by myself can create any special "problems" in the sense you suggest.

You say somewhere that, artistically speaking, you prefer Lolita *to all your other books. Has your new novel* Ada *superseded* Lolita *in your affection?*

Not really. It is true that *Ada* caused me more trouble than all my other novels and perhaps that bright fringe of overlapping worry is synonymous with the crest of love. Incidentally, speaking of my first nymphet, let me take this neat opportunity to correct a curious misconception proffered by an anonymous owl in a London weekly a couple of months ago. "Lolita" should not be pronounced in the English or Russian fashion (as he thinks it should), but with a trill of Latin "l"s and a delicate toothy "t."

Do you feel isolated as a writer?

Most of the writers I have met were Russian émigrés in the nineteen twenties and thirties. With American novelists I have had virtually no contact. In England, I had lunch once with Graham Greene. I have dined with Joyce and have had tea with Robbe-Grillet. Isolation means liberty and discovery. A desert island may be more exciting than a city, but my loneliness, on the whole, has little significance. It is a consequence of chance circumstance—old shipwrecks, freakish tides—and not a matter of temperament. As a private person I am good-natured, warm, cheerful, straightforward, plainspoken, and intolerant of bogus art. I do not mind my own writings being criticized or ignored and therefore think it funny that people not even concerned with literature should be upset by my finding D. H. Lawrence execrable or my seeing in H. G. Wells a far greater artist than Conrad.

What do you think of the so-called "student revolution"?

Rowdies are never revolutionary, they are always reactionary. It is among the young that the greatest conformists and Philistines are found, e.g., the hippies with their group beards and group protests. Demonstrators at American universities care as little about education as football fans who smash up subway stations in England care about soccer. All belong to the same family of goofy hoodlums—with a sprinkling of clever rogues among them.

What are your working methods?

Quite banal. Thirty years ago I used to write in bed, dipping my pen into a bedside inkwell, or else I would compose mentally at any time of the day or night. I would fall asleep when the sparrows woke up. Nowadays I write my stuff on index cards, in pencil, at a lectern, in the forenoon; but I still tend to do a lot of work in my head during long walks in the country on dull days when butterflies do not interfere. Here is a disappointed lepidopterist's ditty:

It's a long climb
Up the rock face
At the wrong time
To the right place.

Do you keep a journal or seek documentary reminders?

I am an ardent memoirist with a rotten memory; a drowsy king's absentminded remembrancer. With absolute lucidity I recall landscapes, gestures, intonations, a million sensuous details, but names and numbers topple into oblivion with absurd abandon like little blind men in file from a pier.

13

Of the fifty-eight questions James Mossman submitted on September 8, 1969, for *Review*, BBC–2 (October 4) some 40 were answered and recorded by me from written cards in Montreux. *The Listener* published the thing in an incomplete form on October 23 of that year. Printed here from my final typescript.

You have said that you explored time's prison and have found no way out. Are you still exploring, and is it inevitably a solitary excursion, from which one returns to the solace of others?

I'm a very poor speaker. I hope our audience won't mind my using notes.

My exploration of time's prison as described in the first chapter of *Speak, Memory* was only a stylistic device meant to introduce my subject.

Memory often presents a life broken into episodes, more or less perfectly recalled. Do you see any themes working through from one episode to another?

Everyone can sort out convenient patterns of related themes in the past development of his life. Here again I had to provide pegs and echoes when furnishing my reception halls.

Is the strongest tie between men this common captivity in time?

Let us not generalize. The common captivity in time is

felt differently by different people, and some people may not feel it at all. Generalizations are full of loopholes and traps. I know elderly men for whom "time" only means "timepiece."

What distinguishes us from animals?
Being aware of being aware of being. In other words, if I not only know that I *am* but also know that I know it, then I belong to the human species. All the rest follows—the glory of thought, poetry, a vision of the universe. In that respect, the gap between ape and man is immeasurably greater than the one between amoeba and ape. The difference between an ape's memory and human memory is the difference between an ampersand and the British Museum library.

Judging from your own awakening consciousness as a child, do you think that the capacity to use language, syntax, relate ideas, is something we learn from adults, as if we were computers being programed, or do we begin to use a unique, built-in capability of our own—call it imagination?
The stupidest person in the world is an all-round genius compared to the cleverest computer. How we learn to imagine and express things is a riddle with premises impossible to express and a solution impossible to imagine.

In your acute scrutiny of your past, can you find the instruments that fashioned you?
Yes—unless I refashion them retrospectively, by the very act of evoking them. There is quite a lot of give and take in the game of metaphors.

As you recall a patch of time, its shapes, sounds, colors, and occupants, does this complete picture help combat time or offer any clue to its mysteries, or is it pleasure that it affords?
Let me quote a paragraph in my book *Ada*: "Physiologi-

cally the sense of Time is a sense of continuous becoming. . . . Philosophically, on the other hand, Time is but memory in the making. In every individual life there goes on, from cradle to deathbed, the gradual shaping and strengthening of that *backbone of consciousness*, which is the Time of the strong." This is Van speaking, Van Veen, the charming villain of my book. I have not decided yet if I agree with him in all his views on the texture of time. I suspect I don't.

Does the inevitable distortion of detail worry you?

Not at all. The distortion of a remembered image may not only enhance its beauty with an added refraction, but provide informative links with earlier or later patches of the past.

You've said that the man in you revolts sometimes against the fictionist. Can you say why? (Note: I'm thinking of your regret at giving items of your past to characters.)

One hates oneself for leaving a pet with a neighbor and never returning for it.

Doesn't giving away past memories to your characters alleviate the burden of the past?

Items of one's past are apt to fade from exposure. They are like those richly pigmented butterflies and moths which the ignorant amateur hangs up in a display case on the wall of his sunny parlor and which, after a few years, are bleached to a pitiful drab hue. The metallic blue of so-called structural wing scales is hardier, but even so a wise collector should keep specimens in the dry dark of a cabinet.

You have written of yourself as looking out "from my present ridge of remote, isolated, almost uninhabited time." Why uninhabited?

Well, for the same reason that a desert island is a more

deserving island than one with a footprint initialing its beach. Moreover, "uninhabited" makes direct sense here, since most of my former companions are gone.

Does the aristocrat in you despise the fictionist, or is it only English aristocrats who feel queasy about men of letters?

Pushkin, professional poet and Russian nobleman, used to shock the *beau monde* by declaring that he wrote for his own pleasure but published for the sake of money. I do likewise, but have never shocked anybody—except, perhaps, a former publisher of mine who used to counter my indignant requests by saying that I'm much too good a writer to need extravagant advances.

Is the capacity to recall and to celebrate patches of past time a special quality of yours?

No, I don't think so. I could name many writers, English, Russian, and French, who have done it at least as well as I have. Funny, I notice that when mentioning my three tongues, I list them in that order because it is the best rhythmic arrangement: either dactylic, with one syllable skipped, "Énglish, Rússian, and Frénch," or anapestic, "English, Rússian, and Frénch." Little lesson in prosody.

Have you ever experienced hallucinations or heard voices or had visions, and if so, have they been illuminating?

When about to fall asleep after a good deal of writing or reading, I often enjoy, if that is the right word, what some drug addicts experience—a continuous series of extraordinary bright, fluidly changing pictures. Their type is different nightly, but on a given night it remains the same: one night it may be a banal kaleidoscope of endlessly recombined and reshaped stained-window designs; next time, comes a subhuman or superhuman face with a formidably growing blue eye; or, and this is the most striking type, I see in realistic detail a long-dead friend turning toward me and melting into another remembered figure against the black velvet of my eyelids' inner side. As to voices, I have described in *Speak, Memory* the snatches of telephone talk which now and then vibrate in my pillowed ear. Reports on those enigmatic phenomena can be found in the case histories collected by psychiatrists but no satisfying interpretation has come my way. Freudians, keep out, please.

Your best memories seem to be golden days, with great green trees, splashes of sun on venerable stone, harmony—a world in which people were going to live for ever. Do you manipulate the past in order to combat life at its less harmonious?

My existence has always remained as harmonious and green as it was throughout the span dealt with in my memoirs, that is from 1903 to 1940. The emotions of my Russian childhood have been replaced by new excitements, by new mountains explored in search of new butterflies, by a cloudless family life, and by the monstrous delights of novelistic invention.

Is writing your novels pleasure or drudgery?

Pleasure and agony while composing the book in my mind; harrowing irritation when struggling with my tools and viscera—the pencil that needs resharpening, the card that has to be rewritten, the bladder that has to be drained, the word that I always misspell and always have to look up. Then the labor of reading the typescript prepared by a secretary, the correction of my major mistakes and her minor ones, transferring corrections to other copies, misplacing pages, trying to remember something that had to be crossed out or inserted. Repeating the process when proofreading. Unpacking the radiant beautiful plump advance copy, opening it—and discovering a stupid oversight committed by me, allowed by me to survive. After a month or so I get used to the book's final stage, to its having been

[145]

weaned from my brain. I now regard it with a kind of amused tenderness as a man regards not his son, but the young wife of his son.

You say you are not interested in what critics say, yet you got very angry with Edmund Wilson once for commenting on you, and let off some heavy field guns at him, not to say multiple rockets. You must have cared.

I never retaliate when my works of art are concerned. There the arrows of adverse criticism cannot scratch, let alone pierce, the shield of what disappointed archers call my "self-assurance." But I do reach for my heaviest dictionary when my scholarship is questioned, as was the case with my old friend Edmund Wilson, and I do get annoyed when people I never met impinge on my privacy with false and vulgar assumptions—as for example Mr. Updike, who in an otherwise clever article absurdly suggests that my fictional character, bitchy and lewd Ada, is, I quote, "in a dimension or two, Nabokov's wife." I might add that I collect clippings—for information and entertainment.

Do you see yourself sometimes as Nabokov the writer isolated from others, flaming sword to scourge them, an entertainer, a drudge, a genius, which?

The word "genius" is passed around rather generously, isn't it? At least in English, because its Russian counterpart, *geniy*, is a term brimming with a sort of throaty awe and is used only in the case of a very small number of writers, Shakespeare, Milton, Pushkin, Tolstoy. To such deeply beloved authors as Turgenev and Chekhov Russians assign the thinner term, *talánt*, talent, not genius. It is a bizarre example of semantic discrepancy—the same word being more substantial in one language than in another. Although my Russian and my English are practically coeval, I still feel appalled and puzzled at seeing "genius" applied to any important storyteller, such as Maupassant or Maugham. Genius still means to me, in my Russian fastidiousness and pride of phrase, a unique, dazzling gift, the genius of James Joyce, not the talent of Henry James. I'm afriad I have lost the thread of my reply to your question. What is your next one, please?

Can political ideas solve any of the big problems of an individual's life?

I have always marveled at the neatness of such solutions: ardent Stalinists transforming themselves into harmless Socialists, Socialists finding a sunset harbor in Conservatism, and so forth. I suppose this must be rather like religious conversion, of which I know very little. I can only explain God's popularity by an atheist's panic.

Why do you say you dislike "serious" writers? Don't you just mean "bad" artists?

Let me put it this way. By inclination and intent I avoid squandering my art on the illustrated catalogues of solemn notions and serious opinions; and I dislike their pervasive presence in the works of others. What ideas can be traced in my novels belong to my creatures therein and may be deliberately flawed. In my memoirs, quotable ideas are merely passing visions, suggestions, mirages of the mind. They lose their colors or explode like football fish when lifted out of the context of their tropical sea.

Great writers have had strong political and sociological preferences or ideas. Tolstoy was one. Does the presence of such ideas in his work make you think the less of him?

I go by books, not by authors. I consider *Anna Karenin* the supreme masterpiece of nineteenth-century literature; it is closely followed by *The Death of Ivan Ilyich.* I detest *Resurrection* and *The Kreuzer Sonata.* Tolstoy's publicistic forays are unreadable. *War and Peace*, though a little too long, is a rollicking historical novel written for that amorphic and limp creature known as "the general reader," and more specifically for the young. In terms of artistic structure it does not satisfy me. I derive no pleasure from its cumbersome message, from the didactic interludes, from the artificial coincidences, with cool Prince Andrey turning up to witness this or that historical moment, this or that footnote in the sources used often uncritically by the author.

Why do you dislike writers who go in for soul-searching and self-revelations in print? After all, do you not do it at another remove, behind a thicket of art?

If you are alluding to Dostoevski's worst novels, then, indeed, I dislike intensely *The Karamazov Brothers* and the ghastly *Crime and Punishment* rigmarole. No, I do not object to soul-searching and self-revelation, but in those books the soul, and the sins, and the sentimentality, and the journalese, hardly warrant the tedious and muddled search.

Is your attachment to childhood specially nostalgic and intense because you were abruptly and forever banished from the place where it evolved by the Russian Revolution?

Yes, that's right. But the stress is not on Russian Revolution. It could have been anything, an earthquake, an illness, an individual departure prompted by a private disaster. The accent is on the abruptness of the change.

Would you ever try to go back there, just to have a look?

There's nothing to look at. New tenement houses and old churches do not interest me. The hotels there are terrible. I detest the Soviet theater. Any palace in Italy is superior to the repainted abodes of the Tsars. The village huts in the forbidden hinterland are as dismally poor as ever, and the wretched peasant flogs his wretched cart horse with the same wretched zest. As to my special northern landscape and the haunts of my childhood—well, I would not wish to contaminate their images preserved in my mind.

How would you define your alienation from present-day Russia?
I loathe and despise dictatorships.

You called the Revolution there "trite." Why?
Because it followed the banal historical pattern of bloodshed, deceit, and oppression, because it betrayed the democratic dream, and because all it can promise the Soviet citizen is the material article, second-hand Philistine values, imitation of Western foods and gadgets, and of course, caviar for the decorated general.

Why do you live in hotels?
It simplifies postal matters, it eliminates the nuisance of private ownership, it confirms me in my favorite habit—the habit of freedom.

Do you have a longing for one place ever, a place in which family or racial continuity has been witnessed for generations, a scrap of Russia in return for the whole of the United States?
I have no such longings.

Is nostalgia debilitating or enriching?
Neither. It's one of a thousand tender emotions.

Do you like being an American citizen?
Yes, very much so.

Did you sit up to watch the Americans land on the moon? Were you impressed?
Oh, "impressed" is not the right word! Treading the soil of the moon gives one, I imagine (or rather my projected

self imagines), the most remarkable romantic thrill ever experienced in the history of discovery. *Of course*, I rented a television set to watch every moment of their marvelous adventure. That gentle little minuet that despite their awkward suits the two men danced with such grace to the tune of lunar gravity was a lovely sight. It was also a moment when a flag means to one more than a flag usually does. I am puzzled and pained by the fact that the English weeklies ignored the absolutely overwhelming excitement of the adventure, the strange sensual exhilaration of palpating those precious pebbles, of seeing our marbled globe in the black sky, of feeling along one's spine the shiver and wonder of it. After all, Englishmen should understand that thrill, they who have been the greatest, the purest explorers. Why then drag in such irrelevant matters as wasted dollars and power politics?

If you ruled any modern industrial state absolutely, what would you abolish?
I would abolish trucks and transistors, I would outlaw the diabolical roar of motorcycles, I would wring the neck of soft music in public places. I would banish the *bidet* from hotel bathrooms so as to make more room for a longer bathtub. I would forbid farmers the use of insecticides and allow them to mow their meadows only once a year, in late August when everyone has safely pupated.

Do you like reading newspapers?
Yes, especially the Sunday papers.

You refer somewhere to your father's study teaching you to appreciate authentic poetry. Is any living poet authentic to you now?
I used to have a veritable passion for poetry, English, Russian, and French. That passion started to dwindle

around 1940 when I stopped gorging myself on contemporary verse. I know as little about today's poetry as about
new music.

Are too many people writing novels?
I read quite a number of them every year. For some odd
reason what authors and publishers keep sending me is the
pseudo-picaresque stuff of cliché characters and the enlarged pores of dirty words.

You parody the poet W. H. Auden in your novel Ada, *I think.
Why do you think so little of him?*
I do not parody Mr. Auden anywhere in *Ada*. I'm not
sufficiently familiar with his poetry for that. I do know,
however, a few of his translations—and deplore the blunders he so lightheartedly permits himself. Robert Lowell,
of course, is the greater offender.

Ada *has a lot of word play, punning, parody—do you acknowledge
influence by James Joyce in your literary upbringing, and do you
admire him?*
I played with words long before I read *Ulysses*. Yes, I love
that book but it is rather the lucidity and precision of its
prose that pleases me. The real puns are in *Finnegans
Wake*—a tragic failure and a frightful bore.

*What about Kafka's work, and Gogol's. I am sniffing about for
early influences.*
Every Russian writer owes something to Gogol, Pushkin, and Shakespeare. Some Russian writers, as for example Pushkin and Gogol, were influenced by Byron and
Sterne in French translation. I do not know German and so
could not read Kafka before the nineteen thirties when his
La métamorphose appeared in *La nouvelle revue française*, and
by that time many of my so-called "kafkaesque" stories had

[151]

already been published. Alas, I am not one to provide much sport for influence hunters.

Tolstoy said, so they say, that life was a "tartine de merde" which one was obliged to eat slowly. Do you agree?
I've never heard that story. The old boy was sometimes rather disgusting, wasn't he? My own life is fresh bread with country butter and Alpine honey.

Which is the worst thing men do? (Note: I'm thinking of your remark about cruelty).
To stink, to cheat, to torture.

Which is the best?
To be kind, to be proud, to be fearless.

14

On June 26, 1969, Allene Talmey, Associate Editor of
Vogue, New York, sent me the questions answered below.
The interview appeared in the Christmas number of that
journal.

*Magic, sleight-of-hand, and other tricks have played quite a role in
your fiction. Are they for amusement or do they serve yet another
purpose?*

Deception is practiced even more beautifully by that
other V.N., Visible Nature. A useful purpose is assigned
by science to animal mimicry, protective patterns and
shapes, yet their refinement transcends the crude purpose
of mere survival. In art, an individual style is essentially as
futile and as organic as a fata morgana. The sleight-of-hand
you mention is hardly more than an insect's sleight-of-
wing. A wit might say that it protects me from half-wits. A
grateful spectator is content to applaud the grace with
which the masked performer melts into Nature's background.

In your autobiography, Speak, Memory, *you describe a series of
concurrent, insignificant events around the world "forming an
instantaneous and transparent organism of events," of which the
poet (sitting in a lawn chair at Ithaca, New York) is the nucleus.*

How does this open out on your larger belief in the precedence of the imagination over the mind?

The simultaneousness of these random events, and indeed the fact of their occurring at all as described by the central percipient, would only then conform to "reality" if he had at his disposal the apparatus to reproduce those events optically within the frame of one screen; but the central figure in the passage you quote is not equipped with any kind of video attached to his lawn chair and must therefore rely on the power of pure imagination. Incidentally, I tend more and more to regard the objective existence of *all* events as a form of impure imagination— hence my inverted commas around "reality." Whatever the mind grasps, it does so with the assistance of creative fancy, that drop of water on a glass slide which gives distinctness and relief to the observed organism.

1969 marks the fiftieth anniversary of your first publication. What do that first book and your latest, Ada, *have in common? What of your intention and technique has changed, what has remained?*

My first publication, a collection of love poems, appeared not fifty, but fifty-three years ago. Several copies of it still lurk in my native country. The versification is fair, the lack of originality complete. Ten years later, in 1926, my first novel, printed abroad, in Russian,* rendered that boyhood romance with a more acceptable glow, supplied, no doubt, by nostalgia, invention, and a dash of detachment. Finally, upon reaching middle age and, with it, a certain degree of precision in the use of my private English, I devoted a chapter of my *Speak, Memory* to the same theme, this time adhering faithfully to the actual past. As to flashes of it in my fiction, I alone can judge if details that look like bits of my "real" self in this or that novel of mine are as authentic as Adam's rib in the most famous of garden scenes. The

*Mashenka, translated as *Mary* (McGraw-Hill, New York, 1970).

[154]

best part of a writer's biography is not the record of his adventures but the story of his style. Only in that light can one properly assess the relationship, if any, between my first heroine and my recent Ada. While two ancestral parks may be *generically* alike, true art deals not with the genus, and not even with the species, but with an aberrant individual of the species. Raisins of fact in the cake of fiction are many stages removed from the initial grape. I have accumulated enough aphorisms here to make it seem that your question about *Ada* has been answered.

You are reported to have said that you live more in the future than in the present or past—in spite of your preoccupation with memory. Can you say why this is so?
I do not recall the exact wording of that statement. Presumably I meant that in professional action I look forward, rather than back, as I try to foresee the evolution of the work in progress, try to perceive the fair copy in the crystal of my inkstand, try to read the proof, long before it is printed, by projecting into an imagined section of time the growth of the book, whose every line belongs to the present moment, which in its turn is nothing but the ever rising horizon of the past. Using another, more emotional metaphor, I might concede, however, that I keep the tools of my trade, memories, experiences, sharp shining things, constantly around me, upon me, within me, the way instruments are stuck into the loops and flaps of a mechanician's magnificently elaborate overalls.

You are often superficially linked to a handful of international writers like Beckett and Borges. Do you feel any affinity with them or with your other contemporaries?
Oh, I am well aware of those commentators: slow minds, hasty typewriters! They would do better to link Beckett with Maeterlinck and Borges with Anatole France. It might prove more instructive than gossiping about a stranger.

You have witnessed extraordinary changes in your lifetime and maintained an "esthetic distance." Would you consider this a matter of your temperament or a quality you had to cultivate?

My aloofness is an illusion resulting from my never having belonged to any literary, political, or social coterie. I am a lone lamb. Let me submit, however, that I have bridged the "esthetic distance" in my own way by means of such absolutely final indictments of Russian and German totalitarianism as my novels *Invitation to a Beheading* and *Bend Sinister*.

Gogol found a most congenial biographer in you. Whom would you choose, free of time, to be your biographer, and why would you make your choice?

This congeniality is another illusion. I loathe Gogol's moralistic slant, I am depressed and puzzled by his utter inability to describe young women, I deplore his obsession with religion. Verbal inventiveness is not really a bond between authors, it is merely a garland. He would have been appalled by my novels and denounced as vicious the innocent, and rather superficial, little sketch of his life that I produced twenty-five years ago. Much more successful, because based on longer and deeper research, was the life of Chernyshevski (in my novel *The Gift*), whose works I found risible, but whose fate moved me more strongly than did Gogol's. What Chernyshevski would have thought of it is another question—but at least the plain truth of documents is on my side. That, and only that, is what I would ask of my biographer—plain facts, no symbol-searching, no jumping at attractive but preposterous conclusions, no Marxist bunkum, no Freudian rot.

The maps and diagrams—your entomological proof that Gregor Samsa was a dung beetle and not a cockroach—are now well-known artifacts of your teaching literature at Cornell. What other refreshing antidotes to current literary criticism might you suggest?

In my academic days I endeavored to provide students of

literature with exact information about details, about such combinations of details as yield the sensual spark without which a book is dead. In that respect, general ideas are of no importance. Any ass can assimilate the main points of Tolstoy's attitude toward adultery but in order to enjoy Tolstoy's art the good reader must wish to visualize, for instance, the arrangement of a railway carriage on the Moscow–Petersburg night train as it was a hundred years ago. Here diagrams are most helpful. Instead of perpetuating the pretentious nonsense of Homeric, chromatic, and visceral chapter headings, instructors should prepare maps of Dublin with Bloom's and Stephen's intertwining itineraries clearly traced. Without a visual perception of the larch labyrinth in *Mansfield Park* that novel loses some of its stereographic charm, and unless the façade of Dr. Jekyll's house is distinctly reconstructed in the student's mind, the enjoyment of Stevenson's story cannot be perfect.

There is a great deal of easy talk about the "death of language" and the "obsolescence of books." What are your views on the future of literature?

I am not overly preoccupied with tomorrow's books. All I would welcome is that in the future editions of my works, especially in paperback, a few misprints were corrected.

Is it right for a writer to give interviews?

Why not? Of course, in a strict sense a poet, a novelist, is not a public figure, not an exotic potentate, not an international lover, not a person one would be proud to call Jim. I can quite understand people wanting to know my writings, but I cannot sympathize with anybody wanting to know me. As a human specimen, I present no particular fascination. My habits are simple, my tastes banal. I would not exchange my favorite fare (bacon and eggs, beer) for the most misspelt menu in the world. I irritate some of my best friends by the relish with which I list the things I hate—

nightclubs, yachts, circuses, pornographic shows, the soulful eyes of naked men with lots of Guevara hair in lots of places. It may seem odd that such a modest and unassuming person as I should not disapprove of the widespread practice of self-description. No doubt some literary interviews are pretty awful: trivial exchanges between sage and stooge, or even worse, the French kind, starting "*Jeanne Dupont, qui êtes-vous?*" (who indeed!) and sporting such intolerable vulgarisms as "*insolite*" and "*écriture*" (French weeklies, please note!). I do not believe that speaking about myself can encourage the sales of my books. What I really like about the better kind of public colloquy is the opportunity it affords me to construct in the presence of my audience the semblance of what I hope is a plausible and not altogether displeasing personality.

15

During a visit in the last week of August, 1970, Alfred Appel interviewed me again. The result was printed, from our careful jottings, in the spring, 1971, issue of *Novel, A Forum on Fiction*, Brown University, Providence, Rhode Island.

In the twelve years since the American publication of Lolita, *you've published twenty-two or so books—new American or Antiterran novels, old Russian works in English,* Lolita *in Russian—giving one the impression that, as someone has said— John Updike, I think—your* oeuvre *is growing at both ends. Now that your first novel has appeared (*Mashenka, 1926), *it seems appropriate that, as we sail into the future, even earlier works should adhere to this elegant formula and make their quantum leap into English.*

Yes, my forthcoming *Poems and Problems* [McGraw-Hill] will offer several examples of the verse of my early youth, including "The Rain Has Flown," which was composed in the park of our country place, Vyra, in May 1917, the last spring my family was to live there. This "new" volume consists of three sections: a selection of thirty-six Russian poems, presented in the original and in translation; fourteen poems which I wrote directly in English, after 1940 and my arrival in America (all of which were published in *The New*

Yorker); and eighteen chess problems, all but two of which were composed in recent years (the chess manuscripts of the 1940–1960 period have been mislaid and the earlier unpublished jottings are not worth printing). These Russian poems constitute no more than one percent of the mass of verse which I exuded with monstrous regularity during my youth.

Do the components of that monstrous mass fall into any discernible periods or stages of development?

What can be called rather grandly my European period of verse-making seems to show several distinctive stages: an initial one of passionate and commonplace love verse (not represented in *Poems and Problems*); a period reflecting utter distrust of the so-called October Revolution; a period (reaching well into the nineteen-twenties) of a kind of private curatorship, aimed at preserving nostalgic retrospections and developing Byzantine imagery (this has been mistaken by some readers for an interest in "religion" which, beyond literary stylization, never meant anything to me); a period lasting another decade or so during which I set myself to illustrate the principle of making a short poem contain a plot and tell a story (this in a way expressed my impatience with the dreary drone of the anemic "Paris School" of émigré poetry); and finally, in the late thirties, and especially in the following decades, a sudden liberation from self-imposed shackles, resulting both in a sparser output and in a belatedly discovered robust style. Selecting poems for this volume proved less difficult than translating them.

Why are you including the chess problems with the poems?

Because problems are the poetry of chess. They demand from the composer the same virtues that characterize all worthwhile art: originality, invention, harmony, conciseness, complexity, and splendid insincerity.

Most of your work in Russian [1920–1940] appeared under the name of "Sirin." Why did you choose that pseudonym?

In modern times *sirin* is one of the popular Russian names of the Snowy Owl, the terror of tundra rodents, and is also applied to the handsome Hawk Owl, but in old Russian mythology it is a multicolored bird, with a woman's face and bust, no doubt identical with the "siren," a Greek deity, transporter of souls and teaser of sailors. In 1920, when casting about for a pseudonym and settling for that fabulous fowl, I still had not shaken off the false glamour of Byzantine imagery that attracted young Russian poets of the Blokian era. Incidentally, circa 1910 there had appeared literary collections under the editorial title of *Sirin* devoted to the so-called "symbolist" movement, and I remember how tickled I was to discover in 1952 when browsing in the Houghton Library at Harvard that its catalogue listed me as actively publishing Blok, Bely, and Bryusov at the age of ten.

An arresting phantasmagoric image of Russian émigré life in Germany is that of film extras playing themselves, as it were, as do Ganin in Mashenka and those characters in your story "The Assistant Producer," whose "only hope and profession was their past—that is, a set of totally unreal people," who, you write, were hired "to represent 'real' audiences in pictures. The dovetailing of one phantasm into another produced upon a sensitive person the impression of living in a Hall of Mirrors, or rather a prison of mirrors, and not even knowing which was the glass and which was yourself." Did Sirin ever do that sort of work?

Yes, I have been a tuxedoed extra as Ganin had been and that passage in *Mashenka*, retitled *Mary* in the 1970 translation, is a rather raw bit of "real life." I don't remember the names of those films.

Did you have much to do with film people in Berlin? Laughter in the Dark [*1932*] *suggests a familiarity.*

In the middle thirties a German actor whose name was Fritz Kortner, a most famous and gifted artist of his day, wanted to make a film of *Camera Obscura* [Englished as *Laughter in the Dark*]. I went to London to see him, nothing came of it, but a few years later another firm, this one in Paris, bought an option which ended in a blind alley too.

I recall that nothing came of yet another option on Laughter in the Dark *when the producer engaged Roger Vadim, circa 1960— Bardot as Margot?—and of course the novel finally reached the no-longer silver screen in 1969, under the direction of Tony Richardson, adapted by Edward Bond, and starring Nicol Williamson and Anna Karina (interesting name, that), the setting changed from old Berlin to Richardson's own mod London. I assume that you saw the movie.*

Yes, I did. That name *is* interesting. In the novel there is a film in which my heroine is given a small part, and I would like my readers to brood over my singular power of prophecy, for the name of the leading lady (Dorianna Karenina) in the picture invented by me in 1931 prefigured that of the actress (Anna Karina) who was to play Margot forty years later in the film *Laughter in the Dark*, which I viewed at a private screening in Montreux.

Are other works headed for the screen?

Yes, *King, Queen, Knave* and *Ada*, though neither is in production yet. *Ada* will be enormously difficult to do: the problem of having a suggestion of fantasy, continually, but never overdoing it. *Bend Sinister* was done on West German television, an opera based on *Invitation to a Beheading* was shown on Danish TV, and my play *The Event* [1938] appeared on Finnish TV.

The German cinema of the twenties and early thirties produced several masterpieces. Living in Berlin, were you impressed by any of the films of the period? Do you today feel any sense of affinity with directors such as Fritz Lang and Josef von Sternberg? The former would have been the ideal director for Despair *[1934], the latter, who did* The Blue Angel, *perfect for* Laughter in the Dark *and* King, Queen, Knave *[1928], with its world of decor and decadence. And if only F. W. Murnau, who died in 1931, could have directed* The Defense *[1930], with Emil Jannings as Luzhin!*

The names of Sternberg and Lang never meant anything to me. In Europe I went to the corner cinema about once in a fortnight and the only kind of picture I liked, and still like, was and is comedy of the Laurel and Hardy type. I enjoyed tremendously American comedy—Buster Keaton, Harold Lloyd, and Chaplin. My favorites by Chaplin are *The Gold Rush* [1925], *The Circus* [1928], and *The Great Dictator* [1940]—especially the parachute inventor who jumps out of the window and ends in a messy fall which we only see in the expression on the dictator's face. However, today's Little Man appeal has somewhat spoiled Chaplin's attraction for me. The Marx Brothers were wonderful. The opera, the crowded cabin [*A Night at the Opera*, 1935], which is pure genius . . . [Nabokov then lovingly rehearsed the scene in detail, delighting particularly in the arrival of the manicurist.] I must have seen that film three times! Laurel and Hardy are always funny; there are subtle, artistic touches in even their most mediocre films. Laurel is so wonderfully inept, yet so very kind. There is a film in which they are at Oxford [*A Chump at Oxford*, 1940]. In one scene the two of them are sitting on a park bench in a labyrinthine garden and the subsequent happenings conform to the labyrinth. A casual villain puts his hand through the back of the bench and Laurel, who is clasping his hands in an idiotic reverie, mistakes the stranger's hand for one of his own hands, with all kinds of complications

[163]

because his own hand is also there. He has to choose. The choice of a hand.

How many years has it been since you saw that movie?
Thirty or forty years. [Nabokov then recalled, again in precise detail, the opening scenes of *County Hospital*, 1932, in which Stan brings a gift of hardboiled eggs to relieve the misery of hospitalized Ollie and consumes them himself, salting them carefully.] More recently, on French TV I saw a Laurel and Hardy short in which the "dubbers" had the atrocious taste to have the two men speak fluent French with an English accent. But I don't even remember if the best Laurel and Hardy are talkies or not. On the whole, I think what I love about the silent film is what comes through the mask of the talkies and, vice versa, talkies are mute in my memory.

Did you only enjoy American films?
No. Dreyer's *La Passion de Jeanne d'Arc* [1928] was superb, and I loved the French films of René Clair—*Sous les Toits de Paris* [1929], *Le Million* [1931], *À Nous la Liberté* [1931]—a new world, a new trend in cinema.

A brilliant but self-effacing critic and scholar has described Invitation to a Beheading [*1935–36*] *as Zamiatin's* We *restaged by the Marx Brothers. Is it fair to say that* Invitation to a Beheading *is in many ways akin to the film comedies we've been talking about?**
I can't make the comparison between a visual impression and my scribble on index cards, which I always see first

*Nabokov's novels abound in the slapstick elements, the cosmic sight gags, as it were, of Keaton, Clair, Laurel and Hardy, and the

when I think of my novels. The verbal part of the cinema is such a hodgepodge of contributions, beginning with the script, that it really has no style of its own. On the other hand, the viewer of a silent film has the opportunity of adding a good deal of his own inner verbal treasure to the silence of the picture.

Although parts were eventually discarded or revised by Stanley Kubrick, you nevertheless did write the original screenplay for Lolita. *Why?*

I tried to give it some kind of form which would protect it from later intrusions and distortions. In the case of *Lolita* I

Marx Brothers. *Pale Fire's* kingdom of Zembla recalls the funhouse palace of *Duck Soup* (1933), with its ludicrous functionaries, uniformed guards and mirror walls, as well as the sequence in *A Night at the Opera* in which, managed by Groucho, the others disguise themselves as the three identically bearded Russian aviators, Chicoski, Harpotski, and Baronoff. Witness Kinbote in *Pale Fire*, as King Charles, modestly "lectur[ing] under an assumed name and in a heavy makeup, with wig and false whiskers" (his real, immense, American-grown beard will earn him his sobriquet, The Great Beaver), or the vision of him making his escape from Zembla, abetted by a hundred loyalists who, in a brilliant diversionary ploy, don red caps and sweaters identical to the King's, in their apprehension packing the local prison, which is "much too small for more kings" (shades of *A Night at the Opera's* crowded cabin!). The activities of The Shadows, that regicidal organization of stooges, recall Mack Sennett's Keystone Cops, and The Shadows' grotesque, bumbling, but lethal agent, assassin Gradus, is a vaudevillian, jet-age Angel of Death, imagined as "always streaking across the sky with black traveling bag in one hand and loosely folded umbrella in the other, in a sustained glide high over sea and land." And in *The Defense* (1930), Luzhin's means of suicide is suggested to him by a movie still, lying on a table, showing "a white-faced man with his lifeless features and big American glasses, hanging by his hands from the ledge of a skyscraper—just about to fall off into the abyss"—the most famous scene in Harold Lloyd's *Safety Last* (1923). I trust you have enjoyed this note, to paraphrase a comment made by Kinbote under very different circumstances.

included quite a number of scenes that I had discarded from the novel but still preserved in my desk. You mention one of those scenes in *The Annotated Lolita*—Humbert's arrival in Ramsdale at the charred ruins of the McCoo house. My complete screenplay of *Lolita*, all deletions and emendations restored, will be published by McGraw-Hill in the near future; I want it out before the musical version.

The musical version?
  You look disapproving. It's in the best of hands: Alan Jay Lerner will do the adaptation and lyrics, John Barry the music, with settings by Boris Aronson.

I notice that you didn't include W. C. Fields among your favorites.
  For some reason his films did not play in Europe and I never saw any in the States, either.

Well, Fields' comedy is more eminently American than the others, less exportable, I suppose. To move from movies to stills, I've noticed that photography is seen negatively (no pun intended, no pun!) in books such as Lolita *and* Invitation to a Beheading. *Are you making a by now traditional distinction between mechanical process and artistic inspiration?*
  No, I do not make that distinction. The mechanical process can exist in a ludicrous daub, and artistic inspiration can be found in a photographer's choice of landscape and in his manner of seeing it.

You once told me that you were born a landscape painter. Which artists have meant the most to you?
  Oh, many. In my youth mostly Russian and French

painters. And English artists such as Turner. The painters and paintings alluded to in *Ada* are for the most part more recent enthusiasms.

The process of reading and rereading your novels is a kind of game of perception, a confrontation of novelistic trompe l'oeil, *and in several novels (*Pale Fire *and* Ada *among others) you allude to* trompe l'oeil *painting. Would you say something about the pleasures inherent in the* trompe l'oeil *school?*

A good *trompe l'oeil* painting proves at least that the painter is not cheating. The charlatan who sells his squiggles to *épatér* Philistines does not have the talent or the technique to draw a nail, let alone the shadow of a nail.

What about Cubistic collage? That's a kind of trompe l'oeil.

No, it has none of the poetic appeal that I demand from all art, be it letters or the little music I know.

The art teacher in Pnin *says that Picasso is supreme, despite his commercial foibles.* Kinbote in Pale Fire *likes him too, gracing his rented house with "a beloved early Picasso: earth boy leading rain-cloud horse," and your Kinbotish questioner recalls a reproduction of Picasso's* Chandelier, pot et casserole émaillée *on your writing desk, 1966 (the same one Kinbote had up on his wall during his reign as King Charles). Which aspects of Picasso do you admire?*

The graphic aspect, the masterly technique, and the quiet colors. But then, starting with *Guernica*, his production leaves me indifferent. The aspects of Picasso that I emphatically dislike are the sloppy products of his old age. I also loathe old Matisse. A contemporary artist I do admire very much, though not only because he paints Lolita-like creatures, is Balthus.

How are you progressing with your book on the butterfly in art?
I am still working, at my own pace, on an illustrated *Butterflies in Art* work, from Egyptian antiquity to the Renaissance. It is a purely scientific pursuit. I find an entomological thrill in tracking down and identifying the butterflies represented by old painters. Only recognizable portraits interest me. Some of the problems that might be solved are: were certain species as common in ancient times as they are today? Can the minutiae of evolutionary change be discerned in the pattern of a five-hundred-year-old wing? One simple conclusion I have come to is that no matter how precise an Old Master's brush can be it cannot vie in artistic magic with some of the colored plates drawn by the illustrators of certain scientific works in the nine-teenth century. An Old Master did not know that in different species the venation is different and never both-ered to examine its structure. It is like painting a hand without knowing anything about its bones or indeed with-out suspecting it has any. Certain impressionists cannot afford to wear glasses. Only myopia condones the blurry generalizations of ignorance. In high art and pure science detail is everything.

Who are some of the artists who rendered butterflies? Might they not attribute more symbolism to the insect than you do?
Among the many Old Masters who depicted butterflies (obviously netted, or more exactly capped, by their appren-tices in the nearest garden) were Hieronymous Bosch (1450–1516), Jan Brueghel (1568–1625), Albrecht Dürer (1471–1528), Paolo Porpora (1617–1673), Daniel Seghers (1590–1661), and many others. The insect depicted is either part of a still-life (flowers or fruit) arrangement, or more strikingly a live detail in a conventional religious picture (Dürer, Francesco di Gentile, etc.). That in some cases the butterfly symbolizes something (*e.g.*, Psyche) lies utterly outside my area of interest.

In 1968 you told me you hoped to travel to various European museums for research purposes. Have you been doing that?

Yes, that's one reason we've been spending so much time in Italy, and in the future will be traveling to Paris and the Louvre, and to the Dutch museums. We've been to small towns in Italy, and to Florence, Venice, Rome, Milano, Naples, and Pompeii, where we found a very badly drawn butterfly, long and thin, like a Mayfly. There are certain obstacles: still-lifes are not very popular today, they are gap-fillers, generally hanging in dark places or high up. A ladder may be necessary, a flashlight, a magnifying glass! My object is to identify such a picture if there are butterflies in it (often it's only "Anonymous" or "School of ——"), and get an efficient person to take a photograph. Since I don't find many of those pictures in the regular display rooms I try to find the curator because some pictures may turn up in their stacks. It takes so much time: I tramped through the Vatican Museum in Rome and found only one butterfly, a Zebra Swallowtail, in a quite conventional *Madonna and Child* by Gentile, as realistic as though it were painted yesterday. Such paintings may throw light on the time taken for evolution; one thousand years could show some little change in trend. It's an almost endless pursuit, but if I could manage to collect at least one hundred of these things I would publish reproductions of those particular paintings which include butterflies, and enlarge parts of the picture with the butterfly in life-size. Curiously, the Red Admirable is the most popular; I've collected twenty examples.

That particular butterfly appears frequently in your own work, too. In Pale Fire, *a Red Admirable lands on John Shade's arm the minute before he is killed, the insect appears in* King, Queen Knave *just after you've withdrawn the authorial omniscience— killing the characters, so to speak—and in the final chapter of* Speak, Memory, *you recall having seen in a Paris park, just before the war, a live Red Admirable being promenaded on a leash of thread by a little girl. Why are you so fond of* Vanessa atalanta?

Its coloring is quite splendid and I liked it very much in my youth. Great numbers of them migrated from Africa to Northern Russia, where it was called "The Butterfly of Doom" because it was especially abundant in 1881, the year Tsar Alexander II was assassinated, and the markings on the underside of its two hind wings seem to read "1881." The Red Admirable's ability to travel so far is matched by many other migratory butterflies.

The painters you admire are for the most part realists, yet it would not be altogether fair to call you a "realist." Should one find this paradoxical? Or does the problem derive from nomenclature?

The problem derives from pigeonholing.

Your youngmanhood coincides with the experimental decade in Russian painting. Did you follow these developments closely at the time, and what were (are) your feelings about, say, Malevich, Kandinsky, or, to choose a more representational artist, Chagall?

I prefer the experimental decade that coincided with my boyhood—Somov, Benois (Peter Ustinov's uncle, you know), Vrubel, Dobuzhinski,* etc. Malevich and Kandinsky mean nothing to me and I have always found Chagall's stuff intolerably primitive and grotesque.

Always?

Well, relatively early works such as *The Green Jew* and *The Promenade* have their points, but the frescoes and windows he now contributes to temples and the Parisian Opera House *plafond* are coarse and unbearable.

*Who, ca. 1912–13, was young Nabokov's drawing master; see *Speak, Memory*, pp. 92–94, and 236.

[170]

What of Tchelitchew, whose Hide and Seek *(another version of* Speak, Memory's Find What the Sailor Has Hidden?) *in part describes the experience of reading one of your novels?*

I know Tchelitchew's work very little.

The latter artist recalls the Ballets Russes. Were you at all acquainted with that circle, painters as well as dancers and musicians?

My parents had many acquaintances who painted and danced and made music. Our house was one of the first where young Shalyapin sang, and I have foxtrotted with Pavlova in London half a century ago.

Mr. Hilton Kramer, in a recent article in the Sunday New York Times (May 3, 1970) writes, "The accomplishments of at least two living artists who are widely regarded as among the greatest of their time—George Balanchine and Vladimir Nabokov—are traceable, despite the changes of venue and language and outlook, to the esthetic dream that nourished Diaghilev and the artists he gathered around him in St. Petersburg in the nineties." This is, I suppose, what Mary McCarthy meant when she characterized Pale Fire *as a "Fabergé gem." Are these analogies just?*

I was never much interested in the ballet. "Fabergé gems" I have dealt with in *Speak, Memory* (Chapter Five, p. 111).* Balanshin, not Balanchine (note the other mistransliterations). I am at a loss to understand why the names of most of the people with whom I am paired begin with a B.

All of which brings to mind another outspoken émigré, Mr. Stravinsky. Have you had any associations with him?

*There the memoirist recalls a morning tour of St. Petersburg with his governess, the majestic Mademoiselle: "We drift past the show windows of Fabergé whose mineral monstrosities, jeweled troykas poised on marble ostrich eggs, and the like, highly appreciated by the imperial family, were emblems of grotesque garishness to ours.

I know Mr. Stravinski very slightly and have never seen any genuine sample of his outspokenness in print.

Whom in Parisian literary circles did you meet in the thirties, in addition to Joyce and the editorial board of Mesures?

I was on friendly terms with the poet Jules Supervielle. Him and Jean Pauhan (editor of *Nouvelle revue française*) I especially remember.

Did you know Samuel Beckett in Paris?

No, I did not. Beckett is the author of lovely novellas and wretched plays in the Maeterlinck tradition. The trilogy is my favorite, expecially *Molloy.* There is an extraordinary scene in which he is crawling through a forest by dragging himself, ⁻by catching the crook of his walking stick, his crutch, in the vegetation before him, and pulling himself up, wearing three overcoats and newspaper underneath them. Then there are those pebbles, which he is busily transferring from pocket to pocket. Everything is so gray, so uncomfortable, you feel that he is in constant bladder discomfort, as old people sometimes are in their dreams. In this abject condition there is no doubt some likeness with Kafka's physically uncomfortable and dingy men. It is that limpness that is so interesting in Beckett's work.

Beckett has also composed in two tongues, has overseen the Englishing of his French works. In which language have you read him?

I've read him in both French and English. Beckett's French is a schoolmaster's French, a preserved French, but in English you feel the moisture of verbal association and of the spreading live roots of his prose.

I have a "theory" that the French translation of Despair *(1939)—not to mention the books she could have read in Russian—exerted a great influence on the so-called New Novel. In his Preface to Mme. Sarraute's* Portrait d'un inconnu *(1947), Sartre includes you among the antinovelists, a rather more intelligent remark—don't you think?—than his comments of eight years before when, reviewing* Despair, *he said that as an émigré writer—landless—you had no subject matter. "But what is the question?" you might ask at this point. Is Nabokov precursor of the French New Novel?*

Answer: The French New Novel does not really exist apart from a little heap of dust and fluff in a fouled pigeonhole.

But what do you think of Sartre's remark?

Nothing. I'm immune to any kind of opinion and I just don't know what an "anti-novel" is specifically. Every original novel is "anti-" because it does not resemble the genre or kind of its predecessor.

I know that you admire Robbe-Grillet. What about some of the others loosely grouped under the "New Novel" tag: Claude Simon? Michel Butor? and Raymond Queneau, a wonderful writer, who, while not a member of l'école, *anticipates it in several ways?*

Queneau's *Exercices de style* is a thrilling masterpiece and, in fact, one of the greatest stories in French literature.* I am also very fond of Queneau's *Zazie*, and I remember some excellent essays he published in *Nouvelle revue française*. We

---

*Nabokov's encomium is not without humor, however, since Queneau's *Exercices* is an anti-story, if not novel: a man is jostled on a bus and is later advised by a friend to add a button to his overcoat, and this "story," such as it is, is retold ninety-nine different times and ways, none of which is as "thrilling" as, say, an episode in James Bond.

met once at a party and talked about another famous *fillette*. I do not care for Butor. But Robbe-Grillet is so unlike the others. One cannot, one should not lump them together. By the way, when we visited Robbe-Grillet, his petite, pretty wife, a young actress, had dressed herself *à la gamine* in my honor, pretending to be Lolita, and she continued the performance the next day, when we met again at a publisher's luncheon in a restaurant. After pouring wine for everyone but her, the waiter asked, "*Voulez-vous un Coca-Cola, Mademoiselle?*" It was very funny, and Robbe-Grillet, who looks so solemn in his photographs, roared with laughter.

Someone has called the New Novel "the detective story taken seriously" (there it is again, the influence of the French edition of Despair*). Parodistic or not, you take it "seriously," given the number of times you've transmuted the properties of the genre. Would you say something about why you've returned to them so often?*

My boyhood passion for the Sherlock Holmes and Father Brown stories may yield some twisted clue.

You once said that Robbe-Grillet's shifts of levels belong to psychology—"psychology at its best." Are you a psychological novelist?

All novelists of any worth are psychological novelists, I guess. Speaking of precursors of the New Novel, there is Franz Hellens, a Belgian, who is very important. Do you know of him?

No, I don't. When was he active, in which period did he write?

The post-Baudelaire period.*

*Nabokov is of course funning the academic proclivity to assign individual artists or writers to neatly, arbitrarily defined "periods,"

[174]

Could you be more specific?

Hellens was a tall, lean, quiet, very dignified man of whom I saw a good deal in Belgium in the middle thirties when I was reading my own stuff in lecture halls for large émigré audiences. *La femme partagee* (1929), a novel, I like particularly, and there are three or four other books that stand out among the many that Hellens wrote. I tried to get someone in the States to publish him—Laughlin, perhaps—but nothing came of it. Hellens would get excellent reviews, was beloved in Belgium, and what friends he had in Paris tried to brighten and broaden his reputation. It is a shame that he is read less than that awful Monsieur Camus and even more awful Monsieur Sartre.

What you say about Hellens and Queneau is most interesting, in part because journalists always find it more "colorful" to stress your negative remarks about other writers.

Yes, "good copy" is the phrase. As a private person, I happen to be good-natured, straightforward, plain-spoken, and intolerant of bogus art. A writer for whom I have the deepest admiration is H. G. Wells, especially his romances: *The Time Machine, The Invisible Man, The Country of the Blind, The War of the Worlds,* and the moon fantasia *The First Men on the Moon.*

"schools," and "–isms" ("there is only one school, that of talent," he says), but his answer turns out to be a sound one. Baudelaire spent the last few years of his life in Belgium, and Hellens was born there in 1881, only 14 years after Baudelaire's death. Now in his ninetieth year, Hellens does indeed embody "the post-Baudelaire period." Hellens' vast *oeuvre* includes eight novels and fourteen volumes of verse. A 1931 volume includes a portrait drawing of him by Modigliani. His *Poésie Complète* was published in 1959, his most recent book, *Objets*, in 1966. The *Nouveau Larousse Universel*, Vol. I (1969), includes a brief entry on him. Nabokov has not seen Hellens for many years. In 1959 he sent Nabokov a presentation copy of his novel, *Oeil-de-Dieu*, warmly inscribed "To the Author of *Lolita*."

And as final food for thought, sir, what is the meaning of life? [*A rather blurry reproduction of Tolstoy's photographed face follows this question in the interviewer's typescript*].

For solutions see p. 000 (thus says a MS note in the edited typescript of my *Poems and Problems* which I have just received). In other words: Let us wait for the page proof.

16

A second exchange with Alden Whitman took place in mid-April, 1971, and was reproduced, with misprints and other flaws, in *The New York Times*, April 23.

You, sir, will be seventy-two in a few days, having exceeded the Biblical three score and ten. How does this feat, if it is a feat, impress you?

"Three score and ten" sounded, no doubt, very venerable in the days when life expectancy hardly reached one half of that length. Anyway, Petersburgan pediatricians never thought I might perform the feat you mention: a feat of lucky endurance, of paradoxically detached will power, of good work and good wine, of healthy concentration on a rare bug or a rhythmic phrase. Another thing that might have been of some help is the fact that I am subject to the embarrassing qualms of superstition: a number, a dream, a coincidence can affect me obsessively—though not in the sense of absurd fears but as fabulous (and on the whole rather bracing) scientific enigmas incapable of being stated, let alone solved.

Has your life thus far come up to expectations you had for yourself as a young man?

My life thus far has surpassed splendidly the ambitions of boyhood and youth. In the first decade of our dwindling century, during trips with my family to Western Europe, I imagined, in bedtime reveries, what it would be like to become an exile who longed for a remote, sad, and (right epithet coming) unquenchable Russia, under the eucalipti of exotic resorts. Lenin and his police nicely arranged the realization of *that* fantasy. At the age of twelve my fondest dream was a visit to the Karakorum range in search of butterflies. Twenty-five years later I successfully sent myself, in the part of my hero's father (see my novel *The Gift*) to explore, net in hand, the mountains of Central Asia. At fifteen I visualized myself as a world-famous author of seventy with a mane of wavy white hair. Today I am practically bald.

If birthday wishes were horses, what would yours be for yourself?
Pegasus, only Pegasus.

You are, I am told, at work on a new novel. Do you have a working title? And could you give me a precis of what it is all about?
The working title of the novel I am composing now is *Transparent Things*, but a precis would be an opaque shadow. The façade of our hotel in Montreux is being repainted, and I have reached the ultimate south of Portugal in an effort to find a quiet spot (*pace* the booming surf and rattling wind) where to write. This I do on scrambled index cards (my text existing already there in invisible lead) which I gradually fill in and sort out, using up in the process more pencil sharpeners than pencils; but I have spoken of this in several earlier questionnaires—a word whose spelling I have to look up every time; my traveling companion, Webster's Collegiate Dictionary, 1970, defines, by the way, "Quassia" as derived from "Quassi," a Surinam Negro slave of the 18th century, who discovered a remedy for worms in white children. On the other hand, none of my own coinages or reapplications appears in this

lexicon—neither "iridule" (a mother-of-pearl cloudlet in *Pale Fire*), nor "racemosa" (a kind of bird cherry), nor several prosodic terms such as "scud" and "tilt" (see my Commentary to *Eugene Onegin*).

There has been a variety of critical reaction to Ada. *Which critics, in your views, have been especially perceptive, and why?*

Except for a number of helpless little hacks who were unable to jog beyond the first chapters, American reviewers have been remarkably perceptive in regard to my most cosmopolitan and poetic novel. As to the British press, the observations of a few discerning critics were also most welcome; the buffoons turned out to be less clever than usual, whilst my regular spiritual guide, Mr. Philip Toynbee, seemed even more distressed by *Ada* than he had been by *Pale Fire*. I am bad at remembering reviews in detail, and for the moment several mountain chains separate me from my files, but generally speaking my wife and I have long stopped stuffing clippings into forgettable boxes, instead of which an efficient secretary pastes them in huge comfortable albums, with the result that I am informed better than before of current gloss and gossip. In direct answer to your question I would say that the main favor I ask of the serious critic is sufficient perceptiveness to understand that whatever term or trope I use, my purpose is not to be facetiously flashy or grotesquely obscure but to express what I feel and think with the utmost truthfulness and perception.

Your novel Mary *is having a success in the United States. What have been your feelings about seeing in print a novel of so long ago in an English version?*

In my preface to the English translation of my first Russian novel, written forty-eight years ago, I point out the nature of the similarities between the author's first love affair in 1915 and that of Ganin who recalls it as his own in the stylized world of my *Mashenka*. Owing perhaps to my having gone back to that young romance in my autobiography begun in the nineteen forties (that is, at the centerpoint of the span separating *Mashenka* from *Mary*), the strangeness of the present resurrection cannot help losing something of its thrill. Yet I do feel another, more abstract though no less grateful, tingle when I tell myself that destiny not only preserved a fragile find from decay and oblivion, but allowed me to last long enough to supervise the unwrapping of the mummy.

If you were writing the "book" for Lolita *as a musical comedy, what would you select as the main comic point?*

The main comic point would have been my trying to do it myself.

17

Israel Shenker sent me his questions on June 10, 1971, three weeks before coming to see me here in Montreux. My written answers were accurately reproduced in *The New York Times Book Review*, January 9, 1972. Their presentation would have been perfect had they not been interspersed with unnecessary embellishment (chitchat about living writers, for instance).

What do you do to prepare yourself for the ordeals of life?
Shave every morning before bath and breakfast so as to be ready to fly far at short notice.

What are the literary virtues you seek to attain—and how?
Mustering the best words, with every available lexical, associative, and rhythmic assistance, to express as closely as possible what one wants to express.

What are the literary sins for which you could be answerable some day—and how would you defend yourself?
Of having spared in my books too many political fools and intellectual frauds among my acquaintances. Of having been too fastidious in choosing my targets.

What is your position in the world of letters?
Jolly good view from up here.

What problems are posed for you by the existence of ego?

A linguistic problem: the singular act of mimetic evolution to which we owe the fact that in Russian the word *ego* means "his," "him."

What struggles these days for pride of place in your mind?

Meadows. A meadow with Scarce Heath butterflies in North Russia, another with Grinnell's Blue in Southern California. That sort of thing.

What are your views about man's upward climb from slime?

A truly remarkable performance. Pity, though, that some of the slime still sticks to drugged brains.

What should we think about death?

"Leave me alone, says dreary Death" (bogus inscription on empty tomb).

What kinds of power do you favor, and which do you oppose?

To play safe, I prefer to accept only one type of power: the power of art over trash, the triumph of magic over the brute.

What are the large issues that you can't get interested in, and what are you most concerned with?

The larger the issue the less it interests me. Some of my best concerns are microscopic patches of color.

What can (should?) we do about elusive truth?

One can (and should) engage a specially trained proofreader to make sure that misprints and omissions do not disfigure the elusive truth of an interview that a newspaper takes the trouble to conduct with an author who is rather particular about the precise reproduction of his phrase.

18

On September 8, 1971, Paul Sufrin came here to conduct a radio interview for *Swiss Broadcast*, European & Overseas Service. I do not know when, or if, our rather odd colloquy was used. Here are a few samples.

You've been quoted as saying that in a first-rate work of fiction, the real clash isn't between the characters, but between the author and the world. Would you explain this?
I believe I said "between the author and the reader," not "the world," which would be a meaningless formula, since a creative artist makes his own world or worlds. He clashes with readerdom because he is his own ideal reader and those other readers are so very often mere lip-moving ghosts and amnesiacs. On the other hand, a good reader is bound to make fierce efforts when wrestling with a difficult author, but those efforts can be most rewarding after the bright dust has settled.

What is your particular clash?
Well, that's the clash I am generally faced with.

In many of your writings, you have conceived what I consider to be an Alice-in-Wonderland world of unreality and illusion. What is the connection with your real struggle with the world?
Alice in Wonderland is a specific book by a definite author with its own quaintness, its own quirks, its own quiddity.

If read very carefully, it will be seen to imply, by humorous juxtaposition, the presence of a quite solid, and rather sentimental, world, behind the semi-detached dream. Moreover, Lewis Carroll liked little girls. I don't.

The mixture of unreality and illusion may have led some people to consider you mystifying and your writing full of puzzles. What is your answer to people who say you are just plain obscure?
To stick to the crossword puzzle in their Sunday paper.

Do you make a point of puzzling people and playing games with readers?
What a bore that would be!

The past figures prominently in some of your writing. What concern do you have for the present and the future?
My conception of the texture of time somewhat resembles its image in Part Four of *Ada*. The present is only the top of the past, and the future does not exist.

What have you found to be the disadvantages of being able to write in so many languages?
The inability to keep up with their ever-changing slang.

What are the advantages?
The ability to render an exact nuance by shifting from the language I am now using to a brief burst of French or to a soft rustle of Russian.

What do you think of critic George Steiner's linking you with Samuel Beckett and Jorge Luis Borges as the three figures of probable genius in contemporary fiction?
That playwright and that essayist are regarded nowadays with such religious fervor that in the triptych you mention, I would feel like a robber between two Christs. Quite a cheerful robber, though.

19

In October, 1971, Kurt Hoffman visited me in Montreux to film an interview for the *Bayerischer Rundfunk*. Of its many topics and themes I have selected a few for reproduction in this volume. The bit about my West European ancestors comes from a carefully executed and beautifully bound *Ahnentafel*, given me on my seventieth birthday by my German publisher Heinrich Maria Ledig-Rowohlt.

ON TIME AND ITS TEXTURE

We can imagine all kinds of time, such as for example "applied time"—time applied to events, which we measure by means of clocks and calendars; but those types of time are inevitably tainted by our notion of space, spatial succession, stretches and sections of space. When we speak of the "passage of time," we visualize an abstract river flowing through a generalized landscape. Applied time, measurable illusions of time, are useful for the purposes of historians or physicists, they do not interest me, and they did not interest my creature Van Veen in Part Four of my *Ada*.

He and I in that book attempt to examine the *essence of Time*, not its lapse. Van mentions the possibility of being "an amateur of Time, an epicure of duration," of being able to delight sensually in the texture of time, "in its stuff and spread, in the fall of its folds, in the very impalpability of its grayish gauze, in the coolness of its continuum." He also is aware that "Time is a fluid medium for the culture of metaphors."

Time, though akin to rhythm, is not simply rhythm, which would imply motion—and Time does not move. Van's greatest discovery is his perception of Time as the dim hollow between two rhythmic beats, the narrow and bottomless silence *between* the beats, not the beats themselves, which only embar Time. In this sense human life is not a pulsating heart but the missed heartbeat.

PERSONAL PAST

Pure Time, Perceptual Time, Tangible Time, Time free of content and context, this, then, is the kind of Time described by my creature under my sympathetic direction. The Past is also part of the tissue, part of the present, but it looks somewhat out of focus. The Past is a constant accumulation of images, but our brain is not an ideal organ for constant retrospection and the best we can do is to pick out and try to retain those patches of rainbow light flitting through memory. The act of retention is the act of art, artistic selection, artistic blending, artistic re-combination of actual events. The bad memoirist re-touches his past, and the result is a blue-tinted or pink-shaded photograph taken by a stranger to console sentimental bereavement. The good memoirist, on the other hand, does his best to preserve the utmost truth of the detail. One of the ways he achieves his intent is to find the right spot on his canvas for placing the right patch of remembered color.

ANCESTRAL PAST

It follows that the combination and juxtaposition of remembered details is a main factor in the artistic process of reconstructing one's past. And that means probing not only one's personal past but the past of one's family in search of affinities with oneself, previews of oneself, faint allusions to one's vivid and vigorous Now. This, of course, is a game for old people. Tracing an ancestor to his lair hardly differs from a boy's search for a bird's nest or for a ball lost in the grass. The Christmas tree of one's childhood is replaced by the Family Tree.

As the author of several papers on Lepidoptera, such as the "Nearctic Members of the Genus *Lycaeides*," I experience a certain thrill on finding that my mother's maternal grandfather Nikolay Kozlov, who was born two centuries ago and was the first president of the Russian Imperial Academy of Medicine, wrote a paper entitled "On the Coarctation of the Jugular Foramen in the Insane" to which my "Nearctic Members *et cetera*," furnishes a perfect response. And no less perfect is the connection between Nabokov's Pug, a little American moth named after me, and Nabokov's River in Nova Zembla of all places, so named after my great-grandfather, who participated at the beginning of the nineteenth century in an arctic expedition. I learned about these things quite late in life. Talks about one's ancestors were frowned upon in my family; the interdiction came from my father who had a particular loathing for the least speck or shadow of snobbishness. When imagining the information that I could now have used in my memoir, I rather regret that no such talks took place. But it simply was not done in our home, sixty years ago, twelve hundred miles away.

FAMILY TREE

My father Vladimir Nabokov was a liberal statesman, member of the first Russian parliament, champion of justice and law in a difficult empire. He was born in 1870, went into exile in 1919, and three years later, in Berlin, was assassinated by two Fascist thugs while he was trying to shield his friend Professor Milyukov.

The Nabokov family's estate was adjacent to that of the Rukavishnikovs in the Government of St. Petersburg. My mother Helen (1876–1939) was the daughter of Ivan Rukavishnikov, country gentleman and philanthropist.

My paternal grandfather Dmitri Nabokov (1827–1904) was State Minister of Justice for eight years (1878–1885) under two tsars.

My grandmother's paternal ancestors, the von Korffs, are traceable to the fourteenth century, while on their distaff side there is a long line of von Tiesenhausens, one of whose ancestors was Engelbrecht von Tiesenhausen of Livland who took part, around 1200, in the Third and Fourth Crusades. Another direct ancestor of mine was Can Grande della Scala, Prince of Verona, who sheltered the exiled Dante Alighieri, and whose blazon (two big dogs holding a ladder) adorns Boccaccio's *Decameron* (1353). Della Scala's granddaughter Beatrice married, in 1370, Wilhelm Count Oettingen, grandson of fat Bolko the Third, Duke of Silesia. Their daughter married a von Waldburg, and three Waldburgs, one Kittlitz, two Polenzes and ten Osten-Sackens later, Wilhelm Carl von Korff and Eleonor von der Osten-Sacken engendered my paternal grandmother's grandfather, Nicolaus, killed in battle on June 12, 1812. His wife, my grandmother's grandmother Antoinette Graun, was the granddaughter of the composer Carl Heinrich Graun (1701–1759).

BERLIN

My first Russian novel was written in Berlin in 1924—this was *Mary*, in Russian *Mashenka*, and the first translation of any of my books was *Mashenka* in German under the title *Sie kommt—kommt Sie?*, published by Ullstein in 1928. My next seven novels were also written in Berlin and all of them had, entirely or in part, a Berlin background. This is the

German contribution to the atmosphere and production of all my eight Russian novels written in Berlin. When I moved there from England in 1921, I had only a smattering of German picked up in Berlin during an earlier stay in the winter of 1910 when by brother and I went there with a Russian tutor to have our teeth fixed by an American dentist. In the course of my Cambridge University years I kept my Russian alive by reading Russian literature, my main subject, and by composing an appalling quantity of poems in Russian. Upon moving to Berlin I was beset by a panicky fear of somehow flawing my precious layer of Russian by learning to speak German fluently. The task of linguistic occlusion was made easier by the fact that I lived in a closed émigré circle of Russian friends and read exclusively Russian newspapers, magazines, and books. My only forays into the local language were the civilities exchanged with my successive landlords or landladies and the routine necessities of shopping: *Ich möchte etwas Schinken.* I now regret that I did so poorly; I regret it from a cultural point of view. The little I ever did in that respect was to translate in my youth the Heine songs for a Russian contralto—who, incidentally, wanted the musically signifi- cant vowels to coincide in fullness of sound, and therefore I turned *Ich grolle nicht* into *Net, zloby net*, instead of the unsingable old version *Ya ne serzhus'*. Later I read Goethe and Kafka *en regard* as I also did Homer and Horace. And of course since my early boyhood I have been tackling a multitude of German butterfly books with the aid of a dictionary.

AMERICA

In America, where I wrote all my fiction in English, the situation was different. I had spoken English with the same ease as Russian, since my earliest infancy. I had already written one English novel in Europe besides translating in the thirties two of my Russian books. Linguistically, though perhaps not emotionally, the transition was endurable. And in reward of whatever wrench I experienced, I composed in America a few Russian poems which are incomparably better than those of my European period.

LEPIDOPTERA

My actual work on lepidoptera is comprised within the span of only seven or eight years in the nineteen forties, mainly at Harvard, where I was Research Fellow in Entomology at the Museum of Comparative Zoology. This entailed some amount of curatorship but most of my work was devoted to the classification of certain small blue butterflies on the basis of their male genitalic structure. These studies required the constant use of a microscope, and since I devoted up to six hours daily to this kind of research my eyesight was impaired for ever; but on the other hand, the years at the Harvard Museum remain the most delightful and thrilling in all my adult life. Summers were spent by my wife and me in hunting butterflies, mostly in the Rocky Mountains. In the last fifteen years I have collected here and there, in North America and Europe, but have not published any scientific papers on butterflies, because the writing of new novels and the translating of my old ones encroached too much on my life: the miniature hooks of a male butterfly are nothing in comparison to the eagle claws of literature which tear at me day and night. My entomological library in Montreux is smaller, in fact, than the heaps of butterfly books I had as a child.

I am the author or the reviser of a number of species and subspecies mainly in the New World. The author's name, in such cases, is appended in Roman letters to the italicized name he gives to the creature. Several butterflies and one moth have been named for me, and in such cases my name is incorporated in that of the described insect, becoming "*nabokovi*," followed by the describer's name. There is also a genus *Nabokovia* Hemming, in South America. All my American collections are in museums, in New York, Boston, and Ithaca. The butterflies I have been collecting during the last decade, mainly in Switzerland and Italy, are not yet spread. They are still papered, that is kept in little glazed envelopes which are stored in tin boxes. Eventually they will be relaxed in damp towels, then pinned, then spread, and dried again on setting boards, and finally, labeled and placed in the glassed drawers of a cabinet to be preserved, I hope, in the splendid entomological museum in Lausanne.

FAMILY

I have always been an omnivorous consumer of books, and now, as in my boyhood, a vision of the night's lamplight on a bedside tome is a promised treat and a guiding star throughout the day. Other keen pleasures are soccer matches on the TV, an occasional cup of wine or a triangular gulp of canned beer, sunbaths on the lawn, and composing chess problems. Less ordinary, perhaps, is the unruffled flow of a family life which during its long course—almost half a century—has made absolute fools of the bogeys of environment and the bores of circumstance at all stages of our expatriation. Most of my works have been dedicated to my wife and her picture has often been reproduced by some mysterious means of reflected color in the inner mirrors of my books.

It was in Berlin that we married, in April, 1925, in the midst of my writing my first Russian novel. We were ridiculously poor, her father was ruined, my widowed mother subsisted on an insufficient pension, my wife and I lived in gloomy rooms which we rented in Berlin West, in the lean bosoms of German military families; I taught tennis and English, and nine years later, in 1934, at the dawn of a new era, our only son was born. In the late thirties we migrated to France. My stuff was beginning to be translated, my readings in Paris and elsewhere were well attended; but then came the end of my European stage: in May, 1940, we moved to America.

FAME

Soviet politicians have a rather comic provincial way of applauding the audience that applauds them. I hope I won't be accused of facetious sufficiency if I say in response to your compliments that I have the greatest readers any author has ever had. I see myself as an American writer raised in Russia, educated in England, imbued with the culture of Western Europe; I am aware of the blend, but even the most lucid plum pudding cannot sort out its own ingredients, especially whilst the pale fire still flickers around it. Field, Appel, Proffer, and many others in the USA, Zimmer in Germany, Vivian Darkbloom (a shy violet in Cambridge), have all added their erudition to my inspiration, with brilliant results. I would like to say a lot about my heroic readers in Russia but am prevented from doing so—by many emotions besides a sense of responsibility with which I still cannot cope in any rational way.

SWITZERLAND

Exquisite postal service. No bothersome demonstrations, no spiteful strikes. Alpine butterflies. Fabulous sunsets— just west of my window, spangling the lake, splitting the crimson sun! Also, the pleasant surprise of a metaphorical sunset in charming surroundings.

All Is Vanity

The phrase is a sophism because, if true, it is itself mere
"vanity," and if not then the "all" is wrong. You say that it
seems to be my main motto. I wonder if there is really so
much doom and "frustration" in my fiction? Humbert is
frustrated, that's obvious; some of my other villains are
frustrated; police states are horribly frustrated in my novels
and stories; but my favorite creatures, my resplendent
characters—in *The Gift*, in *Invitation to a Beheading*, in *Ada*,
in *Glory*, et cetera—are victors in the long run. In fact I
believe that one day a reappraiser will come and declare
that, far from having been a frivolous firebird, I was a rigid
moralist kicking sin, cuffing stupidity, ridiculing the vulgar
and cruel—and assigning sovereign power to tenderness,
talent, and pride.

20

The New York newspaper for which this interview, conducted by correspondence in 1972, was intended, refused to publish it. My interviewer's questions have been abridged or stylized in the following version.

Critics of Transparent Things *seem to have had difficulty in describing its theme.*

Its theme is merely a beyond-the-cypress inquiry into a tangle of random destinies. Amongst the reviewers several careful readers have published some beautiful stuff about it. Yet neither they nor, of course, the common criticule discerned the structural knot of the story. May I explain that simple and elegant point?

You certainly may.

Allow me to quote a passage from my first page which baffled the wise and misled the silly: "When we concentrate on a material object . . . the very act of attention may lead to our involuntarily sinking into the history of that object." A number of such instances of falling through the present's "tension film" are given in the course of the book. There is the personal history of a pencil. There is also, in a later chapter, the past of a shabby room, where, instead of focusing on Person and the prostitute, the spectral observer drifts down into the middle of the previous century and

sees a Russian traveler, a minor Dostoevski, occupying that
room, between Swiss gambling house and Italy.

Another critic has said—
Yes, I am coming to that. Reviewers of my little book
made the lighthearted mistake of assuming that seeing
through things is the professional function of a novelist.
Actually, that kind of generalization is not only a dismal
commonplace but is specifically untrue. Unlike the mysterious observer or observers in *Transparent Things*, a novelist
is, like all mortals, more fully at home on the surface of the
present than in the ooze of the past.

*So who is that observer; who are those italicized "we" in the
fourteenth line of the novel; who, for goodness' sake, is the "I" in its
very first line?*
The solution, my friend, is so simple that one is almost
embarrassed to furnish it. But here goes. An incidental but
curiously active component of my novel is Mr. R., an
American writer of German extraction. He writes English
more correctly than he speaks it. In conversation R. has an
annoying habit of introducing here and there the automatic
"you know" of the German *émigré*, and, more painfully yet,
of misusing, garbling, or padding the commonest American
cliché. A good specimen is his intrusive, though well
meant, admonition in the last line of my last chapter:
"Easy, you know, does it, son."

Some reviewers saw in Mr. R. a portrait or parody of Mr. N.
Exactly. They were led to that notion by mere flippancy
of thought because, I suppose, both writers are naturalized
U.S. citizens and both happen, or happened, to live in
Switzerland. When *Transparent Things* starts, Mr. R. is
already dead and his last letter has been filed away in the
"repository" in his publisher's office (see my Chapter
Twenty-One). Not only is the surviving writer an incom-

parably better artist than Mr. R., but the latter, in his *Tralatitions,* actually squirts the venom of envy at the infuriatingly smiling Adam von Librikov (Chapter Nineteen), an anagrammatic alias that any child can decode. On the threshold of my novel Hugh Person is welcomed by a ghost or ghosts—by his dead father, perhaps, or dead wife; more probably, by the late Monsieur Kronig, former director of the Ascot Hotel; still more probably by Mr. R.'s phantom. This promises a thriller: whose ghost will keep intruding upon the plot? One thing, however, is quite transparent and certain. As intimated already in this exegesis, it is no other than a discarnate, but still rather grotesque, Mr. R. who greets newly-dead Hugh in the last line of the book.

I see. And what are you up to now, Baron Librikov? Another novel? Memoirs? Cocking a snoot at dunderheads?

Two volumes of short stories and a collection of essays are by now almost completed, and a new wonderful novel has its little foot in the door. As to cocking a snoot at dunderheads, I never do that. My books, all my books, are addressed not to "dunderheads"; not to the cretins who believe that I like long Latinate words; not to the learned loonies who find sexual or religious allegories in my fiction; no, my books are addressed to Adam von L., to my family, to a few intelligent friends, and to all my likes in all the crannies of the world, from a carrel in America to the nightmare depths of Russia.

21

Simona Morini came to interview me on February 3, 1972, in Montreux. Our exchange appeared in *Vogue*, New York, April 15, 1972. Three passages (pp. 200–1, 201–2 and 204), are borrowed, with modifications, from *Speak, Memory*, G. P. Putnam's Sons, N. Y., 1966.

The world has been and is open to you. With your Proustian sense of places, what is there in Montreux that attracts you so?

My sense of places is Nabokovian rather than Proustian. With regard to Montreux there are many attractions—nice people, near mountains, regular mails, headquarters at a comfortable hotel. We dwell in the older part of the Palace Hotel, in its original part really, which was all that existed a hundred and fifty years ago (you can still see that initial inn and our future windows in old prints of 1840 or so). Our quarters consist of several tiny rooms with two and a half bathrooms, the result of two apartments having been recently fused. The sequence is: kitchen, living–dining room, my wife's room, my room, a former kitchenette now full of my papers, and our son's former room, now converted into a study. The apartment is cluttered with books, folders, and files. What might be termed rather grandly a library is a back room housing my published works, and there are additional shelves in the attic whose skylight is much frequented by pigeons and Alpine choughs. I am giving this meticulous description to refute a distortion in an interview published recently in another New York magazine—a long piece with embarrassing misquotations, wrong intonations, and false exchanges in the course of which I am made to dismiss the scholarship of a dear friend as "pedantry" and to poke ambiguous fun at a manly writer's tragic fate.

Is there any truth in the rumor that you are thinking of leaving Montreux forever?
Well, there is a rumor that sooner or later *everybody* living now in Montreux will leave it forever.

Lolita is an extraordinary Baedecker of the United States. What fascinated you about American motels?
The fascination was purely utilitarian. My wife used to drive me (Plymouth, Oldsmobile, Buick, Buick Special, Impala—in that order of brand) during several seasons, many thousands of miles every season, for the sole purpose of collecting Lepidoptera—all of which are now in three museums (Natural History in New York City, Comparative Zoology at Harvard, Comstock Hall at Cornell). Usually we spent only a day or two in each motorcourt, but sometimes, if the hunting was good, we stayed for weeks in one place. The main *raison d'être* of the motel was the possibility of walking out straight into an aspen grove with lupines in full bloom or onto a wild mountainside. We also would make many sorties on the way between motels. All this I shall be describing in my next memoir, *Speak On, Memory,* which will deal with many curious things (apart from butterfly lore)—amusing happenings at Cornell and Harvard, gay tussles with publishers, my friendship with Edmund Wilson, et cetera.

You were in Wyoming and Colorado looking for butterflies. What were these places like to you?
My wife and I have collected not only in Wyoming and Colorado, but in most of the states, as well as in Canada.

The list of localities visited between 1940 and 1960 would cover many pages. Each butterfly, killed by an expert nip of its thorax, is slipped immediately into a little glazed envelope, about thirty of which fit into one of the Band-Aid containers which represent, with the net, my only paraphernalia in the field. Captures can be kept, before being relaxed and set, for any number of years in those envelopes, if properly stored. The exact locality and date are written on every envelope besides being jotted down in one's pocket diary. Though my captures are now in American museums, I have preserved hundreds of labels and notes. Here are just a few samples picked out at random:

Road to Terry Peak from Route 85, near Lead, 6500–7000 feet, in the Black Hills of South Dakota, July 20, 1958.

Above Tomboy Road, between Social Tunnel and Bullion Mine, at about 10,500 feet, near Telluride, San Miguel County, W. Colorado, July 3, 1951.

Near Karner, between Albany and Schenectady, New York, June 2, 1950.

Near Columbine Lodge, Estes Park, E. Colorado, about 9000 feet, June 5, 1947.

Soda Mt., Oregon, about 5500 feet, August 2, 1953.

Above Portal, road to Rustler Park, between 5500 and 8000 feet, Chiricahua Mts., Arizona, April 30, 1953.

Fernie, three miles east of Elco, British Columbia, July 10, 1958.

Granite Pass, Bighorn Mts., 8950 feet, E. Wyoming, July 17, 1958.

Near Crawley Lake, Bishop, California, about 7000 feet, June 3, 1953.

Near Gatlinburg, Tennessee, April 21, 1959. Et cetera, et cetera.

Where do you go for butterflies now?

To various good spots in the Valais, the Tessin, the Grisons; to the hills of Italy; to the Mediterranean islands; to the mountains of southern France and so forth. I am chiefly devoted to European and North American butterflies of high altitudes, and have never visited the Tropics. The little mountain trains cogwheeling up to alpine meadows, through sun and shade, along rock face or coniferous forest are tolerable in action and delightful in destination, bringing one as they do to the starting point of a day-long hike. My favorite method of locomotion, though, is the cableway, and especially the chairlift. I find enchanting and dreamy in the best sense of the word to glide in the morning sun from valley to timberline in that magic seat, and watch from above my own shadow—with the ghost of a butterfly net in the ghost of a fist—as it keeps gently ascending in sitting profile along the flowery slope below, among dancing Ringlets and skimming Fritillaries. Some day the butterfly hunter will find even finer dream lore when floating upright over mountains, carried by a diminutive rocket strapped to his back.

In the past, how did you usually travel, when you were looking for butterflies? Did you go camping, for instance?

As a youth of seventeen, on the eve of the Russian Revolution, I was seriously planning (being the independent possessor of an inherited fortune) a lepidopterological expedition to Central Asia, and that would have involved naturally a good deal of camping. Earlier, when I was, say, eight or nine, I seldom roamed further than the fields and woods of our country estate near St. Petersburg. At twelve, when aiming at a particular spot half-a-dozen miles or more distant, I would use a bicycle to get there with my net fastened to the frame; but not many forest paths were passable on wheels; it was possible to ride there on horseback, of course, but, because of our ferocious Russian tabanids, one could not leave a horse haltered in a wood for any length of time: my spirited bay almost climbed up the tree it was tied to one day trying to elude them: big fellows with watered-silk eyes and tiger bodies, and gray little runts with an even more painful proboscis, but much more sluggish: to dispatch two or three of these dingy tipplers with one crush of the gloved hand as they glued themselves to the neck of my mount afforded me a wonderful empathic relief (which a dipterist might not appreciate). Anyway, on my butterfly hunts I always preferred hiking to any other form of locomotion (except, naturally, a flying seat gliding leisurely over the plant mats and rocks of an unexplored mountain, or hovering just above the flowery roof of a rain forest); for when you walk, especially in a region you have studied well, there is an exquisite pleasure in departing from one's itinerary to visit, here and there by the wayside, this glade, that glen, this or that combination of soil and flora—to drop in, as it were, on a familiar butterfly in his particular habitat, in order to see if he has emerged, and if so, how he is doing.

What is your ideal of a splendid grand-hotel?

Absolute quiet, no radio playing behind the wall, none in the lift, no footsteps thudding above, no snores coming from below, no gondoliers carousing across the lane, no drunks in the corridor. I remember one awful little scene (and this was in a five-turret *palace* with the guidebook sign of a red songbird meaning luxury and isolation!). Upon hearing a commotion just outside the door of my bedroom, I poked out my head, while preparing my curse—which fizzled out when I saw what was happening in the passage. An American of the traveling-executive type was staggering about with a bottle of whisky and his son, a boy of twelve or so, was trying to restrain him, repeating: "Please, Dad, please, come to bed," which reminded me of a similar situation in a Chekhov story.

What do you think has changed over the last sixty years in the traveling style? You loved wagons-lits.

Oh, I did. In the early years of this century, a travel agency on Nevski Avenue displayed a three-foot-long model of an oak-brown international sleeping car. In delicate verisimilitude it completely outranked the painted tin of my clockwork trains. Unfortunately it was not for sale. One could make out the blue upholstery inside, the embossed leather lining of the compartment walls, their polished panels, inset mirrors, tulip-shaped reading lamps, and other maddening details. Spacious windows alternated with narrower ones, single or geminate, and some of these were of frosted glass. In a few of the compartments, the beds had been made.

The then great and glamorous Nord-Express (it was never the same after World War I when its elegant brown became a nouveau-riche blue), consisting solely of such international cars and running but twice a week, connected St. Petersburg with Paris. I would have said: directly with Paris, had passengers not been obliged to change from one train to a superficially similar one at the Russo-German frontier (Verzhbolovo-Eydtkuhnen), where the ample and lazy Russian sixty-and-a-half-inch gauge was replaced by the fifty-six-and-a-half-inch standard of Europe, and coal succeeded birch logs.

In the far end of my mind I can unravel, I think, at least five such journeys to Paris, with the Riviera or Biarritz as their ultimate destination. In 1909, the year I now single out, our party consisted of eleven people and one dachs-hund. Wearing gloves and a traveling cap, my father sat reading a book in the compartment he shared with our tutor. My brother and I were separated from them by a washroom. My mother and her maid Natasha occupied a compartment adjacent to ours. Next came my two small sisters, their English governess, Miss Lavington (later governess of the Tsar's children), and a Russian nurse. The odd one of our party, my father's valet, Osip (whom, a decade later, the pedantic Bolsheviks were to shoot, be-cause he appropriated our bicycles instead of turning them over to the nation), had a stranger for companion (Féraudi, a well-known French actor).

Gone the panache of steam, gone the thunder and blaze, gone the romance of the railroad. The popular *train rouge* is merely a souped-up tram. As to the European sleeping-cars, they are drab and vulgar now. The "single" I usually take is a stunted compartment with a corner table conceal-ing inadequate toilet facilities (not unlike those in the farcical American "roomette," where to get at the necessary utensil one has to rise and shoulder one's bed like Lazarus). Still, for the person with a past, some faded charm remains clinging to those international sleepers which take you straight from Lausanne to Rome or from Sicily to the Piedmont. True, the dining-car theme is muted; sand-wiches and wine are supplied by hawkers between stations; and your plastic breakfast is prepared by an overworked, half-dressed conductor in his grubby cubicle next to the car's malodorous W. C.; yet my childhood moments of excitement and wonder are still brought back by the mystery of sighing stops in the middle of the night or by the first morning glimpse of rocks and sea.

What do you think of the super-planes?

I think their publicity department, when advertising the spaciousness of the seat rows, should stop picturing impos-sible children fidgeting between their imperturbed mother and a gray-templed stranger trying to read. Otherwise, those great machines are masterpieces of technology. I have never flown across the Atlantic, but I have had delightful hops with Swissair and Air France. They serve excellent liquor and the view at low elevations is heartbreakingly lovely.

What do you think about luggage? Do you think it has lost style, too?

I think good luggage is always handsome and there is a lot of it around nowadays. Styles, of course, have changed. No longer with us is the kind of elephantine wardrobe trunk, a specimen of which appears in the visually pleasant but otherwise absurd cinema version of Mann's mediocre, but anyway plausible, *Death in Venice*. I still treasure an elegant, elegantly scuffed piece of luggage once owned by my mother. Its travels through space are finished, but it still hums gently through time for I use it to keep old family letters and such curious documents as my birth certificate. I am a couple of years younger than this antique valise, fifty centimeters long by thirty-six broad and sixteen high, technically a heavyish *nécessaire de voyage* of pigskin, with "H.N." elaborately interwoven in thick silver under a similar coronet. It had been bought in 1897 for my mother's wedding trip to Florence. In 1917 it transported from St. Petersburg to the Crimea and then to London a handful of jewels. Around 1930, it lost to a pawnbroker its expensive receptacles of crystal and silver leaving empty the cunningly contrived leathern holders on the inside of the lid. But that loss has been amply recouped during the thirty years it then traveled with me—from Prague to Paris, from St. Nazaire to New York and through the mirrors of more than two hundred motel rooms and rented houses, in forty-six states. The fact that of our Russian heritage the hardiest survivor proved to be a traveling bag is both logical and emblematic.

What is a "perfect trip" for you?

Any first walk in any new place—especially a place where no lepidopterist has been before me. There still exist unexplored mountains in Europe and I still can walk twenty kilometers a day. The ordinary stroller might feel on sauntering out a twinge of pleasure (cloudless morning, village still asleep, one side of the street already sunlit, should try to buy English papers on my way back, here's the turn, I believe, yes, footpath to Cataratta), but the cold of the metal netstick in my right hand magnifies the pleasure to almost intolerable bliss.

22

This interview, conducted by a docile anonym, is preserved in a fragmentary transcript dated October, 1972.

There are two Russian books on which I would like you to comment. The first is Dr. Zhivago. *I understand you never wished to review it?*

Some fifteen years ago, when the Soviets were hypocritically denouncing Pasternak's novel (with the object of increasing foreign sales, the results of which they would eventually pocket and spend on propaganda abroad); when the badgered and bewildered author was promoted by the American press to the rank of an iconic figure; and when his Zhivago vied with my Lalage for the top rungs of the best-seller's ladder; I had the occasion to answer a request for a review of the book from Robert Bingham of *The Reporter*, New York.

And you refused?

Oh, I did, The other day I found in my files a draft of that answer, dated at Goldwin Smith Hall, Ithaca, N.Y., November 8, 1958. I told Bingham that there were several reasons preventing me from freely expressing my opinion in print. The obvious one was the fear of harming the author. Although I never had much influence as a critic, I could well imagine a pack of writers emulating my "eccentric" outspokenness and causing, in the long run, sales to drop, thus thwarting the Bolshevists in their hopes and making their hostage more vulnerable than ever. There were other reasons—but I certainly left out of consideration one point that might have made me change my mind and write that devastating review after all—the exhilarating prospect of seeing it attributed to competitive chagrin by some ass or goose.

Did you tell Robert Bingham what you thought of Dr. Zhivago?
What I told him is what I still think today. Any intelligent Russian would see at once that the book is pro-Bolshevist and historically false, if only because it ignores the Liberal Revolution of spring, 1917, while making the saintly doctor accept with delirious joy the Bolshevist *coup d'état* seven months later—all of which is in keeping with the party line. Leaving out politics, I regard the book as a sorry thing, clumsy, trivial, and melodramatic, with stock situations, voluptuous lawyers, unbelievable girls, and trite coincidences.

Yet you have a high opinion of Pasternak as a lyrical poet?
Yes, I applauded his getting the Nobel Prize on the strength of his verse. In *Dr. Zhivago*, however, the prose does not live up to his poetry. Here and there, in a landscape or simile, one can distinguish, perhaps, faint echoes of his poetical voice, but those occasional *fioriture* are insufficient to save his novel from the provincial banality so typical of Soviet literature for the past fifty years. Precisely that link with Soviet tradition endeared the book to our progressive readers. I deeply sympathized with Pasternak's predicament in a police state; yet neither the vulgarities of the *Zhivago* style nor a philosophy that sought refuge in a sickly sweet brand of Christianism could ever transform that sympathy into a fellow writer's enthusiasm.

The book, however, has become something of a classic. How do you explain its reputation?

Well, all I know is that among Russian readers of today—readers, I mean, who represent that country's wonderful underground intelligentsia and who manage to obtain and distribute works of dissident authors—*Dr. Zhivago* is not prized as universally and unquestioningly as it is, or at least was, by Americans. When the novel appeared in America, her left-wing idealists were delighted to discover in it a proof that "a great book" *could* be produced after all under the Soviet rule. It was for them the triumph of Leninism. They were comforted by the fact that for better or worse its author remained on the side of angelic Old Bolsheviks and that nothing in his book even remotely smacked of the true exile's indomitable contempt for the beastly regime engendered by Lenin.

Let us now turn ——
(The fragment stops here)

Letters to Editors

1

TO THE EDITOR OF *PLAYBOY*
published July, 1961

The amusing memoir by Maurice Girodias (*Pornologist on Olympus, Playboy,* April) contains a number of inaccuracies. My correspondence with Mr. Girodias, and with my literary agent about Mr. Girodias, will soon be published in an appendix to a full account of *Lolita's* tribulations, and will demonstrate what caused the "deterioration" of our relations and reveal which of us was "so absorbed by the financial aspect of the nymphet phenomenon" as to be "blinded to other realities." Here I shall limit myself to the discussion of only one of Mr. Girodias' delusions. I wish to refute Mr. Girodias' bizarre charge that I was aware of his presence at the Gallimard cocktail party in October, 1959. Since I had never met the man, and was not familiar with his face, I could hardly have "identified" him as he "slowly progressed toward" me. I am extremely *distrait* (as Humbert Humbert would have put it in his affected manner) and am liable not to make out mumbled presentations, especially in the hubbub and crush of that kind of affair. One can know obscure mythological or historical figures by their attributes and emblems, and had Mr. Girodias appeared in a punning charade, carrying a plate with an author's head, I might have recognized him. But he came plateless, and, while apologizing for my abstraction, I must affirm here that I did not talk to Mr. Girodias about his brother's translation, or anything else, and that I remained completely and blissfuly ignorant of having exchanged a polite grin with the Olympian Pornologist. Incidentally, in the course of describing our fictitious colloquy, Mr. Girodias compares my physical motions to those of a dolphin. This, I admit, is nicely observed. I do, alas, resemble a dolphin —and can do nothing about it, except remark, in conclusion, that Mr. Girodias speaks of those gentle cetaceans with the frightening appetite of an elasmobranch fish.

Nice, France

2

TO THE EDITOR OF *THE LONDON TIMES*
published May 30, 1962

I find my name listed in the program of the Edinburgh International Festival among those of writers invited to take part in its Writers' Conference. In the same list I find several writers whom I respect but also some others—such as Ilya Ehrenburg, Bertrand Russell, and J. P. Sartre— with whom I would not consent to participate in any festival or conference whatsoever. Needless to say that I am supremely indifferent to the "problems of a writer and the future of the novel" that are to be discussed at the conference.

I would have preferred to bring this to the notice of the Festival Committee in a more private way had I received an invitation to the Conference before my name appeared on its program.

3

TO THE EDITOR OF *ENCOUNTER*
published April, 1966

I am glad that Mr. Fussell has nothing against my notes on prosody provided they remain attached to a work of repelling length and limited appeal. I am amused by his objecting to them when published in the form of a separate, easily available little volume. In my turn, I object to his assuming that my dislike for the French pseudo-classical style as borrowed and reworked by English poets is based "on the eighteenth century's performance in tetrametric verse." Before dragging in Pope's pentameter and Sterne's prose in redemption of a literary era, he should have looked up what I say about Pope and Sterne in my *Eugene Onegin* commentary. I do not know who "Baron Corvo" and (Professor?) Firbank are, or what bearing "Camp" (Campus?) products have on the texture of tetrameters; but I am quite certain that there is no connection between random samples of tetrametric rhythms as discussed in a serious study and what Mr. Fussell comically calls "the overtones of the English Protestant sense of duty." The presence or absence of scuds in a given passage may often be accidental but only a Philistine can assert that the accidental is "undiscussable." If Mr. Fussell is puzzled by my having had to invent terms for new or unfamiliar concepts, it only means that he has not understood my explanations and examples. The purpose of my little investigation was to describe (*not* to "interpret") certain aspects of verse structure. I suspected that my views would irritate the conservative professional in his fondly tilled field, but I was hardly prepared for the sparkling flow of academic kitsch with which Mr. Fussell now regales me.

4

TO THE EDITOR OF *THE SUNDAY TIMES*, LONDON
published January 1, 1967

I strongly object to the remark in "The Red Letter Forgers" (December 18, 1966) about my father who, according to your four investigators, was shot by a monarchist because "he was suspected of being too Left-wing." This nonsense is distasteful to me for several reasons: it is remarkably similar to the glib data distorting truth in Soviet sources; it implies that the chieftains of the Russian emigration were bandits; and the reason it gives for the murder is false.

My father had been one of the leaders of the Constitutional-Democratic party in Russia long before the Revolution, and his articles in the émigré *Rul*—the only influential Russian-language daily in Berlin—merely continued the strain of West European liberalism, in the large sense, that had marked his life since at least 1904.

Although there could be found a number of decent elderly persons among the Russian monarchists in Berlin and Paris, there were no original minds or influential personalities among them. The stauncher reactionaries, Black Hundred groups, votaries of new and better dictatorships, shady journalists who claimed that Kerenski's real name was Kirschbaum, budding Nazis, blooming Fascists, pogromystics, and *agents-provocateurs*, remained on the lurid fringe of Russian expatriation and were not representative in any way of the liberal intelligentsia, which was the backbone and marrow of émigré culture, a fact deliberately played down by Soviet historians; and no wonder: it was that liberal cultural core, and certainly not the crude and ambiguous activities of extreme rightists, that formed a genuine anti-Bolshevist opposition (still working today),

and it was people like my father who pronounced the first
and final verdict on the Soviet police state.

The two sinister ruffians who attacked P. N. Milyukov at
a public lecture in Berlin on March 28, 1922, had planned
to assassinate him, not my father; but it was my father who
shielded his old friend from their pistol bullets and while
vigorously knocking down one of the assailants was fatally
shot by the other.

I wish to submit that at a time when in so many eastern
countries history has become a joke, this precise beam of
light upon a precious detail may be of some help to the next
investigator.

5

TO THE EDITOR OF *ENCOUNTER*
published February, 1967

Sir,

I welcome Freud's "Woodrow Wilson" not only because
of its comic appeal, which is great, but because that surely
must be the last rusty nail in the Viennese Quack's coffin.

6

TO THE EDITOR OF *THE NEW STATESMAN*
Pushkin and Byron
published November 17, 1967

Sir,

Mr. Pritchett (NS, 27 Oct.) says he would have liked Mr.
Magarshack to tell him in what language Pushkin read

Byron and other English authors. I do not know Mr. Magarshack's work or works, but I do know that since neither he, nor anybody else, could answer Mr. Pritchett without dipping into me, a vicious spiral is formed with an additional coy little coil supplied by Mr. Prichett's alluding to the "diverting" article I published in *Encounter* (Feb. 1966). If, however, your reviewer would care to combine the diverting with the instructive I suggest he consult the pages (enumerated in the index to my work on *Eugene Onegin* under Pushkiniana, English) wherein I explain, quite clearly, that most Russians of Pushkin's time, including Pushkin himself, read English authors in French versions.

By a pleasing coincidence the same issue of your journal contains another item worth straightening out. Mr. Desmond MacNamara, writing on a New Zealand novel, thinks that there should be coined a male equivalent of "nymphet" in the sense I gave it. He is welcome to my "faunlet," first mentioned in 1955 (*Lolita*, Chapter 5). How time flies! How attention flags!

7

Answer cabled on March 13, 1969, to William Honon who had asked me, for quotation in *Esquire* magazine, what I would like to hear an astronaut say when landing on the moon for the first time.

Published in the July, 1969 issue of Esquire

"I WANT A LUMP IN HIS THROAT TO OBSTRUCT THE WISECRACK"

8

Answer cabled July 3, 1969, to Thomas Hamilton, who had asked me, for publication in *The New York Times*, what the moon landing means to me. Published *** 1969, with a disastrous misprint in the seventh word.

"TREADING THE SOIL OF THE MOON PALPAT-ING ITS PEBBLES TASTING THE PANIC AND SPLENDOR OF THE EVENT FEELING IN THE PIT OF ONES STOMACH THE SEPARATION FROM TERRA THESE FORM THE MOST ROMAN-TIC SENSATION AN EXPLORER HAS EVER KNOWN"

9

TO THE EDITOR OF *Time* MAGAZINE
published on January 18, 1971

I find highly objectionable the title of the piece ("Profit without Honor," December 21, 1970) on the musical adaptation of *Lolita* as well as your sermonet on the scruples that I once happened to voice concerning its filming (". . . to make a real twelve-year-old girl play such a part would be sinful and immoral. . . ."). When cast in the title role of Kubrick's neither very sinful nor very immoral picture, Miss Lyon was a well-chaperoned young lady, and I suspect that her Broadway successor will be as old as she was at the time. Fourteen is not twelve, 1970 is not 1958, and the sum of $150,000 you mention is not correct.

10

TO JOHN LEONARD, EDITOR OF
THE NEW YORK TIMES BOOK REVIEW
published on November 7, 1971

I seek the shelter of your columns to help me establish the truth in the following case:

A kind correspondent Xeroxed and mailed me pp. 154–162 referring to my person as imagined by Edmund Wilson in his recent work *Upstate*.* Since a number of statements therein wobble on the brink of libel, I must clear up some matters that might mislead trustful readers.

First of all, the "miseries, horrors, and handicaps" that he assumes I was subjected to during forty years before we first met in New York are mostly figments of his warped fancy. He has no direct knowledge of my past. He has not even bothered to read my *Speak, Memory*, the records and recollections of a happy expatriation that began practically on the day of my birth. The method he favors is gleaning from my fiction what he supposes to be actual, "real-life" impressions and then popping them back into my novels and considering my characters in that inept light—rather like the Shakespearian scholar who deduced Shakespeare's mother from the plays and then discovered allusions to her in the very passages he had twisted to manufacture the lady. What surprises me, however, is not so much Wilson's aplomb as the fact that in the diary he kept while he was my guest in Ithaca he pictures himself as nursing feelings and ideas so vindictive and fatuous that if expressed they should have made me demand his immediate departure.

A few of the ineptitudes I notice in these pages of *Upstate* are worth considering here. His conviction that my insis-

* Upstate: Records and Recollections of Northern New York. 386 pages. Farrar, Straus, and Giroux.

tence on basic similarities between Russian and English verse is "a part of [my] inheritance of [my] father . . . champion of a constitutional monarchy for Russia after the British model" is too silly to refute; and his muddleheaded and ill-informed description of Russian prosody only proves that he remains organically incapable of reading, let alone understanding, my work on the subject. Equally inconsistent with facts—and typical of his Philistine imagination—is his impression that at parties in our Ithaca house my wife "concentrated" on me and grudged "special attention to anyone else."

A particularly repulsive blend of vulgarity and naiveté is reflected in his notion that I must have suffered "a good deal of humiliation," because as the son of a liberal noble I was not "accepted (!) by the strictly illiberal nobility"—where? when, good God?—and by whom exactly, by my uncles and aunts? or by the great grim boyars haunting a plebeian's fancy?

I am aware that my former friend is in poor health but in the struggle between the dictates of compassion and those of personal honor the latter wins. Indeed, the publication of those "old diaries" (doctored, I hope, to fit the present requirements of what was then the future), in which living persons are but the performing poodles of the diarist's act, should be subject to a rule or law that would require some kind of formal consent from the victims of conjecture, ignorance, and invention.

11

TO JOHN LEONARD, EDITOR OF
THE NEW YORK TIMES BOOK REVIEW
published March 5, 1972

Puzzled queries from correspondents oblige me to react, with some delay, to the tasteless parody posing as letters (*New York Times Book Review*, Jan. 16, 1972) from "Diron Frieders" and "Mark Hamburg" which I take to be the phony names of one or two facetious undergraduates judging by the style and the piffle. I think, Sir, you would do a service to Mr. Wilson as well as to truth if you were to point out in your next issue that neither he nor I composed those letters.

I might add that I detected in them only one nice point, namely the suggestion that *Schadenfreude*, as used by Mr. Wilson in regard to a special characteristic of mine, really means "hatred of Freud"—but that is poetic justice, not wit.

ARTICLES

1

ON HODASEVICH
(Sovremennyya zapiski LIX, Paris 1939)

This poet, the greatest Russian poet of our time, Pushkin's literary descendant in Tyutchev's line of succession, shall remain the pride of Russian poetry as long as its last memory lives. What makes his genius particularly striking is that it matured in the years of our literature's torpescence, when the Bolshevist era neatly divided poets into established optimists and demoted pessimists, endemic hearties and exiled hypochondriacs; a classification which, incidentally, leads to an instructive paradox: inside Russia the dictate acts from outside; outside Russia, it acts from within. The will of the government which implicitly demands a writer's affectionate attention toward a parachute, a farm tractor, a Red Army soldier, or the participant in some polar venture (*i.e.*, toward this or that externality of the world) is naturally considerably more powerful than the injunction of exile, addressed to man's inner world. The latter precept is barely sensed by the weak and is scorned by the strong. In the nineteen twenties it induced nostalgic rhymes about St. Petersburg's rostral columns, and now, in the late thirties, it has evolved rhymed religious concerns, not always deep but always honest. Art, authentic art, whose object lies next to art's source (that is in lofty and desert places—and certainly not in the over-populated vale of soulful effusions) has degenerated in our midst to the level, alas, of remedial lyricism; and although one understands that private despair cannot help seeking a public path for its easement, poetry has nothing to do with it: the bosom of the Church or that of the Seine is more competent in these matters. The public path, whatever it looks like, is, artistically, always a paltry one, precisely because of its being public. If, however, one finds hard to imagine a poet, in the confines of Russia, refusing to bend under the yoke (such as, for example, declining to translate a Caucasian poetaster's jingles) and behaving rashly enough to put the muse's liberty above his own, one should expect to find more easily in émigré Russia plucky loners who would not wish to unite and pool their poetical preoccupations in a sort of communistery of the spirit.

Even genius does not save one in Russia; in exile, one is saved by genius alone. No matter how difficult Hodasevich's last years were, no matter how sorely the banality of an émigré's lot irked him, no matter, too, how much the good old indifference of fellow mortals contributed to his mortal extinction, Hodasevich is safely enshrined in timeless Russia. Indeed, he himself was ready to admit, through the hiss of his bilious banter, through the "cold and murk" of the days predicted by Blok,* that he occupied a special position: the blissful solitude of a height others could not attain.

Here I have no intention of hitting bystanders with a swing of the thurible.** A few poets of the émigré genera-

---

*In verses written by Blok on the eve of our era:
    If only you knew, oh children you,
    The cold and murk of the coming days
** The metaphor is borrowed from a poem by Baratynski (1800–1844) accusing critics of lauding Lermontov (1814–1841) on the occasion of his death with the unique object of disparaging living poets. Incidentally, the dry little notice accorded to Baratynski in Pavlenkov's encyclopedia (St. Petersburg, 1913) ends with the marvelous misprint: "Complete Works, 1984."

tion are still on their way up and, who knows, may reach the summits of art—if only they do not fritter away life in a second-rate Paris of their own which sails by with a slight list in the mirrors of taverns without mingling in any way with the French Paris, a motionless and impenetrable town. Hodasevich seemed to have sensed in his very fingers the branching influence of the poetry he created in exile and therefore felt a certain responsibility for its destiny, a destiny which irritated him more than it saddened him. The glum notes of cheap verse struck him more as a parody than as the echo of his collection *Evropeyskaya Noch'* (European Night), where bitterness, anger, angels, the gulfs of adjacent vowels—everything, in short, was genuine, unique, and quite unrelated to the current moods which clouded the verse of many of those who were more or less his disciples.

To speak of his *masterstvo, Meisterschaft,* "mastery," *i.e.* "technique," would be meaningless and even blasphemous in relation to poetry in general, and to his own verse in a sharply specific sense, since the notion of "mastery," which automatically supplies its own quotation marks, turns thereby into an appendage, a shadow demanding logical compensation in the guise of any positive quantity, and this easily brings us to that peculiar, soulful attitude toward poetry in result of which nothing remains of squashed art but a damp spot or tear stain. This is condemnable not because even the most *purs sanglots* require a perfect knowledge of prosody, language, verbal equipoise; and this is also absurd not because the poetaster intimating in slatternly verse that art dwindles to nought in the face of human suffering is indulging in coy deceit (comparable, say, to an undertaker's murmuring against human life because of its brevity); no: the split perceived by the brain between the thing and its fashioning is condemnable and absurd because it vitiates the essence of what actually (whatever you call the thing—"art," "poetry," "beauty") is inseparable from all its mysteriously indispensable properties. In other words, the perfect poem (at least three hundred examples of which can be found in Russian literature) is capable of being examined from all angles by the reader in search of its idea or only its sentiment, or only the picture, or only the sound (many things of that kind can be thought up, from "instrumentation" to "imaginization"), but all this amounts to a random selection of an entity's facet, none of which would deserve, really, a moment of our attention (nor could it of course induce in us any thrill except, maybe, obliquely, in making us recall some other "entity," somebody's voice, a room, a night), had not the poem possessed that resplendent independence in respect of which the term "masterly technique" rings as insultingly as its antonym "winning sincerity."

What I am saying here is far from being new; yet one is impelled to repeat it when speaking of Hodasevich. There exists not quite exact verse (whose very blurriness can have an appeal of its own like that of lovely nearsighted eyes) which makes a virtue of approximation by the poet's striving toward it with the same precision in selecting his words as would pass for "mastery" in more picturesque circumstances. Compared to those artful blurrings, the poetry of Hodasevich may strike the gentle reader as an overpolishing of form—I am deliberately using this unappetizing epithet. But the whole point is that his poetry—or indeed any authentic poetry—does not require any definition in terms of "form."

I find it most odd myself that in this article, in this rapid inventory of thoughts prompted by Hodasevich's death, I seem to imply a vague non-recognition of his genius and engage in vague polemics with such phantoms as would question the enchantment and importance of his poetry. Fame, recognition—all that kind of thing is a phenomenon of rather dubious shape which death alone places in true perspective. I am ready to assume that there might have been quite a few people who when reading with interest the weekly critique that Hodasevich wrote for *Vozrozhdenie** (and it should be admitted that his reviews, with all their wit and *allure*, were not on the level of his poetry, for they lacked somehow its throb and magic) simply did not know that the reviewer was also a poet. I should not be surprised if this person or that finds Hodasevich's posthumous fame inexplicable at first blush. Furthermore, he published no poems lately—and readers are forgetful, and our literary critics are too excited and preoccupied by evanescent topical themes to have the time or occasion to remind the public of important matters. Be it as it may, all is finished now: the bequeathed gold shines on a shelf in full view of the future, whilst the goldminer has left for the region from where, perhaps, a faint something reaches the ears of good poets, penetrating our being with the beyond's fresh breath and conferring upon art that mystery which more than anything characterizes its essence.

Well, so it goes, yet another plane of life has been slightly displaced, yet another habit—the habit (one's own) of (another person's) existence—has been broken. There is no consolation, if one starts to encourage the sense of loss by one's private recollections of a brief, brittle, human image that melts like a hailstone on a window sill. Let us turn to the poems.

* An émigré daily in Paris before World War II.

(This article, signed "V. Sirin," the pen-name I used in the twenties and thirties, in Berlin and Paris, appeared in the émigré literary magazine *Sovremennyya zapiski*, LIX, 1939, Paris. I have clung closely to my tortuous Russian text in the present translation into English.)

2

SARTRE'S FIRST TRY
Nausea. By Jean-Paul Sartre. Translated by Lloyd Alexander. 238 pp. New York: New Directions, 1949

Sartre's name, I understand, is associated with a fashionable brand of café philosophy, and since for every so-called "existentialist" one finds quite a few "suctorialists" (if I may coin a polite term), this made-in-England translation of Sartre's first novel, *La Nausée* (published in Paris in 1938) should enjoy some success.

It is hard to imagine (except in a farce) a dentist persistently pulling out the wrong tooth. Publishers and translators, however, seem to get away with something of that sort. Lack of space limits me to only these examples of Mr. Alexander's blunders.

1. The woman who "s'est offert, avec ses économies, un jeune homme" (has bought herself a young husband with her savings) is said by the translator (p. 20) to have "offered herself and her savings" to that young man.

2. The epithets in "*Il a l'air souffreteux et mauvais*" (he looks seedy and vicious) puzzled Mr. Alexander to such an extent that he apparently left out the end of the sentence for somebody else to fill in, but nobody did, which reduced the English text (p. 43) to "he looks."

3. A reference to "*ce pauvre Ghéhenno*" (French writer) is

twisted (p. 163) into "Christ . . . this poor man of Gehenna."

4. The *forêt de verges* (forest of phalli) in the hero's nightmare is misunderstood as being some sort of birchwood.

Whether, from the viewpoint of literature, *La Nausée* was worth translating at all is another question. It belongs to that tense-looking but really very loose type of writing, which has been popularized by many second-raters—Barbusse, Céline, and so forth. Somewhere behind looms Dostoevski at his worst, and still farther back there is old Eugène Sue, to whom the melodramatic Russian owed so much. The book is supposed to be the diary ("Saturday morning," "11.00 P.M."—that sort of dismal thing) of a certain Roquentin, who, after some quite implausible travels, has settled in a town in Normandy to conclude a piece of historical research.

Roquentin shuttles between café and public library, runs into a voluble homosexual, meditates, writes his diary, and finally has a long and tedious talk with his former wife, who is now kept by a suntanned cosmopolitan. Great importance is attached to an American song on the café phonograph: "Some of these days you'll miss me, honey." Roquentin would like to be as crisply alive as this song, which "saved the Jew [who wrote it] and the Negress [who sang it]" from being "drowned in existence."

In an equivocal flash of clairvoyance (p. 235) he visualizes the composer as a clean-shaven Brooklynite with "coal-black eyebrows" and "ringed fingers," writing down the tune on the twenty-first floor of a skyscraper. The heat is terrific. Presently, however, Tom (probably a friend) will come in with his hip flask (local color) and they will take swigs of liquor ("brimming glasses of whisky" in Mr. Alexander's lush version). I have ascertained that in reality the song is a Sophie Tucker one written by the Canadian Shelton Brooks.

The crux of the whole book seems to be the illumination that comes to Roquentin when he discovers that his "nausea" is the result of the pressure of an absurd and amorphous but very tangible world. Unfortunately for the novel, all this remains on a purely mental level, and the discovery might have been of some other nature, say solipsistic, without in the least affecting the rest of the book. When an author inflicts his idle and arbitrary philosophic fancy on a helpless person whom he has invented for that purpose, a lot of talent is needed to have the trick work. One has no special quarrel with Roquentin when he decides that the world exists. But the task to make the world exist as a work of art was beyond Sartre's powers.

[*The New York Times Book Review*, when publishing this piece in its issue of April 24, 1949, left out my fourth example of Mr. Alexander's blunders. From Ithaca, N. Y., where I was teaching at Cornell University, I immediately propelled a fierce telegram accusing the editor of having disfigured my article. On Monday, April 25, I delivered my third and last lecture on Turgenev's *Fathers and Children*. On Tuesday night we had guests at our dreadfully drafty dacha on steep Seneca Street (Lloyd Alexander would have glossed: Lucius Annaeus). I regaled them with a copy of that violent wire. One of my colleagues, a tense young scholar, observed with a humorless chuckle: "Yes, of course, that's what you would *want* to have sent, as we all must have wanted in many similar cases." My retort, I thought, was not unfriendly, but my wife said later I could not have been ruder. On Wednesday I started to analyze, before a torpid class full of vernal languor, Tolstoy's *Death of Ivan Ilyich*. On Thursday I got a letter from *The New York Times Book Review* explaining their action by "considerations of space." I have now reinstated the missing passage from a note in my files. I do not know if the editor was sufficiently farsighted to preserve my typescript and telegram. According to the italicized bit at the bottom of the piece: "Mr. Nabokov is the author of *The Real Life of Sebastian Knight*"—which had been published by New Directions.]

3

POUNDING THE CLAVICHORD

The author of a soon-to-be-published translation may find it awkward to criticize a just-published version of the same work, but in the present case I can, and should, master my embarrassment; for something must be done, some lone, hoarse voice must be raised, to defend both the helpless dead poet and the credulous college student from the kind of pitiless and irresponsible paraphrast whose product * I am about to discuss.

The task of twisting some five thousand Russian iambic tetrameters, with a rigid pattern of masculine and feminine rhymes, into an equal number of similarly rhymed English iambic tetrameters is a monstrous undertaking, and I who have limited my efforts to a plain, prosy, and rhymeless translation of *Eugene Onegin* feel a certain morbid admiration for Mr. Arndt's perseverance. A sympathetic reader, especially one who does not consult the original, may find in Mr. Arndt's version more or less sustained stretches of lulling poetastry and specious sense; but anybody with less benevolence and more knowledge will see how patchy the passable really is.

---

* Alexander Pushkin, *Eugene Onegin*. A new translation in the Onegin stanza with an introduction and notes by Walter Arndt. A Dutton paperback, New York, 1963.

Let me, first of all, present side by side a literal translation of two stanzas (Six: xxxvi–xxxvii) and Mr. Arndt's version. It is a sample of one of those passages in his work that are free from howlers, and that the passive reader (the pet of progressive educators) might accept as a tolerable translation:

1. My friends, you're sorry for the poet	My friends, you will lament the poet
2. in the bloom of glad hopes,	Who, flowering *with a happy gift*,
3. not having yet fulfilled them for the world,	Must wilt before he could bestow it
4. scarce out of infant clothes,	Upon the world, *yet scarce adrift*
5. withered! Where is the ardent stir,	*From boyhood's shore.* Now he will never
6. the noble aspiration,	Seethe with that generous endeavor,
7. of young emotions and young thoughts,	Those *storms* of mind and heart again,
8. exalted, tender, bold?	Audacious, tender or *humane!*
9. Where are love's turbulent desires,	Stilled now are love's unruly urges,
10. the thirst for knowledges and work,	The thirst for knowledge and for *deeds*,
11. the dread of vice and shame,	*Contempt* for vice and *what it breeds*,
12. and you, fond musings,	And stilled you too, ethereal surges
13. you, token of unearthly life,	Breath of a transcendental clime,
14. you, dreams of sacred poetry!	Dreams from the sacred realm of rhyme.

1. Perhaps, for the world's good	Perchance the world would have saluted
2. or, at least, for glory he was born;	In him a *savior or a sage;*
3. his silenced lyre might have aroused	His ly-ere, now forever muted,
4. a resonant, uninter-rupted ringing	Might have resounded down the *age*
5. throughout the ages. There awaited	In ceaseless *thunder,* and have fated
6. the poet, on the stair-way of the world	*Its bearer* to be elevated
7. perhaps, a lofty stair.	To *high rank* on the worldly grade;
8. His martyred shade has carried	Or haply with his martyred shade
9. away with him, per-haps,	Some holy *insight* will they *bury,*
10. a sacred mystery, and for us	A *gem,* perchance, *of wisdom choice,*
11. dead is a life-creating voice,	Now perished with his vital voice.
12. and to his shade beyond the tomb's confines	The hymn of ages will not carry
13. will not rush up the hymn of races,	*Deep into his sepulchral den*
14. the blessing of the ages.	The benedictions of all men.

I have italicized such verbal gobbets as are not found, or found in another form, in Pushkin's text. Omissions, here and throughout the version, are too numerous and too ingrained to be profitably catalogued. Passive readers will derive, no doubt, a casual illusion of sense from Arndt's actually nonsensical line 2 of xxxvi. They will hardly notice that the chancrous metaphor in lines 4–5 inflicted by a meretricious rhyme is not Pushkin's fault, nor wonder at the naive temerity a paraphrast has of throwing in his own tropes when he should know that the figure of speech is the main, sacred quiddity and eyespot of a poet's genius, and is the last thing that should be tampered with. In the second stanza presented here our passive readers may skim over some other added metaphors, such as the "buried insight," the "gem of wisdom," and the "sepulchral den" (which suggests a dead lion rather than a dead poet). They may also swallow the "high rank" (which implies the sort of favor a meek poet like Zhukovski received from the Tsar, and not at all the "lofty stair" which Pushkin invokes); but perhaps the "thunder-bearer" of lines 5–6 shall briefly cause them to stumble.

These, I repeat, are types of the least offensive among Mr. Arndt's stanzas. A closer examination of the actual technique of his various mistranslations brings out the following points:

1. Natural objects changing their species or genus: "flea" turns into "roach," "aspen" into "ash," "birch" and "lime" into "beech," "pine" (many times) into "fir," and "racemose bird cherry" (*cheryomuha*) into "alder" (the harmful drudges who compile Russian-English dictionaries have at least, under *cheryomuha*, "black alder," *i.e.* "alder buckthorn," which is wrong, but not as wrong as Arndt's tree).

2. Transformation of names: "Prince N," Tatiana's husband, turns into "Prince M"; Griboedov's hero "Chatski" into "Chaatsky" (possibly through hybridization with Pushkin's friend Chaadaev); Tatiana's aunt "Pelageya Nikolavna" into "Pelya," an insufferable diminutive; another aunt, "Princess Aline," into the ridiculous "Princess Nancy"; Onegin's housekeeper, "Anisia," into "Mistress Anna," and "Vanya," the husband of Tatiana's nurse, into "Larry."

3. Anachronisms: Triquet's "spectacles" are said to be "gold pince-nez"; the "jams in jars" taken by Mrs. Larin to Moscow become "cans of jelly," and a traveler is introduced as "fresh from the station."

4. Comic scansion: " . . . where ou-er hero lately dwelled"; " . . . and ou-er luckless damzel tasted" (many more "ou-er"s throughout). The same with endings in "ire"; "fi-ere," "squi-ere," "desi-ere," and so on. "Business" is scanned in a Germanic trisyllabic way ("no service, business or wife"), and, in another line, "egoism" is generously granted four syllables as if it were "egoisum."

5. Burlesque rhymes: Feeler–Lyudmila, capital–ball, binoculars–stars, char–Africa, family–me, thrillers–pillows, invaders–days does; and rhymes based on dialect pronunciation: meadow–shadow, message–passage, tenor–manor, possession–fashion, bury–carry, and so on.

6. Crippled clichés and mongrel idioms: "my flesh is parched with thirst," "the mother streaming with tears," "the tears from Tania's lashes gush," "what ardor at her breast is found."

7. Vulgarisms and stale slang: "the bells in décollté creations," "moms," "twosomes," "highbrow," "his women," "I sang of feet I knew before, dear lady-feet," "dear heart, dear all" (Lenski in his last elegy to Olga), "Simon-pure," "beau geste," "hard to meet" (for "unsociable"), "my uncle, decorous old prune" (for "my uncle has most honest principles"), the nurse telling Tatiana "Aye, don't holler," Olga "blended of peach and cream," Tatiana writing to Onegin "my knees were folding" and "you justly dealt with my advances" (Tatiana, Pushkin's Tatiana!). Here too belongs a special little curiosity. The minds of versionists seldom meet but a singular convergence of that sort occurs in Eight: XXXVIII. Pushkin shows Onegin moodily sitting by the fire and dropping into it "now a slipper, now his magazine." Elton, in 1937, vulgarly translated this as " . . . the News drops in the fire or else his shoes" and Mr. Arndt has the almost identical " . . . the News slipped in the fi-ere or his shoes."

8. Howlers and other glaring mistakes. The true howler is a joint product of ignorance and self-assurance. Here are a few of the many examples provided by Mr. Arndt. In

Six: v Pushkin describes Zaretski (formerly a rake, now a placid landowner in the backwoods of northwest Russia). Zaretski several years earlier, during the Napoleonic wars, was taken prisoner by the French and had a pleasant time in Paris—so pleasant in fact that now, in 1820–21, he would not mind being captured again (if there were another war) "so as to drink on credit at Véry's [a café-restaurant in Paris, originally on the Terrasse des Feuillants in the Jardin des Tuileries] two or three bottles every morning." Mr. Arndt completely misses the point, assumes that Véry is a Parisian restaurateur established in Russia (say in Pskov), not too far from Zaretski's country seat, and boldly renders Pushkin's lines as " . . . braving bondage (what bondage in 1821?), enraptured (with what?), he still gallops on his morning sprees to charge three bottles at Véry's." Another howler occurs in his version of Two: xxxv where Pushkin has "the people yawning" on Trinity Day in church, but where Arndt has " . . . Trinity when the peasants tell their beads" (which they do not commonly do in Russia) "and nod at morning service" (which is not easy in the Greek-Orthodox standing position). In Three: iii the meager fare Mrs. Larin offers to her guests ("jams in little dishes are brought; upon a small table, oil-cloth'd [lexically, "waxed"] a jug of lingonberry water is set") becomes a Garg*arndt*uan feast with utensils for giants: " . . . bowls of preserves, then the habitual bilberry water lumbers on (?) in a great wax-sealed [mix-up with the epithet used in the text for the small table] demi-john" [two or three gallons?]. In Three: ix Pushkin alludes to St. Preux ("the lover of Julie Wolmar") but Arndt, who apparently has not read Rousseau's novel, confuses husband with lover: "Julie's adoring swain, Wolmar." In Three: xxviii Pushkin's two learned ladies, one in a yellow shawl, as pedantic as a seminarian, and the other, a bonneted one, as grave as an academician (meaning member of the Academy of Sciences) are replaced in Arndt's version by a Buddhist priest ("the saffron-muffled clerk in orders") and an English don ("a mortar-boarded sage"), which, as boners go, is a kind of multiple fracture. Pushkin's hills which in the beginning of Chapter Five are "softly overspread with Winter's brilliant carpeting" become "mountain summits (in lowland Russia!) softly stretching 'neath Winter's scintillating shawl" (which produces an unexpected American-bosom image); the "sumptuous contact of yielding rugs" (One: xxxi) becomes the rather Freudian "voluptuous embrace of swelling carpets," and the "surgings" of a poet's "heart" (Four: xxxi) are gynandromorphosed into the "deep stirrings of [his] womb." There is no space to list all the glaring mistakes of this sort, and I shall mention only two more. In Six: xix Pushkin has listless Lenski, on the eve of his duel, "sit down at the clavichord and play but chords on it," a melancholy image which Arndt horribly transforms into: "the clavichord he would be pounding, with random chord set it resounding." And finally here is the bloomer in Arndt's version of the end of Three: xl where Pushkin speaks of a hare trembling as it suddenly sees from afar "a shotman in the bushes crouch" but where Arndt changes the weapon and has the hare listen "as from afar with sudden rush an arrow falls into the brush." The source of this blunder will be explained in the next section.

9. Inadequate knowledge of Russian. This is a professional ailment among non-Russian translators from Russian into English. Anything a little too far removed from the *kak-vy-pozhivaete-ya-pozhivayu-khorosho* group becomes a pitfall, into which, rather than around which, dictionaries guide the groper; and when they are not consulted, then other disasters happen. In the abovementioned Three: xl passage, Mr. Arndt has evidently confused the word *strelká*, accusative of *strelok* (shooter, sportsman) with *strélka* (diminutive of *strela*, arrow). *Sed'moy chas* is not "past seven" (p. 149) but only past six. *Podzhavshi ruki* does not mean "arms akimbo" (p. 62) but "with snugly folded arms." *Vishen'e* is simply "cherries" (with which the girls pelt the eavesdropper in their song in Chapter Three) and not

"cherry twigs" and "branches" with which Arndt makes them beat away the intruder. *Pustynnyy sneg* is "desolate snow," not "desert snow" (p. 122). *V puhu* is "covered with fluff" and not "a little dim" (p. 127). *Obnovit'* (Two: XXXIII) is not to "renovate" or "mend" but to "inaugurate." *Vino* in Two: XI is "liquor," not "wine." *Svod* in Four: XXI is not "freight," but "code." *Hory* (Seven: LI) means the upper gallery of a public ballroom, and not "the involved rotations of rounds"—whatever that is.

10. Wobbly English. The phrase "next door" is used to mean "next room" (pp. 122 and 133). A skeleton impossibly "pouts" on p. 122. Lenski in the duel "closing his left eye starts to level" but Arndt (p. 132) makes him take aim with "his left eye blinking" like the corresponding tail light of a turning truck; soon after which (p. 157) "Dead lies our *dim young bard and lover* by friendly *hand and weapon* felled." And the amazon of Six: XLI whom Pushkin pictures as halting her steed before Lenski's grave is hilariously made to "rein in her *charging* horse."

11. Padding. Plug words and rhymes are bound to occur in rhymed versions, but I have seldom seen them used with such consistency and in such profusion as here. A typical example of routine padding (for the sake of a bad rhyme) is the puffing up of the literal "she says: farewell pacific dales, and you, familiar hill tops" (Seven: XXVIII) to become, in Arndt's version; "(she) whispers: Calm valleys where I sauntered, farewell; lone summits that I haunted." When in the same chapter Tatiana is described by Pushkin as avidly reading Onegin's books whereupon "a different world is revealed to her," this becomes with Arndt: "an eager passage (!) door on door (!) to worlds she never knew before." Here simple padding shades into the next category of mistranslation.

12. *Otsebyátina.* This convenient cant word consists of the words *ot*, meaning "from," and *sebya*, meaning "oneself," with a pejorative suffix, *yatina*, tagged on (its *ya* takes improper advantage of the genitive ending of the pronoun,

[238]

coinciding with it and producing a strongly stressed *bya* sound which to a Russian's ear connotes juvenile disgust). Lexically translated, it can be rendered as "come-from-oneselfer" or "from-oneselfity." It is employed to describe the personal contributions of self-sufficient or desperate translators (or actors who have forgotten their speeches). Here are some grotesque examples of *otsebyatina* in Arndt. Pushkin is describing (Eight: xxiv) the guests at Princess N's soirée: "Here were, in mobcaps and roses elderly ladies, wicked looking; here were several maidens —unsmiling faces." This is all there is about those ladies and maidens, but Arndt otsebyatinates thus: " . . . redecorated ladies with caps from France and scowls from Hades; among them here and there a girl without a smile from curl to curl (a fiendish ungrin!)." My other example refers to One: xxxiii where Pushkin has a famous description of "the waves, running in turbulent succession, with love to lie down at her feet"; this becomes "the waves . . . with uproar each the other goading, to curl in love about her feet." One hardly knows what infects one's fancy more painfully here—those waves prodding each other with tridents or that little drain-hole vortex in which their "uproar" ends.

Mr. Arndt's notes to his translation are lean and derivative but even so he manages to make several mistakes. The statement (p. xi) that the third edition of *Eugene Onegin* "appeared on the day of Pushkin's death" is wrong: it appeared not later than January 19, 1837, Old Style, that is at least ten days before the poet's death. He began writing *Eugene Onegin* not "on May 28, 1822," as Arndt (led astray by another bungling commentator and adding his own mistake) notes, but on May 9, 1823. The statuette of Napoleon with folded arms in Chapter Seven is not a "bust" (as stated in a note on p. 191): normal busts do not have arms to fold. The remark on p. 223 that " . . . Prolasov has been proposed" to fill in a gap in the printed text (first line of Eight: xxvi) is nonsense, since "Prolasov" never existed, being merely a comedy name (meaning "climber" or "vile sycophant") preserved in Pushkin's fair copy and misapplied by some editors to Andrey Saburov, director of the Imperial theaters.

Mr. Arndt's most bizarre observation, however, comes on page vi, towards the end of his preface: "The present new translation . . . is not aimed primarily at the academic and literary expert, but at a public of English-speaking students and others interested in a central work of world literature in a compact and readable form."—which is tantamount to proclaiming: "I know this is an inferior product but it is gaily colored and nicely packed, and is, anyway, just for students and such people."

It is only fair to add that this "brilliant" (as said on the upperside of the volume) and "splendid" (as said on its underside) new translation has won one half of the third annual Bollingen prize for the best translation of poetry in English (as the librarian James T. Babb of the Yale University Library announced on November 19, 1963, in New Haven, Conn.). The committee making the awards included Professors Peyre, René Wellek, and John Hollander, of Yale; and Professor Reuben A. Brouwer, of Harvard University. (I rely on Steve Kezerian, Director of the Yale University News Bureau, for the spelling of these names). Representing the permanent committee of administration at Yale was Donald G. Wing, Associate Yale Librarian. One cannot help wondering if any of the professors really read this readable work—or the infinitely remote great poem of their laureate's victim.

Montreux, December 23, 1963

Published in *The New York Review of Books* on April 30, 1964. A "Second Printing, revised" of Arndt's "translation" appeared later (1965?) but despite the note saying (p. v) that "several emendations were suggested by Vladimir Nabokov's criticisms at various times" this "revised" version still remains as abominable as before.

4

REPLY TO MY CRITICS

In regard to my novels my position is different. I cannot imagine myself writing a letter-to-the-editor in reply to an unfavorable review, let alone devoting almost a whole day to composing a magazine article of explanation, retaliation, and protest. I have waited at least thirty years to take notice—casual and amused notice—of some scurvy abuse I met with in my "V. Sirin" disguise, but that pertains to bibliography. My inventions, my circles, my special islands are infinitely safe from exasperated readers. Nor have I ever yielded to the wild desire to thank a benevolent critic—or at least to express somehow my tender awareness of this or that friendly writer's sympathy and understanding, which in some extraordinary way seem always to coincide with talent and originality, an interesting, though not quite inexplicable phenomenon.

If, however, adverse criticism happens to be directed not at those acts of fancy, but at such a matter-of-fact work of reference as my annotated translation of *Eugene Onegin* (hereafter referred to as EO), other considerations take over. Unlike my novels, EO possesses an ethical side, moral and human elements. It reflects the compiler's honesty or dishonesty, skill or sloppiness. If told I am a bad poet, I smile; but if told I am a poor scholar, I reach for my heaviest dictionary.

I do not think I have received all the reviews that appeared after EO was published; I fail to locate a few that I was sure I had in my chaotic study; but judging by the numerous ones that did reach me, one might conclude that literal translation represents an approach entirely devised by me; that it had never been heard of before; and that there was something offensive and even sinister about such a method and undertaking. Promoters and producers of what Anthony Burgess calls "arty translations"—carefully rhymed, pleasantly modulated versions containing, say, eighteen percent of sense plus thirty-two of nonsense and fifty of neutral padding—are I think more prudent than they realize. While ostensibly tempted by impossible dreams, they are subliminally impelled by a kind of self-preservation. The "arty translation" protects them by concealing and camouflaging ignorance or incomplete information or the fuzzy edge of limited knowledge. Stark literalism, on the other hand, would expose their fragile frame to unknown and incalculable perils.

It is quite natural, then, that the solidly unionized professional paraphrast experiences a surge of dull hatred and fear, and in some cases real panic, when confronted with the possibility that a shift in fashion, or the influence of an adventurous publishing house, may suddenly remove from his head the cryptic rosebush he carries or the maculated shield erected between him and the specter of inexorable knowledge. As a result the canned music of rhymed versions is enthusiastically advertised, and accepted, and the sacrifice of textual precision applauded as something rather heroic, whereas only suspicion and bloodhounds await the gaunt, graceless literalist groping around in despair for the obscure word that would satisfy impassioned fidelity and accumulating in the process a wealth of information which only makes the advocates of pretty camouflage tremble or sneer.

These observations, although suggested by specific facts, should not be construed in a strictly *pro domo sua* sense. My

EO falls short of the ideal crib. It is still not close enough and not ugly enough. In future editions I plan to defowlerize it still more drastically. I think I shall turn it entirely into utilitarian prose, with a still bumpier brand of English, rebarbative barricades of square brackets and tattered banners of reprobate words, in order to eliminate the last vestiges of bourgeois poesy and concession to rhythm. This is something to look forward to. For the moment, all I wish is merely to put on record my utter disgust with the general attitude, amoral and Philistine, towards literalism.

It is indeed wonderful how indifferent most critics are to the amount of unwillful deceit going on in the translation trade. I recall once opening a copy of Bely's *Petersburg* in English, and lighting upon a monumental howler in a famous passage about a blue coupé which had been hopelessly discolored by the translator's understanding *kubovyy* (which means "blue") as "cubic"! This has remained a model and a symbol. But who cares and why bother? Mr. Rosen in *The Saturday Review* (November 28, 1964) ends his remarks on rhymed versions of *Eugene Onegin* with the expression of a rapturous hope: "It only remains for a talented poet like Robert Lowell to take advantage [of these versions] to produce a poem in English that really sings and soars." But this is an infernal vision to me who can distinguish in the most elaborate imitation the simple schoolboy howler from the extraneous imagery within which it is so pitifully imbedded. Again—what does it matter? "It is part of the act," as Mr. Edmund Wilson would say. The incredible errors in the translations from the Russian which are being published nowadays with frenetic frequency are dismissed as trivial blemishes that only a pedant would note.

Even Professor Muchnic, who in a recent issue of *The New York Review of Books* delicately takes Mr. Guy Daniels apart as if he were an unfamiliar and possibly defective type of coffee machine, neglects to point out that in both versions of Lermontov's poem which she quotes—Daniels' effort and Baring's very minor (*pace* Mirski) poem—the same grotesque imp blows a strident trumpet. For we have here an admirable example of one of those idiomatic freaks that for reasons of mental balance foreigners should not even try to rationalize. Lermontov's Russian goes: *Sosedka est' u nih odna . . . Kak vspomnish', kak davno rasstalis'*! And the literal sense is: "They have a certain neighbor [fem.] . . . Oh, to think how long ago we parted!" The form *vspomnish'* looks like the second person singular of "remember," but in this intonational arrangement it should be the first person in literal translation since it is addressed by the speaker to himself. Now, both versionists being ignorant of idiomatic Russian did not hesitate to use the second person (though actually the result gives a painfully didactic twist to the sentence, which should have made the translator think twice). Baring's version (which Professor Muchnic, I am sorry to say, calls "a wonderfully precise reproduction of the sense, the idiom") runs: "We had a neighbor . . . and *you remember* I and she . . . " While the more humble Daniels translates: "There was a girl as *you'll recall* . . . " I have italicized the shared boner. The point is not that one version is better than the other (frankly there is not much to choose between the two); the point is that unwittingly *both* use the same wrong person as if all paraphrasts were interconnected omphalically by an ectoplasmic band.

Despite the violent attitude towards literalism, I still find a little surprising the intensity of human passions that my rather dry, rather dull work provokes. Hack reviewers rush to the defense of the orthodox Soviet publicists whom I "chastise" and of whom they have never heard before. A more or less displaced Russian in New York maintains that my commentary is nothing but a collection of obscure trifles and that besides he remembers having heard it all many years ago in Gorki from his high-school teacher, A. A. Artamonov.

The word "mollitude," which I use a few times, has been

now so often denounced that it threatens to become almost a household word, like "nymphet." One of my most furious and inarticulate attackers seems to be an intimate friend of Belinski (born 1811), as well as of all the paraphrasts I "persecute." The fury is, I suppose, pardonable and noble, but there would be no sense in my reacting to it. I shall also ignore some of the slapstick—such as a little item in *The New Republic* (April 3, 1965) which begins "Inspector Nabokov has revisited the scene of the crime in *L'affaire Oneguine*" and is prompted by a sordid little grudge of which the editor, presumably, had no knowledge. A reviewer writing in the *Novyy Zhurnal* (No. 77), Mr. Moris Fridberg—whom I am afraid I shall be accused of having invented—employs a particularly hilarious brand of bad Russian (*kak izvestno dlya lyubogo studenta*, as known "for" every student) to introduce the interesting idea that textual fidelity is unnecessary because "in itself the subject-matter of [Pushkin's] work is not very important." He goes on to complain that I do not say a word about such Pushkinists as Modzalevski, Tomashevski, Bondi, Shchyogolev, and Gofman—a statement that proves he has not only not read my commentary, but has not even consulted the Index; and on top of that he confuses me with Professor Arndt whose preliminary remarks about his "writing not for experts but students" Mr. Fridberg ascribes to me. A still more luckless gentleman (in the *Los Angeles Times*) is so incensed by the pride and prejudice of my commentary that he virtually chokes on his wrath and after enticingly entitling his article "Nabokov Fails as a Translator" has to break it off abruptly without having made one single reference to the translation itself. Among the more serious articles there is a long one in *The New York Times Book Review*, June 28, 1964, by Mr. Ernest Simmons, who obligingly corrects what he takes to be a misprint in One: xxv: 5; "Chadaev," he says, should be "Chaadaev"; but from my note to that passage he should have seen that "Chadaev" is one of the three forms of that name, and also happens to be Pushkin's own spelling in that particular line, which otherwise would not have scanned.

For obvious reasons I cannot discuss all the sympathetic reviews. I shall only refer to some of them in order to acknowledge certain helpful suggestions and corrections. I am grateful to John Bayley (*The Observer*, November 29, 1964) for drawing my attention to what he calls—much too kindly, alas—"the only slip" in my commentary: "*Auf allen Gipfeln*" (in the reference to Goethe's poem) should be corrected to "*Ueber allen Gipfeln*." (I can add at least one other: My note to Two: xxxv: 8 contains a silly blunder and should be violently deleted.) Anthony Burgess in *Encounter* has suddenly and conclusively abolished my sentimental fondness for FitzGerald by showing how he falsified the "witty metaphysical tent-maker's" actual metaphors in "*Awake! for morning in the bowl of Night . . .* ". John Wain, in *The Listener* (April 29, 1965), by a sheer feat of style has made me at once sorry for one of my "victims" and weak with laughter: "This [the discussion of prosody], by the way, is the section in which Arthur Hugh Clough gets described as a poetaster; the effect is like that of seeing an innocent bystander suddenly buried by a fall of snow from a roof . . . ." J. Thomas Shaw, in *The Russian Review* (April 1965), observes that I should have promoted Pushkin after his graduation to the tenth civil rank ("collegiate secretary") instead of leaving him stranded on the fourteenth rung of the ladder; but I cannot find in my copy the misprinted Derzhavin date which he also cites; and I strongly object to his listing James Joyce, whom I revere, among those writers whom I condemn "in contemptuous asides" (apparently Mr. Shaw has dreadfully misunderstood what I say about Joyce's characters falling asleep by applying it to Joyce's readers). Finally, the anonymous reviewer in *The Times Literary Supplement* (January 28, 1965) is perfectly right when he says that in my notes I do not discuss Pushkin's art in sufficient detail; he makes a number of attractive suggestions which, together with those of two other reviewers and several correspondents, would make a fifth volume, or at least a very handsome *Festschrift*. The same reviewer is much too lenient when he remarks that "a careful scrutiny of every line has failed to reveal a single careless error in translation." There are at least two: in Four: XLIII: 2, the word "but" should be deleted, and in Five: XI: 3, "lawn" should be "plain."

The longest, most ambitious, most captious, and, alas, most reckless, article is Mr. Edmund Wilson's in *The New York Review of Books* (July 15, 1965)*, and this I now select for a special examination.

A number of earnest simpletons consider Mr. Wilson to be an authority in my field ("he misses few of Nabokov's lapses," as one hasty well-wisher puts it in a letter to *The New York Review* on August 26), and no doubt such delusions should not be tolerated; still, I am not sure that the necessity to defend my work from blunt jabs and incompetent blame would have been a sufficient incentive for me to discuss that article, had I not been moved to do so by the unusual, unbelievable, and highly entertaining opportunity that I am unexpectedly given by Mr. Wilson himself of refuting practically every item of criticism in his enormous piece. The mistakes and misstatements in it form an uninterrupted series so complete as to seem artistic in reverse, making one wonder if, perhaps, it had not been woven that way on purpose to be turned into something pertinent and coherent when reflected in a looking glass. I am unaware of any other such instance in the history of literature. It is a polemicist's dream come true, and one must be a poor sportsman to disdain what it offers.

As Mr. Wilson points out with such disarming good humor at the beginning of his piece, he and I are old

---

* This is the text readers should consult. It is reprinted in an abridged, emended, and incoherent form in Edmund Wilson's *A Window on Russia*, Farrar, Straus & Giroux, New York, 1972.

friends. I fully reciprocate "the warm affection sometimes chilled by exasperation" that he says he feels for me. When I first came to America a quarter of a century ago, he wrote to me, and called on me, and was most kind to me in various matters, not necessarily pertaining to his profession. I have always been grateful to him for the tact he showed in not reviewing any of my novels while constantly saying flattering things about me in the so-called literary circles where I seldom revolve. We have had many exhilarating talks, have exchanged many frank letters. A patient confidant of his long and hopeless infatuation with the Russian language and literature, I have invariably done my best to explain to him his monstrous mistakes of pronunciation, grammar, and interpretation. As late as 1957, at one of our last meetings, in Ithaca, upstate New York, where I lived at the time, we both realized with amused dismay that, despite my frequent comments on Russian prosody, he still could not scan Russian verse. Upon being challenged to read *Evgeniy Onegin* aloud, he started to perform with great gusto, garbling every second word, and turning Pushkin's iambic line into a kind of spastic anapest with a lot of jaw-twisting haws and rather endearing little barks that utterly jumbled the rhythm and soon had us both in stitches.

In the present case, I greatly regret that Mr. Wilson did not consult me about his perplexities, as he used to in the past. Here are some of the ghastly blunders that might have been so easily avoided.

"Why," asks Mr. Wilson, "should Nabokov call the word *netu* an old-fashioned and dialect form of *net*. It is in constant colloquial use and what I find one usually gets for an answer when one asks for some book in the Soviet bookstore in New York." Mr. Wilson has mistaken the common colloquial *netu* which means "there is not," "we do not have it," etc., for the obsolete *netu* which he has never heard and which as I explain in my note to Three: III: 12, is a form of *net* in the sense of "not so" (the opposite of "yes"). "The character called *yo*," Mr. Wilson continues, "is pronounced . . . more like 'yaw' than like the 'yo' in 'yonder.'" Mr. Wilson should not try to teach me how to pronounce this, or any other, Russian vowel. My "yo" is the standard rendering of the sound. The "yaw" sound he suggests is grotesque and quite wrong. I can hear Mr. Wilson—whose accent in Russian I know so well—asking that bookseller of his for "*Myawrtvye Dushi*" ("Dead Souls"). No wonder he did not get it.

"*Vse*," according to Mr. Wilson (explaining two varieties of the Russian for "all"), "is applied to people, and *vsyo* to things." This is a meaningless pronouncement. *Vse* is merely the plural of *ves'* (masculine), *vsya* (feminine), and *vsyo* (neuter).

Mr. Wilson is puzzled by my assertion that the adjective *zloy* is the only one-syllable adjective in Russian. "How about the one-syllable predicative adjectives?" he asks. The answer is simple: I am not talking of predicative adjectives. Why drag them in? Such forms as *mudr* ("is wise"), *glup* ("is stupid"), *ploh* ("is very sick indeed") are not adjectives at all, but adverbish mongrels which may differ in sense from the related adjectives.

In discussing the word *pochuya* Mr. Wilson confuses it with *chuya* ("sensing") (see my letter about this word in the *New Statesman*, April 23, 1965) and says that had Pushkin used *pochuyav*, only then should I have been entitled to put "having sensed." "Where," queries Mr. Wilson, "is our scrupulous literalness?" Right here. My friend is unaware that despite the different endings, *pochuyav* and *pochuya* happen to be interchangeable, both being "past gerunds," and both meaning exactly the same thing.

All this is rather extraordinary. Every time Mr. Wilson starts examining a Russian phrase he makes some ludicrous slip. His didactic purpose is defeated by such errors, as it is also by the strange tone of his article. Its mixture of

pompous aplomb and peevish ignorance is hardly conducive to a sensible discussion of Pushkin's language and
mine—or indeed any language, for, as we shall presently
see, Mr. Wilson's use of English is also singularly imprecise
and misleading.

First of all it is simply not true to say, as he does, that in
my review of Professor Arndt's translation (*The New York
Review of Books*, August 30, 1964) "Nabokov dwelt especially on what he regarded as Professor Arndt's Germanisms
and other infelicities of phrasing, without apparently being
aware of how vulnerable he himself was." I dwelled
especially on Arndt's mistranslations. What Mr. Wilson
regards as my infelicities may be more repellent to him for
psychological reasons than "anything in Arndt," but they
belong to another class of error than Arndt's or any other
paraphrast's casual blunders, and what is more Mr. Wilson
knows it. I dare him to deny that he deliberately confuses
the issue by applying the term "niggling attack" to an
indignant examination of the insults dealt out to Pushkin's
masterpiece in yet another arty translation. Mr. Wilson
affirms that "the only characteristic Nabokov trait" in my
translation (aside from an innate "sadomasochistic" urge "to
torture both the reader and himself," as Mr. Wilson puts it
in a clumsy attempt to stick a particularly thick and rusty
pin into my effigy) is my "addiction to rare and unfamiliar
words." It does not occur to him that I may have rare and
unfamiliar things to convey; that is his loss. He goes on,
however, to say that in view of my declared intention to
provide students with a trot such words are "entirely
inappropriate" here, since it would be more to the point for
the student to look up the Russian word than the English
one. I shall stop only one moment to consider Mr. Wilson's
pathetic assumption that a student can read Pushkin, or any
other Russian poet, by "looking up" every word (after all,
the result of this simple method is far too apparent in Mr.
Wilson's own mistranslations and misconceptions), or that a

reliable and complete *Russko-angliyskiy slovar'* not only exists (it does not) but is more easily available to the student than, say, the second unabridged edition (1960) of Webster's, which I really must urge Mr. Wilson to acquire. Even if that miraculous *slovar'* did exist, there would still be the difficulty of choosing, without my help, the right shade between two near synonyms and avoiding, without my guidance, the trap-falls of idiomatic phrases no longer in use.

Edmund Wilson sees himself (not quite candidly, I am afraid, and certainly quite erroneously) as a commonsensical, artless, average reader with a natural vocabulary of, say, six hundred basic words. No doubt such an imaginary reader may be sometimes puzzled and upset by the tricky terms I find it necessary to use here and there—very much here and there. But how many such innocents will tackle EO anyway? And what does Mr. Wilson mean by implying I should not use words that in the process of lexicographic evolution begin to occur only at the level of a "fairly comprehensive dictionary"? When does a dictionary cease being an abridged one and start growing "fairly" and then "extremely" comprehensive? Is the sequence: vest-pocket, coat-pocket, greatcoat-pocket, my three book shelves, Mr. Wilson's rich library? And should the translator simply omit any reference to an idea or an object if the only right word—a word he happens to know as a teacher or a naturalist, or an inventor of words—is discoverable in the revised edition of a standard dictionary but not in its earlier edition or *vice versa*? Disturbing possibilities! Nightmarish doubts! And how does the harassed translator know that somewhere on the library ladder he has just stopped short of Wilson's Fairly Comprehensive and may safely use "polyhedral" but not "lingonberry"? (Incidentally, the percentage of what Mr. Wilson calls "dictionary words" in my translation is really so absurdly small that I have difficulty in finding examples.)

Mr. Wilson can hardly be unaware that once a writer chooses to youthen or resurrect a word, it lives again, sobs again, stumbles all over the cemetery in doublet and trunk hose, and will keep annoying stodgy gravediggers as long as that writer's book endures. In several instances, English archaisms have been used in my EO not merely to match Russian antiquated words but to revive a nuance of meaning present in the ordinary Russian term but lost in the English one. Such terms are not meant to be idiomatic. The phrases I decide upon aspire towards literality, not readability. They are steps in the ice, pitons in the sheer rock of fidelity. Some are mere signal words whose only purpose is to suggest or indicate that a certain pet term of Pushkin's has recurred at that point. Others have been chosen for their Gallic touch implicit in this or that Russian attempt to imitate a French turn of phrase. All have pedigrees of agony and rejection and reinstatement, and should be treated as convalescents and ancient orphans, and not hooted at as impostors by a critic who says he admires some of my books. I do not care if a word is "archaic" or "dialect" or "slang"; I am an eclectic democrat in this matter, and whatever suits me, goes. My method may be wrong but it is a method, and a genuine critic's job should have been to examine the method itself instead of crossly fishing out of my pond some of the oddities with which I had deliberately stocked it.

Let me now turn to what Mr. Wilson calls my "infelicities" and "aberrations" and explain to him why I use the words he does not like or does not know.

In referring to Onegin's not being attracted by the picture of family life, Pushkin in Four: XIII: 5 uses the phrase *semeystvennoy kartinoy*. The modern term is *semeynoy kartinoy* and had Pushkin chosen it, I might have put "family picture." But I had to indicate the presence of Pushkin's rarer word and used therefore the rarer "familistic" as a signal word.

In order to indicate the archaic note in *vospomnya* (used by Pushkin in One: xlvii: 6–7 instead of *vspomnya*, or *vspomniv*, or *vspominaya*), as well as to suggest the deep sonorous diction of both lines (*vospomnya prezhnih let romany*; *vospomnya*, etc.), I had to find something more reverberating and evocative than "recalling intrigues of past years," etc., and whether Mr. Wilson (or Mr. N. for that matter) likes it or not, nothing more suitable than "rememorating" for *vospomnya* can be turned up.*

Mr. Wilson also dislikes "curvate," a perfectly plain and technically appropriate word which I have used to render *krivye* because I felt that "curved" or "crooked" did not quite do justice to Onegin's regularly bent manicure scissors.

Similarly, not a passing whim but the considerations of prolonged thought led me to render Four: ix: 5, *privychkoy zhizni izbalovan*, as "spoiled by a habitude of life." I needed the Gallic touch and found it preferable in allusive indefinitude—Pushkin's line is elegantly ambiguous—to "habit of life" or "life's habit." "Habitude" is the right and good word here. It is not labeled "dialect" or "obsolete" in Webster's great dictionary.

Another perfectly acceptable word is "rummer," which I befriended because of its kinship with *ryumka*, and because I wished to find for the *ryumki* of Five: xxix: 4 a more generalized wineglass than the champagne flutes of xxxii: 8–9, which are also *ryumki*. If Mr. Wilson consults my notes, he will see that on second thought I demoted the non-obsolete but rather oversized cups of xxix to jiggers of vodka tossed down before the first course.

I cannot understand why Mr. Wilson is puzzled by "dit" (Five: viii: 13) which I chose instead of "ditty" to parallel "kit" instead of "kitty" in the next line, and which will now,

---

* For reasons having nothing to do with the subject of this essay I subsequently changed the translation, exact in tone but not in syntax, of those two lines (see the epigraph to my *Mary*, McGraw-Hill, New York, 1970).

I hope, enter or re-enter the language. Possibly, the masculine rhyme I needed here may have led me a little astray from the servile path of literalism (Pushkin has simply *pesnya*—"song"). But it is not incomprehensible; after all, anybody who knows what, say, "titty" means ("in nail-making the part that ejects the half-finished nail") can readily understand what "tit" means ("the part that ejects the finished nail").

Next on Mr. Wilson's list of inappropriate words is "gloam." It is a poetic word, and Keats has used it. It renders perfectly the *mgla* of the gathering evening shadows in Four: XLVII: 8, as well as the soft darkness of trees in Three: XVI: 11. It is better than "murk," a dialect word that Mr. Wilson uses for *mgla*, with my sanction, in another passage—the description of a wintry dawn.

In the same passage which both I and Mr. Wilson have translated, my "shippon" is as familiar to anyone who knows the English countryside as Mr. Wilson's "byre" should be to a New England farmer. Both "shippon" and "byre" are unknown to pocket-dictionary readers; both are listed in the three-centimeter-thick Penguin (1965). But I prefer "shippon" for *hlev* because I see its shape as clearly as that of the Russian cow-house it resembles, but see only a Vermont barn when I try to visualize "byre".

Then there is "scrab": "he scrabs the poor thing up," *bednyazhku tsaptsarap* (One: XIV: 8). This *tsaptsarap*—a "verbal interjection" presupposing (as Pushkin notes when employing it in another poem) the existence of the artificial verb *tsaptsarapat'*, jocular and onomatopoeic—combines *tsapat'* ("to snatch") with *tsarapat'* ("to scratch"). I rendered Pushkin's uncommon word by the uncommon "scrab up," which combines "grab" and "scratch," and am proud of it. It is in fact a wonderful find.

I shall not analyze the phrase "in his lunes" that Mr. Wilson for good measure has included among my "aberrations." It occurs not in my translation, which he is discussing, but in the flow of my ordinary comfortable descriptive prose which we can discuss another time.

We now come to one of the chief offenders: "mollitude." For Pushkin's Gallic *nega* I needed an English counterpart of *mollesse* as commonly used in such phrases as *il perdit ses jeunes années dans la mollesse et la volupté* or *son coeur nage dans la mollesse*. It is incorrect to say, as Mr. Wilson does, that readers can never have encountered "mollitude." Readers of Browning have. In this connection Mr. Wilson wonders how I would have translated *chistyh neg* in one of Pushkin's last elegies—would I have said "pure mollitudes"? It so happens that I translated that little poem thirty years ago, and when Mr. Wilson locates my version (in the Introduction to one of my novels*) he will note that the genitive plural of *nega* is a jot different in sense from the singular.

In Mr. Wilson's collection of *bêtes noires* my favorite is "sapajou." He wonders why I render *dostoyno staryh obez'yan* as "worthy of old sapajous" and not as "worthy of old monkeys." True, *obez'yana* means any kind of monkey but it so happens that neither "monkey" nor "ape" is good enough in the context.

"Sapajou" (which technically is applied to two genera of neotropical monkeys) has in French a colloquial sense of "ruffian," "lecher," "ridiculous chap." Now, in lines 1–2 and 9–11 of Four: VII ("the less we love a woman, the easier 'tis to be liked by her . . . but that grand game is worthy of old sapajous of our forefathers' vaunted times") Pushkin echoes a moralistic passage in his own letter written in French from Kishinev to his young brother in Moscow in the autumn of 1822, that is seven months before beginning *Eugene Onegin* and two years before reaching Canto Four. The passage, well known to readers of Pushkin, goes: "*Moins on aime une femme et plus on est sur de l'avoir . . . mais cette jouissance est digne d'un vieux sapajou du dix-huitième siècle.*"

* *Despair*. G. P. Putnam's Sons, New York, 302–303, 1966.

Not only could I not resist the temptation of retranslating the *obez'yan* of the canto into the Anglo-French "sapajous" of the letter, but I was also looking forward to somebody's pouncing on that word and allowing me to retaliate with that wonderfully satisfying reference. Mr. Wilson obliged —and here it is.

"There are also actual errors of English," continued Mr. Wilson, and gives three examples: "dwelled" which I prefer to "dwelt"; "about me," which in Two: xxxix: 14 is used to render *obo mne* instead of the better "of me"; and the word "loaden," which Mr. Wilson "had never heard before." But "dwelled" is marked in my dictionary only "less usual"— not "incorrect"; "remind about" is not quite impossible (*e.g.*, "remind me about it tomorrow"); as to "loaden," which Mr. Wilson suggests replacing by "loadened," *his* English wobbles, not mine, since "loaden" *is* the correct past participle and participial adjective of "load."

In the course of his strange defense of Arndt's version— in which, according to Mr. Wilson, I had been assiduously tracking down Germanisms—he asserts that "it is not difficult to find Russianisms in Nabokov" and turns up *one*, or the shadow of one ("left us" should be "has left us" in a passage that I cannot trace). Surely there must be more than one such slip in a work fifteen hundred pages long devoted by a Russian to a Russian poem; however, the two other Russianisms Mr. Wilson lists are the figments of his own ignorance:

In translating *slushat' shum morskoy* (Eight: iv: 11) I chose the archaic and poetic transitive turn "to listen the sound of the sea" because the relevant passage has in Pushkin a stylized archaic tone. Mr. Wilson may not care for this turn—I do not much care for it either—but it is silly of him to assume that I lapsed into a naive Russianism not being really aware that, as he tells me, "in English you have to listen *to* something." First, it is Mr. Wilson who is not aware of the fact that there exists an analogous construction in Russian *prislushivat'sya k zvuku,* "to listen closely to the sound"—which, of course, makes nonsense of the exclusive Russianism imagined by him, and secondly, had he happened to leaf through a certain canto of *Don Juan,* written in the year Pushkin was beginning his poem, or a certain *Ode to Memory,* written when Pushkin's poem was being finished, my learned friend would have concluded that Byron ("Listening debates not very wise or witty") and Tennyson ("Listening the lordly music") must have had quite as much Russian blood as Pushkin and I.

In the mazurka of Canto Five one of the dancers "leads Tatiana with Olga" (*podvyol Tat'yanu s Ol'goy*) towards Onegin. This has little to do with the idiomatic *my s ney* (which is lexically "we with her," but may mean "she and I") that Mr. Wilson mentions. Actually, in order to cram both girls into the first three feet of Five: XLIV: 3, Pushkin allowed himself a minor solecism. The construction *podvyol Tat'yanu i Ol'gu* would have been better Russian (just as "Tatiana and Olga" would have been better English), but it would not have scanned. Now Mr. Wilson should note carefully that this unfortunate *Tat'yanu s Ol'goy* has an additional repercussion: it clashes unpleasantly with the next line where the associative form is compulsory: *Onegin s Ol'goyu poshyol,* "Onegin goes with Olga." Throughout my translation I have remained a thousand times more faithful to Pushkin's Russian than to Wilson's English and therefore in these passages I did not hesitate to reproduce both the solecism and the ensuing clash.

"The handling of French is peculiar," grimly observes Mr. Wilson, and adduces three instances:

"The name of Rousseau's heroine is," he affirms, "given on one page as Julie and on the next as Julia." This is an absurd cavil since she is named Julie all the thirteen times she is mentioned in the course of the four-page note referring to her (the note to Three: IX: 7), as well as numerous times elsewhere (see Index); but maybe Mr.

Wilson has confused her with Augustus' or Byron's girl (see Index again).

The second "peculiar" example refers to the word *monde* in the world-of-fashion sense copiously described in my note to One: v: 8 (*le monde, le beau monde, le grand monde*). According to Mr. Wilson it should always appear with its "*le*" in the translation of the poem. This is an inept practice, of course (advocated mainly by those who, like Mr. Wilson, are insecure and self-conscious in their use of *le* and *la*), and would have resulted in saying "*le* noisy *monde*" instead of "the noisy *monde*" (Eight: xxxiv: 12). English writers of the eighteenth and nineteenth centuries wrote "the *monde*," not "le monde." I am sure that if Mr. Wilson consults the OED, which I do not have here, he will find examples from Walpole, Byron, Thackeray, and others. What was good enough for them is good enough for Pushkin and me.

Finally, in this peculiar group of peculiar French there is the word *sauvage*, which according to Mr. Wilson should not have appeared in my rendering of Two: xxv: 5, *dika*, *pechal'na, molchaliva*, "*sauvage*, sad, silent"; but apart from the fact that it has no exact English equivalent, I chose this signal word to warn readers that Pushkin was using *dika* not simply in the sense of "wild" or "unsociable" but in a Gallic sense as a translation of "*sauvage*". Incidentally, it often occurs in English novels of the time along with *monde* and *ennui*.

"As for the classics," says Mr. Wilson, "Zoilus should be Zoïlus and Eol, Aeolus." But the diacritical sign is quite superfluous in the first case (see, for instance, Webster) and "Eol" is a poetical abbreviation constantly cropping up in English poetry. Moreover, Mr. Wilson can find the full form in my Index. I am unable to prevent my own Zoilus from imitating a bright and saucy schoolboy, but really he should not tell me how to spell the plural of "automaton" which has two endings, both correct. And what business does he have to rebuke me for preferring Theocritus to Virgil and to insinuate that I have read neither?

There is also the strange case of "stuss." "What does N. mean," queries Mr. Wilson, "when he speaks of Pushkin's addiction to stuss? This is not an English word and if he means the Hebrew word for nonsense which has been absorbed into German, it ought to be italicized and capitalized. But even on this assumption it hardly makes sense." This is Mr. Wilson's nonsense, not mine. "Stuss" is the English name of a card game which I discuss at length in my notes on Pushkin's addiction to gambling. Mr. Wilson should really consult *some* of my notes (and Webster's dictionary).

Then there is Mr. Nabokov's style. My style may be all Mr. Wilson says, clumsy, banal, etc. But in regard to the examples he gives it is not *unnecessarily* clumsy, banal, etc. If in translating *toska lyubvi Tat'yanu gonit* (Three: XVI: 1), "the ache of love chases Tatiana" (not "the ache of loss," as Mr. Wilson nonsensically misquotes), I put "chases" instead of the "pursues" that Mr. Wilson has the temerity to propose, I do so not only because "pursues" is in Russian not *gonit* but *presleduet*, but also because, as Mr. Wilson has not noticed, it would be a misleading repetition of the "pursue" used in the preceding stanza (*tebya presleduyut mechty*, "day-dreams pursue you"), and my method is to repeat a term at close range only when Pushkin repeats it.

When the nurse says to Tatiana *nu delo, delo, ne gnevaysya, dusha moya*, and I render it by "this now makes sense, do not be cross with me, my soul," Mr. Wilson in a tone of voice remindful of some seventeenth-century French pedant discoursing on high and low style, declares that "make sense" and "my soul" do not go together, as if he knows which terms in the nurse's Russian go together or do not!

As I have already said, many of the recurring words I use (ache, pal, mollitude, and so on) are what I call "signal words," *i.e.*, terms meant, among other things, to indicate the recurrence of the corresponding Russian word. Style, indeed! It is correct information I wish to give and not samples of "correct style." I translate *ochen' milo postupil* . . .

nash priyatel', in the beginning of Four: XVIII (which is also the beginning of the least artistic section in Four: XVIII–XXII), by "very nicely did our pal act," and this Mr. Wilson finds "vulgarly phrased"; but Mr. Wilson stomps in where I barely dare to tread because he is quite unaware that the corresponding Russian phrase is also trite and trivial. There simply exists no other way of rendering that genteel *ochen' milo* (Pushkin is imitating here a simpering reader), and if I chose here and elsewhere the signal word "pal" to render the colloquial turn of *priyatel'*, it is because there exists no other way of expressing it. "Pal" retains the unpleasant flippancy of *priyatel'* as used here, besides reproducing its first and last letters. *Priyatel' Vil'son* would be, for instance, a flippant and nasty phrase, out of place in a serious polemical text. Or does Mr. Wilson really think that the passage in question is better rendered by Professor Arndt? ("My reader, can you help bestowing praise on Eugene for the fine part he played with stricken Tanya?")

Mr. Wilson's last example in the series pertaining to "bad style" has to do with the end of Seven: XXXII. When rendering the elegiac terms in which Tatiana takes leave of her country home, I had to take into account their resemblance to the diction of Pushkin's youthful elegy addressed to a beloved country place ("Farewell, ye faithful coppices," etc.), and also to that of Lenski's last poem. It was a question of adjustment and alignment. This is why I have Tatiana say in a stilted and old-fashioned idiom, "Farewell, pacific sites, farewell, secluded [note the old-fashioned pronunciation of the correspondent *uedinennyy*] refuge! Shall I see you?" "Such passages," says Mr. Wilson, "sound like the products of those computers which are supposed to translate Russian into English." But since those computers are fed only the basic Russian Mr. Wilson has mastered, and are directed by anthropologists and progressive linguists, the results would be *his* comic versions, and not my clumsy but literal translation.

[260]

Probably the most rollicking part of Mr. Wilson's animadversions is the one in which he offers his own mistranslation as the perfection I should have tried to emulate.

My rendering of *gusey kriklivyh karavan tyanulsya k yugu* (Four: XLI: 11 and beginning of 12) is "the caravan of clamorous geese was tending southward" but, as I note in my commentary, *kriklivyh* is lexically "screamy"* and the idiomatic *tyanulsya* conveys a very special blend of meaning, with the sense of "progressing in a given direction" predominating over the simple "stretching" obtainable from pocket dictionaries (see also note to Seven: IV: 14). Mr. Wilson thinks that in his own version of the coming of winter in Four, part of which I quote in my Commentary with charitably italicized errors, he is "almost literally accurate and a good deal more poetically vivid than Nabokov." The "almost" is very lenient since "loud-tongued geese" is much too lyrical, and "stretching" fails to bring out the main element of the contextual *tyanulsya*.

A still funnier sight is Mr. Wilson trying to show me how to translate properly *ego loshadka, sneg pochuya, pletyotsya rys'yu kak nibud'* (Five: II: 3–4), which in my literal rendering is "his naggy, having sensed the snow, shambles at something like a trot." Mr. Wilson's own effort, which goes "his poor (?) horse sniffing (?) the snow, attempting (?) a trot, plods (?) through it (?)," besides being a medley of gross mistranslations, is an example of careless English. If, however, we resist the unfair temptation of imagining Mr. Wilson's horse plodding through my trot and, instead, have it plod through Mr. Wilson's snow, we obtain the inept picture of an unfortunate beast of burden laboriously working its way through that snow, whereas in reality Pushkin celebrates relief, not exertions. The peasant is not "rejoicing" or "feeling festive," as paraphrasts have it (not

* In revising my translation for a new edition I have changed "clamorous" to the absolutely exact "cronking."

[261]

knowing Pushkin's use of *torzhestvovat'* here and elsewhere), but "celebrating" (the coming of winter), since the snow under the sleigh facilitates the little nag's progress and is especially welcome after a long snowless autumn of muddy ruts and reluctant cart wheels.

Although Mr. Wilson finds my Commentary overdone, he cannot help suggesting three additions. In a ludicrous display of pseudo-scholarship he insinuates that I "seem to think" (I do not, and never did) that the application by the French of the word "goddams" to the English (which I do not even discuss) begins in the eighteenth century. He would like me to say that it goes back to the fifteenth century. Why should I? Because he looked it up?

He also would have liked me to mention in connection with the "pensive vampire" (Three: xii: 8) of Polidori's novelette (1819) another variety of vampire which Pushkin alluded to in a poem of 1834 suggested by Mérimée's well-known pastiche. But *that* vampire is the much coarser *vurdalak*, a lowly graveyard ghoul having nothing to do with the romantic allusion in Canto Three (1824); besides he appeared ten years later (and three years after Pushkin had finished *Eugene Onegin*)—quite outside the period limiting my interest in vampires.

The most sophisticated suggestion, however, volunteered by Mr. Wilson, concerns the evolution of the adjective *krasnyy* which "means both red and beautiful." May this not be influenced "by the custom in Old Russia, described in Hakluyt's *Voyages*, of the peasant women's painting large red spots on their cheeks in order to beautify themselves?" This is a preposterous gloss, somehow reminding one of Freud's explaining a patient's passion for young women by the fact that the poor fellow in his self-abusing boyhood used to admire Mt. Jungfrau from the window of a water closet.

I shall not say much about the paragraph that Mr. Wilson devotes to my notes on prosody. It is simply not worthwhile. He has skimmed my "tedious and interminable appendix" and has not understood what he managed to glean. From our conversations and correspondence in former years I well know that, like Onegin, he is incapable of comprehending the mechanism of verse—either Russian or English. This being so, he should have refrained from "criticizing" my essay on the subject. With one poke of his stubby pencil he reintroduces the wretched old muddle I take such pains to clear up and fussily puts back the "secondary accents" and "spondees" where I show they do not belong. He makes no attempt to assimilate my terminology, he obstinately ignores the similarities and distinctions I discuss, and indeed I cannot believe he has read more than a few lines of the thing.

My "most serious failure," according to Mr. Wilson, "is one of interpretation." Had he read my commentary with more attention he would have seen that I do not believe in *any* kind of "interpretation" so that his or my "interpretation" can be neither a failure nor a success. In other words, I do not believe in the old-fashioned, naïve, and musty method of human-interest criticism championed by Mr. Wilson that consists of removing the characters from an author's imaginary world to the imaginary, but generally far less plausible, world of the critic who then proceeds to examine these displaced characters as if they were "real people." In my commentary I have given examples and made some innocent fun of such criticism (steering clear, however, of any allusion to Mr. Wilson's extraordinary misconceptions in *The Triple Thinkers*).

I have also demonstrated the factual effect of Pushkin's characterizations as related to the structure of the poem. There are certain inconsistencies in his treatment of his hero which are especially evident, and in a way especially attractive, in the beginning of Canto Six. In a note to Six: xxviii: 7, I stress the uncanny, dreamlike quality of Onegin's behavior just before and during the duel. It is purely a question of architectonics—not of personal interpretation. My facts are objective and irrefutable. I remain with Pushkin in Pushkin's world. I am not concerned with Onegin's being gentle or cruel, energetic or indolent, kind or unkind ("you are simply very kindhearted," says a woman to him quoted in his diary; he is "*zloy*, unkind," says Mr. Wilson); I am concerned only with Pushkin's overlooking, in the interest of the plot, that Onegin, who according to Pushkin is a punctilious *homme du monde* and an experienced duelist, would hardly choose a servant for second or shoot to kill in the kind of humdrum affair where vanity is amply satisfied by sustaining one's adversary's fire without returning it.

The actual cause of the encounter is however quite plausible in Pushkin: upon finding himself at a huge vulgar feast (Five: XXXI) so unlike the informal party promised him by Lenski (Four: XLIX), Onegin is quite right to be furious with his deceitful or scatterbrained young friend, just as Lenski is quite justified in calling him out for flirting with Olga. Onegin accepts the challenge instead of laughing it off as he would have done if Lenski had chosen a less pedantic second. Pushkin stresses the fact that Onegin "sincerely loves the youth" but that *amour propre* is sometimes stronger than friendship. That is all. One should stick to that and not try to think up "deep" variations which are not even new; for what Mr. Wilson inflicts upon me, in teaching me how to understand Onegin, is the old solemn nonsense of Onegin's hating and envying Lenski for being capable of idealism, devoted love, ecstatic German romanticism and the like "when he himself is so sterile and empty." Actually, it is just as easy, and just as irrelevant (yet more fashionable—Mr. Wilson is behind the times), to argue that Onegin, not Lenski, is the true idealist, that he loathes Lenski because he perceives in him the future fat swinish squire Lenski is doomed to become, and so he raises slowly his pistol and . . . but Lenski in malignant cold blood is also raising his pistol, and God knows who would have killed whom had not the author followed wisely the old rule of sparing one's more interesting character while the novel is still developing. If anybody takes "a mean advantage," as Mr. Wilson absurdly puts it (none of the principals can derive any special "advantage" in a *duel à volonté*), it is not Onegin, but Pushkin.

So much for my "most serious failure."

All that now remains to be examined is Mr. Wilson's concern for reputations—Pushkin's reputation as a linguist and the reputations of Sainte-Beuve and others as writers.

With an intensity of feeling that he shares with Russian monolinguists who have debated the subject, Mr. Wilson scolds me for underrating Pushkin's knowledge of English and "quite disregarding the evidence." I supply the evidence, not Mr. Wilson, not Sidorov, and not even Pushkin's own father (a cocky old party who maintained that his son used to speak fluent Spanish, let alone English). Had Mr. Wilson carefully consulted my notes to One: XXXVIII: 9, he would have convinced himself that I prove with absolute certainty that neither in 1821, nor 1833, nor 1836, was Pushkin able to understand simple English phrases. My demonstration remains unassailable, and it is this evidence that Mr. Wilson disregards while referring me to stale generalities or to an idiotic anecdote about the Racvski girls' giving Pushkin lessons in English in a Crimean bower. Mr. Wilson knows nothing about the question. He is not even aware that Pushkin got the style of his "Byronic" tales from Pichot and Zhukovski, or that Pushkin's copying out extracts from foreign writers means nothing. Mr. Wilson, too, may have copied extracts, and we see the results. He complains I do not want to admit that Pushkin's competence in languages was considerable, but I can only reply that Mr. Wilson's notion of such competence and my notion of it are completely dissimilar. I realize, of course, that my friend has a vested interest in the matter, but I can assure him that although Pushkin spoke excellent eighteenth-century French, he had only a gentleman's smattering of other foreign languages.

Finally—Mr. Wilson is horrified by my "instinct to take digs at great reputations." Well, it cannot be helped; Mr. Wilson must accept my instinct, and wait for the next crash. I refuse to be guided and controlled by a communion of established views and academic traditions, as he wants me to be. What right has he to prevent me from finding mediocre and overrated people like Balzac, Dostoevski, Sainte-Beuve, or Stendhal, that pet of all those who like their French plain? How much has Mr. Wilson enjoyed Mme. de Staël's novels? Has he ever studied Balzac's absurdities and Stendhal's clichés? Has he examined the melodramatic muddle and phony mysticism of Dostoevski? Can he really venerate that arch-vulgarian, Sainte-Beuve? And why should I be forbidden to consider that Chaykovski's hideous and insulting libretto is not saved by a music whose cloying banalities have pursued me ever since I was a curly-haired boy in a velvet box? If I am allowed to display my very special and very subjective admiration for Pushkin, Browning, Krylov, Chateaubriand, Griboedov, Senancour, Küchelbecker, Keats, Hodasevich, to name only a few of those I praise in my notes, I should be also allowed to bolster and circumscribe that praise by pointing out to the reader my favorite bogeys and shams in the hall of false fame.

In his rejoinder to my letter of August 26, 1965, in *The New York Review*, Mr. Wilson says that on rereading his article he felt it sounded "more damaging" than he had meant it to be. His article, entirely consisting, as I have shown, of quibbles and blunders, can be damaging only to his own reputation—and that is the last look I shall ever take at the dismal scene.

Completed on January 20, 1966, and published in February of that year in *Encounter*. One or two forced peeps did come after that "last look." The essay was reprinted in *Nabokov's Congeries*, Viking, New York, 1968.

5

LOLITA AND MR. GIRODIAS

From time to time, in the course of the 1960s, there have appeared, over the signature of Mr. Girodias or that of some friend of his, retrospective notes pertaining to the publication of *Lolita* by The Olympia Press and to various phases of our "strained relations." Those frivolous reminiscences invariably contained factual errors, which I generally took the trouble to point out in brief rejoinders; whereupon, as I detected with satisfaction, certain undulatory motions of retreat were performed by our flexible memoirist. An especially ambitious article, with especially serious misstatements, has now been published by him twice—in Barney Rosset's *Evergreen Review* (No. 37, September 1965) under the title "Lolita, Nabokov, and I," and in his own anthology (*The Olympia Reader*, Grove Press, New York, 1965) under the less elegant title of "A Sad, Ungraceful History of Lolita." Since I have religiously preserved all my correspondence with Mr. Girodias, I am able, I trust, to induce a final retraction on his part.

Two clauses from a document in my possession entitled "Memorandum of Agreement" ("made this sixth day of June nineteen hundred and fifty five between Mr. Vladimir Nabokov, Cornell University, Ithaca, N. Y., and Olympia Press, 8, rue de Nesle, Paris") might do very well as a motto for the present occasion. Here they are in strophic form for the reader's convenience:

8

In the event of the Publishers
Going bankrupt
Or failing to make accountings and payments
As herein specified,
Then in either event the present agreement
Becomes automatically null and void
And the rights herein granted
Revert to the Author.

9

The Publishers shall render statement
Of the number of copies sold
On the 30th June and 31st December
Of each year
Within one month from these dates
Respectively
And shall make payment to the Author
At the time of such rendering of account.

The eighth stave, with its opening lines foretelling so plainly what was to happen to Mr. Girodias on December 14, 1964, and that beautiful, eloquent, almost sapphically modulated last verse ("Revert to the Author"), is of great importance for the understanding of what Mr. Girodias calls "our enigmatic conflict." It will be also noted that while devoting a lot of space to the many "disappointments" that my attitude toward him caused him, he never mentions in the course of his article the perfectly obvious reason for a writer's resenting his association with a publisher—namely, the fact of Mr. Girodias' failing repeatedly, with a kind of maniacal persistence, to live up to clause 9 of our agreement. By stressing effects and concealing causes he gives a comic slant to his account of our relations, making it seem that during ten years I kept extravagantly fuming at a puzzled benefactor.

Lolita was finished at the beginning of 1954, in Ithaca, New York. My first attempts to have it published in the U. S. proved disheartening and irritating. On August 6 of that year, from Taos, New Mexico, I wrote to Madame Ergaz, of the Bureau Littéraire Clairouin, Paris, about my troubles. She had arranged the publication in French of some of my Russian and English books; I now asked her to find somebody in Europe who would publish *Lolita* in the original English. She replied that she thought she could arrange it. A month later, however, upon my return to Ithaca (where I taught Russian Literature at Cornell) I wrote to her saying I had changed my mind. New hopes had arisen for publication in America. They petered out, and next spring I got in touch with Madame Ergaz again, writing her (Feb. 16) that Sylvia Beach "might perhaps be interested if she still publishes." This was not followed up. By April 17 Madame Ergaz had received my typescript. On April 26, 1955, a fatidic date, she said she had found a possible publisher. On May 13 she named that person. It was thus that Maurice Girodias entered my files.

Mr. Girodias in his article overemphasizes the obscurity I languished in before 1955 as well as his part in helping me to emerge from it. On the other hand, I shall be strictly truthful when I say that before Madame Ergaz mentioned his name, I was totally ignorant of his existence, or that of his enterprise. He was recommended to me as the founder of The Olympia Press, which "had recently published, among other things, *Histoire d'O*" (a novel I had heard praised by competent judges) and as the former director of the "Editions du Chêne" which had "produced books admirable from the artistic point of view." He wanted *Lolita* not only because it was well written but because (as Mme. Ergaz informed me on May 13, 1955) "he thought that it might lead to a change in social attitudes toward the kind of love described in it." It was a pious although obviously ridiculous thought, but high-minded platitudes are often mouthed by enthusiastic businessmen and nobody bothers to disenchant them.

I had not been in Europe since 1940, was not interested in pornographic books, and thus knew nothing about the obscene novelettes which Mr. Girodias was hiring hacks to confect with his assistance, as he relates elsewhere. I have pondered the painful question whether I would have agreed so cheerfully to his publishing *Lolita* had I been aware in May, 1955, of what formed the supple backbone of his production. Alas, I probably would, though less cheer-fully.

I shall now proceed to point out a number of slippery passages and a few guileful inexactitudes in Mr. Girodias' article. For some reason which presumably I am too naive to grasp, he starts by citing an old *curriculum vitae* of mine which, he says, was sent to him by my agent together with the typescript of *Lolita* in April, 1955. Such a procedure would have been absurd. My files show that only much later, namely on February 8, 1957, *he asked me* to send him "all the biographical and bibliographical material" available for his brochure "L'affaire *Lolita*" (which he published when fighting the ban of the book in France); on February 12, I sent him photographs, a list of published works, and a brief *curriculum vitae*. With the sneer of a hoodlum follow-ing an innocent passerby, Mr. Girodias now makes fun of such facts in it as my father's having been "an eminent statesman" or the "considerable fame" I had acquired in émigré circles. All this he had published himself (with many embellishments and additions gleaned elsewhere) in his brochure of 1957!

On the other hand, he now tones down substantially his proud recollections of having "edited" *Lolita*. On April 22, 1960, I had been obliged to write to the editor of *The New York Times Book Review* (where Mr. Girodias had been comically flattered by a person unknown to me) thus: "Mr. Popkin in his recent article on Monsieur Girodias, the first publisher of my *Lolita*, says that I 'did some rewriting at Girodias' request.' I wish to correct this absurd misstatement. The only alterations Girodias very diffidently suggested concerned a few trivial French phrases in the English text, such as '*bon*,' '*c'est moi*,' '*mais comment*,' etc., which he thought might just as well be translated into English, and this I agreed to do."

I began to curse my association with Olympia Press not in 1957, when our agreement was, according to Mr. Girodias, "weighing heavily" on my "dreams of impending fortune" in America, but as early as 1955; that is, the very first year of my dealings with Mr. Girodias. From the very start I was confronted with the peculiar aura surrounding his business transactions with me, an aura of negligence, evasiveness, procrastination, and falsity. I complained of these peculiarities in most of my letters to my agent who faithfully transmitted my complaints to him but these he never explains in his account of our ten-year-long (1955–65) association.

"I hardly received the proofs back" [he received them in July, 1955], writes Mr. Girodias, "when Nabokov sent me a cable [August 29, *i.e.*, after a month of Girodian silence] saying: "When is *Lolita* appearing. Worried. Please answer my letters'—an entreaty which has been repeated so often in so many cables sent by so many authors to so many [*i.e.*, wise, calm, benevolent] publishers . . . " The would-be wit and delightful flippancy of this remark should not fool anybody. Mr. Girodias alludes here to coy emotions typical of a young author hardly ever published before. Actually, at fifty-six years of age, I had had, since 1925, dealings—

recurrent dealings—with at least a score of publishers and had never been exposed to anything like the tissue of haggling maneuvers and abstruse prevarications in which Mr. Girodias involves his victims (perhaps not deliberately—it just seems to be part of his bizarre nature). In reality, two specific questions were worrying me, and to them I was getting no answer. The main one of the two was the question of the copyright: the book had to be registered in Washington, in the author's name, and for this purpose I had to know the exact date of publication so as to insert it in the application forms. On October 8, 1955, I received, at last, a copy of the published book, but only on November 28, after some more "entreaties," did I learn that *Lolita* had been published on September 15, 1955. The second matter was a financial one—and proved to be the *leit-motif* of what Mr. Girodias terms the "sad, ungraceful history of *Lolita*." My benefactor had agreed to pay me an advance of 400,000 "*anciens*" francs (about a thousand dollars), one half on signature of the agreement (dated June 6, 1955), and the other half on publication. He had paid his first half only one month late. My wire did not help to elucidate the date when Mr. Girodias would have to pay the second half. It was easier for him to leave the matter open. I continued reminding him about that second check. I told him (October 5) that "I write for my pleasure, but publish for money." He paid only on December 27, under strong pressure from my agent, and more than three months after the second payment was due.

My copyright worries were not over. "With blithe unconcern" (to use a phrase Mr. Girodias favors) he had added to "Copyright 1955 by V. Nabokov" on the title page of his edition the words "and the Olympia Press." On January 28, 1956, I learned from the copyright Office in Washington that this matey formula (for which I had not given my permission) might cause trouble at re-publication in the U.S. which had to take place within five years. I was advised to get an "assignment or quitclaim" from Mr. Girodias, and this I at once asked him to send me. I got no reply (as "so many authors" do not get replies from "so many publishers"), wrote to him again and again, but only on April 20 (*i.e.*, three months later) got from him what I asked. It is interesting to conjecture where Mr. Girodias would have been, when "our" book came out in America, had I not had the foresight to protect it there.

By the beginning of 1957, I had still not received from Olympia any statements of accounts since the publication of the book in September 1955. The lapse entitled me to annul the agreement (see Clause 9), but I decided to wait a little longer. I had to wait till March 28, 1957, and when it came, the statement did not cover the entire period for which it was due.

The nuisance of non-statements did not fail to resume. By the end of August, 1957, I had received none for the first semester of that year which was due on July 31. On September 2, Mr. Girodias asked for a postponement of two months, and I agreed to wait till September 30, but nothing happened, and having had enough of that nonsense I advised him (October 5) that all rights had reverted to me. He promptly paid up (44,220 *anciens* francs), and I relented.

In a particularly nasty and silly passage our memoirist juxtaposes my refusal to defend my book in France from the attack of local magistrates and "Philistine readers" (as I wrote to him on March 10, 1957) with my requesting him (a month earlier) to avoid mentioning "Cornell" when referring to me in publicity splashes as a "university professor." I am not sure what he means specifically. Only a very helical mind could twist my request into a semblance of frailty. By signing *Lolita* I had shown my complete acceptance of whatever responsibility an author has to take; but as long as an unhealthy flurry of scandal surrounded my innocent *Lolita*, I certainly was justified in acting as I did, lest a shadow of my responsibility fall on the university that had given me unbelievable freedom in conducting my courses (they were never meddled with by the department or departments under which they were nominally listed); nor did I care to embarrass the close friend who had brought me there to enjoy that true academic freedom.

Nevertheless Mr. Girodias kept urging me to join him in his campaign against French censorship. "Our interests are identical," he wrote; but they were not. He wanted me to defend *Lolita*, but I did not see how my book could be treated separately from his list of twenty or so lewd books. I did not want to defend even *Lolita*. He repeats in his article one of his favorite arguments that without him *Lolita* would have never been published. As I wrote him on August 3, 1957, I was (and am) deeply grateful to him for printing that book. But I must also point out to him that he was not the right person to undertake the thing; he lacked the means to launch *Lolita* properly—a book that differed so utterly in vocabulary, structure, and purpose (or rather absence of purpose) from his other much simpler commercial ventures, such as *Debby's Bidet* or *Tender Thighs*. Mr. Girodias greatly exaggerates his powers. Had not Graham Greene and John Gordon clashed in London in such providential fashion, *Lolita*—especially its second volume which repelled so-called "amateurs"—might have ended in the common grave of Traveler's Favorites or whatever Olympia's little green books were called.

In 1957, the *Lolita* affair entered its American phase, which to me was in every way more important than its Olympia one. Jason Epstein, by championing the publication of a considerable portion of *Lolita* in the summer issue, 1957, of *Anchor Review*, edited by Melvin S. Lasky (Doubleday, New York), and Professor F. W. Dupee by prefacing that portion with a brilliant article, helped to make the idea of an American edition acceptable. Several publishers were interested in it, but the difficulties Mr.

Girodias created in our negotiations with American firms were another source of acute vexation on my part. On September 14, 1957, the head of a distinguished American publishing house flew over to Paris to discuss matters with Mr. Girodias. The latter's account of the interview runs like this in his article: "One publisher spontaneously offered a 20 percent royalty to get the book, but was then apparently frightened away by Nabokov's attitude when he met him later in New York." One part of this passage is inaccurate and the other simply untrue: it was not I who dissuaded this particular publisher, but his partner. The account is inaccurate because Mr. Girodias does not say who was to get most of that 20 percent. "I am prepared to accept this proposal," wrote Mr. Girodias to me (apparently under the impression that he had got a definite offer which was not the case), "if my share is assured at 12$^{1}/_2$ percent. The advance would be shared in the same proportion. Would you accept 7$^{1}/_2$ percent as your share? I consider my claim justified and fair." My agent wrote that she was *"outrée de ces prétentions."* (His contract obliged him to pay me a 10 percent royalty up to ten thousand copies, and 12 percent after that.)

The interim copyright stipulated that no more than 1500 copies should be imported into the U.S. Mr. Girodias rather resented my keeping an eagle eye on his lighthearted transatlantics. I knew for instance that copies of his edition were being sold for $12 and more in New York. He assured me that the difference was pocketed by the retailers. On November 30, 1957, Mr. Girodias wrote in a mellow mood "I admit that I have been wrong on several occasions in the course of our dealings. . . . " He added that he no longer "requested a larger share of the proceeds" of the American edition and that he was canceling his "alternative project" of bringing out his own "American reprint"—a silly threat, the carrying out of which would have been his undoing. But already by December 16, 1957, he was larking again: On that day I learnt with wonder from my agent that Mr. Girodias declared he had sold only *eight* copies in America in three months (April to June) but that since I thought he had done so at a higher price than shown in his statements ($7.50) he was sending me the difference, a check for 50 cents. And he added that he considered all our differences now settled!

It would be tedious to continue giving instances of the delayed or incomplete statements of accounts that marked Mr. Girodias' course of action during the following years or of such misdemeanors as publishing in Paris a reprint of his edition of *Lolita* with his own introduction (in intolerably bad English) without my permission—which he knew I would never have given. What always made me regret our association were not "dreams of impending fortune," not my "hating" him "for having stolen a portion of Nabokov's property," but the obligation to endure the elusiveness, the evasiveness, the procrastination, the dodges, the duplicity, and the utter irresponsibility of the man. This is why, on May 28, 1959, before sailing for Europe after exactly 19 years of absence, I wrote to Mme. Ergaz that I did not wish to make the acquaintance of Mr. Girodias when I came to Paris for the launching of the French translation of *Lolita*. As revealed now by his *Evergreen* article, the depths of his personality are even less attractive than they seemed when showing through our correspondence. I suspect that much of the rudeness in his article is the result of his relying too heavily on a journalistic style, redolent, perhaps, of Gallic levity but sadly wanting in English precision. Anyway, I shall not discuss here the insolent and vulgar remarks he makes in regard to my wife (idiotically insinuating, for instance, that certain editorial comments in *Life International*, July 6, 1959, were written by her though signed "ED").

Let me repeat: I have never met Mr. Girodias. He has been described as "fascinating," and "debonair," and "exuding French charm"; that is about all I have to go upon when trying to picture him to myself as a physical being (his moral aspect I know well enough). However, half-a-dozen years after the beginning of our gappy correspondence, he suddenly proclaimed in a *Playboy* article ("Pornologist on Olympus," April, 1961) that we had been actually introduced to each other at a cocktail party given by Gallimard on October 23, 1959, in Paris, despite my warning my agent I did not want to meet him. The details he gave were so absurd that I saw myself obliged to call his bluff, and did so in the July issue of *Playboy*, 1961. Instead of the stunned silence that I expected would last for ever, Mr. Girodias after brooding on my little note and his imaginary past during the next four years, comes up now with a new version of the event in his *Evergreen* piece. The discrepancies between the two variants are typical of what scholars call "waning" apocrypha. In *Playboy* we have a classical description of "the members of Gallimard family" looking "horrified" while Mr. Girodias "slowly progressed toward the author through a sea of bodies" (a splendid image, that sea). In *Evergreen*, there are no Gallimards, but we find, instead, Monique Grall "doubled over in helpless mirth, in a corner" and another lady, Doussia Ergaz, "hiding in a corner" (*i.e.*, another corner) and, most unconvincingly, "choking on a macaroon." In the *Playboy* codex, Mme. Ergaz is described as Mr. Nabokov's "literary agent and patient supporter." In the *Evergreen* scroll, she has become Mr. Girodias' "dear, suffering, terrified friend." In *Playboy*, he and I exchange a few "not unfriendly" sentences. In *Evergreen*, the great meeting is wordless: I limit myself to a "vacuous grin" and immediately turn away to talk "ardently" to a "Czech reporter" (an unexpected and rather sinister personage of whom one would like to hear more from our chronicler). Finally, and rather disappointingly, the passage in *Playboy* about the quaint way I "plunged backwards and sideways with the easy grace of a dolphin" is now replaced by the "graceful ease of a circus seal"; whereupon Mr. Girodias "went to the bar and had a drink" (plain *Playboy*) or "went to down a few glasses of champagne" (lush *Evergreen*).

As I pointed out in my rejoinder, even *if* Mr. Girodias was introduced to me (which I doubt), I did not catch his name; but what especially invalidates the general veracity of his account is the little phrase he slips in about my having "very obviously recognized" him as he was slowly swimming toward me amid the "bodies." Very obviously, I could not have recognized somebody I had never seen in my life; nor can I insult his sanity by suggesting he assumed I had somehow obtained his picture (in the days of the famous *curriculum vitae*) and had been cherishing it all those years.

I am looking forward to Mr. Girodias' third version of our mythical meeting. Perhaps he will discover at last that he had crashed the wrong party and talked to a Slovak poet who was being fêted next door.

Written on February 15, 1966, and published in *Evergreen Review*, XLV, February, 1967. I have not heard from Mr. Girodias since 1965.

6

ON ADAPTATION

Here is a literal translation of a great poem by Mandelshtam (note the correct form of his name), which appears in the original Russian on pp. 142 and 144 of Olga Carlisle's anthology *Poets on Street Corners* (Random House, New York, 1968). It consists of sixteen tetrametric (odd) and trimetric (even) anapaestic lines with a masculine rhyme scheme *bcbc*.

1 For the sake of the resonant valor of ages to come,
    for the sake of a high race of men,
    I forfeited a bowl at my fathers' feast,
4 and merriment, and my honor.

    On my shoulders there pounces the wolfhound age,
    but no wolf by blood am I;
    better, like a fur cap, thrust me into the sleeve
8 of the warmly fur-coated Siberian steppes,

    ——so that I may not see the coward, the bit of soft
      muck,
    the bloody bones on the wheel,
    so that all night the blue-fox furs may blaze
12 for me in their pristine beauty.

Lead me into the night where the Enisey flows,
and the pine reaches up to the star,
because no wolf by blood am I,
16 and injustice has twisted my mouth.

A number of details in the text are ambiguous (for example, the word translated as "coward" is a homonym of the old Russian *trus*, meaning "quaking" (thus "earthquake"), and the word translated as "injustice" has the additional meaning of "falsehood"), but I will limit myself to discussing some of the quite unambiguous passages misinterpreted, or otherwise mangled, by Robert Lowell in his "adaptation" on pp. 143 and 145 of the same collection.

Line 1, "resonant valor," *gremuchaya doblest'* (nom.): Mandelshtam improves here on the stock phrase "ringing glory" (*gremyashchaya slava*). Mr. Lowell renders this as "foreboding nobility," which is meaningless, both as translation and adaptation, and can be only explained by assuming that he worked out an ominous meaning from the "rumbling" improperly given under *gremuchiy* (see also *gremuchaya zmeya*, rattlesnake) by some unhelpful informer, *e.g.* Louis Segal, M.A., Ph.D. (Econ.), D. Phil., compiler of a Russian-English dictionary.

Line 5, "wolfhound," *volkodav*: lexically "wolf-crusher," "wolf-strangler"; this dog gets transformed by Mr. Lowell into a "cutthroat wolf," another miracle of misinformation, mistransfiguration, and misadaptation.

Line 6, "wear the hide of a wolf" (Lowell) would mean to impersonate a wolf, which is not at all the sense here.

Line 8, actually "of the Siberian prairie's hot furcoat," *zharkoy shuby sibirskih stepey*. The rich heavy pelisse, to which Russia's wild East is likened by the poet (this being the very blazon of its faunal opulence) is demoted by the adapter to a "sheepskin" which is "shipped to the steppes" with the poet in its sleeve. Besides being absurd in itself, this singular importation totally destroys the imagery of the composition. And a poet's imagery is a sacred, unassailable thing.

Lines 11–12: the magnificent metaphor of line 8 now culminates in a vision of the arctic starlight overhead, emblemized by the splendor of gray-blue furs, with a suggestion of astronomical heraldry (cf. Vulpecula, a constellation). Instead of that the adaptor has "I want to run with the shiny blue foxes moving like dancers in the night," which is not so much a pretty piece of pseudo-Russian fairytale as a foxtrot in Disneyland.

Line 13: Why does the adaptation read "there the Siberian river is glass"? Perhaps, because the *techyot* (flows) of the text gives *tekla* in the past tense feminine, and its form *stekla* (flowed down) also happens to be the genitive case of *steklo* (glass)—a really outstanding howler, if my supposition is correct, and an inexplicable cliché, if it isn't.

Line 14, "pine," *sosna*: the adapter has "fir tree," another plant altogether. This is a mistake often committed on both sides of the Bering Strait (and condoned, I note, by Dr. Segal).

Line 16: "or slaver in the wolf trap's steel jaw" (Lowell) —an ending that snaps as it were the very backbone of Mandelshtam's poem.

I am well aware that my laborious literal reproduction of one of the masterpieces of Russian poetry is prevented by the rigor of fierce fidelity from parading as a good English poem; but I am also aware that it is true translation, albeit stiff and rhymeless, and that the adapter's good poem is nothing but a farrago of error and improvisation defacing the even better poem it faces in the anthology. When I think that the American college student of today, so docile, so trustful, so eager to be led to any bright hell by an eccentric teacher, will mistake that adaptation for a sample of Mandelshtam's thought ("the poet compares the sheep-skin sent him from abroad to the wolf hide he refuses to wear"), I cannot help feeling that despite the good intentions of adapters something very like cruelty and deception is the inevitable result of their misguided labors.

Although some of the English versions in Miss Carlisle's collection do their best to follow the text, all of them for some reason or other (perhaps in heroic protection of the main offender) are branded "Adaptations." What, then, is there especially adaptive or adaptational in an obvious travesty? This I wish to be told, this I wish to comprehend. "Adapted" to what? To the needs of an idiot audience? To the demands of good taste? To the level of one's own genius? But one's audience is the most varied and gifted in the world; no arbiter of genteel arts tells us what we can or can't say; and as to genius, nowhere in those paraphrases is the height of fancy made to fuse with the depth of erudition, like a mountain orbed by its reflection in a lake—which at least would be some consolation. What we do have are crude imitations, with hops and flutters of irresponsible invention weighed down by the blunders of ignorance. If this kind of thing becomes an international fashion I can easily imagine Robert Lowell himself finding one of his best poems, whose charm is in its concise, delicate touches (". . . splinters fall in sawdust from the aluminum-plant wall . . . wormwood . . . three pairs of glasses . . . leathery love") adapted in some other country by some eminent, blissfully monolingual foreign poet, assisted by some American expatriate with a not-too-extensive vocabulary in any language. An outraged pedant, wishing to inform and defend our poet, might then translate the adaptation back into English (". . . I saw dusty paint split and fall like aluminum stocks on Wall Street . . . six glasses of absinthe . . . the football of passion"). I wonder on whose side the victim would be.

Written on September 20, 1969, and published on December 4, 1969, in *The New York Review of Books.* I fervently hope that this little essay managed to reach the poet's widow in Soviet Russia.

7

ANNIVERSARY NOTES

My first intention was to write an elaborate paper on this *TriQuarterly* number (17, Winter 1970, Northwestern University, Evanston, Illinois) which is dedicated to me on the occasion of my seventieth birthday. I soon realized, however, that I might find myself discussing critical studies of my fiction, something I have always avoided doing. True, a festschrift is a very special and rare occasion for that kind of sport, but I did not wish to create even the shadow of a precedent and therefore decided simply to publish the rough jottings I made as an objective reader anxious to eliminate slight factual errors of which such a marvelous gift must be free; for I knew what pains the editors, Charles Newman and Alfred Appel, had taken to prepare it and remembered how firmly the guest co-editor, when collecting the ingredients of this great feast, refused to show me any plum or crumb before publication.

BUTTERFLIES

Butterflies are among the most thoughtful and touching contributions to this volume. The old-fashioned engraving of a *Catagramma*-like insect is delightfully reproduced twelve times so as to suggest a double series or "block" of specimens in a cabinet case; and there is a beautiful photograph of a Red Admirable (but "Nymphalidae" is the family to which it belongs, not its genus, which is *Vanessa*—my first bit of carping).

ALFRED APPEL, JR.

Mr. Appel, guest co-editor, writes about my two main works of fiction. His essay "Backgrounds of *Lolita*" is a superb example of the rare case where art and erudition meet in a shining ridge of specific information (the highest and to me most acceptable function of literary criticism). I would have liked to say more about his findings but modesty (a virtue that the average reviewer especially appreciates in authors) denies me that pleasure.

His other piece in this precious collection is "*Ada* Described." I planted three blunders, meant to ridicule mistranslations of Russian classics, in the first paragraph of my *Ada*: the opening sentence of *Anna Karenin* (no additional "a," printer, she was not a ballerina) is turned inside out, Anna Arkadievna's patronymic is given a grotesque masculine ending; and the title of Tolstoy's family chronicle has been botched by the invented Stoner or Lower (I must have received at least a dozen letters with clarifications and corrections from indignant or puzzled readers, some of them of Russian origin, who never read *Ada* beyond the first page). Furthermore, in the same important paragraph, "Mount Tabor" and "Pontius" allude respectively to the transfigurations and betrayals to which great texts are subjected by pretentious and ignorant versionists. The present statement is an amplification of Mr. Appel's remarks on the subject in his brilliant essay "*Ada* Described." I confess that his piece was a great pleasure to read, but one error in it I really must correct: My Baltic Baron is totally and emphatically unrelated to Mr. Norman Mailer, the writer.

SIMON KARLINSKY

Mr. Karlinsky's "N. and Chekhov" is a very remarkable essay, and I greatly appreciate being with A. P. in the same boat—on a Russian lake, at sunset, he fishing, I watching the hawkmoths above the water. Mr. Karlinsky has put his finger on a mysterious sensory cell. He is right, I do love Chekhov dearly. I fail, however, to rationalize my feeling for him: I can easily do so in regard to the greater artist, Tolstoy, with the flash of this or that unforgettable passage (". . . how sweetly she said: 'and even very much' "—Vronsky recalling Kitty's reply to some trivial question that we shall never know), but when I imagine Chekhov with the same detachment all I can make out is a medley of dreadful prosaisms, ready-made epithets, repetitions, doctors, unconvincing vamps, and so forth; yet it is *his* works which I would take on a trip to another planet.

In another article—on "N.'s Russified Lewis Carroll"—the same critic is much too kind to my *Anya in Wonderland* (1924). How much better I could have done it fifteen years later! The only good bits are the poems and the word-play. I find an odd blunder in the "Song of the Soup": *lohan'* (a kind of bucket) is misspelt by me and twisted into the wrong gender. Incidentally, I had not (and still have not) seen any other Russian versions of the book (as Mr. Karlinsky suggests I may have had) so that my sharing with Poliksena Solovyov the same model for one of the parodies is a coincidence. I recall with pleasure that one of the accidents that prompted Wellesley College to engage me as lecturer in the early forties was the presence of my rare *Anya* in the Wellesley collection of Lewis Carroll editions.

ROBERT ALTER

Mr. Alter's essay on the "Art of Politics in *Invitation to a Beheading*" is a most brilliant reflection of that book in a reader's mind. It is practically flawless so that all I can add is that I particularly appreciated his citing a passage from *The Gift* "that could serve as a useful gloss on the entire nature of political and social reality in the earlier novel."

STANLEY EDGAR HYMAN

Mr. Hyman in his first-rate piece "The Handle" discusses *Invitation to a Beheading* and *Bend Sinister*, the two bookends of grotesque design between which my other volumes tightly huddle. I am a great admirer of Ransom's poem about Captain Carpenter aptly mentioned by Mr. Hyman.

DABNEY STUART

I must point out two fascinating little mistakes in Mr. Stuart's very interesting "*Laughter in the Dark*: Dimensions of Parody": (1) The film in which my heroine is given a small part in the 1920s has nothing to do with Garbo's *Anna Karenina* (of which incidentally I have only seen stills); but what I would like my readers to brood over is my singular power of prophecy, for the name of the leading lady (Dorianna Karenina) in the picture invented by me in 1928 prefigured that of the actress (Anna Karina) who was to play Margot forty years later in the film *Laughter in the Dark*; and (2) Mr. Stuart cleverly toys with the idea that Albert Albinus and Axel Rex are "doubles," one of his main clues being that Margot finds Albinus' telephone number not under "A" but under "R" in the directory. Actually that "R" is a mere slip or typo (the initial corresponds correctly to the man's name in the first English-language edition of the novel, London, 1936).

GEORGE STEINER

Mr. Steiner's article ("Extraterritorial") is built on solid abstractions and opaque generalizations. A few specific items can be made out and should be corrected. He absurdly overestimates Oscar Wilde's mastery of French. It is human but a little cheap on his part to chide my Van Veen for sneering at my *Lolita* (which, in a transfigured form, I magnanimously turned over to a transposed fellow author); it might be wiser for him to read *Ada* more carefully than did the morons whom he rightly condemns for having dismissed as hermetic a writer's limpid and precise prose. To one piece of misinformation I must strongly object: I never belonged to the "*haute bourgeoisie*" to which he grimly assigns me (rather like that Marxist reviewer of my *Speak, Memory* who classified my father as a "plutocrat" and a "man of affairs"!). The Nabokovs have been soldiers and squires since (at least) the fifteenth century.

BARBARA HELDT MONTER

In her otherwise impeccable little piece "*Spring in Fialta*: The Choice that Mimics Chance," Mrs. Barbara Monter makes a slight bibliographic mistake. She implies that I wrote the Russian original of the story sometime around 1947, in America. This is not so. It was written at least a dozen years earlier, in Berlin, and was first published in Paris ("Vesna v Fial'te," *Sovremennyya Zapiski*, 1936) long before being collected in the Chekhov House edition, New York, 1956. The English translation (by Peter Pertzov and me) appeared in *Harper's Bazaar*, May, 1947.

JEFFREY LEONARD

I am not sure that Mr. Leonard has quite understood what Van Veen means by his "texture of time" in the penultimate part of *Ada*. First of all, whatever I may have said in an old interview, it is not the entire novel but only that one part (as Alfred Appel correctly points out elsewhere) in which the illustrative metaphors, all built around one viatic theme, gradually accumulate, come to life, and form a story turning on Van's ride from the Grisons to the Valais—after which the thing again disintegrates and reverts to abstraction on a last night of solitude in a hotel in Vaud. In other words, it is all a structural trick: Van's theory of time has no existence beyond the fabric of one part of the novel *Ada*. In the second place, Mr. Leonard has evidently not grasped what is meant by "texture"; it is something quite different from what Proust called "lost time," and it is precisely in everyday life, in the waiting-rooms of life's stations that we can concentrate on the "feeling" of time and palpate its very texture. I also protest against his dragging "Antiterra," which is merely an ornamental incident, into a discussion whose only rightful field is Part Four and not the entire novel. And finally I owe no debt whatsoever (as Mr. Leonard seems to think) to the famous Argentine essayist and his rather confused compilation "A New Refutation of

Time." Mr. Leonard would have lost less of it had he gone straight to Berkeley and Bergson.

NINA BERBEROVA

In Miss Berberov's excellent article on *Pale Fire* I find a couple of minute mistakes: Kinbote begs "dear Jesus" to relieve him of his fondness for faunlets, not to cure his headache, as she implies; and Professor Pnin, whose presence in that novel Miss Berberov overlooks, *does* appear in person (note to line 949, *Pale Fire*), with his dog. She is much better, however, at delineating the characters in my novels than in describing V. Sirin, one of my characters in "real" life. In her second article, on "N. in the Thirties" (from her recent memoirs, *The Italics Are Mine*), she permits herself bizarre inaccuracies. I may be absentminded, I may be too frank about my literary tastes, okay, but I would like Miss Berberov to cite one specific instance of my having read a book that I had never read. In my preface (June 25, 1959) to the English-language edition of *Invitation to a Beheading* I have more to say about that kind of nonsense. Then there is a sartorial detail in her memoir that I must set straight. Never did I possess, in Paris or elsewhere, "a tuxedo Rachmaninov had given [me]." I had not met Rachmaninov before leaving France for America in 1940. He had twice sent me small amounts of money, through friends, and I was eager now to thank him in person. During our first meeting at his flat on West End Avenue, I mentioned I had been invited to teach summer school at Stanford. On the following day I got from him a carton with several items of obsolete clothing, among which was a cutaway (presumably tailored in the period of the Prelude), which he hoped—as he said in a kind little note—I would wear for my first lecture. I sent back his well-meant gift but (gulp of *mea culpa!*) could not resist telling one or two people about it. Half a dozen years later, when Miss Berberov migrated to New York in her turn, she must have heard the anecdote from one of our common friends, Karpovich or Kerenski, after which a quarter of a century elapsed, or rather collapsed, and somehow, in her mind, the cutaway was transformed into a "tuxedo" and transferred to an earlier era of my life. I doubt that I had any occasion in Paris, in the thirties, when the short series of my brief encounters with Miss Berberov took place, to wear my old London dinner jacket; certainly not for that dinner at *L'Ours* (with which, incidentally, the "Ursus" of *Ada* and the *Medved'* of St. Petersburg have nothing to do); anyway, I do not see how any of my clothes could have resembled the doubly anachronistic hand-me-down in which the memoirist rigs me out. How much kinder she is to my books!

PETER LUBIN

The multicolored inklings offered by Mr. Lubin in his "Kickshaws and Motley" are absolutely dazzling. Such things as his "*v ugloo*" [Russ. for "in the corner"] in the igloo of the globe [a blend of "glow" and "strobe"] are better than anything I have done in that line. Very beautifully he tracks down to their lairs in Eliot three terms queried by a poor little person in *Pale Fire*. I greatly admire the definition of tmesis (Type I) as a "semantic petticoat slipped on between the naked noun and its clothing epithet," as well as Lubin's "proleptic" tmesis illustrated by Shakespeare's glow-worm beginning "to pale his ineffectual fire." And the parody of an interview with N. (though a little more exquisitely iridized than my own replies would have been) is sufficiently convincing to catch readers.

LUCIE LÉON NOEL

The extent to which I was concerned with the fragility of my English at the time of my abandoning Russian in 1939 may be gauged by the fact that even after Mrs. Léon had gone over the manuscript of my *Sebastian Knight* in Paris where it was written, and I had moved to the USA, I begged the late Agnes Perkins, the admirable Head of the English Department at Wellesley, to assist me in reading the galleys of the book (bought for $150 in 1941, by New Directions), and that later, another kind lady, Sylvia Berkman, checked the grammar of my first English stories that appeared in *The Atlantic* in the early forties.

I am sorry that Lucie Léon in her amiably modulated "Playback" does not speak more than she does of her brother Alex Ponizovski of whom I was very fond (I particularly like recalling the streak of quiet eccentricity that endeared him to fellow students at Cambridge, such as the time he casually swallowed the contents of a small bottle of ink that happened to be within reach while we sat and talked by the fire). In her account of a dinner with James Joyce in Paris, I found it refreshing to be accused of bashfulness (after finding so frequently in the gazettes complaints of my "arrogance"); but is her impression correct? She pictures me as a timid young artist; actually I was forty, with a sufficiently lucid awareness of what I had already done for Russian letters preventing me from feeling awed in the presence of any living writer. (Had Mrs. Léon and I met more often at parties she might have realized that I am always a disappointing guest, neither inclined nor able to shine socially.)

Another little error occurs in the reference to the palindrome that I wrote in her album. There was nothing new about a reversible sentence in Russian: the anonymous sandglass "*a roza upala na lapu Azora*" ("and the rose fell upon Azor's paw") is as familiar to children as, in another nursery, "able was I ere I saw Elba." The first line of my *Kazak* is, in fact, not mine (I *think* it was given me by the late Vladimir Piotrovski, a wonderfully skillful poet); what I claimed was new referred to my expanding the palindrome into a rhymed quatrain with its three last verses making continuous sense in spite of each being reversible.

IRWIN WEIL

Curiously enough, the note appended to my *Kazak* by Irwin Weil (who contributes an interesting essay on my "Odyssey" elsewhere in the volume) also requires correction. His statement that "the third and fourth lines are each palindromes if one excludes the last [?] syllables" is quite wrong; all four lines are palindromes, and no "last syllables" have to be excluded.* Especially regrettable is Mr. Weil's mistranslation of one of them. He has confused the Russian word for aloes (a genus of plant) with *aloe*, which means "red" or "rosy," and that, too, is mistranslated, becoming "purple"!

I must also question an incomprehensible statement in Mr. Weil's article "Odyssey of a Translator." The Russian lawyer E. M. Kulisher may well have been "an old acquaintance" of my father's, but he was not "close to the Nabokov family" (I do not remember him as a person) and I have never said anywhere what Mr. Weil has me indicate in the opening paragraph of his article.

---

* This error is due to a faulty transcription of the palindrome on p. 218 of *TriQuarterly* 17. The Russian word *rvat'*, the first word of line four, has been placed at the end of line three. The errors in the transcription and note (p. 217) will be corrected in the paperback edition of the volume, to be published this fall by Simon and Schuster.

MORRIS BISHOP

My old friend Morris Bishop (my only close friend on the campus) has touched me very deeply by his recollections of my stay at Cornell. I am assigning an entire chapter to it in my *Speak On, Mnemosyne*, a memoir devoted to the 20 years I spent in my adopted country, after dwelling for 20 years in Russia and for as many more in Western Europe. My friend suggests that I was bothered by the students' incompetence in my Pushkin class. Not at all. What bothered and angered me was the ineptitude of the system of Scientific Linguistics at Cornell.

ROSS WETZSTEON

I remember most of the best students in my Cornell classes. Mr. Wetzsteon was one of them. My "*Bleak House* diagram," which he recalls so movingly, is preserved among my papers and will appear in the collection of lectures (*Bleak House, Mansfield Park, Madame Bovary*, etc.) that I mean to publish some day. It is strange to think that never again shall I feel between finger and thumb the cool smoothness of virgin chalk or make that joke about the "gray board" (improperly wiped), and be rewarded by two or three chuckles (RW? AA? NS?).

JULIAN MOYNAHAN

Mr. Moynahan in his charming "*Lolita* and Related Memories" recalls his professor of Russian, the late Dr. Leonid Strakhovski (most foreign-born lecturers used to be "doctors"). I knew him, he did not really resemble my Pnin. We met at literary parties in Berlin half a century ago. He wrote verse. He wore a monocle. He had no sense of humor. He dwelt in dramatic detail on his military and civil adventures. Most of his yarns had a knack of fading out at the critical point. He had worked as a trolley car driver and had run over a man. The rowboat in which he escaped from Russia developed a leak in the middle of the Baltic. When asked what happened then, he would wave a limp hand in the Russian gesture of despair and dismissal.

ELLENDEA PROFFER

Ellendea Proffer's report on my Russian readers is both heartening and sad. "All Soviet age groups," she observes, "tend to feel that literature has a didactic function." This marks a kind of dead end, despite a new generation of talented people. "*Zhalkiy udel* (piteous fate)," as the *Literaturnaya Gazeta* says *à propos de bottes* (March 4, 1970).

STANLEY ELKIN

Several passages in Mr. Elkin's "Three Meetings," a parody of an "I remember . . ." piece, are extremely funny, such as the farcical variety of repetition or the casual reference to the "lovely eggal forms" he and I encountered on "an expedition up the Orinoco." And our third meeting is a scream.

ROBERT P. HUGHES

Mr. Hughes in his "Notes on the Translation of *Invitation to a Beheading*" is one of the few critics who noticed the poetry of the Tamara terraces with their metamorphosed tamaracks. In the trance of objectivity which the reading of the festschrift has now induced in me, I am able to say that Mr. Hughes' discussion of the trials and triumphs attending that translation is very subtle and rewarding.

CARL R. PROFFER

Mr. Proffer, who discusses another translation, that of my much older *Korol', Dama, Valet,* tackles a more ungrateful task, first because *King, Queen, Knave* "does not surmount its original weaknesses," and secondly because revision and adaptation blur one's interest in faithfulnesses. He wonders what "worse sins" (than planning the murder of his uncle) cowardly and brutal Franz could have committed between the twenties and sixties in Germany, but a minute's thought should reveal to the reader what the activities of that type of man could have been at the exact center of the interval. Mr. Proffer ends his "A New Deck for Nabokov's Knaves" by saying he expects the English version of *Mashenka* to be quite different from the Russian original. Expectation has been the undoing of many a shrewd gambler.

W. B. SCOTT

I had read and hugely enjoyed Mr. Scott's essay on my *EO* translation, "The Cypress Veil," when it first appeared in the Winter, 1965, issue of the *TriQuarterly.* It is a most refreshing piece. My improved cab is now ready for publication.

Mr. Scott is also responsible for the last item in the volume, a letter addressed by Timofey Pnin to "Many respected Professor Apple [sic]," a stunning affair in which scholarship and high spirits interlace to produce the monogram of a very special masterpiece. And that frozen frenzy of footnotes!

SAUL STEINBERG

There is magic in every penstroke and curlicue of the delightful diploma that Saul Steinberg has drawn for my wife and me.

R. M. ADAMS

Mr. Adams' letter about me addressed to "M. le Baron de Stendhal" is an extremely witty piece—reminding me, I do not know why, of those macabre little miracles that chess problemists call suimates (White forces Black to win in a certain number of moves).

ANTHONY BURGESS

In Mr. Burgess' poem I particularly appreciate his Maltese grocer's cat that likes to sit upon the scales and is found to weigh 2 rotolos.

ALBERT J. GUERARD

"Not even Colette," says Mr. Guerard in his tribute to *Ada*, "rendered fleshly textures and tones with such grace." The lady is mentioned in *Ada*.

HERBERT GOLD

Blending fact and fiction in a kind of slat-sign shimmer, Mr. Gold recalls our meetings in upstate New York and in a Swiss hotel. I recall with pleasure my correspondence with the puzzled editor of the *Saturday Evening Post* for which he had written what I had thought was to be an interview with me—or, at least, with the person I usually impersonate in Montreux.

RICHARD HOWARD

Mr. Howard's poem "Waiting for Ada" contains a wonderful description of a Grand Hotel du Miroir very like some of the "nearly pearly nougat-textured art-nouveau" places where I have been "working wickedly away" during recent *séjours* in Italy.

JOHN UPDIKE

I am grateful to Mr. Updike for mentioning, in his stylish tribute, the little Parisian prostitute whom Humbert Humbert recalls so wistfully. On the other hand there was no reason at all for that harsh and contemptuous reference to a small publishing house which brought out excellent editions of four books of mine.

R. H. W. DILLARD

Mr. Dillard's poem "A day, a country home" is most attractive—especially the "light through the leaves, like butterflies" in the fourth stanza.

[298]

HORTENSE CALISHER

Miss Calisher's contubernal contribution expresses in a sophisticated metaphor her readiness to share the paranoia of her fellow writers. Oddly enough, even the best tent is absolutely dependent on the kind of country amidst which it is pitched.

JACK LUDWIG

I remember, not without satisfaction, how fiercely and frequently, during my last year of high school in Russia (which was also the first year of the revolution), most of my teachers and some of my schoolmates accused me of being a "foreigner" because I refused to join in political declarations and demonstrations. Mr. Ludwig in his splendid little article indicates with great sympathy and acumen the possibility of similar accusations being made by my new fellow-citizens. They could not vie with Vladimir Vasilievich Gippius, my fiery, redhaired teacher of Russian literature.

J. BARTH

Dear Mr. B.:
  Thanks for your birthday greetings. Let me wish you many returns of the same day. How many nice people crowd around my cradle! It is pleasant to know you like Max Planck. I rather like him, too. But not Cervantes!

Yours cordially,
V. N.

CLARENCE BROWN

Lines 31–32 of Mr. Brown's fascinating poem in Russian display a looping-the-loop inversion of which old Lomonosov might have been proud: "Why, better of Dante's Hell for him to burn in the seventh circle" if translated lexically. His cartoons in a British weekly are marvelous.

CHARLES NEWMAN

The editor of the *TriQuarterly*, in "Americanization of V. N." (an exhilarating physical process in the present case!) recalls taking *Pale Fire* "to Basic Training in hot Texas," tearing it from its binding, and keeping it "pure and scrolled in my Fatigues' long pocket like a Bowie knife" safe from the Barracks Sergeant. It is a beautifully written, and most touching, epic.

DAVID WAGONER

Laughter in the Dark is paid a suitable tribute in Mr. Wagoner's sinister poem.

RICHARD STERN

I like the epithets "opulent, triplicitous," in Mr. Stern's lines, but I am not sure that any of the four Karamazovs (grotesque, humorless, hysterical, and jejune, respectively) can be defined as "triste."

ANDREW FIELD

My good friend, Mr. Field, has contributed some brilliantly worded remarks, one of which refers to V.N.'s being "counted upon to observe the hoisting of his statue (Peter the Great seated upon an invisible horse)." This reminded me suddenly of a not-unsimilar event in California where some fancy statuary, lovingly erected by a Russian group to commemorate Pushkin's duel, partly disintegrated after a couple of years' exposure, removing Pushkin but leaving intact the figure of magnificent Dantes pointing his pistol at posterity.

BROCK BROWER

The "socio-political nature" of Mr. Brower's tribute to *Lolita*, far from being repugnant to me (as he modestly assumes), is more than redeemed by the specific precision of his artistic touch.

IRWIN SHAW

In his "Advice to a Young Writer," Mr. Shaw draws his examples from the life, labors, and luck of "Vladimir N., perched on a hill in Switzerland." To Irwin S., perched on a not-too-distant hill, I send by Alpine Horn my best greetings.

JAY NEUGEBOREN

In a very pretty little poem, Mr. Neugeboren seems to

rhyme, somewhat surprisingly, "Nabokov" and "love." I would suggest "talk of" or "balk of" as more closely conforming to the stressed middle vowel of that awkward name ("Nabawkof"). I once composed the following rhyme for my students:

> The querulous gawk of
> A heron at night
> Prompts Nabokov
> To write

RICHARD GILMAN

Mr. Gilman's tribute to *Ada* comes at a time when I still think that of all my books it is the one that corresponds most exactly to its fore-image; and therefore I cannot help being affected by his kind words.

GEORGE P. ELLIOTT

Among my short stories, "Signs and Symbols" still remains an old favorite of mine. I am happy that Mr. Elliott has singled it out for comment with a phrase from *Ada* heading his pithy piece.

ALFRED KAZIN

A final splendid salute comes from one of my friendliest readers. It ends on an emotional note which I inwardly respond to without being able to formulate my response with Mr. Kazin's force and feeling.

Written on March 10, 1970, and published in the *Supplement to TriQuarterly 17*, Northwestern University Press, 1970.

8

ROWE'S SYMBOLS

"It appears," says Mr. Rowe* in his Introduction, "that Nabokov—partially by means of the mechanisms revealed below—will continue to flutter the pulses of his readers for some time."

"The mechanisms revealed below" is a pretty phrase, suggesting perhaps more than its author intends, but it does not quite apply to me. The purpose of the present review is not to answer a critic but to ask him to remove his belongings. The book consists of three parts. Whilst I have no great quarrel with the first two, entitled "A Touch of Russian" and "N. as Stage Manager," I must protest vehemently against a number of indecent absurdities contained in the third part, entitled "Sexual Manipulations."

One may wonder if it was worth Mr. Rowe's time to exhibit erotic bits picked out of *Lolita* and *Ada*—a process rather like looking for allusions to aquatic mammals in *Moby Dick*. But that is his own choice and concern. What I object to is Mr. Rowe's manipulating my most innocent words so as to introduce sexual "symbols" into them. The notion of symbol itself has always been abhorrent to me, and I never

* William Woodin Rowe: *Nabokov's Deceptive World*. New York University Press, 1971, 193 pp.

tire of retelling how I once failed a student—the dupe, alas, of an earlier teacher—for writing that Jane Austen describes leaves as "green" because Fanny is hopeful, and "green" is the color of hope. The symbolism racket in schools attracts computerized minds but destroys plain intelligence as well as poetical sense. It bleaches the soul. It numbs all capacity to enjoy the fun and enchantment of art. Who the hell cares, as Mr. Rowe wants us to care, that there is, according to his italics, a "man" in the sentence about a homosexual Swede who "had embarrassing *man*ners" (p. 148), and another "man" in "*man*ipulate" (*passim*)? "Wickedly folded moth" suggests "wick" to Mr. Rowe, and "wick," as we Freudians know, is the Male Organ. "I" stands for "eye," and "eye" stands for the Female Organ. Pencil licking is always a reference to you know what. A soccer goal hints at the vulval orifice (which Mr. Rowe evidently sees as square).

I wish to share with him the following secret: In the case of a certain type of writer it often happens that a whole paragraph or sinuous sentence exists as a discrete organism, with its own imagery, its own invocations, its own bloom, and then it is especially precious, and also vulnerable, so that if an outsider, immune to poetry and common sense, injects spurious symbols into it, or actually tampers with its wording (see Mr. Rowe's crass attempt on his page 113), its magic is replaced by maggots. The various words that Mr. Rowe mistakes for the "symbols" of academic jargon, supposedly planted by an idiotically sly novelist to keep schoolmen busy, are not labels, not pointers, and certainly not the garbage cans of a Viennese tenement, but live fragments of specific description, rudiments of metaphor, and echoes of creative emotion. The fatal flaw in Mr. Rowe's treatment of recurrent words, such as "garden" or "water," is his regarding them as abstractions, and not realizing that the sound of a bath being filled, say, in the world of *Laughter in the Dark*, is as different from the limes

[305]

rustling in the rain of *Speak, Memory* as the Garden of Delights in *Ada* is from the lawns in *Lolita.* If every "come" and "part" on the pages of my books is supposedly used by me to represent "climax" and "genitals," one can well imagine the naughty treasures Mr. Rowe might find in any French novel where the prefix "*con*" occurs so frequently as to make every chapter a veritable compote of female organs. I do not think, however, that his French is sufficient for such feasts; nor is his Russian good enough for his manipulations if he believes that "*otblesk*" (confused apparently with *otliv*) means "low tide" (page 111) or that the nonexistent "*triazh*" stands for "tyranny" (page 41) when actually the word that I used (and that he wrongly transcribed), *tirazh*, is merely a publisher's term for "circulation."

One can excuse a critic for not finding "stillicide" and "ganch" in his abridged dictionary and concluding that I invented those words; one can understand a dull reader of *Invitation to a Beheading* thinking that the executioner develops a homosexual tenderness for his victim when actually that affectionate look reflects only the lust of a glutton coveting a live chicken; but what I find unpardonable, and indeed unworthy of a scholar, is Mr. Rowe's twisting my discussion of prosody (as appended to my translation of *Eugene Onegin*) into a torrent of Freudian drivel, which allows him to construe "metrical length" as an erection and "rhyme" as a sexual climax. No less ludicrous is his examination of Lolita's tennis and his claim that the tennis balls represent testicles (those of a giant albino, no doubt). Passing on to my reference to chess problems in *Speak, Memory* Mr. Rowe finds "sexual analogies" in such phrases as "mating devices" and "groping for a pawn in the box"—all of which is as much an insult to chess as to the problemist.

The jacket of Mr. Rowe's book depicts a butterfly incongruously flying around a candle. Moths, not butterflies, are attracted to light but the designer's blunder neatly illustrates the quality of Mr. Rowe's preposterous and nasty interpretations. And he will be read, he will be quoted, he will be filed in great libraries, next to my arbors and mists!

Written at Gstaad, Bernese Oberland, on August 28, 1971, and published in *The New York Review* on October 7 of the same year.

9

INSPIRATION
(written on November 20, 1972, for Saturday Review*)*

> The awakening, quickening, or creative impulse, esp. as
> manifested in high artistic achievement.
> > Webster, Second Ed., unabridged, 1957

> The enthusiasm that sweeps away (*entraîne*) poets. Also a term
> of physiology (*insufflation*): ". . . wolves and dogs howl only by
> inspiration; one can easily ascertain this by causing a little dog
> to howl close to one's face (Buffon)."
> > Littré, *éd. intégrale*, 1963

> The enthusiasm, concentration, and unusual manifestation of
> the mental faculties (*umstvennyh sil*).
> > Dal, Revised Ed., St. Petersburg, 1904

> A creative upsurge. [Examples:] Inspired poet. Inspired
> socialistic work.
> > Ozhegov, Russian dictionary, Moscow, 1960

A special study, which I do not plan to conduct, would
reveal, probably, that inspiration is seldom dwelt upon
nowadays even by the worst reviewers of our best prose. I
say "our" and I say "prose" because I am thinking of
American works of fiction, including my own stuff. It
would seem that this reticence is somehow linked up with a
sense of decorum. Conformists suspect that to speak of

"inspiration" is as tasteless and old-fashioned as to stand up for the Ivory Tower. Yet inspiration exists as do towers and tusks.

One can distinguish several types of inspiration, which intergrade, as all things do in this fluid and interesting world of ours, while yielding gracefully to a semblance of classification. A prefatory glow, not unlike some benign variety of the aura before an epileptic attack, is something the artist learns to perceive very early in life. This feeling of tickly well-being branches through him like the red and the blue in the picture of a skinned man under Circulation. As it spreads, it banishes all awareness of physical discomfort—youth's toothache as well as the neuralgia of old age. The beauty of it is that, while completely intelligible (as if it were connected with a known gland or led to an expected climax), it has neither source nor object. It expands, glows, and subsides without revealing its secret. In the meantime, however, a window has opened, an auroral wind has blown, every exposed nerve has tingled. Presently all dissolves: the familiar worries are back and the eyebrow redescribes its arc of pain; but the artist knows he is ready.

A few days elapse. The next stage of inspiration is something ardently anticipated—and no longer anonymous. The shape of the new impact is indeed so definite that I am forced to relinquish metaphors and resort to specific terms. The narrator forefeels what he is going to tell. The forefeeling can be defined as an instant vision turning into rapid speech. If some instrument were to render this rare and delightful phenomenon, the image would come as a shimmer of exact details, and the verbal part as a tumble of merging words. The experienced writer immediately takes it down and, in the process of doing so, transforms what is little more than a running blur into gradually dawning sense, with epithets and sentence construction growing as clear and trim as they would be on the printed page:

Sea crashing, retreating with shuffle of pebbles, Juan and beloved young whore—is her name, as they say, Adora? is she Italian, Roumanian, Irish?—asleep in his lap, his opera cloak pulled over her, candle messily burning in its tin cup, next to it a paper-wrapped bunch of long roses, his silk hat on the stone floor near a patch of moonlight, all this in a corner of a decrepit, once palatial whorehouse, Villa Venus, on a rocky Mediterranean coast, a door standing ajar gives on what seems to be a moonlit gallery but is really a half-demolished reception room with a broken outer wall, through a great rip in it the naked sea is heard as a panting space separated from time, it dully booms, dully withdraws dragging its platter of wet pebbles.

This I jotted down one morning at the very end of 1965, a couple of months before the novel began to flow. What I give above is its first throb, the strange nucleus of the book that was to grow around it in the course of the next three years. Much of that growth obviously differs in coloration and lighting from the foreglimpsed scene, whose structural centrality, however, is emphasized, with a kind of pleasing neatness, by the fact that it now exists as an inset scene right in the middle of the novel (which was entitled at first *Villa Venus*, then *The Veens*, then *Ardor*, and finally *Ada*).

Reverting to a more generalized account, one sees inspiration accompanying the author in his actual work on the new book. She accompanies him (for by now we are in the presence of a nubile muse) by means of successive flashes to which the writer may grow so accustomed that a sudden fizzle in the domestic illumination may strike him as an act of betrayal.

One and the same person can compose parts of one and the same story or poem, either in his head or on paper, pencil or pen in hand (I am told there exist fantastic performers who actually *type out* their immediate product or, still more incredibly, *dictate* it, warm and bubbly, to a typist or to a machine!). Some prefer the bathtub to the study and the bed to the windy moor—the place does not matter much, it is the relationship between the brain and the hand that poses some odd problems. As John Shade says somewhere: "I am puzzled by the difference between two methods of composing: *A*, the kind which goes on solely in the poet's mind, a testing of performing words, while he is soaping a third time one leg, and *B*, the other kind, much more decorous, when he's in his study writing with a pen. In method *B* the hand supports the thought, the abstract battle is concretely fought. The pen stops in mid-air, then swoops to bar a canceled sunset or restore a star, and thus it physically guides the phrase toward faint daylight through the inky maze. But method *A* is agony! The brain is soon enclosed in a steel cap of pain. A muse in overalls directs the drill which grinds, and which no effort of the will can interrupt, while the automaton is taking off what he has just put on or walking briskly to the corner store to buy the paper he has read before. Why is it so? Is it, perhaps, because in penless work there is no pen-poised pause . . . Or is the process deeper, with no desk to prop the false and hoist the picturesque? For there are those mysterious moments when, too weary to delete, I drop my pen; I ambulate—and by some mute command the right word flutes and perches on my hand."

This is, of course, where inspiration comes in. The words which on various occasions, during some fifty years of composing prose, I have put together and then canceled may have formed by now in the Realm of Rejection (a foggy but not quite unlikely land north of nowhere) a huge library of scrapped phrases, characterized and concorded only by their wanting the benison of inspiration.

No wonder, then, that a writer who is not afraid to confess that he has known inspiration and can readily distinguish it from the froth of a fit, as well as from the humdrum comfort of the "right word," should seek the bright trace of that thrill in the work of fellow authors. The bolt of inspiration strikes invariably: you observe the flash in this or that piece of great writing, be it a stretch of fine verse, or a passage in Joyce or Tolstoy, or a phrase in a short story, or a spurt of genius in the paper of a naturalist, of a scholar, or even in a book reviewer's article. I have in view, naturally, not the hopeless hacks we all know—but people who are creative artists in their own right, such as, say, Trilling (with his critical opinions I am not concerned), or Thurber (*e.g.* in *Voices of Revolution*: "Art does not rush to the barricades").

In recent years numerous publishers have had the pleasure of sending me their anthologies—homing pigeons really, for all of them contain samples of the recipient's writings. Amongst the thirty or so of those collections, some flaunt pretentious labels ("Fables of Our Time" or "Themes and Targets"); others are presented more soberly ("Great Tales") and their blurbs promise the reader that he will meet cranberry pickers and hunkies; but almost in each of them there are at least two or three first-rate stories.

Age is chary, but it is also forgetful, and in order to choose instantly what to reread on a night of Orphic thirst and what to reject for ever, I am careful to put an A, or a C, or a D-minus, against this or that item in the anthology. The profusion of high marks reconfirms me every time in the exhilarating belief that at the present time (say, for the last fifty years) the greatest short stories have been produced not in England, not in Russia, and certainly not in France, but in this country.

Examples are the stained-glass windows of knowledge. From a small number of A-plus stories I have chosen half-a-dozen particular favorites of mine. I list their titles below and parenthesize briefly the passage—or one of the passages—in which genuine afflation appears to be present, no matter how trivial the inspired detail may look to a dull criticule.

John Cheever's "The Country Husband" ("Jupiter [a black retriever] crashed through the tomato vines with the remains of a felt hat in his mouth." The story is really a miniature novel beautifully traced, so that the impression of there being a little too many things happening in it is completely redeemed by the satisfying coherence of its thematic interlacings.)

John Updike's "The Happiest I've Been" ("The important thing, rather than the subject, was the conversation itself, the quick agreements, the slow nods, the weave of different memories; it was like one of these Panama baskets shaped underwater around a worthless stone." I like so many of Updike's stories that it was difficult to choose one for demonstration and even more difficult to settle upon its most inspired bit.)

J. D. Salinger's "A Perfect Day for Bananafish" ("Stopping only to sink a foot in a soggy, collapsed castle . . ." This is a great story, too famous and fragile to be measured here by a casual conchometrist.)

Herbert Gold's "Death in Miami Beach" ("Finally we die, opposable thumbs and all." Or to do even better justice to this admirable piece: "Barbados turtles as large as children . . . crucified like thieves . . . the tough leather of their skin does not disguise their present helplessness and pain.")

John Barth's "Lost in the Funhouse" ("What is the story's point? Ambrose is ill. He perspires in the dark passages; candied apples-on-a-stick, delicious-looking, disappointing to eat. Funhouses need men's and ladies' rooms at interval." I had some trouble in pinning down what I needed amidst the lovely swift speckled imagery.)

Delmore Schwartz's "In Dreams Begin Responsibilities" (". . . and the fatal merciless passionate ocean." Although there are several other divine vibrations in this story that so miraculously blends an old cinema film with a personal past, the quoted phrase wins its citation for power and impeccable rhythm.)

I must add that I would be very pleased if a Professor of

Literature to test his students at the start or the close of the term would request them to write a paper discussing the following points:

1. What is so good about those six stories? (Refrain from referring to "commitment," "ecology," "realism," "symbols," and so forth).

2. What other passages in them bear the mark of inspiration?

3. How exactly was that poor lap dog made to howl in those lace-cuffed hands, close to that periwig?

LEPIDOPTERA PAPERS

For nearly fifteen years after moving, in 1940, to America I devoted a tremendous amount of time (more in fact than I did to writing and teaching) to the study of lepidoptera, a study consisting of three parts: working out certain microscopic structures in the laboratory of the Museum of Comparative Zoology, Harvard; contributing scientific papers to entomological journals; and collecting during summer vacations. At least three of those papers have sufficient literary interest to deserve a place in this volume and to them I have added two book reviews, the last one published quite recently.

10

THE FEMALE OF *LYCAEIDES* *SUBLIVENS* NAB.*

Last summer (1951) I decided to visit Telluride, San Miguel County, Colorado, in order to search for the unknown female of what I had described as *Lycaeides argyrognomon sublivens* in 1949 (*Bull. Mus. Comp. Zool.*, vol. 101: p. 513) on the strength of nine males in the Museum of Comparative Zoology, Harvard, which had been taken in the vicinity of Telluride half a century ago. *L. sublivens* is an isolated southern representative (the only known one south of northwestern Wyoming, southeast of Idaho, and east of California) of the species (the holarctic *argyrognomon* Bergstr.=*idas auct.*) to which *anna* Edw., *scudderi* Edw., *aster* Edw., and six other nearctic subspecies belong. I bungled my family's vacation but got what I wanted.

Owing to rains and floods, especially noticeable in Kansas, most of the drive from New York State to Colorado was entomologically uneventful. When reached at last, Telluride turned out to be a damp, unfrequented, but very spectacular cul-de-sac (which a prodigious rainbow strad-

---

* Now known as *Plebejus* (*Lycaeides*) *idas sublivens* or *Lycaeides sublivens* Nab.; it has been dubbed "Nabokov's Blue" by F. Martin Brown (1955).

dled every evening) at the end of two converging roads, one from Placerville, the other from Dolores, both atrocious. There is one motel, the optimistic and excellent Valley View Court where my wife and I stayed, at 9,000 feet altitude, from the 3rd to the 29th of July, walking up daily to at least 12,000 feet along various more or less steep trails in search of *sublivens*. Once or twice Mr. Homer Reid of Telluride took us up in his jeep. Every morning the sky would be of an impeccable blue at 6 A.M. when I set out. The first innocent cloudlet would scud across at 7:30 A.M. Bigger fellows with darker bellies would start tampering with the sun around 9 A.M., just as we emerged from the shadow of the cliffs and trees onto good hunting grounds. Everything would be cold and gloomy half an hour later. At around 10 A.M. there would come the daily electric storm, in several installments, accompanied by the most irritatingly close lightning I have ever encountered anywhere in the Rockies, not excepting Longs Peak, which is saying a good deal, and followed by cloudy and rainy weather through the rest of the day.

After 10 days of this, and despite diligent subsequent exploration, only one sparse colony of *sublivens* was found. On that one spot my wife found a freshly emerged male on the 15th. Three days later I had the pleasure of discovering the unusual-looking female. Between the 15th and the 28th, a dozen hours of windy but passable collecting weather in all (not counting the hours and hours uselessly spent in mist and rain) yielded only 54 specimens, of which 16 were females. Had I been younger and weighed less, I might have perhaps got another 50, but hardly much more than that, and, possibly, the higher ridges I vainly investigated between 12,000 and 14,000 feet at the end of July, in the *magdalena-snowi-centaureae* zone, might have produced *sublivens* later in the season.

The colony I found was restricted to one very steep slope reaching from about 10,500 to a ridge at 11,000 feet and towering over Tomboy Road between "Social Tunnel" and "Bullion Mine." The slope was densely covered with a fine growth of lupines in flower (*Lupinus parviflorus* Nuttall, which did not occur elsewhere along the trail) and green gentians (the tall turrets of which were assiduously patronized by the Broad-Tailed Hummingbird and the White-Striped Hawkmoth). This lupine, which in the mountains of Utah is the food-plant of an alpine race of *L. melissa* (*annetta* Edw.), proved to be also the host of *L. sublivens*. The larva pupates at its base, and in dull weather a few specimens of both sexes of the imago could be found settled on the lower leaves and stems, the livid tone of the butterflies' undersides nicely matching the tint of the plant.

The female of *sublivens* is of a curiously arctic appearance, completely different from the richly pigmented, regionally sympatric, locoweed- and alfalfa-feeding *L. melissa* or from the *melissa*-like females of Wyoming and Idaho *argyrognomon* (*idas*) races, and somewhat resembling *argyrognomon* (*idas*) forms from northwestern Canada and Alaska (see for instance in the above-mentioned work, p. 501 and plate 8, fig. 112). It also recalls a certain combination of characters that crops up in *L. melissa annetta*.

Here is a brief description of *L. sublivens* female: Upperside of a rather peculiar, smooth, weak brown, with an olivaceous cast in the living insect; more or less extensively dusted with cinder-blue scales; triangulate greyish blue inner cretules generally present in the hindwing and often accompanied by some bluish or greyish bleaching in the radial cells of the forewing; aurorae reduced: short and dullish in the hindwing, blurred or absent in the forewing, tending to disappear in both wings and almost completely absent in 3 specimens; lunulate pale greyish blue outer cretules very distinct in both wings; underside similar to that of the male.

Deposited: 20 males and 10 females in the Cornell

University collection, and 18 males and 6 females in the
Museum of Comparative Zoology, Harvard University.

Published in *The Lepidopterists' News*,
New Haven, Conn., Vol. 6, August 8, 1952, pp. 35–36.

11

ON SOME INACCURACIES IN
KLOTS' *FIELD GUIDE*

In connection with "Blues," I wish to correct two or three slips in Professor Alexander B. Klots' important and delightful book (*A Field Guide to the Butterflies of North America, East of the Great Plains*, Houghton Mifflin, Boston, 1951).

On p. 166 there is a misprint: "Center (formerly Karner)" should be, of course, "Karner (formerly Center)." Incidentally I visit the place every time I happen to drive (as I do yearly in early June) from Ithaca to Boston and can report that, despite local picnickers and the hideous garbage they leave, the lupines and *Lycaeides samuelis* Nab. are still doing as fine under those old gnarled pines along the railroad as they did ninety years ago.

On p. 165, another, more unfortunate transposition occurs: "When fawn colored, more vivid in tone" should refer not to *Lycaeides argyrognomon* [*idas*] but to *L. melissa*, while "wings beneath, when fawn colored, duller in tone" should refer not to *L. melissa* but to *L. argyrognomon* [*idas*] (see my "Nearctic Lycaeides," *Bull. Mus. Comp. Zool.*, vol. 101: p. 541: 1949).

On pp. 162–164, the genus *Brephidium* (in company with two others) is incorrectly placed between *Hemiargus* and

Lycaeides. I have shown in my paper on Neotropical Plebejinae (*Psyche*, vol. 52: pp. 1–61; 1945) that *Hemiargus* (*sensu lato*) and *Lycaeides* belong to the same group (subfamily Plebejinae—or supergenus *Plebejus;* the rank does not matter but the relationship does). *Brephidium*, of course, stands on the very outskirts of the family, in a highly specialized group, immeasurably further removed from *Hemiargus* or *Lycaeides* than, say, *Lycaena.* This is where my subfamilies come in handy since at least they keep related things in one bunch and eject intruders. Views may differ in regard to the hierarchic element in the classification I adopt, but no one has questioned so far the fact of the structural relationship and phylogenetic circumstances I mean it to reflect. The whole interest of *Hemiargus* is that it is allied to *Lycaeides* etc., while bearing a striking superficial resemblance to an African group with which it does not have the slightest structural affinity. Systematics, I think, should bring out such points and not keep them blurred in the haze of tradition. I am perfectly willing to demote the whole of my "subfamily" Plebejinae to a supergenus or genus *Plebejus* (*Plebejus ceraunus, isola, thomasi, idas, melissa, aquilo, saepiolus,* etc.) but only under the condition that it include exactly the same species, in the same groupings ("subgenera" or numbered sections, as you will) and in the same sequence of groups, without intrusions from groups assigned structurally to other "subfamilies" (and then, of course, *lygdamus, battoides,* and *piasus* should be all in *Scolitantides* or its equivalent). However, I still think that the formality of generic names for the groupings is a better method than going by numbers, etc. Names are also easier to handle in works on zoological distribution when it is important to bring out the way a group is represented in different regions of the world. Generally speaking, systematics is not directly concerned with the convenience of collectors in their dealings with small local faunas. It should attempt to express structural affinities and divergences, suggest certain

[320]

phylogenetic lines, relate local developments to global ones—and help lumpers to sort out properly the ingredients of their lumps.

The Lepidopterists' News, Vol. 6, August 8, 1952, p. 41

12

BUTTERFLY COLLECTING IN WYOMING, 1952

A visit to Wyoming by car in July–August 1952 was devoted to collecting in the following places:

Southeastern Wyoming: eastern Medicine Bow National Forest, in the Snowy Range, up to approximately 10,500 ft. alt. (using paved road 130 between Laramie and Saratoga); sagebrush country, approximately 7,000 ft. alt., between Saratoga and Encampment, east of paved highway 230; marshes at about the same elevation between eastern Medicine Bow National Forest and Northgate, northern Colorado, within 15 miles from the Wyoming State Line, mainly south of the unpaved road 127; and W. Medicine Bow National Forest, in the Sierra Madre, using the abominable local road from Encampment to the Continental Divide (approximately 9,500 ft. alt.).

Western Wyoming: sagebrush, approximately 6,500 ft. alt. immediately east of Dubois along the (well-named) Wind River; western Shoshone and Teton National Forests, following admirable paved road 26, from Dubois towards Moran over Togwotee Pass (9,500 ft. alt.); near Moran, on Buffalo River, approximately 7,000 ft. alt.; traveling through the construction hell of the city of Jackson, and bearing southeast along paved 187 to The Rim

(7,900 ft. alt.); and, finally, spending most of August in collecting around the altogether enchanting little town of Afton (on paved 89, along the Idaho border), approximately 7,000 ft. alt., mainly in canyons east of the town, and in various spots of Bridger National Forest, Southwestern part, along trails up to 9,000 ft. alt.

Most of the material collected has gone to the Cornell University Museum; the rest to the American Museum of Natural History and the Museum of Comparative Zoology.

The best hunting grounds proved to be: the Sierra Madre at about 8,000 ft. alt., where on some forest trails I found among other things a curious form (? *S. secreta* dos Passos & Grey) of *Speyeria egleis* Behr flying in numbers with *S. atlantis hesperis* Edw. and *S. hydaspe purpurascens* H. Edw., a very eastern locality for the latter; still better were the forests, meadows, and marshes about Togwotee Pass in the third week of July, where the generally early emergences of the season were exemplified by great quantities of *Erebia theona ethela* Edw. and *E. callias callias* Edw. already on the wing; very good, too, were some of the canyons near Afton.

Here are a few notes on what interested me most in the field: *Boloria, Colias*, certain Blues, and migratory or at least "mobile" species.

Of *Boloria* I got seven species, of the eight (or possibly ten) that occur within the region. Plunging into the forest south of route 130 on the western slopes of the Snowy Range, I found *B. selene tollandensis* B & McD. not uncommon on a small richly flowered marsh at about 8,000 ft. alt.; also on marshes north of Northgate and on Togwotee Pass. On July 8, I spent three hours collecting a dozen fresh specimens of *B. eunomia alticola* B & McD., both sexes, on a tiny very wet marsh along the eastern lip of the last lake before reaching Snowy Range Pass from the west, possibly the same spot where Klots had taken it in 1935 (*Journ. N. Y. Ent. Soc.* 45: p. 326; 1937). I met with the same form on a marsh near Peacock Lake, Longs Peak, Colorado, in

1947. Forms of *B. titania* Esp. (mostly near ssp. *helena* Edw.) were abundant everywhere above 7,500 ft. alt. By the end of July *B. freija* Thunb. was in tatters near Togwotee Pass (it had been on the wane in June, 1947, on marshes near Columbine Lodge, Estes Park; and on Hoback River, Tetons, in early July, 1949). Of the beautiful *B. frigga sagata* B. & Benj. I took two ♂♂ (fresh but frayed) near Togwotee Pass. Of *B. toddi* Holland ssp. I took a very fresh ♂ in early July in the Snowy Range at 8,000 ft. alt. and a couple of days later, acting upon a hunch, I visited a remarkably repulsive-looking willow-bog, full of cowmerds and barbed wire, off route 127, and found there a largish form of *B. toddi* very abundant—in fact, I have never seen it as common anywhere in the west; unfortunately, the specimens, of which I kept a score or so, were mostly faded—and very difficult to capture, their idea of sport being to sail to and fro over the fairly tall sallows that encompassed the many small circular areas (inhabited only by *Plebeius saepiolus* Boisd. and *Polites utahensis* Skin.) into which the bog was divided by the shrubs. Another species I had never seen to be so common was *B. kriemhild* Strecker which I found in all the willow-bogs near Togwotee Pass.

In regard to *Colias* I could not discover what I wanted—which was some geographical intergradation between *C. scudderi* Reakirt, which I suggest should be classified as *C. palaeno scudderi* (Reakirt) (common everywhere in the Medicine Bow National Forest), and *C. pelidne skinneri* Barnes (locally common near Togwotee Pass and above Afton). I was struck, however, by the identical ovipositing manners of *C. scudderi* and *C. skinneri* ♀♀ which were common in the densest woods of their respective habitats, laying on *Vaccinium*. I found *C. meadi* Edw. very common on Snowy Range Pass. It was also present at timberline near Togwotee Pass and east of it, below timberline, down to 8,000 ft. alt. in willow-bogs, where it was accompanied by another usually "Hudsonian" species, *Lycaena snowi* Edw.,

[324]

the latter represented by undersized individuals. (In early July, 1951, near Telluride, Colorado, I found a colony of healthy *Colias meadi* and one of very sluggish *Pargus centaureae freija* Warren in aspen groves along a canyon at only 8,500 ft. alt.) On a slope near Togwotee Pass at timberline I had the pleasure of discovering a strain of *C. meadi* with albinic ♀♀. The species was anything but common there, but of the dozen ♀♀ or so seen or caught, as many as three were albinic. Of these my wife and I took two, hers a dull white similar to *C. hecla* "pallida," mine slightly tinged with peach (the only other time I saw a white *C. meadi* was at the base of Longs Peak, 1947, where the species was extremely abundant).

In 1949 and 1951, when collecting *Lycaeides* in the Tetons, all over Jackson Hole, and in the Yellowstone, I had found that to the north and east *L. argyrognomon* (*idas*) *longinus* Nab. turns into *L. argyrognomon* (*idas*) *scudderi* Edw. but I had not solved the problem of the *L. melissa* strain so prominent in some colonies of *L. argyrognomon longinus* (i.e. Black Tail Butte near Jackson). I had conjectured that hybridization occurs or had occurred with wandering low elevation *L. melissa* (the rather richly marked "Artemisian" *L. melissa*—probably in need of some name) that follows alfalfa along roads as *Plebeius saepiolus* does clover. In result of my 1952 quest the situation appears as follows. The most northern point where typical *L. longinus* occurs is the vicinity of Moran, seldom below 7,000 ft. alt. and up to 11,000 at least. It spreads south at those altitudes for more than a thousand miles to the southern tip of Bridger National Forest but not much further (I have not found it, for instance, around Kemmerer). I have managed to find one *L. melissa*, a fresh ♂, in August, 1952, in a dry field near Afton, less than a mile from the canyon into which both sexes of *L. longinus* descended from the woods above. At eastern points of the Bridger and Shoshone Forests, *L. longinus* stops definitely at The Rim, west of Bondurant, and at Brooks Lake (about 7,500 ft. alt.) some twenty miles west of Dubois. Very small colonies (seldom more than half-a-dozen specimens were taken in any one place) of *L. melissa* were found around Dubois at 6,500 ft. alt. or so (agricultural areas and the hot dry hills). A colony of typical (alpine) *L. melissa melissa* as described by Edwards, was found just above timberline in the Sierra Madre. The search for *L. melissa* in various windy and barren localities in the sagebrush zone in mid-July led to the finding of a rather unexpected Blue. This was *Plebeius* (*Icaricia*) *shasta* Edw., common in the parched plain at less than 7,000 ft. alt. between Saratoga and Encampment flying on sandy ground with *Phyciodes mylitta barnesi* Skinner, *Satyrium fuliginosa* Edw., and *Neominois ridingsi* Edw. It was also abundant all over the hot hills at 6,500 ft. alt. around Dubois where nothing much else occurred. I have not yet been able to compare my specimens with certain series in the Museum of Comparative Zoology, Harvard, but I suggest that this low-altitude *P. shasta* is the true *P. minnehaha* Scudder while the alpine form which I found in enormous numbers above timberline in Estes Park (especially, on Twin Sisters) and which collectors, following Holland's mislead, call "*minnehaha*," is really an undescribed race.

As to migratory species observed in Wyoming, 1952, I distinguish two groups: (1) latitudinal migrants—moving within their zones of habitat mainly in a west–east (North America) or east–west (Europe) direction and capable of surviving a Canadian Zone winter in this or that stage. Mobile, individually wandering species of *Plebeius* and *Colias* belong to this group as well as our four erratically swarming *Nymphalis* species which hibernate in the imaginal stage. In early August the trails in Bridger National Forest were covered at every damp spot with millions of N. *californica* Boisd. in tippling groups of four hundred and more, and countless individuals were drifting in a steady stream along every canyon. It was interesting to find a few specimens of the beautiful dark western form of N. *j-album* Boisd. & Lec. among the N. *californica* near Afton. (2) longitudinal migrants—moving early in the season from subtropical homes to summer breeding places in the Nearctic region but not hibernating there in any stage. *Vanessa cardui* L. is a typical example. Its movements in the New World are considerably less known than in the Old World (in eastern Europe, for instance, according to my own observations, migratory flights from beyond the Black Sea hit the south of the Crimea in April, and females, bleached and tattered, reach the Leningrad region early in June). In the first week of July, 1952, this species (offspring mainly) was observed in colossal numbers above timberline in the Snowy Range over which the first spring flock had passed on May 28, according to an intelligent ranger. A few specimens of *Euptoieta claudia* Cramer were in clover fields around Afton, western Wyoming, in August. Of *Leptotes marina* Reakirt, one ♂ was observed near Afton in August, with *Apodemia mormo* Felder and "*Hemiargus*" (*Echinargus*) *isola* Reakirt. Both *A. mormo* and *E. isola* plant very isolated small summer colonies on hot hillsides. The *H. isola* specimens, which I took also in Medicine Bow National Forest, are all tiny ones, an obvious result of seasonal environment, not subspeciation. *H. isola* (incidentally, this is not a Latin adjective, but a fancy name— an Italian noun originally—and cannot be turned into "*isolus*" to comply with the gender of the generic name, as done by some writers) belongs to a neotropical group (my *Echinargus*) with two other species: *E. martha* Dognin, from the Andes, and a new species, described by me but not named, from Trinidad and Venezuela (see *Psyche*, 52: 3–4). Other representatives of neotropical groups (*Graphium marcellus* Cramer, "*Strymon*" *melinus* Hübner, *Pyrgus communis* Grote, *Epargyreus clarus* Cramer—to name the most obvious ones) have established themselves in the Nearctic more securely than

H. isola. Among the migratory Pierids, the following were observed: single specimens of *Nathalis iole* Boisd. all over Wyoming; one worn ♂ of *Phoebis eubule* L. in the Sierra Madre (Battle Lake), July 9; one worn ♂ of *Eurema mexicana* Boisd., between Cheyenne and Laramie (and a worn ♀ near Ogallala, Neb.), first week of July.

The Lepidopterists' News,
Vol. 7, July 26, 1953, pp. 49–52.

13

AUDUBON'S BUTTERFLIES, MOTHS AND OTHER STUDIES
Compiled and edited by Alice Ford

Anyone knowing as little about butterflies as I do about birds may find Audubon's lepidoptera as attractive as his bright, active, theatrical birds are to me. Whatever those birds do, I am with them, heartily sharing, for instance, the openbilled wonder of "Green Heron" at the fantastic situation and much too bright colors of "Luna Moth" in a famous picture of the "Birds" folio. At present, however, I am concerned only with Audubon's sketchbook ("a fifteen-page pioneer art rarity" belonging to Mrs. Kirby Chambers of New Castle, Kentucky) from which Miss Ford has published drawings of butterflies and other insects in a handsome volume padded with additional pictorial odds and ends and an account of Audubon's life. The sketches were made in the 1820s. Most of the lepidoptera which they burlesque came from Europe (Southern France, I suggest). Their scientific names, supplied by Mr. Austin H. Clark, are meticulously correct—except in the case of one butter-fly, p. 20, top, which is not a *Hamaeris* but a distorted *Zerynthia*. Their English equivalents, however, reveal some sad editorial blundering: "Cabbage," p. 23, and "Miller," p.

91, should be "Bath White" and "Witch," respectively; and the two moths on p. 64 are emphatically not "Flesh Flies." In an utterly helpless account of the history of entomological illustration, Miss Ford calls Audubon's era "scientifically unsophisticated." The unsophistication is all her own. She might have looked up John Abbot's prodigious representations of North American lepidoptera, 1797, or the splendid plates of eighteenth- and early-nineteenth-century German lepidopterists, or the rich butterflies that enliven the flowers and fruit of the old Dutch Masters. She might have traveled back some thirty-three centuries to the times of Tuthmosis IV or Amenophis III and, instead of the obvious scarab, found there frescoes with a marvelous Egyptian butterfly (subtly combining the pattern of our Painted Lady and the body of an African ally of the Monarch). I cannot speak with any authority about the beetles and grasshoppers in the Sketchbook, but the butterflies are certainly inept. The exaggerated crenulation of hindwing edges, due to a naive artist's doing his best to render the dry, rumpled margins of carelessly spread specimens, is typical of the poorest entomological figures of earlier centuries and to these figures Audubon's sketches are curiously close. Query: Can anyone draw something he knows nothing about? Does there not exist a high ridge where the mountainside of "scientific" knowledge joins the opposite slope of "artistic" imagination? If so, Audubon, the butterfly artist, is at sea level on one side and climbing the wrong foothill on the other.

The New York Times Book Review,
December 28, 1952.

14

L. C. HIGGINS AND N. D. RILEY
Field Guide to the Butterflies of Britain and Europe

In my early boyhood, almost sixty-five years ago, I would quiver with helpless rage when Hofmann in his then famous *Die Gross-Schmetterlinge Europas* failed to figure the rarity he described in the text. No such frustration awaits the young reader of the marvelous guide to the Palaearctic butterflies west of the Russian frontier now produced by Lionel C. Higgins, author of important papers on Lepidoptera, and Norman D. Riley, keeper of insects at the British Museum. The exclusion of Russia is (alas) a practical necessity. Non-utilitarian science does not thrive in that sad and cagey country; the mild foreign gentleman eager to collect in the steppes will soon catch his net in a tangle of barbed wire, and to work out the distribution of Eversmann's Orange Tip or the Edda Ringlet would have proved much harder than mapping the moon. The little maps that the Field Guide does supply for the fauna it covers seem seldom to err. I note that the range of the Twin-spot Fritillary and that of the Idas Blue are incorrectly marked, and I think Nogell's Hairstreak, which reaches Romania from the east, should have been included. Among minor shortcomings is the somewhat curt way in which British butterflies are treated (surely the Norfolk race of the Swallowtail, which is so different from the Swedish, should have received more attention). I would say that alder, rather than spruce, characterizes the habitat of Wolfensberger's and Thor's Fritillaries. I regret that the dreadful nickname "Admiral" is used instead of the old "Admirable." The new vernacular names are well invented— and, paradoxically, will be more attractive to the expert wishing to avoid taxonomic controversy when indicating a species than to the youngster who will lap up the Latin in a trice. The checklist of species would have been considerably more appealing if the names of authors had not been omitted (a deplorable practice of commercial origin which impairs a number of recent zoological and botanical manuals in America).

The choice of important subspecies among the thousands described in the last hundred years is a somewhat subjective matter and cannot be discussed here. In deciding whether to regard a butterfly as a race of its closest ally or as a separate species the *Field Guide* displays good judgment in re-attaching Rebel's Blue to Alcon, and in tying up the Bryony White with the Green-veined White: anyone who has walked along a mountain brook in the Valais, the Tessin, and elsewhere must have noticed the profusion and almost comic muddle of varicolored intergrades between those two Whites. In a few cases, however, the authors seem to have succumbed to the blandishments of the chromosome count. For better or worse our present notion of species in Lepidoptera is based solely on the checkable structures of dead specimens, and if Forster's Furry cannot be distinguished from the Furry Blue except by its chromosome number, Forster's Furry must be scrapped.

In many groups the *Field Guide* accepts the generic splitting proposed by various specialists. The resulting orgy of genera may bewilder the innocent reader and irritate the conservative old lumper. A compromise might be reached by demoting the genitalically allied genera to the rank of subgenera within one large genus. Thus, for instance, a large generic group, called, say, *Scolitantides*, would include 6 subgenera (pp. 262–271 of the *Field Guide*, from Green-underside Blue to Chequered Blue) and a large generic group, called, say, *Plebejus*, would include 15 subgenera (pp. 271–311, Grass Jewel to Eros Blue); what matters, of course, is not naming or numbering the groups but correctly assorting the species so as to reflect relationships and distinctions, and in that sense the *Field Guide* is logical and scientific. On the other hand, I must disagree with the misapplication of the term "f." (meaning "form"). It is properly used to denote recurrent aberrations, clinal blends, or seasonal aspects, but it has no taxonomic standing (and available names for such forms should be quote-marked and anonymous). This the authors know as well as I do, yet for some reason they use "f." here and there as a catchall for altitudinal races and minor subspecies. Particularly odd is "*Boloria graeca balcanica* f. *tendensis*," which is actually *Boloria graeca tendensis* Higgins, a lovely and unexpected subspecies for the sake of which I once visited Limone Piemonte where I found it at about 7000 ft. in the company of its two congeners, the Shepherd's and the Mountain Fritillaries. Incidentally, the drabbish figure hardly does justice to the nacreous pallor of its underside.

These are all trivial flaws which melt away in the book's aura of authority and honesty, conciseness and completeness, but there is one fault which I find serious and which should be corrected in later printings. The explanation facing every plate should give the exact place and date of capture of every painted or photographed specimen—a principle to which the latest butterfly books rigidly adhere. This our *Field Guide* omits to do. In result the young reader will not only be deprived of a vicarious thrill but will not know if the specimen came from anywhere near the type locality, whilst the old lepidopterist may at once perceive that the portrait does not represent an individual of the typical race. Thus one doubts that the bright female of the Northern Wall Brown (Pl. 49) comes from the North, and it is a pity that the Poplar Admirable shown on Pl. 15 should belong to the brownish, blurrily banded West European sub-species rather than to the black Scandinavian type race with pure white markings.

The red-stained Corsican Swallowtail (front end-paper) is surely a printer's freak, not the artist's fancy, and no doubt will be repaired in due time. Many of Brian Hargreaves' illustrations are excellent, some are a little crude, a few are poor; all his butterflies, however, are recognizable, which after all is the essential purpose. His treatment of wing shape is sometimes wobbly, for instance in the case of the Heaths (Pl. 47), and one notes a displeasing tendency to acuminate the hind-wing margins of some Ringlets (Plates 37, 41, 44). In some groups of closely allied butterflies Nature seems to have taken capricious delight in varying from species to species the design of the hind-wing underside, thinking up fantastic twists and tints, but never sacrificing the basic generic idea to the cunning disguise. Brian Hargreaves has not always followed this interplay of thematic variations within the genus. For example, in the *Clossiana* hind-wing undersides the compact jagged rhythm of the Polar Fritillary's markings, which intensifies and unifies the Freya scheme, is weakly rendered. The artist has not understood the affinity with Frigga that dimly transpires through the design of the Dusky-winged, nor has he seen the garlands of pattern and the violet tones as connecting the Arctic Fritillary with Titania, and the latter with Dia. Otherwise, many such rarely figured butterflies as the Atlas White, the Fatma Blue, and Chapman's Hairstreak, or such tricky creatures as the enchanting Blues on Pl. 57 came out remarkably well. The feat of assembling all those Spanish and African beauties in one book is not the least glory of Higgins' and Riley's unique and indispensable manual.

Times Educational Supplement,
London, October 23, 1970

One Teacher in 10

LGBT Educators Share Their Stories

Second Edition

Edited by
Kevin Jennings

alyson books
los angeles

THIS TRADE PAPERBACK IS PUBLISHED BY ALYSON PUBLICATIONS,
P.O. BOX 4371, LOS ANGELES, CALIFORNIA 90078-4371.
DISTRIBUTION IN THE UNITED KINGDOM BY TURNAROUND PUBLISHER SERVICES LTD.,
UNIT 3, OLYMPIA TRADING ESTATE, COBURG ROAD, WOOD GREEN,
LONDON N22 6TZ ENGLAND.

ISBN 0-7394-5273-8

CREDITS
COVER PHOTOGRAPHY BY ANDY SACKS/PHOTOGRAPHER'S CHOICE/GETTY IMAGES.
COVER DESIGN BY MATT SAMS.

For Jeff,
who has been there every step of the way
for the past 10 years

Contents

Part Two
Lessons Taught...and Learned

Part Three
May–September

Part Four
Change Agent

Acknowledgments

I'd first like to thank Angela Brown of Alyson Publications, who reached out to me with the idea of doing a new collection of stories by LGBT educators on the 10th anniversary of the publication of *One Teacher in 10* by Alyson in 1994. It has been fascinating to see how times have changed, and I thank Angela and Alyson for giving me the opportunity to do this work again.

Numerous individuals and organizations helped with outreach for this collection, but one deserves special thanks: Jamison Green, through his personal arm-twisting, made sure that this anthology included the voices of transgender educators. For the second book in a row, Jamison, you have come through. Thank you!

More than anyone else, my assistant Tim Pappalardo deserves the credit for this book seeing the light of day. He has stayed on top of innumerable details, tracking the progress of the various edits of the different stories, proofing my illegible handwriting and incomprehensible two-finger typing, and generally just cheering me on when I felt like this would never get done. Thanks, Tim, you are a star.

In many ways, the changes documented in this collection are due at least in part to the work of GLSEN, the Gay, Lesbian, and Straight Education Network. I have been privileged to work with an extraordinarily dedicated group of staff, Board members, and volunteers at GLSEN for the past decade: I could never, ever say thank you enough to them for all of they have done, nor could I ever adequately express my gratitude to the extraordinarily generous individuals whose financial support has made this work possible. I want to specially thank our board president, Christie Vianson, for her leadership and support, and my deputy executive director, Eliza Byard, for whom I give thanks every day. I could not have two finer partners in leading this organization. I hope everyone associated with GLSEN is as proud as I am of what we have accomplished together.

Finally, I want to thank those who contributed their stories to this collection, especially to Judee King, who lost her battle with breast cancer shortly after submitting her story in 2004. I could never thank them enough for their bravery, their patience with the editing process, and most of all their willingness to put themselves on the firing line in defense of their students and the ideals of "liberty and justice for all" that we make students pledge allegiance to every day in our schools. We're not finished, but we're getting there.

Preface

What a difference a decade makes.

When I edited *One Teacher in 10* in 1994 it was a profoundly different time. Only two states (Massachusetts and Wisconsin) banned discrimination and harassment based on sexual orientation in their schools. There were probably fewer than 50 gay-straight student alliance clubs in the nation. Educational organizations generally wouldn't acknowledge the existence of lesbian, gay, bisexual, and transgender (LGBT) people or their concerns in schools, and LGBT organizations didn't make schools or young people much of a priority.

In this climate, most LGBT teachers adhered to the "don't ask, don't tell" policy, which governed our professional lives long before Clinton proposed it for the military. Finding enough teachers to fill a collection was a challenge. Many chose to use pseudonyms as they were too afraid to be known as LGBT in their schools or communities. While many stories in *One Teacher* did have "happy endings," those were often won at the price of considerable struggle.

Ten years later, the world has changed. A movement to make sure our schools are safe and effective educational environments for all students, staff, and families—regardless of sexual orientation or gender identity—has grown explosively throughout the United States. Today eight states (California, Connecticut, Massachusetts, Minnesota, New Jersey, Vermont, Washington, and Wisconsin) ban discrimination and harassment based on sexual orientation or gender identity in their schools. Over 2,000 gay-straight student alliance clubs are now registered with GLSEN, with at least one in every state in the nation.

Not that everything in 2004 is "all better." The 2003–2004 GLSEN National School Climate Survey found that four out of five LGBT high school students routinely experiences verbal, physical, or sexual harassment at school. But the education world is increasingly aware of this fact and more and more willing to take responsibility for doing something about it.

It is thus unsurprising that this second edition should be a very different book than the first edition was. First off, there was no problem in finding enough submissions this time: Over 100 people submitted stories, and the selection process was extraordinarily difficult due to the high quality of the submissions. The diversity of this collection is also far greater than its predecessor; there are many more voices from people of color and transgender educators.

But most of all, it is the tone of the stories that marks the greatest change. It is still not easy to be an LGBT educator, but a general sense of hope pervades the stories of this book. There are certainly still tales of struggle, but on the whole more LGBT teachers are able to be open and honest about their identities in the same way that non-LGBT teachers routinely are. There are many more "happy endings" this time around.

When I reflect on the reason for this change, one jumps out at me: the attitudes of the students themselves. While editing the collection I was struck by the number of stories in which students themselves were pushing LGBT educators to do more, in which LGBT educators were surprised to find how accepting their students were, in which the "gay thing" turned out to be much less of a big deal than the teachers had expected.

With such a diverse array of stories, it's a challenge to organize them in a way that makes sense. In an effort to help the reader navigate the many stories included herein, I have divided the stories into four major groupings:

Come Out, Come Out, Wherever You Are. While "coming out" is a feature of many of these stories, in this section it's the central theme. A diversity of individuals and settings are represented so that the reader can readily contrast educator experiences with this rite of passage.

Lessons Taught...and Learned. Many educators found themselves both teaching profound lessons to their students and, in many cases, learning such lessons from them. The stories in this section document these journeys.

May to September. Contributors were in all different stages of their careers, from rookies to retirees. The contrasting perspectives of "newbies" versus "old hands" makes for interesting reading!

Change Agents. Oftentimes contributors found themselves in leadership roles where they were leading a process of change in their schools, communities, or districts. How they found themselves in these roles and what they experienced is enlightening.

The level of dedication and professionalism among these contributors is stunning. Their commitment to the education and the lives of the students they serve shines through every story like a beacon.

No one goes into teaching for the money. In 2001 the average first-year teacher earned a salary of just under $29,000. This placed them well below the typical 2001 college graduate, who earned a first-year salary of $42,712—nearly 50% more than a first-year teacher. Add on to the low pay the struggle any LGBT person faces in a profession where homophobia is still pervasive, and you have a sense of the sacrifices the contributors to this book make daily to serve the needs of their students. In the end, people go into teaching because they want to help young people. And the contributors in *One Teacher in 10* are some of the most outstanding examples of that kind of dedication I have ever seen in our profession. Their students are lucky to have them, and it has been my privilege to work with them on this collection.

—Kevin Jennings, founder and executive director of the
Gay, Lesbian, and Straight Education Network

Prologue

CONVERSATIONS WITH JESUS
Steve Trujillo
English teacher
Skyline High School
Oakland, California

"Porque es usted un joto, Señor Trujillo?"

The words caused me a moment of discomfort, moving me from frenetic first-period preparations to freeze-frame. But only for a moment. This time. How many times would I have to deal with this question?

Jesus wanted absolution. He absolutely had to know why I was a fag. As the teacher of his U.S. history class, I was a history-making event in his eyes.

"I never had a gay teacher before."

The classroom was still mostly empty, and there were a few more minutes left before the opening of another day in 1988 at Alisal High School in Salinas, California. Before me stood Jesus, one of 35 juniors with a strong desire to learn about his newly adopted home and those people of significance in it.

Another Jesus was with me. This one I consulted daily. I was in conference with him now, while I stood with my student Jesus,

1

formulating an answer that was both honest and measured within the school district policy.

"Jesus, I know that you have many questions about why I am the way I am," I began.

As I spoke, I thought of the day I came out to my coworkers at a faculty meeting. Our administrators had decided to do a day of sensitivity training at our campus, and they'd invited a team of people to our all-day in-service to help improve faculty-administrator-student-parent relationships. Each one of us was asked to take a risk and share something personal with the staff at lunch. *OK,* I thought. *Be brave.* It was 1978, and voters had recently defeated the Briggs initiative, which would have banned gays from teaching in California. Surely Salinas was not the *most* redneck rodeo town west of the Sierras, was it? Surely we had moved forward since the John Steinbeck era…

"Jesus, I know this is confusing for you. You were raised as a good Catholic boy, like me. I knew I was gay in high school, but I couldn't talk to anybody about it. Now I can be myself, and I can talk to students who are not sure what they are or who want to know why I am the way I am. I didn't choose this way—it chose me. If you trust me as your teacher, then you know I'm the same person you knew me to be before you knew I was gay."

Which Jesus was I talking to? Maybe both.

I was the one seeking absolution this time. I remembered the day I told my coworkers my big secret. I was hoping that Jesus was listening that day as well. I needed him to hear me.

"I've wanted to share this with you for some time," I began. "I have worked here for a few years now, and most of you know who I am and what I do here. Many of you have encouraged me, and some of you have noted that I attend all evening school functions alone. You don't see any family pictures on my desk. The reason for all that would make for a rather long movie, so I will give you just the part that might appear in the trailer of coming attractions: I am gay."

I never imagined that school cafeteria could get that quiet with more than 100 live bodies in it. It appeared much like the farm-worker mural on the wall: Suspended animation. Suspension of disbelief. Suspense of anticipation.

Then, one by one, each of the staff slowly stood up and applauded. I felt as if I was being held up by an invisible presence. I felt hot, dry-mouthed, and dizzy.

Was Jesus speaking to me? Any Jesus?

After that watershed day, I knew I could talk with Jesus, Jose, Maria, or any of my students about who I am. I knew that I had moral support from different places. Maybe even places I had never seen. Places I had only heard about in Sunday school as a kid.

I was able to get my student Jesus to allow me to continue our conversation at lunch that day. Without getting graphic, or too personal, I was able to help him understand why I was a "*joto*." But I made sure windows and doors were open, for all to see and hear. My welcome mat, so to speak, was always out. Just like me.

Jesus later joined our MECHA club (which stands for Movimiento Estudiantil Chicano de Aztlan). He told me he felt at ease with me.

I hope beyond hope that any and all Jesuses will always feel the same.

Part One
Come Out, Come Out, Wherever You Are

A GOOD DAY

Joel M. Freedman
English language arts and dramatic arts teacher
King/Drew Magnet High School of Medicine and Science
South Central Los Angeles, California

This being as good a day as any to die, the little man in my head is already on heightened alert. But first there is the phone call.

"Hey, Joel." It's Judd, the former tax auditor turned teacher. It's 7:30. I only just got in the door.

"Yeah, Judd?"

"D'you get a load of what's goin' on outside?"

I had seen dense L.A. traffic coming in, a dead dog in the dirt, the brownish dinge in the sky. "No, Judd. What're you talking about?"

"There's all these parents leafleting."

"Huh? Why?" There are no pedestrians outside our school or the state-of-the-art trauma and gunshot wound wards of the King/Drew Medical Center.

"I got one of their flyers right here. They're sayin' there's an emergency meeting tonight."

"There's no emergency. It's the regular Parent Advisory Council (PAC) meeting."

He sends the flyer down to my room. Sure enough: "Emergency meeting tonight." "Our children's future is at stake." "Our sons' and daughters' education is in jeopardy." Among other assorted cryptic nonsense.

My banana from breakfast begins its own leafleting of my stomach.

Just yesterday, I'd been e-requested by our Parent Advisory Council president to address the parents at tonight's monthly meeting. I wasn't informed why. It was just last month, dusty September, when I gave my annual spiel. This is dusty October.

I have the distinction of holding the position of Title IX Coordinator. Title IX, of course, is concerned with equity for men and women in schools. Being a magnet high school without a ball field of any sort, presumably, students—actually, their parents—elect to attend our school in pursuit of science, math, and our school-to-work program with the hospital. Our staff is five-to-one women to men; gender equity is not our major diversity issue. I, therefore, deem my responsibility to provide dignity and safety for all students, sexual minorities included, and their right to a hate-free, intimidation-free, harassment-free, and a free-access-to-relevant-information education.

A former actor who maintains his propensity for drama, I take my titular roles seriously. Recently, I had broadcast throughout the school the approaching Models of Pride event, a daylong confer-ence for gay, lesbian, bisexual, transgender, and questioning youth held at Occidental College. "See Mr. Freedman for details." There's usually one parent who expresses the desire that his or her child not have to hear of such goings-on.

Homo announcements? Irate leafleting parents? Calls to arms? Coincidence? I don't think so. Neither does my principal. This is not simply a disconcerted parent on the phone. And there's only one day—a full schedule of classes and three hours, to be exact—to circle the wagons and get the cavalry in.

I start by recruiting all the colleagues I can to attend tonight's meeting and be a visible show of support. I'm asking a lot. "Stay in school till 6 o'clock for the meeting. Then stay longer."

As per instructions from the PAC president, I will be addressing the parents at this meeting. I still have no idea what I am expected to say, and I'm afraid to ask.

If we've got trouble, I shouldn't be surprised. My principal shouldn't be miffed. I'm an out gay teacher, the only one in our school (the only one out, that is); so I must be looking for trouble. Looking or not, it looks like trouble found me.

The decision to return to education at the age of 45 was made while standing on the porch of a thatched-roofed hut on stilts extended out over the South China Sea, facing Venus and the dawn sun. I simply did not want to return to L.A. and work the equivalent of three jobs for miserable pay just so I could continue to slave at my art. I was fed up. I figured I'd do something relatively easy, enjoyable, and rewarding, a job with normal work hours and appropriate pay. I'd go back to teach. That would fix everything.

What a jerk.

The overwhelming challenges of teaching notwithstanding, I knew what I was doing. I had taught all my life: swimming; reading; camp counseloring; student teaching in college; substitute teaching upon graduating with a lifetime teaching certification in Massachusetts; landing a permanent sub position, even; speakers bureau for the AIDS Coalition to Unleash Power (ACT UP); discussing anti-AIDS activism with college students and community groups.

However, at age 22, it was a breeze walking away from education to pursue theater. It was Boston, 1975, and I parted easily from a bureaucracy where the school librarian informed me that a library is not a classroom. I was witness to the frequent police activity that facilitated the busing of students from their local neighborhoods to distant places to satisfy Supreme Court demands for racial integration of public schools. The people needed armed military protection from one another, and I had to maintain tallies of how many students in each class were white, black, white Latino, black Latino, and "other."

"Tyrone Jones."

"Here." He sees I'm counting. "I'm black."

And the little man in my head is screaming, "Are you sure? How

do I know you're telling me the truth and not simply saying what you think I want to hear? How mortifying *is* this?"

I walked away before I figured out how I was going to manage being gay and a teacher. I migrated home to New York City to pursue a career in theater.

Fast-forward 23 years, and my husband of 13 years and I are returning home to L.A. from a half-year trip around the globe so that I might reenter the world of academia.

What is remarkable about my coming out in our high school is that it was unremarkable. After my first year of teaching, endeavoring to make myself indispensable, I approached my principal and told him that I was a gay teacher who considered personal disclosure an educational option. (Don't ask me how long I rehearsed that one.)

I gaped, amazed, as my principal acknowledged he had worked with many homosexual people in education. I feigned flabbergast to find that we probably have a number of students who might be gay. But what did I plan to do? Announce it to the whole school?

I honestly had no idea how I would inform students of my sexual orientation. Truthfully, it didn't seem appropriate. Certainly it has nothing to do with my job…except that, closeted, I'm working in an atmosphere much less dignified than that of my straight colleagues. Except that, without my husband and a life outside of school, I am bloodless flesh and bone to my students. Except that, if I'm closeted, my gay students have no role model, no validation of their very existence or recognition of shared experience, no adult to talk to when they have boy or girl troubles or problems at home, no place to go where they are certain they won't be negatively judged. Except that gay and lesbian family members and friends of my students are otherwise not represented or appreciated in the microcosm that is the public school.

Being out has nothing to do with my work except that, were I to be outed as gay, my prior silence would be interpreted as shame, fear, or both.

Until this discussion with my principal, I had lied to my students by omission. "No, I am not single." "I have family in San Francisco." "I'm not playing in the student-teacher basketball game due to a condition."

I'm not a very good liar. I write that not from pride; it's not due to any lack of trying. I write that because my authority in the classroom was being undermined by my vagaries. I needed to come up with a good truth, and soon.

To my principal's credit, he agreed. Dr. Ernie Roy also gave me what I think he believed to be Herculean tasks to perform first. One, come out to colleagues. Done; like, from the first day; after all, I'm from New York, I'm an atheist Jew, a leftish theatrical type, kinetic, opinionated, *and* verbose, you do the math. Two, get to know useful people in the district. An ongoing process since Day 1. Three, ingratiate myself with the parents and volunteers of the PAC. Already happening. And, four, do an in-service with teachers and staff on campus.

As a developing instructor going up before my coteachers, I set out to gather the blandest speakers I could find and sacrifice them in the least creative, least stimulating format: the one-hour panel discussion. The little man in my head was hollering, "What is wrong with you? I never agreed to a suicide pact."

Expertly proffering vital information, first-hand tales of challenges, victories, and loss, were representatives of Lambda Legal Defense; Parents, Families, and Friends of Lesbians and Gays; and the director of intergroup relations for the Los Angeles Unified School District (LAUSD). My normally comatose-at-in-services colleagues were conscious and kind to our guests. Dr. Roy even cracked a smile when I gave vent to the little man in my head by finding justification to speak the words "Damn you, Ernie."

I began coming out to students with a lesson on the impact of words, particularly epithets, created by Beverly Hills teacher Marla Weiss and published in a book of lesson plans I purchased through GLSEN-L.A. One student, daughter to the PAC vice president, stormed out of my class. Our newly appointed principal, J. Michelle Woods (a young former VP and protégé to Dr. Roy, who

groomed her for the job knowing he was losing his life to cancer), requested that I inform parents in advance of such "controversial" lessons. I wasn't happy about it, but I decided I could do that and suffer that small indignity. I also suffered a one-hour-plus phone conversation with the PAC VP mom of the storming student. Her Christian beliefs permitted her—despite herself—to allow for our differences and to recognize that, by some fluke of nature, politics, and TV programming, I had sound ethics, political correctness, law, and *Will & Grace* on my side. The daughter has since graduated, but the mom still e-mails me and greets me like an old friend.

Other results of my coming out: My husband's photo sits prominently on my desk; it seems that every one of my school's 1,643 students knows me; now and then a student will peer into my room and flee without a word; despite my being in-your-face confrontational, I still hear "shut up," "nigga," "stupid," and profanity in our classroom, but never "faggot," "dyke," or "that's so gay"; a student—or two, on occasion—will demonstrably, physically distance himself from me as if I were contagious; a sub was immediately removed from a class and banned from our school after publicly addressing one of our gay students with "What, are you gay or something?"; a parent joined me for a performance of my husband's improv and sketch comedy group, *The Gay Mafia*; books from my classroom library, many with titles that reference gay themes or information, fly from the shelves; students talk to me, some come out to me; teachers talk to me, some come out to me; my room is constantly filled with children. These are all opportunities—those elusive, enriching "teachable moments."

It gets tiresome confronting everything. On good days I respond with patience, understanding, and clarity. On less-than-good days I go Bronx on their heads. I teach in a school with a near total minority student body. Our students usually know firsthand the isolation due to stereotyping and the dehumanizing effects of discrimination. They understand when they are dignified with respect and a response.

I don't say it's been easy. When asked, I recommend to closeted teachers they cease considering coming out. From my experience, I'm going broke on antacids and aspirin. But, if the horror stories I've heard are any indication, I've been extremely lucky—until today.

Today, all day long, I teach on autopilot. "Yes, whatever I just said."

Teachers, if you prepare well for class and have a little man (or woman) in your head, you don't have to think about what you're doing or what you're saying. You can conduct your lesson while simultaneously planning for your retirement, figuring out the meaning of life, or rehearsing what you are going to say to the villagers when they arrive at the schoolhouse door waving pitchforks and flaming torches.

Immediately upon classes ending, I meet with my principal and a vice principal. We strategize how we will handle the vitriolic tirades of homophobic parents. We are basically on our own. The director of intergroup relations for our school district was appropriately sympathetic, though regrettably unavailable to attend our meeting; he cried audibly to me at his inability to reschedule the detailing of his SUV. My contact at LAUSD's celebrated Project 10, also unable to attend, fortified me by insisting I had legal might and moral right on my side, then promised to light a candle on my behalf.

And so…into the meeting.

The PAC monthly meeting, traditionally lightly attended, has managed on this night to pack the lecture hall. There is a cadre of more than one dozen of my colleagues present. My informant, Judd, the former tax auditor turned teacher, is not one of them. He's comfortable being the harbinger of bad news but doesn't have the guts to stick it out.

Some people stand up, move around, say things. None of it registers with me. The little man in my head is howling, "Get me out of here."

And, then, "Mr. Freedman, if you please." *That* I hear just as the little man in my head clams up.

I rise. My upper lip's the size of a walnut. With the sharpest canines in all humanity, I had repeatedly chomped down on it

during lunch. I still don't know what I'm expected to say. I'd been looking for a sign all day to no avail.

I mechanically go into my spiel, the same one I gave a month ago. "We here at King/Drew are committed...blah, blah, blah...regardless of race, religion, ethnicity, gender, sexual orientation, abilities either physical or mental, real or perceived...blah, blah, blah...blah, blah, blah, blah, blah...any questions?"

A hand goes up. Here it comes. The little man in my head is howling, "No-o-o."

"Yes?"

"How do we go about getting rid of a teacher?" And, of course, she's looking straight at me. The little whimpering man in my head quakes as he attempts to hide.

Huh? Uh. I don't know. Catch me in a sting operation? Offer me any job with respectable pay and reasonable hours? Explain to me the Amway Opportunity? Tell me "Shoo, go away"?

"There is a certain protocol..." This is my principal Mrs. Woods stepping in.

But the lady's not done. "He's failing my daughter. He's throwing chairs in the classroom. How does he do his grading? I really don't know."

Intrepid Mrs. Woods again: "This is a matter for private discussion. We have a rule whereby we don't speak of individual concerns in this public forum..."

Wait a second. This isn't about me.

"No, you hold on," someone else pipes in, "we've been trying to get rid of this guy for two years—"

Another lady has found her courage, "He's ruined my child's chances of going to a decent college."

There is cacophony of voices concurring and personalizing their concerns.

This is not about me. This is about Judd—the former tax auditor turned teacher.

"Joel. Get over here," mentor teacher Yvonne is hissing at me. "Sit your fool ass down."

I make like a Slinky going down stairs by pouring myself into my chair as all hell breaks loose. I leave Mrs. Woods to the lions. I am gloriously uninvolved.

Uninvolved, yet I get to continue to introduce students to the work of some of my gay and lesbian brothers and sisters: Sor Juana Inés de la Cruz, Walt Whitman, Emily Dickinson, Claude McKay, Langston Hughes, Countee Cullen, Hart Crane, Thornton Wilder, Aaron Copland, Samuel Barber, Willa Cather, W.H. Auden, Tennessee Williams, James Baldwin, Adrienne Rich, Anne Sexton, Lorraine Hansberry, Edward Albee, Audre Lorde, Alice Walker, Samuel Delaney, Robert Patrick, Richard Rodriguez, Jacqueline Woodson, Essex Hemphill, to name a few. I hesitate, at times, to mention their sexual orientation in class ("You say that about everybody, Mr. Freedman,") and sometimes I don't, for fear of appearing biased.

Five years teaching some of the finest and funniest youngsters in the nation. Five years learning from some of the most talented educators in the country. Fifty years of age. Eighteen years in love. Extraordinary good fortune and good health—I'd say it's a good day to be gay.

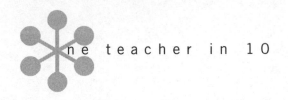

IF ELLEN CAN DO IT, SO CAN I

Patricia A. Nicolari
Health and PE teacher, administrator for alternative education
Ansonia High School
Ansonia, Connecticut

It was April of 1997 when Ellen DeGeneres came out on TV. There I was, at a New Haven restaurant, surrounded by other like-minded individuals who were equally thrilled about watching Ellen's brave step, when a photographer from the *New Haven Register* announced her presence. She was covering the *Ellen* episode and would be taking pictures; she would respect our wishes, however, if we didn't want to be photographed. One by one people stepped forward in fear, pleading to her to remember their face and not take their picture. These people included doctors, lawyers, and teachers. I sat back and silently observed.

After 15 years of teaching at Ansonia High School, the high school I had also attended as a student in the 1970s, I was exhausted by the energy it took to hide my sexual orientation. I was tired of pretending to be someone else, tired of dodging cameras, tired of not answering uncomfortable questions from teachers and students, and tired of losing respect for myself. So I decided to come out. I wasn't sure how or when this would happen, but I knew I was ready to let go of the fear and energy it took to hide. I saw the fear in those people the night of the *Ellen* episode and I knew I could not continue my teaching career in fear. I just wanted to teach.

In September of 1996 I requested a fireside chat with my

boss. Although it was her first year as principal, I needed to share with her that I was gay. I wasn't asking her permission to come out—I was simply wondering if I had her support, and it turned out I did. Like many others she suspected I was gay but had never hinted at such.

It felt reassuring to know the principal was in my corner. Of course I didn't know at that time how I would come out, but I knew if it felt right, I was ready.

In hindsight, I knew I was getting my ducks in a row and testing the waters. How safe was my school environment? Who would be my support system? When the topic of homosexuality came up in my classroom, I stopped discouraging discussion. If a student called someone a fag or a dyke, I addressed it—something I'd been afraid to do when I was in the classroom closet.

For 15 years as an "in" teacher, I lived in fear of being "found out." I lived with this silent, "less than" feeling. Occasionally situations would occur that would magnify this feeling. One afternoon I had a student after school serving a detention—and detentions always turned into a "what's going on in your life" discussion. He told me he had real problems at home. When I asked if he was comfortable enough to share them with me, he responded with disgust: "I have a mother who is lesbian, Ms. Nic, a *lesbian!*" He was so distraught. As a lesbian trying to conceal my own identity, I could only muster up an "It could always be worse" response. To this day I wonder the difference it would have made in his life if I could have had the strength to say, "Well, Tommy, I too am a lesbian. I know you respect me as your teacher; let's talk."

I had another student stop by my room many times after school; she was struggling to understand her sexual orientation yet appeared quite confident in doing so. As much as I wanted to be a support for her, she raised my anxiety level with her strong sense of self. Consequently, I always pretended to be busy, shuffling papers and avoiding her eyes. The reality that I couldn't be a support system for *all* of my students—especially the LGBTQ students—was taking its toll on me. My own homophobia was a

self-imposed barrier that I didn't know how to break.

Unfortunately, students seem to have the power when a teacher has something to hide. I now know that I gave them that power. When I was on stage in front of the entire school hosting the school-wide talent show, I was anxious that a student might shout, "Get off the stage, you dyke!" After the show I would ask another colleague, who is also a lesbian, if she heard anyone say anything about me being gay.

As I entered my freshman health class in September of 1986, I found a note on my desk. The note said "We, the freshman class, want to know if it is true that you are gay?" While 28 students sat quietly observing me as I read this anonymous note, I listened to the inner dialogue. *Please, face, don't turn red, or for sure you will look like you are gay. Just relax, be calm, and pretend it is a joke. Should I address it or ignore it?* I decided to pretend it was a joke. "Who wrote this note?" I asked. "Oh, come on now, there are always rumors about teachers. Let's now turn to page 125." I had extreme difficulty focusing on any health lessons that day.

At the end of school one winter day, I walked out to my car to check out the work that the boys from shop had completed. As I approached the car I saw LES scratched into the entire side door panel. My heart raced, my head pounded, and I thought, "How could I drive this car around?"

When I brought it up to the shop teacher, he looked at me with this shocked expression and asked why the kids would do that. So I let it go. It took too much energy to pursue; along with the risk of exposing too much of myself, it wasn't worth it.

Another day, I unfortunately intercepted a note from another student in a health class. The note said, "No wonder she likes teaching PE; this way she can check out all the girls in the locker room." Honestly, I felt my character was being defamed in the eyes of my students because of my sexual orientation. How could I ever let them know that being gay has nothing to do with one's character? I felt so alone, and so alone in this harassment.

Faculty rooms didn't offer me much respite either. One day

during lunch, a veteran teacher of 32 years walked in, saying, "Hey, how about that three-dollar bill we had presenting at yesterday's professional development workshop? If he said he was gay one more time I was going to leave." Some other teachers laughed along with him. I am embarrassed to admit this, but I may have even smiled along with the joke.

Another teacher would joke with his students about wearing green on Thursdays. "Don't you know, if you wear green on Thursdays, you must be gay?" As innocent as he thought this statement was, he didn't know that on Thursdays I would make sure not to wear green. I felt so incredibly unsafe.

Feeling brave one day, I did bring my struggle up to the principal at that time. She seemed extremely uncomfortable when I told her about the harassment and could offer no direction other than, "Just try to ignore it and don't let it get to you..." and "Why would they be saying that?" Of course I could not say: Because it is true.

I began to question whether or not I could keep teaching. Would I always face this harassment? All this was happening without my students knowing for sure that I am gay. What would I face if I actually came out? What support systems did I have? There were other gay teachers in my building, but they were just as persecuted as I was. I began to feel hopeless.

So when a position for a K–3 "self-esteem teacher" was created, it seemed just for me. My six years of hearing myself attempting to impress upon my high school students the value of feeling good about "who you are" finally caught up with me: If I wasn't feeling good about who I was because I was hiding a part of my identity, how could I expect my students to feel good about who they were? I just wasn't practicing what I was preaching.

Upon my return to teaching at the high school—six years later, in 1996—I felt more confident. But I was still paranoid about my sexual orientation when I was at school. I wanted to let go of this extra negative energy, but how?

That April 1997 night provided the answer. It must have been

fate that landed me on the front page of the morning newspaper. I hadn't dodged the camera like so many others had that evening. When the photographer perched herself in front of me, finally, I was ready for some controversy. And now I had it: There I was, smack in the middle of the group cheering away as we watched the events unfold. The headline read, "Ellen's Out, Gays Hail Historic Night."

Since my father was the former superintendent of schools in Ansonia, and my mom was in real estate there as well, I wanted to tell them about this before people approached them with the news. So at 6 A.M. we had a conversation about how my day might unfold. My parents and three sisters were fearful of what I might encounter in a homophobic world. They warned me that if I had a negative experience, I couldn't change my mind and say I was only kidding. My youngest sister said that I should tell people I'd just been out with some gay people, that I was not gay.

Throughout the years people always warned me not to disclose my sexual orientation, especially in a town like Ansonia, which many felt was not very progressive. So in all honesty, I did fleetingly consider using my 162 accumulated sick days. In the end, however, I decided I'd already spent far too much of my professional life in fear.

On the way to work I saw every newspaper box with my picture in it. My heart was racing. As I entered the main office, I could sense that the secretaries, along with the teachers present, did not know how to handle this awkward situation. I was sure they wondered if Ms. Nic had gotten "caught" and been outed in the paper? As their eyes looked elsewhere, anywhere but at me, I sensed their silence was out of respect. So I took the bull by the horn and said, "Hey, did anyone see this morning's paper? Ellen is out and so is Ms. Nic, and it feels great!" A few came up and hugged me, asked me a few questions, and we laughed; and it did feel great. Just then the principal, who had not yet seen the morning paper, said, "Why is everyone so gay this morning?" As our laughs grew even louder, I responded, "I don't know about the others being gay, but this teacher is." Then I left to continue on my new journey as an out teacher.

The first student to address the photo said, "Hey, Ms. Nic, was that your picture on the front of this morning's paper?" With 10 other students listening as they filed into an English class I said, "Yes, it is, Christy." With her thumbs up, she responded with the ubiquitous high school phrase, "Cool." I walked away with tears in my eyes, wondering where Christy found the strength to give me her approval in front of her peers. Later that day Christy told me her aunt is gay, something I had not known.

Upon entering the media center, I noticed the newspapers were not in the usual place, out on the counter. When I asked the media specialist where that day's *New Haven Register* was, she said, "Oh, are you sure you want them out?" Confidently I responded, "Yes, I have waited 15 years for this day, *please* put them out." As we continued our discussion, she hugged me, as did another teacher who was privy to the conversation.

One boy, upon entering our health issues class, stopped to quietly warn me that this class was going to be tough on me. He said the discussion about my sexual orientation in the previous class had some students in it who were going to give me a hard time. He also said, "Ms. Nic, did you know my mother is gay?" I was surprised by his admission, especially considering the vulnerable environment my classroom was about to become. He continued, "Well, she thinks you are very cute and wants to know if you are single." I told him to tell his mother that I was flattered but that I was already in a relationship. Another student stood in the hallway telling me—loud enough for all to hear—that his sister is a lesbian and she lives with her life partner in Florida, and if anybody gives me a hard time to let him know about it. He was a popular football player, and his allegiance to his sister, and his teacher, was admirable.

Once the bell rang and class began, I knew I had to be strong, not only for myself but for the student who had to remain silent about his own mother being a lesbian. The football player felt he

could talk openly about his sister, but many others have not yet reached that level of empowerment to share about a gay relative. The more confidently I handled this situation, the better they might feel about themselves. I knew that my coming out broke the barriers and gave people permission to—whether privately or in public—share with me about their gay relatives or themselves. The school was feeling safer for me, and I'm sure it was for others as well.

Former students stopped by school that day to say congratulations. The superintendent called to offer her support and to ask how I was holding up. The president of the board of education came to my class to inquire about my well-being and offered her support as well. I came out to each class that day, and more students came out to me about their relatives who are gay. Some teachers approached me and quietly disclosed that they suspected their child might be gay and wished they came to this school so they could have me for a teacher. Other colleagues shared about their gay relatives. My buddy in the gym, Gennaro, a strong Italian with conservative views, hugged me and offered to cover my classes if I was having a difficult time.

This all happened in a six-hour school day. It was such an emotional high yet totally draining. All the fear I had bottled up for 15 years was now being released. If I had known the support would be so overwhelming, I would never have wasted so much time.

That day I went home in tears—tears of relief. When I called my dad and shared my stories, I could hear his tears of relief as well. I also contacted the reporter at the *New Haven Register* to let him know that I appreciated his story of the *Ellen* event, and that I thought the photo was in good taste. My appreciation was especially personal, I told him, because I'd come out today at my high school as a result of his work. There was silence at the other end. He was amazed that, as a teacher, I'd allowed myself to be photographed. In his quick reporter mode, he asked if I would be willing to let them do a follow-up story. I told him I needed time to think about that.

After asking the opinion of family, friends, and colleagues—who all advised me against it—I called back and said yes. I had learned to let my own intuition be my guide. I felt that a picture of the high school substance-abuse teacher at a bar surrounded by people with beer bottles didn't best represent me. This was an opportunity to attach a story to my picture, and I did.

With an entire page dedicated to "Today's Woman," my coming out of the classroom closet story was beautifully captured in the *New Haven Register*. The title of the article read, "Thanks to Ellen, Ms. Nic found the courage to come out the same night DeGeneres did."

The weeks that followed, I had received phone calls from radio stations wanting to do interviews, letters from teachers all around Connecticut telling me they wished they could come out at their school, a call from Robin Roberts from *20/20* interested in doing a segment, and public TV wanting an interview. It was hard to comprehend that all this was happening simply because I said I am gay. I quietly thought, *It will be nice when it is not newsworthy simply because a teacher is gay.*

After coming out in 1997 I became a GLSEN Connecticut member when I stumbled upon their booth at a conference. Shortly thereafter, I became a board member, then cochair. (Those involved with GLSEN know how quickly this transition occurs.) I was now developing and presenting teacher training seminars on creating safe school environments for all students regardless of sexual orientation or gender identity/expression throughout schools in Connecticut.

I also developed workshops for LGBT educators titled "Educator's Empowerment." I have presented this workshop for GLSEN National at the Teaching Respect for All conferences as well as at the Boston and Connecticut conferences. Hearing concerns and questions and sharing fears about coming out from teachers and administrators in Atlanta, Los Angeles, Boston, Chicago, and Connecticut is powerful stuff. No workshop ever ended without tears. Often I would get an e-mail from a teacher after these workshops telling me they came out on the Monday

morning after their return to school, and they were elated.

Teachers who come out usually feel like a more complete human being. Being more complete impacts our teaching, which in turn impacts students. It is a powerful ripple effect that changes the school climate.

Coming out is a powerful transition. It allows you to be in control by taking the power away from others. I can now confidently handle any situation that comes my way regarding LGBT issues. Every September with a new freshman class is another opportunity for "teachable moments." When a student asked me during freshman homeroom what I did with my boyfriend this weekend, I calmly stated, "I don't have a boyfriend, but I went to the movies with my girlfriend." The class was speechless. I asked how many were shocked by that information; not one student raised their hand. Unassumingly one girl said, "I already knew you were gay; I was just shocked you said it." Then the student who had asked about my boyfriend confessed that he'd known I was gay, he just wanted to see my reaction.

We now have a GSA (gay-straight alliance) at our high school. Our first project was the Day of Silence, with 107 students out of 650 and 10 teachers out of 45 participating. No longer do teachers make inappropriate comments about being gay. No longer will I remain silent if they do.

I am now part of a support system for all students, including LGBT students or those with a gay relative. As an out teacher I have released my fears; I will be fine. I was even selected for Teacher of the Year for the 2004 school year and hired in March as the administrator for the alternative education program. It is my hope that someday all teachers and students feel comfortable coming out. It is my hope that one day GLSEN will not need to exist because its mission will have been accomplished.

THE MARRIAGE QUESTION

Brian Davis

Seventh and eighth grade language arts and social studies teacher

Claire Lilienthal School

San Francisco, California

"Mr. Davis, are you married?" asked the saucy eighth grader, eyeing my bear fetish ring on the telltale finger.

"No," I replied, unthinkingly giving the correct legal answer.

Thus suddenly arrived and rapidly departed the first opportunity to come out to my students at my new school. My resolve to not miss any chance to reveal my sexual orientation was momentarily derailed due to my confusion about how to answer this unexpected and, for me, complex question.

I had been prepared to answer the "Are you gay?" question with a calm and confident "Yes," but somehow I had never prepared to answer the marriage question. Throughout my previous four years, during the late 1990s at three tough inner-city middle schools in the San Francisco Unified School District, I had never had a student ask about my marriage status.

I had occasionally faced the "Are you gay?" question from some class disrupter who wanted to embarrass me. Always on those occasions I had stuck with the standard party line recommended to me by every teacher, counselor, or administrator, gay or straight: "That's a personal question. Personal questions are inappropriate…" The equivalent, if I were to judge by the students' faces, of: "Yes, I am gay,

but I don't want you to know about it. So I'm avoiding the question."

I was cautious partly because, as a long-term substitute teacher for my first three years, I could theoretically be fired on a moment's notice for any reason. ("Long-term substitute" was a designation formerly used by my district to keep the "dime a dozen"—as one administrator interviewer once referred to us—fully credentialed language arts and social studies teachers from gaining any job security, despite our regular classroom status.)

Now, I know what you're thinking: *He was teaching in San Francisco, the land wrapped up in the rainbow, and he was afraid of being fired for being gay?*

What you have to realize is that many of the students and parents at these schools were anything but supportive of LGBT issues. But if I made an issue out of this, given my tenuous employment status, I was afraid I might rile up enough parents that the principal would find some excuse other than my sexuality to get rid of me just to avoid the hassle. I was also reluctant to be open because these students were often difficult to control under the best of circumstances, and I didn't want to do anything that could potentially make things worse.

However, when I became a probationary teacher at the start of my fourth year, which was also my first chance to teach at the same school for a second year in a row, I began to seriously consider opening up to my students. That year I had the misfortune of being assigned an extremely difficult group of seventh graders. I was not alone in this regard. Teachers who had been there for 30 years said that student behavior was the worst they had ever seen. Students frequently made both thinly veiled and completely unveiled insinuating comments. MR. DAVIS IS GAY appeared on the side of a desk and on the blackboard on two separate occasions.

I addressed the issue, of course, discussing the Matthew Shepard murder, doing antislur activities, but I continued to stick to the party line regarding my own sexuality, despite the knowing look in their eyes.

When I consulted a trusted colleague, asking if I should come out, she felt that I should consider what my motivations were—was I wanting to do it for myself or for my students? At the time I wasn't sure how to answer that. I knew that I felt dishonest, and that I could not expect students to open up to me if I concealed such an important part of my identity. For some reason I was not able to recognize the real reason I needed to come out—so that I could be a positive role model for LGBT students. Perhaps this was because I wasn't sure whether they were capable of seeing me in a positive light at this point. At any rate, I decided to finish the year unrevealed. But I did finish the year, which I considered quite an accomplishment, under the circumstances.

Feeling burned out, I decided to take a year's leave to look into other career options. During this time, I spent much of my time volunteering on a campaign to legalize same-sex marriage in California, which reaffirmed my commitment to teach the public that those of us in the queer community are ordinary people deserving of equal rights and respect. The slogan I wrote, which the organization adopted—"Marriage: Anything Less Is Less Than Equal"—sums up my perspective on this issue.

I decided that I would return to the district only if I could find a job in a less challenging environment. As much as I wanted to work with the kids who needed the most help, I knew that I couldn't survive in that kind of school any longer. Fortunately I found work at a K–8 "alternative" school with a more manageable student population. I knew that I had come to a different place when, during a discussion about racial discrimination related to a story we were reading early on in my seventh-grade language arts class, I asked whether they could describe other kinds of discrimination, and a pair of students spoke about gay friends of their parents in a positive way. I also loved my new principal, had good relations with other staff members and parents, and I had finally gained tenure, so it seemed that the time and the place were finally right for my students to find out that they had a gay teacher.

I decided that I didn't want to make a big deal out of coming out because I wanted the message to be that my being gay was a

totally normal everyday thing, rather than some kind of terrible secret that needed to be couched in an air of dramatic revelation. I have since come to a different conclusion, as I will discuss later, but at the time I felt that this particular school in San Francisco in the new millennium was ready for this kind of casual approach.

I had hoped that I would one day make an offhand comment to the students along the lines of "My partner and I went to a movie the other day…" but somehow the words wouldn't leave my lips. Next I decided that I would wait for the inevitable "Are you gay?" question, but I had not counted on the less-predatory nature of my new students. The question never came.

After the aforementioned eighth grader caught me off guard with the marriage question, I considered how I would answer if given another opportunity. "No" was not a truthful answer since my partner, Ted, and I had been together longer than these students had been alive and were married in every way but legally. "Yes" was also untrue, as we did not have a marriage license. Eventually I came up with an answer that I thought would do the trick.

My opportunity finally arrived. During a semiprivate moment on a field trip, a seventh-grade girl (the product of a racially mixed marriage) inquired, "Are you married, Mr. Davis?"

"In a way," I replied cagily.

After looking at me curiously for a moment, she followed up with "What are you, then?"

"I'm domestic partnered."

"Oh. What's his name?"

"Ted."

"How old is he?"

"Thirty-one."

This seemed to satisfy her curiosity. Just as I'd hoped, it had been very relaxed. An ordinary conversation.

Word spread quickly at our small school. The next day two students came up to me independently and asked if I was gay. When I said yes they nodded and smiled. One exclaimed, "Cool!"

Only one student sought to taunt me with this new information:

a sixth-grade girl, whom I knew to be a troublemaker, waited in ambush for me in the schoolyard at the end of the day. Just as I was about to exit the yard on my bicycle I caught her out of the corner of my eye as she shouted: "Are you gay?!"

I turned my bike around, rode up to where she was hiding behind a lunch table, evidently expecting a tongue-lashing, and simply stated, "Yes, I'm gay." I then wished her a good afternoon and went on my way.

I wish I could say that we all lived happily ever after, but unfortunately that was not the case. Three times during the last three years I have found the word FAG written on or in my classroom—two of those times were just this past year. The most recent occasion was on the second-to-last day of school, written on the outside of my bungalow door.

I have taught the students that the word *faggot* originally referred to a bundle of sticks used for kindling, and that during the middle ages when women accused of witchcraft were burned at the stake, sometimes men accused of homosexuality were covered in oil and used to start the fire, thereby serving as the kindling or "faggot." "So when you call someone a fag you are saying that they deserve to be burned alive," I tell them in the hope that this will impress upon them the horrific evil of the word.

Yet this last incident has opened my eyes to the reality that my casual "Yeah, I'm gay. So what?" attitude, an occasional discussion or article related to the subject once or twice a year, a yearly visit to the health class by members of a gay speakers bureau, and a general air of tolerance for all groups that are discriminated upon in our society is not enough to completely defeat the ingrained homophobia that still persists among some of the best-educated children in this most enlightened of cities.

So during the summer I contacted Kevin Gogin and Olivia Higgins at the Support Services for Sexual Minority Youth and the School Health Programs Department, the dedicated people who provide the LGBT education services in our district. With their help, I became the Sexual Minority Youth Liaison for my school,

which means that signs are posted in every classroom letting kids know that I am there if they need to talk about issues of sexual orientation. My new responsibility also requires me to start a "diversity club," which I have begun with the help of the after-school program coordinator, and to organize Violence Prevention Month and gay pride. I am also a resource for my fellow teachers, providing them with age-appropriate materials to help them teach students to understand and respect LGBT people.

And so the school year began. Now once again I was faced with a new version of the age-old question: How and when would I come out to this new batch of students? And how could I do it in a way that would help them not only to understand and respect LGBT people, but also to make valuable connections to their own lives so that the message would sink in? I had an idea about how to approach it, but I needed a catalyst, something that would set the proper tone and help pave the way.

Fortunately, Olivia had recommended a novel called *The Misfits* by James Howe, the main characters of which are all different in some way from their seventh-grade peers. One of them, Joe, is an out and proud gay boy, who improbably but wonderfully finds that the boy he has a crush on likes him too. Together, the group of outcasts start a campaign to stop name-calling at their school.

Each of my seventh graders read this book, and we discussed the issues it raised. When one of my classes started an impromptu discussion about whether people are born gay or lesbian, I knew that the time had come to make my big speech.

"Today I have something to tell you about myself," I began. "I'm a misfit too. I'm a misfit in the same way as Joe. I'm gay.

"Now, my experience was different from Joe's. When I was a teenager during the '70s I didn't accept myself the way he does. When I was growing up the only gay people I knew about were the men marching in the gay pride parade wearing dresses that I would see for a few moments on the news. I thought that that was what it meant to be gay, and since I had no interest in wearing dresses I thought that I was some kind of freak that didn't belong anywhere.

"Everything around me told me that it was wrong to like boys, and that I was supposed to like girls. So from around the time when I was about 11 to around 21 I would go to bed every night wishing that in the morning I would wake up attracted to girls instead of boys.

"But eventually I came to realize that I was not alone, that gay men and lesbian women were all different kinds of people, most of whom were like me: just like everyone else in every way except that we are emotionally attracted to people of the same sex. I came to accept and celebrate who I was instead of fearing and hating my feelings because society had taught me that what I was was 'wrong.'

"Then I met a man that I now share my life with. We held a commitment ceremony that all of our friends and family members attended. We've been together for 16 years now.

"Now, I'm not telling you this because I have some need to unburden myself to you. I am telling you this because I want you to have what I didn't have: a gay role model, a successful, respected member of the community whom you know personally and whom you can't stereotype or easily dismiss as some kind of oddball but whom you are getting to know as a fully rounded individual.

"I am also telling you this to make it very clear that I will not allow anyone to use the word *fag* or *gay* as an insult in this class, just as I will not allow anyone to use words which insult people of different races, cultural backgrounds, genders, religions, or abilities.

"I am also telling you this because I want the children in this classroom who have family members or friends who are lesbian or gay to know that their families will be respected in this room.

"Also, statistically speaking, about one in 10 people all over the world are lesbian, gay, bisexual, or transgender, and so, statistically, there are students in this school who are, or someday will be, dealing with this issue. I want those students to know that they are safe here.

"I am saying to all of you that no matter what kind of misfit you are, whether you think you are overweight, or too short, or not good-looking enough, or anything that makes you feel different, be

proud of who you are. Don't let anyone tell you that you aren't a good person, or that you have to be something that you aren't. Be proud to be yourself. That's my message to you today."

This particular class applauded heartily when I finished, and I spent the rest of the period answering some very insightful questions about my experiences and opinions. The responses of the other classes, when I gave them the same speech, ranged from enthusiasm to indifference, but I felt that I had done all I could to come out in a way that would connect with their lives and help them to understand and respect LGBT people.

As you might expect, I got a little flack from parents for this. I heard from some supportive parents that there had been "discussions" among the parents about me, and one parent wrote a very detailed anonymous letter to the principal demanding that I be reprimanded. My principal was very supportive and gave a great deal of her valuable time helping make certain that nothing came of this.

Out of all of this has also come what for me is a rather astonishing thing. Throughout my teaching career I have always had difficulty feeling truly relaxed and comfortable around my students. There has always been a distance between us, which I believed to be because of the needs of classroom discipline and my demanding academic requirements.

Yet suddenly, I have become aware that the wall separating my students from me has disappeared, even though the need for discipline and my high academic expectations remain. Now, for the first time ever, I am able to laugh and joke with my students without feeling awkward. I am my naturally silly self with them, and they have responded by showing affection in return.

Why has this finally happened during my eighth year of teaching? There may be many reasons, yet I cannot help but think that finally opening up to them fully, baring my heart to them without fear or restraint, might have something to do with it. I feel confident and secure with my students in a way I've never felt before. I no longer have to be afraid that something I say will trigger a raised eyebrow and a question that I don't feel ready to answer.

Ironically, it may be the act of opening up, perhaps more than the message itself, which will hopefully keep someone from writing FAG on my wall again. But if someone does, I will know that it isn't in any way because I have failed to do everything I can to prevent it.

*

The preceding was written during 2003. It is now late February 2004 and Ted and I are legally married! On February 12 we went to the annual Valentine's Day protest at San Francisco City Hall: A group of us ask for marriage licenses; they say no; we demonstrate and make speeches. Except, as everyone now knows, this year they said yes, and we were among the first 20 same-sex couples in the country to be officially wed. We were stunned and overjoyed.

Afterward, I told my students about it, but it turned out many of them had already seen me on the news. Parents have been coming up to me every day since to offer their congratulations. I have told the students that we are living in truly historic times, and that is how it feels, like we are being carried along in an unstoppable flood of freedom and equality.

And so the marriage question can finally be answered, with no ambiguity or asterisks attached. The struggle for true equality is just beginning, of course, both inside and outside of the classroom. Hopefully, someday in the near future, when a student asks if I am married, and I answer "Yes, to a man," every middle schooler in the room will have the same thought: "Whatever. Big deal."

LIVING SIMPLY AND OPENLY

Kathleen Crawford
Math teacher, drama teacher
Jefferson County public schools
Louisville, Kentucky

I think the biggest reason I became a teacher is because I knew if I did, I would never stop learning. In college I could not decide on one specific content area to major in, and I would routinely take 18–19 hours each semester because I enjoyed the coursework and academic environment. I loved to read and spend time pondering, sharing great thoughts in study groups, and quoting Ralph Waldo Emerson: "What lies behind us, and what lies before us, are tiny matters compared to what lies within us."

I was so young, yet I thought I was so wise. Ha! As I have grown older—I've taught for 19 years now—I've realized that academic work is a tiny matter compared to the life experiences on my journey. So, if I may borrow from the *Gilligan's Island* theme song, "Now, sit right back and you'll hear a tale…"

During the summer of 2001, I realized, accepted, and embraced the fact that I am a lesbian.

When I look back on my life, I know that I felt those first inklings in junior high, but I was a tomboy and athletic and it was the mid '70s, so I just didn't pay too much attention to those feelings. I viewed the boys in the neighborhood and at school mostly as competitors. I was determined to always show them up in one way or another. I don't remember having true feelings for them—though I "played" that I did. I enjoyed my friendships with girls and remember having crushes; but in that time of innocence, I thought of those feelings as admiration. I did have a fascination with Wonder Woman's background as an Amazon princess. I remember fantasizing about a world, a community of strong and beautiful women. But I never consciously thought of myself as homosexual. Whenever the topic of homosexuality came up, it was typically something joked about or talked about in hushed tones.

Back then, I didn't spend much time concerned about what I was feeling. I just sort of went along with what was considered "acceptable" and "normal." So I finished my undergraduate degree and married a nice guy. I was drawn to his gentle manner, plus he was not macho and condescending like so many guys I had met and known. I wanted children and a good life.

But there was an emptiness deep within me.

To fill this void, I developed a pattern of throwing myself into things, learning as much as I could, and getting very involved in my children, work, church, and personal development. This culminated after attending an educational conference in 1998, when I seized a new venture that came my way—writing, editing, consulting, and new professional opportunities with a Catholic publishing house. I cut back to part-time teaching at the Catholic high school where I'd been employed for the past 11 years.

The world had opened up! I was learning and growing so much in my new work and meeting some amazing people. Over the course of three years, I grew very close to one amazing person in particular, the design director at the publishing company. We clicked intellectually from the very beginning. I often traveled on business to Minnesota, where she lived. Over the course of time, we began carving out time for just the two of us, and so our emotional and spiritual connection grew. The friendship was pure joy.

However, it was still a big surprise when I realized that I was falling in love with this amazing woman, Cindi.

Neither one of us were consciously aware of what was happening when we dove deeply into an intimate, whole, and connected relationship. However, when the physical dimension developed,

everything made sense to me. I had never known what it was like to feel so whole, so complete, so *me*. I realized that I was a lesbian.

By this time, Cindi and I had fallen in love. We wanted to spend the rest of our lives loving each other. It sounds simple; it seems like a fairy tale and the beginning of a beautiful love story. But to get to what our vision of a relationship would be, it was not going to be easy because of what we not-so-jokingly called the "practicalities." We were colleagues at a Catholic publishing company. I had been teaching at a local Catholic high school for 11 years. I loved my classes and my students. We were both women with heterosexual pasts. I was in a 15-year marriage and had three kids. We knew that if we were to really be together, both of us would need to find new jobs. This would mean Cindi leaving Minnesota and moving 600 miles to Kentucky. Not your typical love story.

One October afternoon as we walked, I was keenly aware that we were choosing what was choosing us. She said, "We'll live it simply and openly."

I looked into my beloved's blue eyes and repeated what she had said. "Yes, we'll live it simply and openly."

Two weeks later, after we made the commitment to live *it*—our lesbian relationship—simply and openly, the major life changes began. We knew that it would mean some painful situations and endings in our lives, but the seven months between that late October and May were more difficult than I had imagined. I came out to a husband, three children (then ages 13, 11, 8), friends, and family. And it was not an accepting and positive experience. I heard the most hateful things.

The following month, while I was on a business trip, my ex-husband scheduled a meeting and outed me to an administrator at the Catholic school where I taught. When I got back to town I had a conversation with the assistant principal that was very painful. I was told that I was touched by "an evil spirit." I was told that I would live the story of Hamlet and "leave nothing but dead bodies in my wake." She questioned my spirituality, my teaching ability, and whether or not I could actually teach in a Catholic school.

I was filled with hurt, disbelief, and anger. How could I go from celebrated teacher at the school one day to the next day having my life judged? I had already come to the conclusion that I would leave the school at the end of the academic year because I knew if I didn't it would be impossible to live openly in my relationship with Cindi. But after hearing such hateful things and knowing that it would create a "scandal," I resigned in the middle of the year. I was not asked to leave, but I would have been if I'd stayed there and claimed my homosexuality. I handled a hard situation the best I could, but looking back on it it still feels raw and painful.

In the late spring, Cindi left her position as design director and moved to Kentucky. It was wonderful to finally be together. We began the process of becoming a family. Shortly after Cindi's arrival I resigned from my editing position and applied for a job in the public school system. I got the job almost immediately.

I started teaching drama at Westport Middle School and Fine Arts Academy and was filled with enthusiasm. I started to network, wanting to meet other teachers in the system who were gay and out of the closet. I talked to Natalie, a friend who was the director of the Louisville Youth Group, a support group for LGBTQ teens, and she gave me the names of two teachers at my school that she had heard good things about. I looked these teachers up immediately and found they were out to colleagues, but not students; both were in long-term relationships and were wonderful, healthy individuals. We became a good support system for one another.

But I wanted to network beyond my school, so I went to a couple of meetings of a Gay-Lesbian Teacher Caucus that was sponsored by the teacher's union. I found teachers who were out to colleagues but not students to be the norm. Throughout the year I had conversations with only two teachers who were out to their students—one of whom told me that the more out you were, the more protected you would be.

That was not what I heard at my school. I heard various "warnings" from my principal about not sharing my sexual orientation with colleagues, and certainly not students. She said her concern

was that I would not be accepted and that I could get hurt. The principal also made comments about parents and the community not accepting gays and lesbians. I remember telling her that after all I had lived through over the past year or so, I could handle some remarks at the copy machine. Later that year we had a conversation in which she told me not to deny or affirm or validate when asked about my sexual orientation. She also told me not to promote it.

I felt a profound sense of sadness and frustration at the injustice and craziness of it all. I had left Catholic institutions where the "don't ask, don't tell" policy was securely in place—along with teachings on homosexual activity being sinful. I was not prepared for the same "policy" in a public school system in a city with a fairness ordinance that protects LGBTQ individuals from discrimination.

As the school year went on I became deeply aware of the hatred, prejudice, and stereotypes that pervaded our school. In the halls, at lunch, on the buses, and even in my well-managed and engaging classroom, students would not think twice about calling each other "gay" or "fag." While I would also hear racist and sexist remarks, or even comments on another student's cognitive ability, I heard more homophobic remarks than anything. I began keeping track of how many times I heard these slurs, put-downs, jokes, and comments, and it was averaging about 10–15 times a day. I even heard students make comments about a few of the male teachers using these words.

I knew that there were many teachers who would not address the comments, but I was not one of them. From the first comment I heard that August, I found myself constantly saying to my students, "That is inappropriate and not respectful to your classmate or to this group of people." "I take personal offense at that comment." "We need to respect all people."

Since I was teaching drama, I gave students the opportunity to plan role-plays and participate in improvisational scenarios. During performances, students would often bring stereotypical and prejudiced bias to characters they were developing. They also knew, without a shadow of a doubt, that I would deal with comments, have conversations with them, stop a performance, and penalize their grade if they crossed a line. I felt like I was making some headway, but it was a daily commitment to be consistent and aware. Still, I was not out to students. I had never gone from a reprimand to anything on a more personal level, other than my mantra of "I take personal offense at that comment."

But one early spring day in March 2003, that all changed.

We had been studying character development for more than two weeks. As a springboard for one last character study performance, I wanted students to do some analysis of the movie *Harriet the Spy*. I set the focus, talked about dramatic and production elements, specifically about the stylized Nickelodeon approach to the film, and then began a 25-minute clip from the movie.

During one scene the main character, Harriet, is getting ready for bed and talking to Golly, her nanny, played by Rosie O'Donnell. Once Harriet begins bouncing on the bed, Golly shoos her off the bed, tickling and teasing her on the way to her own bedroom.

The class was quiet, watching and enjoying the movie. Then an eighth-grader (who I'll call Brad) yelled out, "Lesbian!" First laughter, then side conversations started.

I had a student turn on the light and then I asked, "Brad, can you help me understand what would possess you to yell that out? It has nothing to do with the movie."

He then began to explain, "Well, Rosie is a lesbian, right? And so, I was wondering if the people who made the movie knew that. I mean, look at how she is touching that girl."

I said, "Brad, that is inappropriate, and I honestly don't know if your comment is rooted in ignorance, or fear, or what. I do find it personally offensive."

He then said, "But Ms. Crawford, I mean she's touching that girl all like…"

There was growing laughter, conversations, and smirking.

Something inside me just could not let it go with simply reciting my chosen mantra. I was sickened by the connection my young student was making with lesbianism and pedophilia. I was also

keenly aware of the moment being a teachable one—and one that would be memorable for my students and for me.

I quietly and calmly said, "I find your comments personally offensive. Do you know why?"

He shook his head no. I took a deep breath and was aware of my heart beating quickly and the catch in my voice. I looked out at my students and gazed into their eyes. Then I focused on Brad.

"I am a lesbian. It hurts my heart, my ears, and my feelings when you say things like that. The role that Rosie is playing is that of a caring nanny. There is nothing about her being a lesbian that would make shooing a child off to bed inappropriate or sexual or anything like that. I don't know what these hateful comments are based upon or why you think they are funny. I really don't."

It was so quiet in the classroom. Eyes were wider than I had seen them all year. Some students did not make eye contact. I saw Brad gulp.

Then I finished, "I want you to be more careful when you choose words. You do not know who you could be offending. I am a good teacher, a good mom, and a lesbian. The slurs, the put-downs, and the misconceptions you have are not who I am or what I am about. I want you to understand where I am coming from. I want you to think about a real, live gay person's face when you say homophobic remarks. They hurt *me*. Do you understand?"

He said, "Yes, Ms. Crawford. I'm sorry."

I then continued on with the movie. The class was quiet, did the analysis questions at the end, and was dismissed.

As I moved to the door to see students out, I noticed Brad hanging back. When everyone had left the room, he looked down at me—he was over 6 feet tall—and said to my face, "I'm sorry. I didn't know. I don't have anything against gay people."

I said, "I hope not."

He continued, "I was just trying to be funny. I am really sorry, Ms. Crawford."

I told him that I accepted his apology and I thanked him for his maturity.

During my planning period, I immediately scripted the events of the class and put them in a memo to my principal, just in case there was an onslaught of parent calls. I said I would discuss what had happened with her, provided that my union representative was with me. Once my principal read the memo, she came up to my room. I could tell she was not pleased with what had happened, but she surprised me and said that she saw it was a teachable moment and she would support me.

The onslaught of parent calls never came. I was later told of an "anonymous" parent complaint, but when I asked to speak to the parent, it was not brought up again.

The next day or two, the class seemed a little different. I told them that Brad had apologized and I thanked them for handling that moment in a mature way. A little comic relief later and the class went back to dramatic presentations. The major difference was that the homophobic remarks became the exception, as opposed to the norm, as they had been before. Students had a good-natured rapport with me about not "crossing the line" and we enjoyed one another so much during those last two months. On my final exam, I asked a question about what they had learned during the trimester about respect and diversity. A number of students commented on my coming out in class and said that as a result they stopped prejudging people or making fun of them. Brad's answer was most poignant: He commented that before, he'd made homophobic remarks 10 times a day, whereas in the past two months he had only said them twice, and afterward regretted it.

As the semester went on, kids being kids, the word got out about Ms. Crawford being gay. There were whispers and looks— but of course, in middle school, you never know what those whispers and looks mean. In April I came out to my sixth-grade class in a similar teachable moment that stemmed from students calling a male teacher on the floor a "faggot." I sent a memo to my principal, and even though my assistant principal told me of another anonymous parent phone call, I was never called into the office for a conversation.

One other defining moment came in May, during the week of statewide testing in Kentucky. I was proctoring a class in another teacher's room and all the students had finished testing except one in the back. The test booklets were collected, and students were getting restless. I moved to the center of the room and as I did so, there was a lot of commotion and noise from the right side. And then a voice yelled out, "Hey, lesbian." I was surprised and tried to locate the student who said it.

I asked who said it and a couple of girls said, "Don't tell her."

Then I heard more comments and words like "nasty," "gross," "lesbo," "filthy" and full sentences such as, "Being gay is gross. I've seen *Jerry Springer.*" "It's nasty, wrong, just bad."

The noise level was starting to build and becoming unmanageable. Students on the other side of the room were playing and bugging one another. As I walked to the side of the room with all the comments, a girl named Alexandra started speaking: "Yeah, I heard you were gay. I don't care. Shouldn't matter what people do."

I asked, "So, you've heard all this where?"

She said, "On the bus, in the halls, all over the place. It doesn't matter to me."

I told Alexandra I respected her beliefs and complimented her on a mature understanding of diversity. Then another student asked, "You are gay?"

And I said, "Yes. I don't believe it matters. I'm a good person and a good teacher."

While some students were obnoxious, still muttering words like "gross" and "nasty," other students added some positive comments about respect.

After that experience, whenever comments occurred in any of my classes, I would have conversations with small groups about the use of the word *gay* as an adjective, asking them why they choose that word, and what other words really describe what they are saying. I explained to them how sad it makes me to hear them using that word as an adjective meaning "weird," "gross," "bad," "disgusting."

*

I believe in these young people and I think our society commonly sells them short. I value my relationships with my students and colleagues. I am hopeful that each school will be a place of growth for young minds and attitudes. They are questioning and can be taught, but we must model for them what is appropriate and right. How? By addressing the issue of verbal violence and harassment, by educating students about the connection between attitudes and thoughts and words and behavior, by modeling and witnessing what it sounds like and means to speak in respectful and dignified ways. Gay and straight teachers need to speak out. It really doesn't seem as much of a gay issue as one about basic respect, human dignity, and tolerance—values that are always age-appropriate, values that will make the world a better place.

*

A couple of girls stayed after one of my classes one day and said that they had heard some students talking about me being gay. She and the other girl told me that they said to their peers, "Yes, she is, but it doesn't matter. Leave the judging to God."

I said, "Exactly."

*

My relationship with Cindi is one of profound happiness and joy. We are creating new circles of friends and extended family. My children have adjusted well and are thriving in a loving home. I am teaching math at a different school in my neighborhood, and I enjoy it a good deal. My parents and siblings keep moving more to a place of acceptance and love. Life is good.

I want to live authentically.

I want to live my life openly and simply.

I will. I am.

WHY I DO WHAT I DO
Roberto Wheaton
Ninth grade earth science teacher
Cathedral City High School
Cathedral City, California

It seems like dealing with my sexual orientation began in (of all places) a small university in northern Idaho in 1984. My final education class assignment was to identify a controversial issue in education and to present an argument for or against, with a personal opinion supporting my argument. Growing up as a Latino/Native American mix in an inner-city barrio and on a reservation, the one thing I knew was how to fight, so being one of two males in a class of 75 women (and gay at that), I decided to write my paper on the issue of gays in education.

After three hours of typical education talk, my presentation really woke up the class and the professor. Every word I uttered seemed to flow with conviction. When I was finished, the class gave me a standing ovation. The professor called me into his office to tell me that he would be giving me an A for the class and thanked me for addressing a unique issue we would all have to face someday.

In many ways this was the my first "coming out," but I knew it wasn't going to be the last time I would stand among strangers and admit I was a gay teacher. Why this is necessary, I don't know. Perhaps I have always felt like I didn't quite fit into either the Latino or Native cultures completely, but my sexual orientation always seemed to be a complete fit.

In 1984 I left the reservation with a bag of clothes in the trunk of my old Ford Fairmont and headed for Seattle, where I accepted a teaching position at a Native American high school in south Seattle. During my first two years of teaching, I didn't address my sexual orientation—one, because it never came up and, two, because I was too busy surviving from day to day as a beginning teacher. Then one day in class I overheard two 16-year-old boys talking about meeting in front of a bar on Capitol Hill to find a "runner" and score. I knew from my days on the reservation that finding runners was a way for teens to have adults buy alcohol, in return for money or sex. These boys were talking of giving up their bodies for alcohol and drugs, and they knew exactly where to loiter. I knew this because coincidentally, I was moonlighting at this particular bar at night, and I knew what was taking place outside its front doors.

I casually asked the boys to remain after class, but they left as soon as the bell rang. After class I stopped by to speak with the counselor and nurses about my concern. The nurse told me she would speak to the boys, but the school had few resources to deal with these kinds of problems.

That same week, I received a note in my box from the visiting physician at our school about a meeting I might be interested in attending. A group of physicians, therapists, and administrators were forming a group to work on LGBT issues for adolescents. I was invited to join but was told not to tell anyone about the group.

I attended the meeting; indeed, there was a support group starting at the local university and a possible youth group for teens. I was impressed with the group, but admission to it was a very private affair as they wanted to keep out any possible pedophiles. I was accepted because I was a gay teacher (although not an out one at time).

My journey toward coming out was just beginning.

In 1989 I left the school for another small community public school where I knew there were a number of out gay students. The teachers seemed supportive and tolerant as all the rooms had signs

of some type advocating peace or "Diversity Welcomed Here." I met a couple of gay teachers, but they were in the closet and seemed to have no intentions of ever coming out—even though in their dress and behavior they embodied every gay stereotype. The students and staff "knew"; the teachers themselves seemed to be the only ones who didn't think that they were "out." While it was healthy for the school to have out gay and lesbian students, I was told that for teachers, the answer was a clear "no." I took their advice and decided to feel out the community before making any decision about coming out.

During this time my work with the LGBT group seemed to increase, as we did community trainings, established an information line, and sponsored dances and a support group. I began to identify library resources and reached out to my own school librarian. She greeted the LGBT books I brought with open arms and invited me to bring even more resources. Eventually she even set up an LGBT presentation to the school librarians and developed a LGBT resource list for the school district.

Then one winter day in my ninth-grade environmental class, a young girl with an ACT UP shirt ask me if I was gay. Shocked, I responded with a loud "No," then watched her face shift from anticipation to disappointment.

That day was one of my lowest points. I had compromised my advocacy and the beliefs that drove it to hold on to my job. I had not been truthful to the very students for whom I was advocating in my community work. I had let fear guide my decision, rather than my principles. And I don't think I fooled anyone: Gay students know which teachers are gay from the first day of the school year. I vowed never to lie to students again about my sexual orientation.

The moment of truth came the following October.

I can remember that fall day like it was yesterday. I arrived early to school, parked my car, and was gathering my book bag when a teacher parked beside me yelled, "Great job, Bob!" I replied "Thanks," even though I didn't know what had motivated his comment. Then, as I proceeded through the parking lot, another teacher commented how proud she was of my work. I was still puzzled at these comments. It wasn't until I entered the school and was greeted by another colleague with a hug and "Nice interview! We're so proud of you," that I remembered the interview I'd done with a local public radio station back in the spring about LGBT youth issues. Apparently, it had finally aired the day before.

I guess I had outed myself on National Public Radio—without even knowing it.

Walking down the hallway toward the office, I felt a sense of relief about coming out to my colleagues. I knew too that I had to deal with my fears about losing my job, what my administrator would say, and what to expect inside the office—it could be the warmest of places or sheer hell, especially when you had a SEE ME! posted on your box. I wasn't in the mood for a SEE ME! day, so I tried to sneak by unnoticed. But my friend, the attendance secretary, saw me and yelled "Bobby, I just knew you were! I am so proud of you." My heart started racing as I tried to quiet her down and not draw attention from the principal. I knew it was only a matter of time before a SEE ME! would appear on my box; I just wanted it to come another day. I was feeling so good, thanks to the support from my peers, and I wasn't ready for the heavy-handed reprimand I was so sure I would receive.

Making my way up the stairs to my classroom, I realized that some students had probably heard the interview, and I pondered how I would respond. My first three periods were 7th–8th grade, and I was hoping that they didn't hear it or simply forgot, since that's what they commonly do at that age. As expected, no one said a word for three periods.

Then my fourth period—a 10th-grade class—came stumbling in. I could hear them talking about the interview and knew the question was coming. Most of these students had been in my 9th-grade class the year before, when had I denied the question; now they were unusually silent. Ten minutes into the class, a young man raised his hand to ask, "Hey, Bob, were you on the radio today?" I

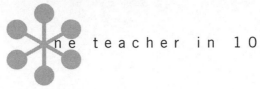

responded with a "As a matter of fact, I was," and I complimented him for listening to NPR. Then the class went dead again and a young woman (who was holding her girlfriend's hand) asked, "Are you gay?" I responded that "I would love to answer that question, but not during class time." I invited them to stay after class during part of their lunch, when I would give them the answer they wanted to hear.

The hour seemed to fly by. My nervousness was building, but knew that I had to be truthful with the students, even if it might mean I'd lose my job, my career, my reputation in education. When the lunch bell rang, I expected the class to bolt, but every last student sat quietly in their seats, with their eyes fixed on me. Trying not to sweat or show any emotion in my voice, I waited for the young girl to ask the question again. This time I took a few seconds to breathe and answered, "Yes, I am." It was the most empowering moment of my teaching career.

I broke down and apologized for the previous year's denial. I explained my fears about job security, but mostly I spoke about my feelings of my own betrayal of my beliefs—and of my students, who are the reason I was teaching in the first place.

The next 15 minutes were filled with stories about dads, moms, friends, and family, and the pain and fear they all had to live with on a daily basis. A male student yelled, "It shouldn't matter what a teacher is, but how they do their job." One girl, who identified herself as a lesbian, spoke of her fears at our school and how she had no place or person to go to for help. Another student described how her sister, an A student in an outlying high school, had come out and been beaten up and hassled until she dropped out of school. When the second lunch bell rang, I fell to my chair in disbelief that the students had been so supportive. They'd had so much more compassion than I expected. That is when I realized that the youth of today are pretty genuine about acceptance: It's the family and organizational leaders (school administrators) that create the intolerance for LGBT students.

For the next couple of weeks, students stopped by at lunch or during passing time to ask if "it" was true. I always answered that it was, and asked if this was a problem. I received no negative responses. I thought that my coming out was a nonevent—until Halloween weekend.

When I returned on the Monday after Halloween and entered my classroom, I was shocked to find my desk turned upside-down and the room scrawled with antigay graffiti. I knew that there might be consequences for coming out, but I hadn't anticipated anything like this. I called security to report the incident. They did the usual district write-up and went their way.

I went downstairs to the office and asked to meet with the principal. I informed her what had happened. She looked at me and said, "Now you know what women teachers go through when they find BITCH scrawled on their blackboards, or are called it to their faces." I tried to explain this incident was different than that, but the principal replied, "I can barely deal with teenage pregnancy, let alone this issue." And the meeting was over. I left feeling completely on my own and knowing that I would have to find some other way to report this incident if I didn't want it to happen again.

It's interesting how fate works when you least expect it. The next month, a student placed a poster for a city-sponsored LGBT dance on the bulletin board at another school and was harassed by the principal. I was called to help advocate for the student. After calling ACT UP, the Gay News, and other activists, I called the district office and demanded a meeting with the superintendent, telling them that we were going to blow this story to the press and unleash ACT UP if we didn't get an immediate response. Within hours we had a meeting with the superintendent and two school lawyers. We came up with a plan that included a letter of reprimand for the administrator's file and mandatory training for all administrators on LGBT issues. The district agreed. Guess which out gay teacher was asked to serve on the panel for these trainings? You got it. And my story was used in the training sessions.

the teacher in 10

Interestingly, none of the administrators from my building made it to any of those sessions.

In the following years I experienced few antigay incidents, other than having my windows egged a couple times and finding BOB'S A FAGGOT written in the boys bathroom. I found myself working under a constant pressure from my unsupportive principal. Nevertheless I hung in there, feeling that my presence was important both for my students and so that our school might become a safe place for LGBT youth, families, and teachers.

During my 12 years in Seattle I was fortunate to have colleagues who were supportive, compassionate, caring, and loving individuals who spoke up for LGBT rights without hesitation. I now think of my coming-out as being like the experience of a student on the first day of a new school year. You enter with many fears and hesitations but if the building is affirming, supportive, and respectful, you have opportunities to grow.

For me there is nothing more beautiful than to see at graduation that LGBT youth who arrived at our school door battered, defeated, and neglected has grown and blossomed thanks to a nurturing, caring, and loving staff. I smile as these confident, proud adults leave the stage with a diploma and college admissions and a will to make a better world. They are why I do what I do.

ONE OF THE BOYS FROM THE BAND

Michael Fridgen
Music teacher
Pinecrest Elementary School
Hastings, Minnesota

"Mr. Fridgen, I want to ask you a question," said Zach after class. "Some of the other kids say you're gay. On the playground I heard this one kid say that you're a fag. Is that true?"

"What?" I replied, pretending I did not hear him. Actually, I'm a music teacher with above-average hearing, but I needed to buy some time to consider my answer. Zach repeated his question as my mind raced to discover a reply.

Man, this kid's got guts, I thought to myself as I looked at his extremely serious face. I was openly gay to most everyone who knew me, but this was the first time a student had broached the subject. I had lived under the assumption that as an elementary teacher my students were too young to be concerned with the intimate details of my personal life; I'd thought that was for high school teachers to deal with. However, Zach's question immediately informed me that fifth graders are definitely not too young to be wondering why their handsome music teacher is unmarried.

Times have changed since I was in fifth grade 18 years ago.

When I was Zach's age I sang with the St. John's Boys Choir in Collegeville, Minnesota. Twice each week my parents drove me to St. John's Abbey to rehearse with 35 other boys; I loved every minute of it. It's true that I liked to sing; it's true that I liked the serenity of St. John's; and it's true that I liked learning from the Benedictine monks. But none of these reasons explained why I loved the boys choir with all my heart.

I grew up wanting to play with dolls rather than dump trucks and being extremely careful not to get my dress clothes dirty. Until I joined the boys choir, I was not the typical "snakes and snails" kind of guy. But now, for the first time, I was one of the boys. That is why I loved it so much. Nobody thought I was strange for wanting to go to rehearsal; nobody thought it odd that I dressed in a tuxedo and smiled for the audience. In the boys choir, we all looked and acted the same.

Damn that puberty! I was at my peak enjoyment of being one of the guys when adolescence hit and took it all away. First, my voice changed; goodbye boys choir. Then, as I entered high school, it became obvious that I was no longer one of the guys. I needed to seek out a new place to hide. I found it on the street.

I loved marching band: the pageantry, the music, the chance to wear a huge feather on my head. It was absolutely my favorite thing to do. By the time I was a junior I became drum major. People respected me as I marched down the street in front of thousands of spectators. Wearing my white uniform, I was one of the guys again. In the marching band we all looked and acted the same.

Damn that graduation! Leaving high school meant leaving marching band. Once again I was in search of a safe place to exist. I found it one Sunday at church. It seemed so obvious to me; I would love to be part of the clergy. Priests get to sing all the time; they are respected; they're invited to dinner parties; and they get to wear gaudy outfits in front of thousands of people. It would be perfect.

I began going on retreats and meeting with vocation directors; I started hanging out with seminarians. I was one of the boys again and was anxious to put on the Roman collar; all the clergy looked and acted the same.

During this time of discernment I was compelled to finish my degree in music education, a degree that has turned out to be my greatest blessing. God works in mysterious ways, and He knows what is best for our future. While waiting for the appropriate time to enter the seminary, I began teaching elementary music. After a few years of watching the children interact with one another I made the greatest discovery of my life: If you are feeling like you're not one of the boys, perhaps you should change your concept of how boys look and act.

I had spent my life attempting to look and act like everyone else, when what I really needed was to simply look and act like me.

✻

"Mr. Fridgen," said Zach. "I'm not going to get in trouble for asking you this, am I?"

"Of course not, Zach," I replied. "In fact, I'm proud of you for having the courage to talk *with* me instead of going to the playground to talk *about* me."

After considering my life, I knew how to answer him. More importantly, I learned that gender identification issues cannot wait until high school; I needed Zach to know that you do not have to be what society says you are. I stood before him not as a choirboy, drum major, or priest, but simply as me.

"Zach, yes, I am gay. I have been for all my life, and I do not wish to be any different; this is how God made me. I am not the only gay teacher in this school, and you may someday learn that many of your classmates are gay. In fact, you are going to meet gay people everywhere you go throughout your whole life.

"I know that you are a great kid, Zach, and I hope you will remember that there are many different kinds of people on this planet: black, white, blond, brunette, the list goes on and on. There are men, like your dad, who want to make their lives with women.

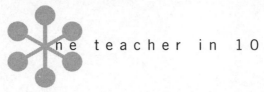

There are women, like your mom, who want to be with men. But, Zach, don't forget that there are also women who want to make their lives with other women, and men who want to be with men. There is enough love in God's heart for all the different kinds of people; I hope you will have enough love in your heart as well."

I could tell from his face that Zach had been expecting a simple yes or no answer; he got much more. As a teacher of primary students, the impact I make on academic skills can be observed daily. But the difference I make in personal development is never immediately evident. It may be years—if ever—before I find out whether Zach learned my real lesson: Don't worry so much about being one of the boys. Just be.

MY DOG DYKE

Julia Haines
Music teacher
Stratford Friends School
Havertown, Pennsylvania

As an out teacher working with elementary-age children with learning differences, I always look for that teachable moment. My students, never ones to disappoint, gave me a teachable moment that I will always cherish.

One morning in the spring of 2003 one of my most challenging students, A., came into my room muttering "dyke...dyke" over and over again. He was really taken with this word and kept remarking on it, sometimes under his breath, sometimes in a stage whisper.

I asked him if he knew what it meant. In fact, I asked the whole class of 10- and 11-year-olds if anyone knew what it meant. One student, Z., raised his hand. " I think it means demented," he said.

"No," I told them. "There are two meanings of the word *dyke*. One meaning is a wall to prevent flooding."

I then asked if anyone had ever heard of the story from Holland about the boy who prevented a disaster by putting his finger in a leaking dike. None of my students had heard this story. I found this to be very interesting as this was an archetypal story that had been repeatedly told to many of my contemporaries in the baby-boom generation when we were kids. I had grown up with this story, a parable about a young person who suffers discomfort in order to help safeguard his community. (I later found out that this was a

fictional story by the American writer Mary Mapes Dodge but that it had so much impact that the Dutch actually built a statue to commemorate the story.)

The students started looking askance; they had no relationship to this story. Meanwhile, A. kept muttering "Dyke…dyke…I like this word, I think I'll name my dog Dyke."

Then, one of the other students asked: "Teacher Julia, what is the other meaning?"

I looked around and said: "It is a slang word for *lesbian*."

The silence was delicious as you could see the students digesting this new information. Then A. started muttering "Dyke, Dyke, I'm going to call my dog Dyke. Hey, Dykey, come here…that will sound good in the park." His fascination with the word seemed to be fueled with this new information.

At this point, I told him directly that no, he couldn't do that, as it was offensive and inappropriate. He looked shocked and asked "Why, Teacher Julia?"

So I said: "I am a lesbian, and I don't want to hear you using the word in that manner."

Now the silence rang deeper. All the students, including one who had lesbian moms, were looking at me incredulously. I waited.

And then, dear Z. raised his hand and said quite sincerely: " But Teacher Julia, how come you didn't tell us this at the beginning of the year?" This question got some of the other students nodding and talking in agreement. It was all I could do to contain my delight.

Now I had the floor. I just looked at my students and said, "Oh, right, I'm going to stand up in front of the class in September and say, 'Hi, I'm Teacher Julia, your lesbian music teacher.'"

Everybody started laughing except for A., who looked flustered. He sat back for a minute and then raised his hand. "Why do they let you teach here?" he asked.

"Because I am a good teacher," I replied.

He then asked, "But, um, don't you, um, bother, um, you know, the other girl teachers, don't they get, um, upset...um, ah, because you, um, bother..." to which I asked him, "Do you mean harass?" This young boy knew this word quite well, as he had been to the assistant principal's office more than once for harassing girls at the beginning of the year, and he nodded his head vigorously. I looked at him again and said, "No, I am a good teacher, and good teachers don't harass other people."

Then he wanted to know if he should tell his mother. I told them all that this was a good topic they could go home and talk to their families about. Later, I heard from one of the parents that her daughter had come home and said, "I've known Teacher Julia all my life, and I can't believe that she never told me this before. How come I didn't know?"

But A. still wanted to know how I could teach at the school. I let the whole class know that not only was I a lesbian, but we also had gay and lesbian parents, and it was important for our school community to be welcoming to all families.

Then E., who is usually very quiet, raised her hand and said, "My moms are lesbians." Almost all the class knew that, as her moms had visited their classes to talk about their family and many students had been over to her house. To empower E. to speak her truth was the most rewarding part of this experience.

When I am open to my students, it makes it safer for them to be open in our school community. I know it is essential for me to continue this journey, not only working with teachable moments, but also making sure that I bring my experience to the students so that they can feel safe and affirmed in our school community.

MY JOURNEY IN EDUCATION

Jannette Manuel
Family and consumer science education department head
Garfield High School
Seattle, Washington

I was 10 years old when I realized something about me was different from all of the other girls in the neighborhood. It wasn't a question, nor something I needed to rationalize, but rather a statement to my own self: "I am gay!" At the same time, though, I knew that I wanted to be a teacher one day, and that brought up so many more questions—it was more of a complicated process than my own coming out. Am I going to be a teacher in my native Philippines? What subject could I possibly teach?

Throughout my life I have always admired my teachers and thought of nothing more profoundly significant than to be a teacher myself. They have in their many ways given me so much hope and support and such a sense of belonging. It's amazing how even their smiles at times allowed me to not feel not so alone.

When my family and I moved to Seattle in 1989 I found a "home" in Eileen Knobbs's classroom at Ballard High School. Though I can't remember much of my high school years, I'll never forget Ms. Knobbs. I was extremely shy and even though I could speak English, the difference in language and culture made school difficult. In her classroom she allowed me to be who I am and to succeed at my own pace.

It wasn't until I was attending North Seattle Community

College, when I worked as a mentor for the Higher Education Project, that I knew for sure that I would become a high school teacher. Working with those high school students was a revelation: It brought me immense satisfaction. Their energy, curiosity, and growth were something I wanted to be a part of. I finally settled on a degree in human development, specifically family and consumer science education (FACSE) at Washington State University. I couldn't wait to get started. I knew that from then on, my life would be full of excitement, growth, and revelations.

I began my teaching career at Garfield High School in Seattle. It is one of the most diverse inner-city schools in the state of Washington, with more than 1,700 students. Though I was not extremely excited to be at Garfield (simply because I had my heart set on teaching at the high school I went to, Ballard), I really didn't have time to mull over the situation. Not only was it my first year of teaching but also the department head and one of the teachers in the Seattle School District who were just starting ProStart, a culinary-hospitality program for high school students. It was a crazy year, but support from my administration, my mentor—Mona Mendoza—and my FACSE colleagues allowed me to survive and also grow from the experience.

Though I knew that I was different from everyone else, it was more apparent than ever when I first went to a conference for vocational educators. I walked into a room full of FACSE educators who were mostly Caucasian middle-age women. I felt self-conscious of the fact that I was a Filipina and that I was probably the only gay woman in the room. Although there were many who were welcoming, there were (and still are) women who give me second looks or question my presence at these conferences. It irks me when this happens, yet I have to stop myself from becoming upset, for I have to realize that some of these women have never seen the likes of me in their daily lives. I have to educate them.

I feel quite fortunate to be working with a group of women in my school that is extremely supportive. Since FACSE is comprised of a specialized group of vocational educators, we find ourselves

working together in many different situations. I know that I can approach anyone with anything. How many people can say that their colleagues offer them advice on artificial insemination and give them a turkey baster to use during the insemination process? How many can say that their colleagues are offering them their husband's or boyfriend's sperm? In fact, even Ms. Knobbs, my former high school teacher and now my colleague, offered to ask her son for a "donation." I never really had to come out to these women; it was simply a fact that needed to be known. It was as simple as the day I told myself that I am gay.

It is hard to see some of my colleagues who are extremely scared of others finding out who they are. Their fears consume their energy and constrain their ability to function properly in their careers and in their lives. It makes me feel free and scared at the same time. I am glad that I long ago acknowledged and accepted who I am, and it is that comfort that makes me free to be who I am as a person and as a teacher. Consequently I find it easy to encourage my students to be who they are and to become what they want to be and to be happy. I find it easy to be honest—sometimes brutally—to those around me. I find it easy to be able to point out to my students that sometimes their behaviors are not that appropriate.

Though it is not common knowledge, it is also not a big secret in school that Ms. Manuel is gay. Some students figure it out the first day in class. For some, their friends tell them. Yet, there are those that do not have a clue and still to this day ask me if I have a boyfriend. I have never pretended to be anything less than who I am. I am not the most feminine woman, which I suppose makes it easier for them to guess.

I have come out to a number of students, male or female—sometimes out of need and necessity. During my second year of teaching, I had a student who I suspected was gay. She showed signs of a person who was going through the coming-out process and I noticed that she was spending a lot of time in my room. She needed and wanted someone to talk to. One afternoon she stopped by my room with another female student. She looked extremely sad and before she left, she informed me that she would not be here the following day. I told her that things would get better and that she would survive whatever it was that was bothering her. I didn't think much of what she said until the next day when I didn't see her in class. I started panicking and soon found out that indeed, she had tried to hurt herself. She was in the hospital for about three weeks, and during that time I made sure that I was there for her. I was one of the few people she allowed to visit her, and at times we even talked about what happened. Even though she survived, to this day I feel guilty about ignoring what she said to me that day in class. I promised myself that after that incident, never again would I ignore such comments. From then on I've created an environment that is more welcoming and a "home" to my students.

Since then I have had the opportunity to have real conversations with students about feelings, relationships, and family. Yet there are still times when fear outweighs everything else. Sometimes nothing is guaranteed. My confidence as a person and as a teacher was tested a couple of months ago. It was one of those things that teachers would consider as their worst nightmare—certainly as a gay teacher I considered it my worst nightmare. A student started a rumor that a female student had a crush on me. When I found out, I was more scared that I'd ever been in my life. Though it wasn't as bad as if I was the one rumored to have a crush on a female student, I still felt completely paralyzed. And even though the student assured me that whoever started the rumor was just an immature and selfish person, and that this was just a moment where we were being "tested," it was still hard to function properly with something like that looming over my head. For months I kept waiting for something to happen—difficult conversations with the administration, perhaps an investigation, perhaps even losing my job.

Though none of these things happened, I felt vulnerable that something like this can happen again. I could be shattered so easily. Even with the support system I have, there are still many things unclear and undefined as I continue my journey as an educator.

Though I have never considered myself an activist, I have found myself becoming more and more vocal about diversity, acceptance, and tolerance. Whether it is talking to a student about why he or she called someone a "fag" or advocating the need for the inclusion of LGBT issues in the family and consumer science education curriculum, I have started to make these things my responsibility and will continue to do so. I do it not only for the sake of my students but also for my colleagues. As I am about to end my fourth year of teaching, I am excited. Even with all the uncertainties of this world, I know that I can count on the excitement, growth, and revelations that this teaching brings. I look forward to the day when I can say that I have journeyed a million miles, a journey that has been full of rich experiences and lessons, all of which started because I wanted to become a teacher.

I'LL SEE YOU THERE

Malana Summers
Eighth grade core teacher
Rivera Middle School
Merced, California

L'audace, encore de l'audace, toujours l'audace! I can't believe that I'm actually doing this. By now, of course, I'd heard this refrain from the little voice inside me too many times to count. The Rubicon had long since been crossed. The only thing left was to follow through.

It had been months since I'd somewhat reluctantly told Sallie, my therapist, that I needed to transition fully. Already having been sobered by a painful divorce as well as the estrangement of my children, countless hours of electrolysis, and more than two years of hormone replacement therapy, I'd had plenty of opportunities to reflect. Somehow, this had to work.

Outing myself was not something I really wanted to do, but it had to be done. There was no other way now. I had seen others try and fail, had learned from witnessing those mistakes, and I had a plan. I would go straight to the most senior officials, promise to avoid publicity whenever possible, and be a team player. And so on May 11, 2000, I met with my superintendent and his personnel associate. Holding my hand was a union representative who also happened to be a colleague and friend. Pushing copies of a letter outlining my clinical history and professional assessments across the table in reply to a "Why are we here?" was like the opening ante

of some surreal poker game. (I would come to realize just how apt the analogy was as spring warmed into summer.)

By August my assignment had morphed from eighth-grade teacher at the school I'd been working at for 20 years to being squirreled away as a teacher on special assignment in the district's profession development center. The concept wasn't so terrible. Both the district and I had sought a "win-win" situation—that is, of course, after both they and I had sought legal advice. The reality turned out to be less appealing. My duties were not very well thought-out. One long year was spent in a series of largely menial functions. One particularly frustrating example was spending several days removing staples from collated paper packets so that the paper could be recycled. Was I being nudged into giving up? I thought so.

Meanwhile, word of my transition didn't take long to spread through the local educational community. During the months of my mutually agreed exile, I endured looks of questioning, astonishment, and disgust. Lord only knows what was going on behind my back. I tried not to imagine. During this phase, the worst thing was being condescended to. No longer a respected veteran educator, I was now a neophyte bimbo. I thought I was mentally prepared for what would happen. I was not.

I should interject at this point that I am no transsexual poster girl. In my 40s, over 6 feet tall, and by any objective assessment quite the plane Jane, I was attempting what even kind supporters in the trans community would suggest was nearly impossible.

My "passing" was called into question. Well-meaning friends privately suggested that I needed more time to present convincingly. Ironically, stealth—a prized attribute among many transsexuals—is nonexistent in any on-the-job transition. I would probably never completely pass in an environment where coworkers at my school were so grounded in my "him" past. Regardless of any cosmetic image, how could I ever pass in those people's eyes?

Further, I would not be in an insulated private setting. The prospect of public scrutiny, ridicule, and condemnation was quite real. More than one sister predicted that right-wing protests would make themselves felt in one way or another. Ultimately, so conventional wisdom ran, even if I could personally endure the stress, the school system would bow to pressure from parents and other outside forces with political and moral agendas.

Finally, I had a long history in the educational community here. Never mind that it was a positive one. How would the whispers of siblings, ex-students, colleagues, parents, and staff allow me to successfully function teaching adolescents? Problematic or not, I had to try.

By the spring of 2001 I was ready to return to the classroom. Senior school officials still seemed unsure as to how to proceed. On the one hand, I was told to apply for any and all transfer vacancies. On the other, middle-level administration privately suggested to me that I should consider the more low-profile field of grant writing. (For my own sake.) This was the central San Joaquin Valley, after all, the reasoning went, "And you know how people are." At one point I was even called into the assistant superintendent's office for an exploratory conversation as to whether I might be interested in a two-year severance package. Thank you, no.

I'm a Capricorn, and stubborn as any goat. I teach middle school. It's what I know; it's what I do. I'd like to think I'm pretty good at it—every evaluation I've received in my career has said so. Therefore, it's not surprising that I should be determined to return to the classroom. Curiously, this made sense to virtually no one that I talked to.

In any case, after prioritizing the available vacancies, and though I preferred a new school, I was informed that I would be returning to my original school and assignment. Oh, joy! To face people, some of who'd known "Butch" (couldn't you just die?) for two decades, now as Malana—fresh from breast augmentation and on the verge of the big snip-snip—was daunting. Where were Toto and that wizard when I really needed them?

During the first few days, if I hadn't had a sense of humor, all

would have been lost. Reactions from staff ran the entire gamut. I'm still awaiting the appropriate offer of a doctorate in humanities. Seriously. One of my favorite reactions was from a sincerely concerned colleague and friend who took me aside and in a quiet moment asked, "Haven't you thought about moving to San Francisco?" Another was, "Now you know how it feels to be black." That one took a while to grasp as I'm one pale-complexioned, fair-haired honky girl.

I was going back to the classroom, though. Or was I? At the 11th hour, the school district got cold feet. I was called in and begged to accept an on-campus position as a nonteaching programs facilitator. I would learn later that downtown was getting phone calls from "concerned citizens." Another Chernobyl? Sensing the pervasive mood—that the sky was indeed falling—I reluctantly agreed. This time—with the demand that I be given a signed memorandum of understanding that should I so desire, I would be able to return to full-time teaching duties for the 2002–2003 school year—I agreed. Patience can be a virtue. It was noted that this would facilitate a less-demanding recovery from my scheduled gender reassignment surgery, set for December 2001. This was in my best interest...at least that's what I was told.

Fast-forward to today.

At the time of this writing, March 2004, I am in the middle of my second year back in the classroom—at my original assignment, eighth-grade language arts and social studies, at my original school. My students seem to have forgotten, if they ever knew, that I was a "him." Occasionally, other students will hear the rumors and catcall my former name and gender from a distance in an attempt to get a reaction. And yes, it hurts.

Even though California's education and legal codes protect me from harassment and employment discrimination, I can't pretend that it doesn't exist. School officials are wary of taking forceful response for fear of opening a can of worms—and I understand their plight, to a degree. One needs a thick skin to transition on the job!

Nobody would choose my life. At one point a school official spoke of my journey as a lifestyle choice, and I nearly became unglued. Anyone who would suggest that is, to put it tactfully, ill-informed. To spend the first half of my life in the anguish of the wrong gender was ghastly. To try and fashion a "normal" life in denial of a powerful internal reality was destructive, not only to me but ultimately to those I cared most deeply for. And then to risk all that I had managed to acquire—love, family, friendship, career, economic security, and respect—in a leap of faith that seemed akin to leaping from a Cessna without a parachute. There was no choice involved, only an imperative.

Today I am consoled by the fact that I have persevered. I never went on *Oprah,* and I haven't even been mentioned in what passes for a newspaper in my locale. People who were radically opposed to my return to the classroom have receded into the forgiving veil of time. I have lost friends and made new ones on my journey. Those who I thought would rally behind me didn't. But supporters from unexpected quarters have shown great compassion. In each case, they know who they are.

If, in some small measure, my experience can make it easier, or provide some inspiration for the next trans person, then maybe I've helped. I'm still looking for "Happily Ever After," and I hope to see you there.

FEELING ALL RIGHT ON THE RELIGIOUS LEFT

Patricia Lyons
Religion teacher
St. Stephen's and St. Agnes's School
Alexandria, Virginia

Seniors in high school used to wait for the mailman to hear responses from colleges to which they applied. I hear that now you can find out on the Internet, which is an amazing change. Back in 1990 I thought I was a high-tech senior because, rather than stalk letter carriers near the official notification date, I picked up the phone and called the only college to which I had applied.

"Harvard University, Office of Undergraduate Admissions. Can I help you?" What an understated request. I gave my social security number while I listened to my parents whispering in the next room, waiting to hear the news. I had called from the privacy of my bedroom on my Garfield the Cat telephone. I remember spending the time on hold by looking at the bulging white eyes of that faux feline and thinking, *Why I am making such an important call on this ridiculous phone?* Then, out of the silence, the words: "You were admitted. Do you have any other questions?" I gently hung up Garfield, looked at myself in that old full-length mirror, and whispered the words, "They can't touch me now."

What a sad first reaction to such wonderful news—especially since I've always been known as a lighthearted and hopeful person. To this day I know my parents would be shocked to think that when I entered that room to share my college news, the smile on my face did not represent the first emotion I had felt. I applied to Harvard for many reasons, most of which my parents and my friends knew about and understood. But no one but Garfield had any idea that on the top of that list of reasons was: armor in my adult life.

How naive I was to think that an Ivy League education would somehow take away the threat and dread I felt as a teenager when I thought about how the world would see me and treat me for being a homosexual. I did not have the word *homosexual* back then for my feelings, but I knew even as a child that I was different than most of my female peers, and I felt that difference getting stronger and not weaker with every new day of my life. Who was I afraid of? Everybody, I guess. But most of all, as a person of strong faith since childhood, I was afraid of those who would reject me in the name of God. Growing up as a Catholic and looking at crucifixes all the time, I was a very young child when I first thought about what religious people do to people whom they reject. I never questioned God's love for me, but every glance at Jesus on the cross was a kind of signpost to me of where my future might lead.

Today, I am a much-loved teacher in my school. I enjoy what older teachers call "the young-teacher honeymoon." This is the phenomenon of students seeing young teachers as infinitely cooler and more hip than any gray-haired teacher could ever be, no matter how interesting their classroom actually is. Every time I find a lonely gray hair in my head, I pluck it out quickly and am forced to admit that these honeymoon days may soon come to an end.

I also think the subject I teach also makes for easy friends among students. All religion classes in my Episcopal school are electives, which the students must take a number of in order to graduate. The idea of mandatory religion classes is a chore for many, but it can also be a break from the major academic subjects that they have been taking for years. I have always seen the unpopularity of religion as a challenge to take on. I bring in doughnuts

and engage in near stand-up comedy acts to introduce the topics and ideas of my classes. I run my religion classes like philosophy seminars, with lots of debating, laughing, and talking about contemporary films and television shows. We talk about music videos, Internet surfing, politicians, and professional sports figures. We talk about Thomas Aquinas, Martin Luther, Nietzsche, Foucault, and *The Simpsons*. I will use any medium to generate interest in spiritual ideas.

I am committed to making the classroom a space of safety and enjoyment—where the talk is not of the dogmatic force of religion but rather of the dynamic creativity of spiritual ideas. I go out to dinner with students of other faiths to hear about their upbringings; I read the religious texts that communicate their faith traditions; I go to synagogue with Jewish students to affirm their faith; I attend the confirmations of Christian students; and I have seized every opportunity to speak at youth conferences in the area on interfaith dialogue with Muslim, Sikh, and Hindu teenagers. I do all this to show every student that the Christianity I practice does not fear the faiths of others but, on the contrary, rejoices in common ground.

Most of my students are Christians, and many are politically center-right Catholics or Protestant evangelicals of many flavors. Most have had a fairly conservative upbringing on social issues. Prior to this past year, I had never considered coming out to this community because I'd convinced myself that I could do more to broaden their understanding of Christianity by becoming their (heterosexual) hero. I have always known the importance of teachers coming out to their students and to their schools, but my deep fear of being attacked for being different led to many years of hiding and rationalizations. I convinced myself that my circumstances—and not my actual fears of being rejected—were the reason that I could not speak. After all, I am a teacher of religion in a church-affiliated Christian high school. Nevertheless, teachers who dared to come out have always inspired me. But whenever educator friends of mine would question me about why I had not taken that step, I would launch into an explanation of The Strategy.

The Strategy was to get kids excited about a version of Christianity that is inclusive of people of all sexual orientations. I worried that "waving my banner" could start rumors and ruin The Strategy. I rationalized that I could do more "on the inside" of conservative Christian circles, rather than coming out and being banished from that subculture for good. I believed that if I came out, many of my students and their parents would shut out my voice and put up walls around their spirituality to avoid my influence on their fairly rigid religious assumption that homosexuality is, at best, displeasing to God.

Hiding my sexual identity by trying to be a spiritual superhero was exhausting. I preached at our weekly school chapel sermons, full of jokes and stories and accessible spiritual messages. I prayed at football season opening dinners, led a community service trip to Honduras, trekked across Europe with history students, chaperoned dances, visited students who were sick or depressed in their homes, baked brownies for student birthdays, and went to the funerals of parents and grandparents. I walked the sidelines of sporting events and approached parents about their moral concerns for their kids, or even for themselves. I took all the esteem that came from this superhero reputation as a sign that The Strategy was working.

It has pained me, though, to be in the middle of conversations with parents and students and to listen to them spew rants against "pro-gay books in the library," "sex-promoting gays," "the homosexual agenda," and "the abomination of homosexuality." I have had dozens of students and parents say point-blank that "a person cannot be a true Christian and a practicing homosexual." I would try not to blink while offering tacit thoughts on inclusion and then changing the subject. I never lied about my sexual orientation, but I never spoke of it either.

But this last year the students have pulled me to a new place. In my Christian ethics class, I ask kids every year what mentors or role models they did not have but needed along the way. More than one

student wrote anonymously, "I wish I had a gay teacher." The handwriting alone made me skip a breath. Another student wrote on an anonymous form, "I wish the gay teachers here would say it, because when they don't it sends the message that they are ashamed."

I don't think these students were baiting me to come out. I felt like I had betrayed them. The Strategy required silence so as not to lose any popularity or influence with the students and parents who already enjoy the privileged status of heterosexual and Christian in America. My conscience began to whisper, *Whose side are you on?*

What began last year was a maddening conversation in my head. For the first time since I began teaching Christian theology to young people, I was seriously questioning The Strategy, which said that telling people I was gay would do more damage than good by possibly limiting my audience. I thought back to the people who had made the most difference in my own spiritual understanding of myself and God and how they had handled the issue of coming out. One name and one moment walked to center stage in my memory.

I had been a freshman at Harvard for one month when my father died of a long illness. The morning after his funeral I left my home in New York and flew back to college to try and restart my college experience and the rest of my life. I did not have any real peers as friends yet, but I had made a connection at the University Church, where a dynamic seminarian had gotten me involved in teaching Sunday school. I had also heard three weeks of incredible preaching from Harvard's famous chaplain, the Reverend Professor Peter J. Gomes. I loved his vision of life and God from the start. Working in his church was the most exciting decision I made that first month. I was too scared to shake his hand at any public event, though, and felt it would be a year or two before I got up the courage to introduce myself.

When I came back to college after my dad's funeral, I was stunned to be approached by Reverend Gomes at the coffee hour after church the following Sunday. He had heard about my dad, and he expressed his deepest condolences. I was speechless. And then he really shocked me by inviting me over to his house for tea the following day. Of course I accepted. His house even had a name: Sparks House. I had never been personally invited to a house with its own name. I was definitely one of the most famous freshmen in my dorm.

I paced the floor for hours before the meeting, then walked to his residence so elated and so nervous that my palms were sweating. What could I possibly say to one of Harvard's most renowned professors? I practiced conversation ideas all the way over.

Tea, as I remember it, was not long, but it was definitely an oasis of attention and warmth. It was a very rainy day, and Reverend Gomes met me at his front door with a loud but warm greeting, whisked me in, and took my coat before I could say a word. He poured out words about New England weather, and by the way, did I like sugar in my tea and would I please, please, please take a seat anywhere I felt comfortable. His house was a totally overwhelming and poorly lit museum of artifacts, 19th-century furniture, and photographs on every surface. Every available space bore some honorary plaque or signed paper or framed image. There was more than one picture of Reverend Gomes with every president since I was born, members of royal families, military figures, social activists, the Archbishop of Canterbury, and dozens of mysterious people who looked important and whose identities I hoped a Harvard education would someday reveal to me.

Although I had worried about what we could talk about, I should have remembered that this preacher was, according to *Time* magazine, one of the best talkers in the world, and so the time passed quickly and gracefully. Soon, I was at the door saying good-bye and walking on air back to my dorm.

Perhaps because I was still dealing with my father's death or maybe because I was focused on adjusting to college life, I do not remember too many of the details of the following tumultuous week at Harvard. However, the whole country would soon be embroiled in the events that would occur.

There was a student-run conservative political publication called *Peninsula* that few people read, though it had a loyal following among conservatives of all ages at the university. The November issue came out on more or less the same day as my tea with Reverend Gomes. The entire issue was devoted to homosexuality—essay after essay attacking the gay community with rhetoric from every academic discipline. It was cold, calculating, and disturbing, with lots of talk of "tough love" and "eternal truth." I found the whole issue scary because of its systematic warnings and shady statistics that presented homosexuality as our society's most pressing social evil.

Needless to say, the university was up in arms. I was walking back to my dorm one day that week when I came upon a support rally for gay, lesbian, and transgender members of the university community. The crowd had gathered on the steps of Memorial Church. I only stopped to listen because I saw my new friend Peter Gomes standing on the stage near the microphone. When he took the microphone, I expected to hear kind words of support from a minister who had long been known to be politely supportive of minority groups.

His first words were of sadness about hatred in all forms. He spoke of a more loving and inclusive Christianity. Then I heard his historic words fly through the air of Harvard Yard: "I stand here a Christian and a gay man…that which is irreconcilable for some, is reconcilable for me." There are no words to describe the reaction of the crowd. People were just plain stunned. The Plummer Professor of Christian Morals, the Preacher to Harvard University for over 20 years, a man who had prayed at the inaugurals for both Reagan and George H.W. Bush, had just announced that he was a homosexual. I remember thinking that I had just witnessed a man change his life forever.

Looking back, I am sure Peter Gomes had something of The Strategy for himself during those two decades of stunning popularity in all theological circles across the globe. But one day he dropped The Strategy—and in so doing, radically changed my life and countless others. He was a teacher of the Christian faith who did more than send coded messages of support for all: He also spoke the words to name his life and its vocation as a gay man.

The sad cries for gay role models from my students and the memory of Peter Gomes's coming-out slowly brought me to a point where I realized that my Strategy had to go. I did not know how I could ever find the courage or even the opportunity to come out, but I could feel in the depth of my being that it was the right thing to do.

Then I was asked to speak on a panel with three students at a schoolwide assembly on diversity. The invitation was to speak for three to five minutes about a personal experience of prejudice and/or why it is important for people to be allies in social justice. From the second the offer was made, that voice of conscience started screaming at my fears: *Why not?*

It was a Thursday afternoon, and I'd been asked to speak the following Monday morning. I didn't sleep that night. I thought of every senior class that had graduated in past years and how guilty I had felt at every graduation to say goodbye to students who I knew felt ashamed of their sexual identity and to whom and for whom I had said nothing. By sunrise Friday morning, I knew I had to come out. I met with the Head of School, who spoke kind words of respect for me as a teacher and wise words of confidence in me as a professional to speak appropriately about my sexual orientation.

Looking back on that weekend, I think I was in a state of mourning for the coming death of the safety that had always come from The Strategy. I went to every athletic event that Friday afternoon and hung around with every parent and child I could until I was the last person to leave the fields. I went to more school events on Saturday; in fact, I just hung around the school building and exchanged small talk with anyone I could because I believed that such mindless and pleasant chatter would never be possible after the assembly. It was a busy weekend of what felt like packing for a trip or moving away. I felt more determined as each hour passed

and each to-do item was crossed off the long list, but also I felt sad at every step. The long honeymoon, in my imagination, was going to come to an abrupt end.

Monday morning came and I was nervous beyond description. I sat on the stage during that assembly and listened to the three students speak before me about their experiences of economic and racial discrimination. Their words were beautiful and I tried hard to listen to them with full attention and forget my own impending words, which were boiling in my head and causing my sweat to drip from my neck down my back and chest. What kept me sane was looking at all of my students. I hoped they would hear what I'd heard that day from Peter Gomes: that honesty is a greater gift than strategy.

After sharing my story, in which I spoke the words, "I am a homosexual," I ended by saying,

> Those of you who are minorities of color are my heroes. It drives me crazy with anger that people hate me for the way God has made me, but I can hide the truth if I want to. It makes me so sad that some people don't believe me when I say that God and I have studied, prayed, and talked together a great deal about the person I am and that we are both proud of it. But people of color cannot hide their oppressed status like I can. That's what this word *privilege* is all about. I have the privilege of hiding what people might discriminate against if I want to, and that means I have more power to protect myself than those of you who cannot hide. But today I have decided to lay down that privilege and walk away from it so that we can work together in honesty about the fact that we all need allies, and that we all need allies desperately.
>
> You asked me what I think "being an ally" means. I think it means giving up the power of any arbitrary privilege or any unearned opportunity to hide from the ugliness of prejudice. When those of us who can hide, do hide, we do it to save ourselves, although it means sitting by and watching others who cannot hide their differences drown in discrimination. Days like today help to break that cycle here and now. Today I jump into the waters of discrimination with you, which means I am going to need as much support as I plan to offer. But that equality feels better than safety. I dare all of you to jump in. Thank you.

The applause came strong and long. Microphones were open for questions, and the first came from one of my Hindu students, who looked right at me as he grabbed the microphone. He spoke loudly, "I do not have a question, I just wanted to say, Miss Lyons, I'll be your ally." I choked as I tried to smile and keep down the sob that lunged up to my throat with my first breath. The applause came again, but now just for him and for me. One thought came to me as I watched him sit down: If *that* is the only student who is left loving me after all this, if that is the only kind of parent or colleague left, if that is how the few who are left talking to me after this day think and love, then just a handful is more than I need to live an incredible life.

The end of the assembly brought a crowd of students to the podium. I thought that they would all have things to say, but instead they wanted to give hugs and kisses and tears, from boys and girls and colleagues alike. I will never forget their embraces. The very first class I had after the assembly had written on the board, MISS LYONS, YOU ROCK. I had no idea that throwing away so much could feel so good.

Who knows what the future will bring for me at this school. The assembly came just before exams, so everyone quickly went back to the business of schooling within a few hours of the event that was life-changing for me. In earlier years there would perhaps have been an outcry, and yet this day seemed to pass as a great success but also as a sort of nonevent as far as scandal goes. The notes and letters kept coming, but the school also just moved on.

Two weeks later I delivered that sermon to seniors at their last chapel, and it was such a wonderful moment. I did not mention anything about sexual orientation, but for the first time I didn't have to. The issue no longer needed to be the silent but forced subtext in every word. Rather, the real truth is now the text of everything I say in this community. In that sermon I shared my hopes and prayers that those seniors see themselves as children of God and people of dignity, and I did it as the person who knows what I know because of, and not in spite of, who I really am. And for the

first time, I know many kids and adults had to face the reality that any spiritual wisdom they get (or ever got) from my words or deeds grows out of my loving and serving God as a gay person.

For many, I know that this fact will cause confusion about their religious assumptions, faith commitments, and Biblical convictions. Teachers usually aim to bring people out of confusion. In this case, however, I think some confusion might be a good thing for social or religious conservatives and their ignorance and fears about homosexuality. Who knows, maybe some of them—like the slave owners, antisuffragists, or pro-segregationists before them—might have to face the possibility that much of what they define as "pleasing to God" might instead be a complex collection of cultural wishes pleasing to the Western tradition.

On the last day of school I sat in the same crowded auditorium for an end-of-the-year awards assembly. I listened to the reading of the dedication of the yearbook by its student editors. They don't say the teacher's name until the end, but by the end of the first sentence of the dedication, I knew, and I bowed my head in my hands and whispered, "Oh, my God." As I walked to the stage on which I had shed my armor for love of those kids two weeks before, the standing ovation was enough to make my steps wobbly. I hugged those seniors and knew I was living in a moment that few people will ever experience. That moment, made possible by the love of so many students and colleagues, is why I teach.

Part Two
Lessons Taught...
and Learned

I STARTED OUT BY NOT TALKING TO ANYONE...

Mike Fishback
Language arts and social studies teacher
The Park School of Baltimore
Brooklandville, Maryland

"When I came here in fifth grade, I had a really bad stuttering problem," began Davon.

For all of his 13 years, "Davon" was a wise kid. Our social studies class, which focused on the theme of identity, provided an outlet for Davon to discuss his own unique situation—as a new student, as an African-American in a mostly white school, as a Muslim in the wake of September 11. And now he saw it as his duty to respond when his classmate "Amy" asked, "Why does Mr. Fishback feel it's so important to tell people he's gay? Why can't gay people just keep it to themselves?"

"I started out by not talking to anyone," Davon continued, his voice quivering a bit. "I was too scared to let anyone know I stuttered, so basically I hid. And then I came home one day and my mom told me that I needed to just talk, and once people got to know me they'd be OK with the stuttering and realize that I was a really cool person even though I stuttered, and that's exactly what happened. And now I'm more confident and I don't even stutter as much anymore. And that's sort of why Mr. Fishback needed to come out."

❋

Looking back on my own middle and high school years, I see a closeted gay boy who never seemed to get bullied yet nonetheless felt like a victim. I spent those years passing as straight and worrying about my future. I tried to figure out how I'd keep my dirty secret the rest of my life. Fortunately, my younger brother—whose natural affect made passing as straight more of a challenge—came out during our teenage years, and slowly, with his help and the guidance of a few other friends and family members in whom I confided, I was completely out by my senior year of college.

Yet not one year later, the closet door beckoned once more. I was hired to be an intern teacher at the Park School, an independent school in the Baltimore area. Although I was just getting used to being openly gay, I decided that in my new school environment, I had to proceed cautiously. That winter, scandal broke out within the Catholic Church, and the terms "gay male" and "child abuser" were thrown about interchangeably in the media. And even though our school was "progressive," few teachers were out to their fellow faculty, and none were out to their students.

My youth and Ivy League credentials quickly earned me—or, more accurately, won me—respect among my colleagues. As I gradually came out to my fellow interns, and then to my faculty mentor, I sensed a desire in our community for a more open dialogue about homosexuality. When I was hired that spring to continue as a full-time middle school teacher, to craft a combined language arts and social studies curriculum, the principal suggested that I include a history of the civil rights movement.

"I'd love to," I responded, "and I want to focus not only on issues of race, but also on women's rights, and gay rights…"

The sentence continued in some random, unmemorable direction, but the words "gay rights" lingered in the air, waiting patiently to be seized and dealt with in whatever way fate intended. When

I finally concluded whatever I was rambling on about, she smiled and said, "That sounds exciting. We've never had a social studies class about gay rights before."

✼

Having gained the support of my administration, I entered my first year of solo teaching while planning the first gay rights unit.

Throughout the fall and winter, I kept asking myself the obvious question: Should I come out to my students? I had been developing a very positive rapport with my seventh graders; was it worth risking it all to provide them with a good role model? Or would it be enough to simply teach about gay issues?

I was made aware of the possible pitfalls of becoming an openly gay teacher. My parents, who have always been completely supportive of me, were worried that I could become a target of false allegations of sexual abuse, like other teachers about whom they had read. Some colleagues were cautious about my becoming the sole representative for all things gay. And in a recent school-wide survey, most students had expressed a belief that if someone were to be openly gay or lesbian at Park School, he or she would have a very difficult time being accepted.

But I also received words of encouragement, not only from my parents and colleagues, but also indirectly from students. In March, as part of an eighth-grade unit on persuasive writing, one student presented a speech to her classmates and teachers about homophobia. She argued that the only way to rid Park School of homophobia was for a faculty member to come out. The audience applauded, and I understood that she was right.

✼

By the first week of May, my seventh graders were well versed in identity, differences, and social justice. We had created individual "identity charts" to explore how we fit into society. We had read *To*

Kill a Mockingbird and "The Lottery" to examine the impact of tradition on human behavior. We had studied the meaning of race and the history of Jim Crow. One Friday I gave them a typical homework assignment: They were to read an article about the Florida adoption controversy and summarize the arguments for and against allowing gay couples to adopt children.

That same Friday, after consulting with the Head of School, I notified my colleagues that Monday would be the day when I would come out to my students. I requested that they encourage dialogue rather than stifle it, and I also pointed them to a section of the GLSEN Web site with suggestions for discussing such issues with students.

I started class a few minutes late Monday morning. My emotions floated somewhere in that realm between excited and nervous, recognizable in that it drains all the saliva from one's mouth. I eyed the full bottle of water that I had placed next to me. I would need it. The kids quieted down, and I began to speak.

"Before we begin discussing the homework, I'd like to say a few words about why we are studying the gay rights movement, because many schools in our country are afraid to teach about this topic. I think one reason is that many people see gay rights as being about sex—because the word *sex* is conveniently placed in the center of the word *homosexuality*—and many schools are afraid to talk about sex. But this is not about sex at all; it's about identity, and respecting differences in our society, which is exactly what we've been studying all year. So one reason we're looking at gay rights is that it's very relevant to our class's curriculum.

"A second reason is that the topic is extremely current. The article you read over the weekend was published less than two years ago. The Supreme Court is currently considering a major gay rights case, and just last week a high-ranking senator was criticized for making antigay remarks. We see these issues covered in the media all the time. In the grand scope of the civil rights movement, gay issues are the current battleground."

I took a sip of water.

"And a third reason, which is perhaps the most important one to me personally, is that I myself am gay."

I paused for a long moment to look around the classroom and allow this news to sink in. Some students returned a blank stare, others smiled, and still others began to get teary-eyed, even before I uttered my next words:

"I decided to teach this course on identity and respecting differences because I deal with these issues every day of my life. I'd also like to say that I am open about my sexuality with everyone in my life, including the Park faculty. Over the course of this year, I've realized that I admire and respect my students deeply, and that I can share this part of me with you and feel comfortable doing so. It's really a testament to how great you guys are."

I then opened the floor for questions and comments. I encouraged my students to ask me about anything, no matter how personal, with the exception of questions about sex itself.

The very first question was, "Are you going to adopt a baby from America or from overseas?"

Here are some of the other questions and comments I remember:

"Is being gay scientific or is it something you choose?"

"Isn't it hard to find someone to be with if everyone who's also gay is hiding who they are?"

"Do you hate people who are homophobic?"

"That guy who visited our class...is he...?" ("Yes, he's my boyfriend.")

"Do gay men like a different kind of guy than straight women do?"

"Did you get girlfriends when you were in school to cover up that you were gay?"

"I heard there are kids in the lower school who have same-sex parents."

"What do your parents think of you being gay?"

"What do you do about being Jewish, if the Bible says homosexuality is a sin?"

"How did you and your boyfriend meet?"

"At my old school there was a lesbian teacher who got fired when a student said she tried to hit on her."

"Are you going to get married?"

"What do you mean you're not allowed to get married?"

"When did you know you were gay?"

"Is it true that all bisexual women are really straight?"

"Did you ever like girls?"

"Were you nervous telling us?"

"You should add GAY to your identity chart now that you're out."

My seventh graders explored this issue with incredible maturity, thoughtfulness, and—most important—open minds. In retrospect, I should not have expected anything less. The week we spent studying the gay adoption battle, examining the life of Harvey Milk, and illustrating essays by adolescents about coming out was by far my most exhilarating and inspiring experience as a teacher.

That Thursday happened to be Grandparents Visiting Day. Members of the "Greatest Generation" observed a dynamic classroom conversation about gays in the military, for which my students and I earned many compliments. In fact, I received only positive feedback about the week, from parents, colleagues, and students. I am still dreading the first negative note, but it has yet to arrive.

But Amy, who was one of the deepest and most articulate thinkers in the class, and who never shied away from taking opposing viewpoints, was a bit uneasy about our study of homosexuality: "Why does Mr. Fishback feel it's so important to tell people he's gay? Why can't gay people just keep it to themselves?"

Yet rather than hiding her confusion or erupting in angry outcries over our lessons, Amy returned to class each day to ask her question again, each time in a sincere attempt to "get it." And each day I attempted to help her get it. I rehashed the hardships of my life. I referred back to the stories we'd read and the films we'd seen, trying to draw parallels. But it finally took 13-year-old

Davon, sitting her down at the end of class to tell her about his stuttering, to give it to her.

What I realized in that moment was that, as much of an advocate as I thought I had become, I was really only a teacher—a teacher with a powerful message and trusting students. The real advocates in that classroom were the students themselves. One who got it helped give it to his classmate. And the next Monday, that classmate, Amy, excitedly reported on the weekend's conversations, in which she had enlightened her family about homosexuality. She had gotten it and given it to others.

WHAT DO LECTURERS WEAR?

Josephine Allison Wilson
Guest lecturer
The London School of Economics
London, England

"What do lecturers wear?" is the question that I half-screamed at my flatmates the night before the first lecture I would ever give. I had been going to university lectures for six years at that point, I had been a full-time student all that time, and I had very rarely missed a scheduled lecture. However, on that particular night, I simply could not dredge up from all that experience what it was that these lecturers actually adorned themselves with before stepping up before any number of students to impart upon them the information that they had garnered from their years of experience—I had no idea what to put on.

Let me clarify.

I am a Ph.D. student at the Gender Institute located in the London School of Economics. My thesis concerns the construction of a theoretical framework, which can adequately account for the variety in trans subjectivities. This probably requires a much longer (and possibly quite dull to some, possibly even many, maybe even most) explanation, but suffice to say I am writing what I know about—namely trans people and their variety, being as I am quite a varied trans person.

One of the things that I have always wanted to do is teach. Luckily, being a Ph.D. student, I'd been encouraged to teach, which suited me fine—at least right up until the point someone actually asked me to do it. It was a lucky accident, really. An e-mail came through the ether to all the Ph.D. students in the Gender Institute asking if there was anyone interested in lecturing on qualitative methodology part-time at the South Bank University. Well, I quite like a bit of qualitative methodology—I have studied it, utilized it in a lot of work to date, and had even published a working paper the previous year on the difficulties in research methodology (specifically qualitative) as it relates to studying trans people. So I thought, well, I'll send her a quick e-mail. "Great," came the response, "We would like you to give a lecture/seminar on Visual Analysis in a few months time. Oh, and we like our lecturers, if they are researching, to utilize their own research as an example or case study."

I wrote back and agreed and then promptly forgot about it (primarily, I think, so I would forget to worry about it) and continued with my day-to-day Ph.D. work. When it came to be about a month away, I started to think about writing the lecture. A lot of things started to cross my mind, in fact. This wasn't a "gender" seminar, this was a lecture/seminar which was part of a qualitative methodology course at the prestigious (and therefore likely "serious" in a sensible-haircut, tie-wearing, briefcase-carrying kind of way) South Bank University. That's not to say that the London School of Economics doesn't have a similar reputation. But I live in the Gender Institute —something of a safe space for varied trans types like myself, and while there are some here with sensible haircuts, ties, and briefcases, they are very friendly and don't intimidate unless required to do so.

My worries began something like this: The person running the course at South Bank knew that I was going to talk about images of trans people, but nonetheless this is a classroom full of people who likely have never met a trans person, let alone considered studying them. I mean, maybe they aren't even sympathetic to the idea.

Let me clarify (further).

I consider myself to be lucky in many ways. I am aware that I

have managed to avoid, so far, many of the pitfalls and discriminations in opportunity that trans people often face in all walks of life, let alone in academic or educative spheres. I certainly know of cases—from trans friends, from the media, through the "grapevine" and so forth—that prove I could have it a hell of a lot worse than I do. Don't get me wrong: I have had a trouble or two that I have had to overcome. But that's another story, which I will leave for another time. I have been accepted and allowed to work on my Ph.D., I have a job that pays for my rent and food, occasionally I have an opportunity to have a social life, and now I have been asked to lecture and teach—which, as I have already noted, is something I have always wanted to do.

I started to worry not only about this one lecture/seminar but also about my whole career. Through my own studies and through my own life (as it were), I am aware of the discrimination faced by trans people in any form of employment. Am I asking for too much? I mean, I think of myself as a pretty open trans person. But does this make me completely unemployable? Will this first lecture be my very last?

There have certainly been people in my life who have told me that I will not be employable anywhere, that if I don't "change back" I am going to end up in the gutter ("they" can be very melodramatic, can't they). I try not to listen. But maybe in this instance I am asking for too much. To be openly trans, to talk about social science to sensible, suited people, to talk about bringing the study of trans people and its implications into their sensible sciences…am I going to be taken seriously? Are they even going to listen to me? Who am I kidding?

What am I going to wear?

Now, I am not much of a psychologist these days (I studied it for my first degree, quite some time ago), but I think there may have been some psycho-ma-logical stuff transpiring when I poured all of my insecurities and doubts into the question of what I was going to wear that night before my first lecture, the lecture that I was now not sure I had the courage to go through with. I was starting to question myself in lots of ways, but the only way in which I seemed to be able to communicate this at that moment was through my inability to dress.

Was there something I could wear, I frantically tried to think, that would make these people see beyond what I was sure were their preconceived notions of who—or even what—they thought I was? Was there a special outfit for such an occasion? I didn't know, and I am a little embarrassed to say that I was literally running around, far too late the night before the lecture, shouting at my flatmates. It was one of them, Verena, who came to my rescue. She stopped me in my tracks, sat me down, and started to pull garments out of my closet after I quickly and incoherently tried to explain my dilemma. She pulled out a calf-length black pencil-skirt, my only black "suit" jacket, a cream blouse, and a red scarf. She told me to wear my knee-length boots to add a touch of "funk." This would let them take me seriously, she thought, and allow me to feel "professional" and "confident."

I had never worn these things together. I didn't even know I owned a "suit," and so I'd never considered myself to be someone who could or would wear one. So it was thus, suited and booted, if you will, that I went to my first lecture—essentially appearing as a serious, tie-wearing (or, in my case, scarf-wearing) professional.

I was terrified going into the building. I had straightened my scarf several times before even entering the lobby of the reception that I had been directed to. The lovely person at the desk had called the person that I was to be meeting and I waited, quaking in my boots, as the person descended the stairs to meet me. She seemed OK. Said very pleasant things about being interested in my topic and asked me whether I needed anything. But I had yet to meet the students. That was going to be a whole other thing.

They were lovely.

They were attentive, interested, and vocal. I started the lecture and felt that I had their complete attention as I ran through the theories of Visual Analysis, feminist uses thereof, and finally its application to trans people. They didn't seem to drop off at all

when I started to talk about the varieties in trans people's experiences and identifications. I talked about the ways in which trans people often do battle with doctors, psychologists, social scientists, and sometimes even some feminists and lesbian/gay/queer theorists. I talked about the stereotypes of trans people, how they are perceived in academia, the media, politics, and law. And finally I talked about myself, as an educator. The students had responded so well and seemed so invested that I felt comfortable letting them in on my little secret: I wasn't really a suit-wearer by nature. I had constructed this image in order to overcome the prejudices that I imagined they might have. To create an acceptable image in their minds so that they would at least give me a chance. To combat their images of what trans people are like.

The lecture ran late because we had so much to talk about, and I am elated to say that it was a success. It made me feel that I could talk about these issues, to try and educate in these environments, and also to work in academia in general. I was very happy when a few months later I was invited to give the lecture again because the faculty who ran the course had received such good feedback.

It hasn't eliminated all my concerns, but this experience has gone a long way toward making me feel confident about teaching. Of course, I still know that there will be challenges ahead. I still work in a field where trans people are not fully accepted, but I have been lucky to find my niche here, supported as I am, and I feel like I have a real opportunity to change people's minds. I feel lucky in that respect and grateful to those who have helped me get here. I hope that that I can help other people who, like me, love to work in these and other areas of education. I know that is a bit of a grand mission, but if I can achieve that, I think I would be a very happy woman indeed.

PROUD TO BE A FAGET

Dan Woog
Varsity soccer coach
Staples High School
Westport, Connecticut

As an openly gay soccer coach and writer on gay issues, I often talk with students about my experiences, and about gay issues in general. The discussions that follow are intriguing, but the questions are often predictable. So are the notes I receive afterward: "Thanks for coming. I learned a lot. I'll try not to say 'That's so gay' anymore."

Not long ago, however, I spent the day at a Connecticut middle school, talking with eighth-grade classes. Their responses were a bit less scripted. In fact, they were so honest and raw that I saved them. Here are my favorites, along with my reactions to them.

> Dear Dan Woog,
>   Thank you for coming to our class the other day. Although some people in the class didn't agree with you (Matt), who cares because he is stupid. I think its all right so keep going! To me there is nothing wrong with it. Thank you! —Bridget

Ah, eighth graders! They are nothing like the audiences of adults (mental health professionals, fellow teachers, church members) and high school students I am used to. Eighth graders inhabit their own planet—if not an entirely separate universe.

Dear Mr. Woog,

Thank you for informing me about homosexuality. Some of the things you told me informed me. Thank you very much. You have a lot of courage to be gay. Some people would kick your butt if you told them. It should be left that way. Just to let you know, I think that some people in our class are gay. Sincerely, ?

I agree with his or her last comment. I am thinking of the boy in that class who sat directly in front of me. Throughout the entire 40 minutes he never made eye contact—but the tilt of his head told me he was absorbing every word. Come to think of it, perhaps "?" is that boy.

Dear Dan,

Hi! Thanx for coming. I really injoyed you talk about gay people yesterday. I really learned that there can be different people in life, and sorry for laughen at you because It was the first time I ever talk to a gay guy like you so I hope you forgive me. Sincerly, Chamone

All is forgiven. I also forgive the two boys who walked into class holding hands and smirking. I hope they didn't mind when I casually mentioned that many times the ones who make fun of gay people are those who are least sure of their own sexuality.

Dear Dan,

Thanks for coming in and telling us how it is in the gay life. And from now on I won't make fun of people like you. Well try to come back. See ya, Casey

P.S. I am not gay.

Interesting, isn't it, that Casey felt compelled to add that postscript. I hope the next time he hears a homophobic joke—or encounters a homosexual classmate—he remembers my talk, and his pledge.

Dear Dan Woog,

Thank you for coming into our class and talking about gay and lesbian people. I am homophobic, but if you want to be gay you can be gay. Sincerely, Mr. Sullivan's 8th grade class student

Well, eighth graders are nothing if not honest—and uncertain. They also do not censor themselves. When they wrote anonymous questions on note cards during my talk, one youngster wanted to know, "Do you masturbate frequently?" However, that question does not even come close to the one at the end of this note:

> Dear Daniel Woog,
> Thank you for coming into our class and informing us about homosexuality. I know that it must have been hard to admit your homosexuality to our eighth grade class. Not many people would have had the courage to do this. Sincerely, A Student
> P.S. Do you think that size matters?

But my favorite thank-you note of all was written by this girl:

> Dear Mr. Woog,
> Thank you very much for comming to visit us. Your talk was very interesting. I'm glad that your proud to be a faget. There aren't many people who are. I feel bad for the people who tease gay people. They're regular people. No different. Except for who they like. But I really respect gays as well as others. —Kimberly

Kimberly does not quite get it yet—she must have zoned out during the part in my talk when I mentioned the power of words like "fag" and "homo," especially when spat out by middle-school boys and girls—but she clearly is on her way.

It's notes like hers—and those by Bridget, Casey, and "?"—that keep me going back to talk to eighth graders, year after year. I know I shouldn't stereotype, but it continues to be true: They're funny. They're energetic. They're eager to learn. And—most important—they give me great hope for the future.

CHASING MY OWN TALE

Judee King
Director of after-school programs
Redwood Day School
Oakland, California

1989

Around and around I go, in my career in education, staying just this side of straight and, narrowly, missing. Coworkers, questioning. "We should all go out for a drink after work. Want to?" "Do you have to check with your man?" "*Are* you married?" The eyebrows rise curiously in sync with the virtual theatrical curtain of *The Judee Show* as I mentally and physically rev up to begin the chase.

The tale gains momentum when I find myself needing to quicken the pace as I lose sight of what the actual end of my tale truly is. The sound of laughter soothes my uneasy discomfort of yet again passing for straight. I slyly sigh and slowly grin as questions are soon forgotten.

School events and coworker's parties required being surrounded by a pit crew of my gay male friends. Hair, wardrobe, made up and over from lesbian to thespian. Priming my selected male companion with the script of the screenplay of "our life." Depending on the depth of the current relationship, my girlfriend would be sulking on the couch or pacing and cursing about what a lie I live in order to be in the low-paying field of education. Oh, the exhaustion of make-believe.

Ten years later...1999

The exhaustion of chasing my own tale caught up with me in 1999. I was stopped in my tracks with the news I had breast cancer. I contracted three separate cases of breast cancer within a four-year period! Initially, I went spinning out of control, questioning all rhyme and reason. The direction of my chase took a 180-degree turn. It was time to reevaluate the "who's," "what's," and "where's." The "who": me, a woman educated both formally and by social experience into a real understanding of the challenges of being true to yourself and your sexual orientation and what the denial of the latter can cause to the essence of one's soul. With my newfound awareness, the "what" seemed so clearly defined. As a three-time breast cancer survivor I could use my new lease on life to help others begin their journey. As a second-generation San Franciscan, I wanted to stay local and have the "where" be in the Bay Area. So I sought out opportunities.

The new direction of my chase has drawn me to seek opportunities to support LGBT adolescents through a variety of venues. My experience as a chaperone for the Gay Prom, where teens and young adults from all over California came to share the authentic experience of attending a spring high school prom. That warm spring night was filled with the sweet scent of jasmine carried on the same breeze as the venomous voices of the Caucasian, conservative, corrosive contingency that pressed in mass against the legal barriers, shouting, "God hates you queers, you're all going to hell!" Waving their ignorance on signs that read the same. I joined the welcoming committee, and in our formal wear we made a human barricade encircling the elegant teens in tuxes and gowns, shouting our greetings and compliments over the protesters with their hateful eyes and surgical masks—to keep from getting AIDS, they yelled. Inside, I paused to smile at the young happy couples, capturing memories, posing for prom pictures.

Frannie's voice still rings in my ears filled with sorry surprise, hurt, and anger. "Judee, you're gay! Hey, how come you never said anything? Especially when I came out to the therapist and then

they wouldn't let me be alone or near any girls after that." The accusations stung; I remembered how I'd shrunk away when the administration was up in arms and so disgusted and obviously homophobic. Before I could respond, Frannie exclaimed, "Wow, I wonder who else at our school was." I felt so feeble when I explained how much I regretted being forced by our unspoken school policy, "If you are gay or lesbian, you'd better stay in the closet and never disclose your sexual identity to the children or you will be terminated immediately." We hugged and Frannie smiled, forgave me, and danced off into the night to the beat from the turntables of famous San Francisco disc jockey Page Hodel. As the classy-clad crowd moved to the rhythm, I felt the pull of the chase quicken: *It's time...*

I put pen to paper and devised a plan, complete from career to courtship of the woman I'll share my life-dream beside. Shortly after my blueprint was drawn, a beautiful woman walked into my life, bringing love, laughter, and inspiration. All these qualities helped me keep an eye on the prize during agonizing hours of operations and recoveries. Just last December, grinning and kissing, we exchanged rings on the warm sands of Waikiki Beach. Hibiscus and plumeria softly scented the tropical breeze as the moonlight followed the gentle rhythm of the waves as they slid upon the sand. One day we will live together on the island in the sun.

In a fast-paced series of events, I discovered my "where." After chasing my tale through a variety of challenging career choices, I was ready for Redwood Day School in Oakland, California. Their mission statement is in line with my motivation to make a difference in our children's life experience: "Engage, Prepare, Inspire." During my second interview, I stood and watched beautiful children of diverse backgrounds playing in and around the shadows of the filtered sunlight of the towering redwood trees. It was then that I knew this was the place. When I received my new hire packet I nearly choked in an astonished excitement akin to that of a dog who finally has achieved the perceived unachievable: "catching my own tale." For there, printed under the section of "Frequently

Asked Questions," was the answer I have been looking for over the past 22 years of my educational career:

> *Do you have any gay and lesbian staff and families in your current school community?*
> We have faculty, staff, and parents from these communities who are active and vital members of our school. We support community understanding of many kinds of families through curriculum, assemblies, and Gallery displays.

2004

As the dust from my chase begins to settle, my purpose for reaching and teaching is so clearly defined. I have joined Redwood Day School at the right time. My coworkers, both gay and straight, are in the initial planning stages of creating a GSA for our growing community of children and adolescents. I welcome the challenge of making a difference. Timing is everything. I've just been notified I have stage IV breast cancer, my fourth case in five years. I am now more determined than ever that my tale ends with LGBT and straight students and educators all living happily ever after...

TWO YEARS IN THE LIFE OF A QUEER TEACHER

Tarah Ausburn
Language arts teacher
Rose Linda Elementary School
Phoenix, Arizona

October 29, 2001

"Instructor Ausburn, I have a question."

"What is it, Carlota?"

"Are you a lesbian?"

My plan was never to fight this battle so directly. My first battle did not start with my "coming out" at school, nor did it start with "concerned" parents; it started with my car. I take pride in decorating my beautiful silver Honda Civic with progressive bumper stickers, dealing with issues such as animal rights, education, feminism, homophobia, military policies, and racism. To date, there are 62, and I have 18 more sitting in my glove compartment, waiting for the opportunity to make their debut on my moving billboard.

Everywhere I go, my car makes an impact; experiences range from people refusing to park next to me, to throwing gum on my windshield, to asking me out, to thanking me for stating my opinion, to expressing dismay at the lowered resale value, to groups crowding around my car in dozens of parking lots, to honks and thumbs-up on an almost-daily basis. At school, the students competed to find out who owned the car, and then when they figured it out, they bombarded me throughout the year to ask for clarification of my purpose, as well as the meaning behind some of the phrases plastered to the doors, hood, trunk, and bumpers. I once gave my language arts students the opportunity to gain 50 points if they could find the simile on my car; surely enough, Suzanne proudly handed me a slip of paper the very next morning: "A woman without a man is like a fish without a bicycle."

The administration's relationship with my car has not been nearly as friendly.

We were sitting in my classroom, our small bodies easily lounging in two students' desks. Ann, our school's coprincipal, was barely five feet tall, a tiny pale creature with flaming red hair, yet she possessed a respectful air of authority about her.

"I've been asked to talk to you about your bumper stickers," she said.

"What about them?" I asked.

"I want you to know that I'm only passing along a message to you, that this doesn't have anything to do with my own beliefs. Dr. Stanley [our superintendent] is furious about your bumper stickers. He wants you to remove them."

"Well, that's not an option." My blazing eyes challenged her to argue with me, not quite realizing whose side she was on.

"I know what you're going through…" My skeptical expression indicated I thought otherwise of this seemingly straitlaced principal in her gray suit and bright-pink, collared shirt. "No, I do. When I first started teaching I used to get in trouble all the time for my clothing. Even though I was a music and theater teacher, and we were always sitting on the floor in a circle, they thought my overalls and jeans were inappropriate. I constantly got into battles with my supervisor. In the end, you just have to figure out whether the battle is worth fighting."

I hardly recognized the underlying synonymy between wearing jeans to work and being ordered to remove bumper stickers from one's car, but I struggled to keep the cold fury out of my eyes.

She continued, "I want you to know that I support you, but I am not going to fight this battle for you."

Something in the way she told me this softened my hard defense. Perhaps I thought that her status as an administrator automatically put her on "their" side. Knowing her support—albeit silent—was there enabled me to open myself up enough to talk to her. I understood the precarious position she was in. She had been given orders from her boss, and it was not in her own best interest to help me fight the battle. So she passed along the message, while subtly giving me another message of her own.

"So, he wants my bumper stickers removed. Did he say which ones?"

"He did single out two," she admitted, "but I am not sure how many he wants you to remove. He did mention VEGETARIANS TASTE BETTER, and he was particularly outraged by SORRY I MISSED CHURCH. I WAS BUSY PRACTICING WITCHCRAFT AND BECOMING A LESBIAN. He said that it was 'offensive.' Anyway, like I said, I am just passing along a message from him. It's your decision what you want to do. He wants to know your decision tomorrow."

I did not give a decision the next day, simply because I had not had enough time to discuss the situation with any private attorneys or the ACLU. Luckily, a First Amendment rights specialist did return my e-mail, and he provided me with support and ammunition as to why the school district could not force me to remove my bumper stickers. When Ann approached me again to ask what my decision was, based on suggestions from the specialist, I told her that I would not remove any bumper stickers, that all requests or mandates needed to be put into writing, and that they needed to come from the person making the orders.

But Dr. Stanley would not contact me directly, despite my request. He told Ann to tell me to park off campus, on a side street. I refused to do that as well and again reiterated that I needed all mandates in writing.

His next step was ordering Ann to write me a formal directive—in her name, not his—requiring me to write out a list of all my bumper stickers and the interpretation of their meanings. This list was to be turned in by the next school day, less than 24 hours later. At this point I knew I was being harassed and again sought legal counsel. I ended up writing the school district a three-page letter detailing why I thought this was inappropriate and unethical. I did submit a then-current list of my bumper stickers and an interpretation of their meanings. The meaning was the same for each bumper sticker: "Guaranteeing freedom of speech for all humans and animals." At the end of the letter, I announced firm intentions to legally fight this battle, if the school district was that adamant about forcing me to remove my bumper stickers.

I waited for a reply, which never came. Weeks went by, and not another word was said about my bumper stickers. After six weeks, I knew that there would be a new form of harassment in the future and waited for it to arise. I was not disappointed. Throughout the rest of the year, I was shunned by my coworkers and mistreated by the administration. At one point, when I questioned a shady decision made by the assistant superintendent regarding one of my ED (emotionally disturbed) students, I was written up for "questioning authority."

My reaction was to put a bumper sticker on my car that stated in bold, red letters: QUESTION AUTHORITY.

❊

"Shut the fuck up, stupid faggot!" Dishawne yelled at Doug, seemingly for no reason other than the fact that Doug kept walking around the room talking to himself in that naturally psychotic way of his. My blood went cold, and my underarms immediately started to sweat. This was the first time I would address queer-related hate speech with my students, and I wanted to make an impression that lasted. Amazingly, my voice remained calm and unwavering.

"Dishawne, how would you feel if I called you a nigger?"

He stopped dead in his tracks. My assistant stared at me with wide eyes. Was some white girl teacher from Pennsylvania really going to open her mouth and say "the *n* word" in front of black

people? Other students who had not yet left to go to their buses whipped their heads around toward Dishawne to see what he would do.

"But you wouldn't, Instructor, because you're not like that." Still, his face showed disbelief and outrage.

"Dishawne, you calling Doug a faggot is no different than me calling you a nigger."

"That's not the same at all," he said. But I had his eye contact, and he was engaging in conversation. I pressed on, hoping to get through to him. He knew I was angry—he could hear it in my icy voice—but he did not understand why.

"*Faggot* is a word that was used in the Middle Ages. Gay men were rounded, tied together, and set on fire. They called homosexuals 'faggots' because the word *faggot* means 'a bundle of sticks,' and they tied them up just like they were a bunch of sticks."

"It's still not the same as *nigger*. It's just not right for you to call black people niggers."

I had used so much passion in my explanation that I felt defeated when he didn't immediately make the connection. I turned my back to him and said, "Go home, Dishawne," in a frustrated voice. He knew I was mad and did not know what to do. "Sorry, Instructor," he whimpered and ran out of the room, relieved to be away from my disappointment and my historical references.

The next morning, Dishawne tentatively approached me in class before school started.

"Can I talk to you, Instructor?"

The previous day's events had already washed away in my dreams, stored away as memories to potentially be retrieved later. I knew better than to take the whole matter personally; I was fighting a battle that was far older and stronger than I was. "Of course you can talk to me. What's up, Dishawne?"

"I told my mom last night about what happened yesterday."

A range of thoughts sped through my head. She misunderstood my reference with "the *n* word." She didn't like that I was teaching homosexual history at school. She was angry and was going to take it to the principal or the school board. These are the paranoid thoughts that float daily through the mind of any teacher who fights for LGBT rights on school grounds.

"It turns out my uncle is…that way."

"That way, Dishawne?"

"He's…you know…gay. He has one of those key chains with all the colors on it, like yours. He has a bunch of rainbow stuff, but I didn't know that meant he was gay. My mom and I sat down and talked about it. She told me it was OK. She still loves him, and I should too, and there isn't anything wrong with him being gay."

"Do you love your uncle?"

"Yeah."

"Even if he's gay?"

"I don't care!"

"I think that's great, Dishawne. Not everyone would be so mature about it. I'm proud of you."

Dishawne can't handle compliments, and he grew quite flustered. "I'm sorry about yesterday, Instructor."

"Thank you, Dishawne. It's not easy to apologize. And thanks for telling me about your uncle. I won't tell anyone, though—don't worry. That's your business."

He left to go hang out with his friends before the morning bell rang, and I spent the rest of my morning prep time floating on clouds. I'd finally gotten through to *someone*.

Throughout the year, I had intentionally treated my sexual preference as a mundane characteristic, hoping to normalize such a taboo concept. I never had a formal coming-out speech, but I answered my students' questions honestly. When they asked why I didn't have a boyfriend, I told them. When they wanted to know about my girlfriend, I gave them any requested information that did not relate to sex. The assistant superintendent did not agree that sexual orientation or preference and sexuality are completely different matters. She also

did not see the connection between having positive LGBT role models and a subsequent campus decrease in hate speech, homophobic attitudes, and middle school children getting beaten to a pulp simply because they are or are perceived to be queer. I was reprimanded for letting my students know about my sexual preference and given the formal directive not to discuss sexuality with any student on campus.

❋

"Dishawne, what's wrong?"

"My mom went to go see my uncle. He's in the hospital, and he has AIDS."

"Is this the uncle you were telling me about before, the one with the rainbow key chain?"

"No, this is another one. But he's that way too."

"Are you upset that he has AIDS?"

"I don't know him…but my mom goes to visit him in the hospital, and she hugs him. I don't want her to catch what he's got."

"Dishawne, you can't catch AIDS from hugging someone who has it."

"Yeah, but she kisses him too."

"You can't catch it that way either."

"How can you catch it, then?" he challenged, fighting back the tears forming in his eyes.

There it was, that paralyzing fear of saying the "wrong" thing and being written up or sued for it later. Why does the truth carry such fear and risk of consequence? Why can't I just answer a question to a scared teenage boy who thinks his mom is going to die just because she visits her sick brother in the hospital?

❋

At the end of the year, the assistant superintendent informed me that my contract would not be renewed because she did not think that I could "deal well with children."

Never mind that, according to our state's Department of Education guidelines, this was illegal, for the simple reason that they told me they would not renew my contract after the state-mandated deadline. Never mind that their statement did not even make any sense, as my most significant gain that year had *not* been standardized test scores, grades, attendance, or objective assessments but rather a connection with a group of special-needs students who had so few positive experiences in a public-school setting. Never mind that their statement is also ridiculous and irrational because it is ambiguous and lacking in any concrete support; she could not give me one example to support her slander. Never mind that this administration was lying about the real reason they wanted to get rid of me, but they needed an excuse that was somehow related to the children. Never mind that this administration is scared to tell me the real reason because they are already sitting on two potential lawsuits—due to the fact that two of our students had committed suicide in the previous three weeks—and they wanted to avoid a third potential legal battle. Never mind that they could have gotten away with telling me, "We are firing you because you are a lesbian." Never mind that the statement is preposterous for the additional reason that my cumulative end-of-year evaluation by my school principal states: "Instructor Ausburn clearly has an exceptional ability for handling troubled youth."

Never mind that what the assistant superintendent really meant to tell me was, "It is not that you cannot deal well with children. It is that we cannot deal well with you."

※

If I had not been only 22 years old—and devoid of union representation, financial support, or higher connections—I might have fought back. Instead, I left quietly and applied at another school district. I felt kicked down and humiliated, but I rationalized that there would come a time when I would have to fight again; next time I would be stronger. In some ways the next year

was better. I accepted a teaching position at another school in South Phoenix, with a population that had similar demographics.

My reading class was made up of mainstream junior high students. They were a delight to interact with; unlike my previous students, they weren't imprisoned in a self-contained ED classroom. I became that positive role model I hoped to be, and I had some impact on their language choices. Most of my students would not have even considered calling someone else "gay," "faggot," "dyke," or "homo," at least not in my presence. I also became the confidante to about half a dozen questioning eighth-graders. I even received community support when I discussed a controversial curriculum with two dozen parents and guardians. When I wanted to implement a yearlong diversity curriculum into my junior high reading class, complete with a month on gay and lesbian history, I began to circulate amongst students' guardians, trying to gauge their reaction. In some cases, I met with guardians in their homes; others came to meet me in my classroom. I discussed my intentions with 23 guardians altogether; only one mother refused to support my curriculum. The other 22 mothers, fathers, and guardians signed a written statement, asserting their support.

✳

It had been a particularly difficult day. A parent came in to yell at me about his daughter's math grade on her progress report. I didn't drink water all day because the vending machine kept spitting out Minute Maid Fruit Punch in a can when I pushed the button for purified water. I was coming down with a cold *again,* drained by stress, moldy classrooms, polluted air, and germy kids. It was only 11:55, and I still had hours of teaching and grading ahead of me. Kids were in my classroom—writing on my white board, gossiping about friends and new dating partners, eating and making a mess, and manipulating the surroundings in order to get my attention. Even though it was lunchtime, and the students should have been eating in the cafeteria, there was always a select group of students who would eat lunch in my room and spend their "recess" sitting inside the classroom rather than soaking up the sun's vitamins out on the playground or basketball courts.

I always tried to appear busy when I was in a foul mood, hoping the students would not talk to me as much when I needed the solitary downtime that simply was not available. Walking toward my desk, I stopped at a white table that held our classroom suggestion box. Shaking it, I heard the scratching sound of paper hitting cardboard, so I flipped the latch and opened the lid. Two papers, white, each folded and refolded half a dozen times, lay in stark contrast compared to the fluorescent orange bottom, and I opened each paper, always curious to read what the students thought they wanted, needed, or deserved in order to make this a better class.

"We need some tissues, Instructor. Real tissues not hard toilet paper."

Fair enough. If I don't blow my nose using bulk supply toilet paper, I should not expect my students to. I made a mental note to stop at the grocery store on the way home.

"Do you date students? My friend likes you. Hint-hint, it's a girl."

I looked around, paranoid that this was a joke and I was not going to handle it properly. Everyone was immersed in her or his own business, and no one but me felt the pounding in my chest. I folded that paper back up and stuck it in my purse. There was no point in trying to deal with the comment until my head was clear.

Two days later, Mireya mentioned it over a delicious cafeteria-provided lunch of taco boats, one of the few vegetarian dishes provided at RL Elementary. Mireya always tried to keep secrets, but the truth was she had no will power. She also wanted to be the important person who spread the grade's gossip, so I learned many a story and junior-high truth from her.

"How often do you read your notes in the suggestion box, Instructor?"

"I check it twice a week, on Tuesdays and Fridays."

Carlota and Mireya exchanged a look, and Mireya continued to pry. "Did you check it this Tuesday?"

"Yes. Why?"

No answer. No answer. Still, no answer. I repeated my question, more persistently this time. "Why, Mireya?"

"I know who wrote it."

"Who wrote what?"

"The note."

"What note?" I could see her frustration, and it was the highlight of my entire day.

"You know."

"Mireya, I get notes almost every day [this was a lie]. What note are you talking about? Did *you* write me a note?"

"No!"

"Oh, OK then. What note are you talking about?"

Mireya had had enough. "It was Darlene. She wrote it. She wrote it for Melosa, because Melosa likes you. She's like that, you know."

"Oh."

She obviously expected a bigger reaction than that. I knew I was torturing her. It's not often an eighth-grade teacher has the upper hand over her students, so it's important to take advantage of every available opportunity.

"Are you going to answer her?"

"I don't date students, Mireya. That's against the law, and it's not right for a teacher to date her student anyway. Then, that teacher might give the student special treatment...or fail the student when they break up."

It wasn't the answer that Mireya wanted. "Would you date her if she wasn't your student?"

"Not if she was 14."

"If she *wasn't* 14?" Mireya planned to push this conversation until she extracted the information she wanted; that much was clear.

"That depends on how much we had in common."

"Instructor, you're like that?"

"Like what?"

"You know."

"If you want to have a conversation, Mireya, you need to be able to say what's on your mind."

"Melosa's a girl."

"That's true. Rose Linda Elementary is giving you a wonderful education."

"Aw, Instructor! Do you date girls?"

"I date people, Mireya. Would you date someone who was black?"

"Yes."

"Native American?"

"Yes."

"Poor?"

"Who cares if they're poor?"

"That's the way I feel about dating girls. Who cares? They're people, all the same."

"I don't care either," Carlota piped up. "What difference does it make?" It was the first and only thing she said during the entire conversation.

Of course, the students are not really the problem; it is the society and the system that engulf and train them to repeat history's mistakes. I cannot say that my administration was any better this year. They would not permit me to teach Gay and Lesbian History Month as part of my yearlong diversity curriculum; when I put up a fight and started gaining community support, they switched me mid-year from being the junior high reading teacher to teaching eighth-graders math. Throughout the year, my homeroom students read stories from a book published by Teaching Tolerance; the stories focused on struggles and achievements made by various minority groups. We read the stories together, discussed their implications, and followed up with relevant projects. When my principal

heard that we read a true story about a Utah lesbian teacher fighting against a gag order her school district issued her, I was reprimanded for not getting prior approval of the book first, despite the fact that the assistant principal had approved the book for the social studies teacher the prior year. The discrimination was not as blatant the second time around, but that did not make it any better; it actually made it more difficult to deal with. I would have preferred the in-your-face, "I don't like you because you're a queer" approach, rather than the more subtle tactics used by this second administration to silence me and all LGBTAQ students on school grounds.

✳

This morning one of my students approached me before school. The night before, she had gotten a phone call from her aunt. Apparently, two teachers approached Ebony's aunt Tanisha, who also works at our school, to discuss some accusations concerning Ebony and me. There were two comments mentioned: (1) Ebony sits between my legs at the school basketball games; and (2) Ebony hangs out with me, alone, in my classroom.

Tanisha called another one of Ebony's aunts, who proceeded to call Ebony. According to Ebony, this conversation consisted of her aunt passing along the information and warning her to stop doing anything, if she was.

Ebony was embarrassed to admit this, and she usually confided all of her 14-year-old secrets to me. I tried to appear lackadaisical, hoping it would rub off. Casually I questioned, "Did you tell her there is nothing going on between us?"

"Of course!" she exclaimed. "All she said was, 'Well, you'd better stop, if there is.'"

I knew exactly who had started this, as there were only two teachers who consistently attended the basketball games: the cheerleading coaches. I had been informed on more than one occasion that they had a problem with me teaching at the school; they thought it was "inappropriate." By this time I was used to the fact that teachers used my sexual orientation as an argument to declare me "unfit" for teaching. Up until now I never bothered to approach any of the teachers, as I knew all would vehemently deny having made such bigoted remarks. This time I immediately approached Tanisha to discuss these allegations. She agreed with me, so we went and talked it over with the administrators. It turned out that the administrators had already been approached, and my principal informed me that he had looked into the situation.

Incredulously, I asked, "You heard this too? Why doesn't anyone inform *me* of these accusations?"

A strange look passed across the principal's face—guilt, mixed with...disappointment?—before he lamely replied, "Well, I looked into it and didn't find anything. If there had been a problem, then you would have known about it." I couldn't help but wonder if he was disappointed that he found nothing to persecute me for. I left the office continuing to feel suspicious but proud that I handled the rumor directly and efficiently to the best of my ability. Nothing ever came of the rumor, but I did start to notice the way certain teachers watched me whenever I talked to Ebony outside of the classroom.

The relatively supportive response from my principal made it quite an interesting turn of events when I discovered that my principal did not plan to renew my contract. It was déjà vu: For the second year in a row, my contributions to my students were thwarted by politics and irrational fears—and the administration had again failed to follow legal procedures required for not renewing my contract. According to the law, I should have been informed by April 15, via writing, if they did not plan for my return to their school.

It was more than simple legal procedures that frustrated me, however; it was, of course, principle. My standardized test scores

on the SAT-9s rivaled that of the two other eighth-grade teachers, who had decades of experience compared to my two years. My math test scores alone were a vast improvement from the 0% of students who had achieved grade level in the past three years; my classes' test scores indicated that 17% of the eight-graders at RL Elementary were now on grade level, mathematically speaking. In my homeroom, I tripled the number of honor roll students. I was popular with the students; they both trusted and respected me, a difficult feat to achieve simultaneously amongst kids of their age. I averaged 11-hour days and 60-hour weeks, working overtime to find ways to get my students interested in learning.

None of that mattered, though, when the administration was dealing with a polysexual-but-lesbian-to-them teacher who had the audacity to drive a car saturated with "offensive" bumper stickers, teach gay and lesbian history, and not feel ashamed of her sexual preferences.

Remember, though—the past year's experiences had made me stronger, and I took advantage of that strength to fight back this time. After discovering that my contract would not be renewed, I involved my union and made plans to sue the district, battling loudly enough that my principal rescinded his decision; he filed a "Recommendation to Hire" form at the district. I signed my contract. I did not even want to return there, but there was no way I was going to allow them to make that decision for me, not when I'd dedicated a year of my life to helping those kids achieve beyond their perceived capabilities.

If there is one thing all of this has taught me, it is the importance of developing patience. I want to make change overnight in my classroom and on school grounds, and of course I cannot. If I do not learn patience, my frustration will erode both my idealism and any chance I have of improving conditions. I also understand now that I am seriously not going to have any impact if I am in this alone. I would like to think I am important and extraordinary enough that I could be that *one teacher* who changed my students' lives. The truth is, unless there are other teachers, leaders, adults, and peers confirming my lessons on diversity and tolerance, my progress will be minimal. It is often disheartening to look around at my staff meetings and see the walls of intolerance that have been built around the public education system. It is frightening to see other queer colleagues look away in silence instead of speaking up. I see that I am literally the only one at our school fighting against gender conformity, sexism, and heterosexism.

I do feel alone. I am lucky because I don't need to have a lot of support in order to have my beliefs validated. Not everyone feels that way. Validation aside, though, I know I cannot make the necessary progress if I fight alone. We need other teachers also paving the rainbow way for true diversity and tolerance when it comes to sexual orientation or preference. We need people in power, working on the system from the inside. We need resources, volunteers, secure organizations, and community support in order to make any of this work. Change is not going to naturally occur *for* us. If we are not actively working toward solving the problem, then we remain a part of the problem.

Dario and Chale approach me, the smirks on their faces an obvious sign that they are up to something. Chale, always the more outspoken one of the pair, speaks up first. "Have you ever heard of Flexx, Instructor Ausburn?"

"No. What is it?"

"It's a gay club practically right across the street from me."

"How do you know it's a gay club?"

Dario jumps into the conversation, eager to contribute. "'Cause there are all these guys walking around funny and holding hands with other guys."

"What do you mean, 'walking around funny'?"

This time, it's Chale's turn. "You know how gay guys walk...all funny, and then they talk with that weird lisp, and they do that hand thing..." Chale proceeds to make one of his wrists go limp,

and Dario bursts out laughing: "Chale, you look so...flexx...when you do that."

It was blatantly clear by now that they were baiting me, so I decided to retaliate in my own way. "Well, Chale looks flexx no matter what he does."

There are definite benefits to working with adolescents who are old enough to appreciate sarcasm. Before Chale could recover with a witty remark of his own, I reminded both of them, "There are some gay people who 'look' gay, but there are also lots of people you'd never know were gay. Don't go thinking all gay people look and act the same."

"That's messed up, Instructor," whined Chale. "I don't look flexx."

"Hey, you never know, Chale," I replied. "You never know who's flexx and who's not. That's the point I'm trying to make." I walked away, leaving two students who love to antagonize me standing there, mouths agape and at a loss for any retaliation. The battles I win are slow in coming and seemingly miniscule—but I'm making progress.

ARE THOSE REAL?

Anafaith Lubliner
Theater teacher
César Chávez Elementary
San Francisco, California

I can still remember the moment before I came out as a lesbian to my students. I was sitting on the dirty floor of the cafeteria/auditorium. There was that familiar strange aroma of garbage and kids. It was dark, with dingy faux theater lighting. I looked around at their distracted faces, poking one another, thinking today would be just another day in acting class. I was anxious. But there was a little glimmer of hope. Hope that I was about to do something…good. Life-changing. They had no idea what was about to hit them.

How did I come to this decision? I came out because of a realization. I am an after-school theater teacher in the Mission District at César Chávez Elementary in one of the most gay-friendly cities in the country, possibly the world.

Now, let me tell you, scratch the surface of any school in San Francisco and you will find a large queer population—from the teachers to any part of the administration. So many people have migrated to this gay mecca in order to be free and open about their sexual orientation. Yet here is the conundrum. While most of the people on the staff are out to one another, they are still closeted with the students and the parents. In general we know who is a cross-dresser, who is a lesbian, and who is raising a son that has

117

two daddies. But we're hush-hush when it comes to the students we see day in and out.

This may not seem so strange in Utah, but in San Francisco? Why would we be afraid here? This is the town where we see men in dresses and dyke lesbian leather daddies with their "boi" and we do not bat an eye. Yet the teachers and staff are still afraid to tell their students.

Why are we hiding from children? I believe the answer is internal. It is the inner child that still lives in the schoolyard—the child that has been bullied and pummeled into corners and hard pavement for being different. Too swishy, too butch, too, too, too anything…just too. We do not want to be teased, to be the weak one, to be taunted and humiliated again and again, or worse, to be the one totally left out. We are afraid if we are exposed, the parents, the teachers, and the kids will hate us. We won't be allowed to play with our friends anymore.

I came out because I finally decided that I did not want to let these old fears win. It was time for me to face the bully in the schoolyard. The day I made this decision, a student of mine made a gay slur toward another boy. Instead of responding immediately, I became numb and did not say anything at all. I froze.

Afterward, I was very disappointed in myself and tried to look at why I had been so unable to respond. Had the slur been toward any racial group, I would have acted immediately. Yet a gay slur hit my core: He was talking about me. This was when I realized the depth of my hiding. I had to take action. If I believe in freedom and equality for all, what better place to start than in my own classroom?

My first plan of action was to speak with the staff at Jamestown. I told my supervisor, Katie Brackenridge. I sat her down in the school therapy section, surrounded by little toys, African-American and Latina dolls, and various stuffed animals. Katie was a phenomenal supervisor: sharp, strong, and an excellent educator. She still floored me with her response. Katie looked at me and immediately told me she would completely support me. She even offered to sit in with the kids when I came out. I was thrilled.

I also spoke with my teaching assistant, who was only 15 and had been raised Catholic. She was intelligent and scrappy and the kids loved her, but her Catholic upbringing made me cautious. She quietly told me that she had been raised to accept everyone, that her uncle is gay, and that it was no big deal to her. She also offered to support me. This had been one of my anxieties around coming out in my school. So many children in the Mission District are raised in a Catholic or Christian environment, which I assumed was generally homophobic. Once again I was happily surprised. Together we picked a specific date.

When that day finally came, only half the kids showed up, so we decided to wait until my next teaching day. That was when the anxiety and tension began to build. I had to wait two more days!

Finally the day came. I sat in a circle with the kids, Katie, and my TA. My first line was "I need to talk to you all about something that upset me." They were immediately on alert, sure they were in trouble. I assured them they were not in trouble. Then I said, "There was something that one of you said that hurt my feelings. When I heard one student say to another student they were gay in a mean way, that hurt my feelings. Because you were talking about me; I am a lesbian."

Shocked looks, silence, gasps, and wide-open eyes.

"Who did it?" they asked, looking around.

"I am not going to say who did it, but does anyone have a question?" That is when the flood of questions began. Their curiosity was amazing.

Question: Who is the girl and who is the boy? Answer: We are both girls, no one plays the boy.

Question: Are you really a man? Answer: No.

Question: Do you kiss her? Answer: I don't talk about private things...

Question: At what age did you know that you liked girls? Answer: About 18.

Then, my favorite question: While pointing at my breasts, one girl asked: Are those real? Answer: Yes, my breasts are real, and I am a woman!

One student said, "That's OK, Ana, you are still the nice person you always were…"

Then they asked why Katie was there. Katie said, "Because I want everyone to know I support Ana. She is gay, and it doesn't matter—she is still my friend."

Another student said, "My uncle is gay." A few others chimed in with stories about gay relatives, or how their parents relate to gay people. We were done.

Then the most extraordinary thing happened. Afterward, I was still anxious, my heart was tight, my breathing shallow. I was afraid that I would be rejected, thrown out of the house, so to speak. We went outside for our break, to let the kids play in the yard, and two of the girls kept on hugging me over and over, giving me "love bombs." It was as if they felt closer to me because I had opened up to them.

Then came the biggest surprise of all: The kids decided to improvise a play in a talk show format. Here was the setup:

Title: *Bullies on the Playground*
Characters: An upper-class English girl, a Southern girl, a bully, best friend to the English girl, two talk-show hosts, a *gay character,* and the studio audience.
Story: Gay character and all the others had been mercilessly mistreated by the school bully. Characters come up to be interviewed by the hosts. One by one they tell the story of how they have been bullied. The bully comes onstage. The studio audience all began to boo. Then when the gay student is telling his story onstage, they all began to cheer. Then they all began to chant "Gay is good, gay is good." Then the bully apologizes to the gay kid and all of his other victims. The end.

It was unbelievable. I could not have planned it better myself. That was how the day ended.

The following week the resistance began. One of the children, Pablo (all of the children's names have been changed to protect their privacy), was absent the day I had come out. When he returned he came back to *Bullies in the Playground* being played out again. He began to turn the chant around into "Gay is bad," and some of the students joined in. We had to stop class to talk about it.

The honeymoon was over. It seemed like a metaphor for society. Often when there is an opening, there is also a closing down in fear.

It was not all easy after that. That same student, Pablo, was mysteriously and suddenly pulled out of my class. My own identity issues came up: I am married to a woman, and yet I consider myself bisexual. Should I have come out as bisexual? Or would that have been too much for me? For the kids? I do not know. Maybe I was still hiding.

Still, the ice had been broken. They all expressed an interest in meeting my partner, Katrine. They were as intrigued with her being a juggler as with her being my partner. A week later I brought in Katrine to meet them, and as promised she taught them how to juggle. They all seemed both intrigued and shy. They were thrilled with the juggling.

My being out eventually faded into the background of plays and sets and regular day-to-day activities. I have since come out three other times, with varying degrees of drama.

Years later, the third time I came out, there was an interesting development. I told this new class that they could meet Katrine as well. But Katrine was not able to make it that semester. Yet one student, Angelica, bothered me over and over. She was beyond fascinated: She was borderline obsessed. She bothered me every time she saw me. "When am I going to meet Katrine?" "When am I going to meet Katrine?" Finally Katrine came to a performance to meet her. When she met Katrine, Angelica was shy beyond belief.

Will Angelica be a lesbian? I do not know, but her level of interest made me believe that by coming out I had stirred some possible inner recognition in her. She also told me she wants to be a teacher. If she is a lesbian, she will have a role model of an out gay teacher who was not ashamed of the fact that she loves a woman.

I believe without a shadow of a doubt this is the best lesson I have ever given.

TRUE COLORS

Chip James
School social worker
Clarkstown Schools
New City, New York

Having cleaned up their places at the table, my fifth-grade boys, in a five-member group for children of divorced parents, bounded out the door to recess. I faced my desk to phone my friend Jane—also a school social worker—and tell her I'd be a bit late for our lunch date. When I turned to leave the office, however, I discovered that Jason remained seated at the table. I'd known Jason since he was 9, early in fourth grade; he was referred by his teacher due to his "poor self-image" and ongoing conflicts with peers. At times the conflicts were initiated by other boys' taunting, and at other times they were initiated by Jason's vigilant defensiveness. Underneath the conflicts, however, was the pain and confusion of his perception of himself as "different." A slight, olive-skinned boy under a pile of dirty-blond hair (complete with a hastily made cow-lick in front, a feeble attempt to fit in), he sat waiting for words to come. Below his faded blue T-shirt and his jeans were the new sneakers he'd negotiated with his mother as an early birthday present. Already he'd learned from a classmate that the stripes were "all wrong."

He said nothing and didn't look up at me. I pretended to arrange some things on my desk to give him some time to get his nerve up. Finally, given my time constraints, I offered, "So, Jason, usually when someone stays at my table, they either have something they need to say, or something they need to hear."

"First," replied Jason. The sound of spittle punctuated his speech, which had been increasingly pensive and measured and was especially so today.

"OK," I continued, "is it about school or home?"

"Home," he said, nodding his head, lips pursed in anticipation and concern.

"Is it about something that happened or something you wish would happen?"

"Something I wish." His direct eye contact told me that I had his full attention. We might actually get somewhere. With each answer known and expressed, he was closer to something that's difficult to get at. He turned a corner to find a corridor, and not a dead end.

"Does it involve Mom's house or Dad's?" I continued.

"Mom's."

"So, Jason, what is it that you wish would happen with you and your Mom?" The right question is always more than half the battle.

"I want her to watch a movie with me."

"Is this about the movie or about spending some time with her?"

"Well, kind of both, but more about the movie," he clarified.

"So, what's the movie, and what's important about it?" I asked.

"Have you seen *Bring It On,* Mr. James? It's about professional cheerleaders and what they go through to compete. It's really, really hard to do."

"I haven't seen it, Jason, but I'd like to. What is it that you'd like your Mom to get from watching this movie with you?"

" I want her to see how hard that stuff is. I want her to know that's what I want to do."

"Wow, so you want your Mom to respect what you want to do."

"*Exactly,*" exclaimed Jason, awed by my insight.

"Have you tried to tell her before?" I asked.

"Well, yes, but she didn't have time to listen to me." While this

may be the perception of many kids, I knew it to be true in Jason's situation.

"Then that's what we have to work on first, right?" I asked, with Jason's immediate agreement. "We have to come up with time when you're alone with your mom. How about homework time?"

"No, that's crazy time in my house."

"OK, how about some time in the car?"

"Yes, that's it—before we pick up the others!" Ah, my crystal ball is in tune now. "But I don't know what to say."

"All right, it's best to be clear when making a request. I'll try it on you and you see if it fits. You drive, and I'll be you. If the radio's on, you may want to turn it down so your mom hears and listens. It's a good signal that you're going to say something serious. 'Mom, I really want you to watch a movie with me, because I want you to learn something about me.'"

"That's perfect, Mr. James!"

"Now I'll drive, and you're you...go," I directed.

"Mom, I really *need* you to watch a movie with me, because I want you to know something about me and what I want to do." This time he personalized and empowered the request with his substitution of "need."

"Great. Jason, is there any reason why you've hesitated about doing this?"

"Well, most people think that cheerleading is only for girls, but there are boys who do it," he answered.

"Of course there are boys who do it. Is that why you want your mom to know that it's hard to do?" I asked.

"Yes."

"Brilliant," I replied, "and very creative."

"Mr. James, why do people think that cheerleading is only for girls?"

"I think it's because cheerleaders cheer for players, and originally all the players could only be men. So, the women took over cheering. After a long time of seeing it this way, people just think that's the way it is...even though it's not that way anymore. It's pretty dumb, and, unfortunately, some people believe a lot of

124

dumb things, just because it's what they've learned. A dumb thing about how somebody's supposed to be is called a stereotype. Stereotypes confuse people because they always have a little piece of truth, so it seems like it could be true. But, a stereotype also has lies. I'm always proud of people who follow their own heart and don't let a stereotype boss them around. I'm proud of girls who join the little league team, and I'm proud of boys who follow their interest onto the cheerleading squad. I'm proud of you."

"Thank you, Mr. James."

"I'm also proud of being chosen for this discussion, and I'm glad that you want your family to know you better…and to respect you for it. Will you let me know how it goes?"

"Yes."

"Good luck, and let me know if you need more from me?"

"I will." He thanked me and went off to join his class.

When I arrived at the diner, Jane was already seated. "I just had an amazing conversation with one of my fifth-grade boys," I began, and proceeded to tell the story. As I continued, step by step, Jane's eyes widened, as did her pearly smile.

"I can't believe this!" she exclaimed. "I just can't believe this." She was laughing. "My son, the fifth grader, had me sit down with him this past week to watch *Bring It On*." More bursts of laughter, and tearing eyes. "He wanted me to know that he wants to be a cheerleader, and that it's hard work."

"You've got to be kidding me." I took her hand, and we both squeezed through heartfelt laughter.

Jane continued. "He asked me where there's a high school that has a coed cheerleading squad, and whether he could go there one day. I told him we'd explore it, and that if it didn't happen in high school, he could take gymnastics and we'd look for a college where he could do it." I could only hope that Jason would receive half as supportive a reception from his mother.

When I saw Jason the next week for his regular group meeting,

I asked him to stay behind after the other boys left. He wanted to get to recess and could only spare me a few minutes, his coolness belying some potential discomfort.

"You're wondering if I spoke to my mom…well, I did. And no, we haven't watched the video yet, because my mother can't find the time," he said, rolling his eyes dramatically.

"Jason, I'm proud of you for following through, and sad that she's disappointing you. She doesn't even get it that she's missing out. Do I call her for an appointment, or do you want to step it up and try a note this time? You see, if you give up, you join her. You both deserve for her to listen to you."

"I'll write a note. If it still doesn't work, you can call," he decided. I admired his desire to handle it himself and told him so.

"But that's not the only reason I asked you to stay," I broke in as he darted a glance at the door, recess still beckoning. "I wanted to tell you about an interesting conversation I had recently with a friend of mine." This potential window into my personal life stole his attention away from recess and he settled himself on the chair. "You see, after our last talk, I had lunch with a friend of mine who is also a school social worker like me. I was still thinking about what you and I discussed and thought that it was an important talk. So, without using any names, I told her the story. She became stunned and couldn't believe what she was hearing. It turns out that she has a son in the fifth grade, and this past week he asked her to watch *Bring It On* with him."

This time Jason's eyes enlarged as his mouth hung open in absolute disbelief. "Really? Did she do it?" he asked with hope and anticipation.

I momentarily considered whether I could do harm by answering this question, concerned that his mother's reception may not be as fulfilling. Understanding that he still needed to know that *some* mom would be supportive, I answered him, "Yes, she did, and now she knows that her son wants to be a cheerleader, and she wants to help find ways to make it happen."

Jason grew quiet, as I watched his shoulders drop with his silent pondering. "You know, Mr. James, maybe he and I could get along." (An important consideration for someone who felt largely alien with regard to his peers.)

"I bet it's a good possibility," I said. Then I dismissed him, and he floated to recess in a stream of new consciousness. It struck me that he was a new boy—a boy who knows there's another boy in the world like him, with a mother who supports him.

After a faculty meeting, I walked Jane to her car. We both started speaking simultaneously. I let her go first.

"When I got home on the day of our lunch date, I told my son about our conversation and the story you told me. He was so excited to hear that there's another fifth-grade boy who wants to be a cheerleader. His very first response was 'Maybe we could get along.' "

Now it was my turn for the wide eyes and the slack jaw. Jane's son said what Jason had said verbatim. Now there are two boys in the world who will never be alone again, regardless of whether they meet.

Rigid social expectations regarding gender roles have been so unfair to human beings for a long time, and kids pay the price. At the potential costs of taunting, rejection, and isolation, kids are often fumbling their way through the "mind" field of gender roles that don't reflect them either as individuals or, more basically, as people. While taking on the complexities and contradictions of Western gender politics and sexism as a whole would overwhelm these young pilgrims, trimming off the crust and cutting it up into chewable pieces can change the world…one bite at a time.

"Hey! Mr. James, how can you do that?" asked a boy in the third grade, first to arrive of six boys and girls in a weekly counseling group. I had no idea what he was referring to. "Your cup, you're drinking out of a pink cup!" With his permission, I brought the question to the group when they arrived with lunch bags and styrofoam trays of mass-produced food. "Yeah," they chided,

"how *can* you drink out of a pink cup?" Their incredulity was unanimous.

"Well," I told them, "it's got a bottom, a handle, and it's filled with coffee exactly the way I like it, so I don't have any problem drinking out of it. What could be the problem with me drinking out of it?"

"It's a girl color," they agreed.

"Oh," I said, "you mean there are things only for girls and only for boys?"

"*Yes*! Duh!" I clearly needed some training on the matter.

"OK, so let's do this so I can get really clear." I drew a line down the center of the black board, labeling one side BOYS and the other GIRLS. Then I said, "Let's list as many girl things and boy things as we can." They instantly began calling out items for the lists—seemingly without dispute. Of course, the lists began with colors. Girl colors were pink, red, yellow, and purple, while boy colors were blue, green, brown, and black. Boys are faster, stronger, better at and more interested in sports, and they like tools and cars. Girls, on the other hand, like to play with dolls, dance, clean, cook, and sew, and they care more about their looks.

Though there were no overt challenges to individual items, as the lists lengthened the group became increasingly polarized, and the tension was palpable. They began corralling their lunch materials into small, identifiable "territories," circling the wagons. Accidental foot touching under the table became kicking, and a defensive atmosphere enveloped the room.

"OK, stop," I said. "Let's forget about the list for a minute. What's happening in this room at this table?"

Silence. They looked at me and at one another.

"We're getting angry at each other," offered Anna firmly.

"Why?" I asked.

"Because there are things wrong on those lists," she said. I breathed a private sigh of relief. Perhaps we had moved somewhat beyond those antiquated and limiting stereotypes after all.

"So," I proposed, "how about we go back to the lists, and if you can tell me what's wrong with an item, we'll agree to take it off the list." We began to dismantle the lists. The girls were quick and clear about owning things on the boys' list. Girls can also be strong, fast, and can like and be good at sports. After all, that very morning Claire had beaten Thomas at a race in the schoolyard…three times! With examples agreeable to all, these items were removed from the list. The boys sat silently as their list grew shorter. None of the three boys attempted to dispute any items on the girls' list. I wondered if they were feeling emasculated. They needed help.

Knowing them all rather well, I encouraged the boys to own something on the girls' list—something they needed but were terrified to do. "Now, listen here, you guys," I cajoled, "I happen to know how long it takes to make those perfect little spikes on top of your heads with gel, tie laces like that, and make sure that pants hang right up top and at the bottom. I also happen to know that you wouldn't even *think* of leaving your house unless they were all perfect. So don't even try to tell me otherwise. Am I right?"

The boys looked at one another, blushing, with chirps of suppressed giggles. The girls were thrilled with the suggestion, and they joined the boys' chirping, till they were all laughing together at the truth of the situation. They seemed thrilled and supportive of the boys' acceptance of my use of humor to weather the vulnerability of potential humiliation in owning girls' list items. "Girls care more about their looks" was removed from the girls' list without opposition.

I pushed again. "And you, Tony, brought me spaghetti that you made so I would know what a good cook you are, right?" Again, laughter, and still lighter spirits. "Cooking" was removed from the girls' list.

There were only a few items left on the lists, and time was running out. "I have another idea," I said. "Tell me what you think about this." I erased the line dividing the board into two lists.

"That's it," Anna cried out, "we'll have only one list!" She got it immediately. They all excitedly agreed. All seemed relieved to find a solution that saved them from the limitations and pain of the rigid and unrealistic lists.

I continued. "If it's going to be one list, it has to have one title," I stated. "What will we title the list?"

Again, silence. Then, Anna (on a roll...and I swear I didn't pay her...though I was moved to!) stated with certainty, "Let's call it 'Humankind.'"

"Yes, yes. Humankind," the rest chimed in. I wrote HUMANKIND over the remnants of the torturous lists, turning the remaining items into one list.

They literally bounced, giggling, out of my room, like they had just won a team sport. They looked as though pounds of extra weight had been taken off of them. There was such relief in surviving and even flourishing through the process of constructing, then consciously *de*constructing a system that is experienced as oppressive. As it turns out, there are all kinds of boys and all kinds of girls, all kinds of things for them to like and do, *and* it feels good to remember that.

Two weeks later I played a board game with this same group of kids. Anna stopped the play for a moment, saying, "Hey, look what we did!" She pointed to the plastic pawns on the board. "We all chose opposite colors." We all looked at the pieces to see that, indeed each child had chosen a color from the "other" side of the original two lists. We all laughed, and we reminisced about how fun that meeting had been in the end. Privately, I feared that once attention was called to their "gender-atypical" choices, something tantamount to a crime, they would rectify this by trading colors. They laughed and maintained their "new" color choices. They seemed gratified, as I certainly was.

Early in my career as a school social worker, I couldn't imagine being out. Now it's hard to imagine not being out. This doesn't mean that I make a general and regular announcement, but rather that self-censorship is not an automatic process. My being out is much more about comfort in my own skin while being out on the issues as an advocate, mental health consultant, educator, and colleague.

Well, time for a cup of coffee...in my pink cup. Join me?

AN UNCERTAIN AND BRILLIANT WORLD

Elizabeth Katz
Teacher
Phillips Exeter Academy
Exeter, New Hampshire

For my teachers, and my students

When I was in high school it felt like almost nothing outside my books was true. I looked out the windows of my school library into the abandoned parks of Boston, and the world seemed distant and unreal. My own life too did not seem real; it was a combination of hiding myself and hiding other people. I had just figured out that I was gay and that I could tell no one. In the library, I sat underneath desks and read Walt Whitman and Adrienne Rich. I had to believe in books; if it was my furtive life that was true, I would have to listen to the radio through headphones for the rest of my life, lie about the people I talked to on the phone, hide the magazines I bought. Every morning, I put on my jeans and my black T-shirt. It was easy, invisible. I could save my thinking for the brave lives I wanted to learn about in books.

The only people who seemed to live beyond the stories that surrounded me were my teachers, and especially the women who taught me English. It was my teachers who convinced me that my own life was full of possibilities, who showed me lives full of integrity and courage outside the books they taught.

Seven years after my own graduation, I came back to high school, this time as a teacher myself, with memories of what my own teachers had been to me. I started my second year of teaching, September 2002, in limbo. I had taken this position in the English department at Cranbrook Kingswood Upper School to be near my partner, who was still in graduate school at the University of Michigan. Eight months after she moved in with me, she left. I was alone, almost a thousand miles away from my family and friends, in a school and a profession where I wasn't sure I belonged. My summer had been spent trying to put my life back together, filling the holes in the apartment where her books and picture frames had been. I knew this year would be my last in this school.

As the school year began, the English teachers settled into our first department meeting. We ran through book orders, department policies, and class sizes, and then one of my colleagues announced a visiting author, an alumnus, a man who had made his reputation by writing novels about being gay. My colleague ran through the publications, the prizes the writer had won, and then paused. Because this writer was "a proponent of the gay lifestyle," he said, we could mention the writer's lecture in class but could distribute none of his writing.

I did not know what to do. I wanted to cry and, realizing I couldn't stop myself, I left the meeting. The only place to go was the bathroom, just like all those times in high school when my friends and I fled to the girls' room for an inadequate privacy. I was ashamed to be part of a school that did not want students to read about people like me. The school had invited this man back because of the recognition he had received as a writer, and yet they wouldn't allow students to read his writing.

I thought about my own visibility; I had never lied to my students, and when they asked about the ring I had worn on my left hand, or the woman who answered the phone at my apartment, I had told them about my partner. I had been visible when necessary. Now, it felt like what was necessary was changing. Angry and sad, I went to my friend Tim, one of the faculty advisers to our school's gay-straight alliance. As we talked, I could feel him becoming outraged.

A few days later, Tim confronted an administrator in the faculty room. "Why can't we pass out excerpts from the books? We know what's appropriate," he said.

The administrator shuffled his feet. "We're just not ready for this yet," he said. Tim looked him straight in the eye. He did not raise his voice. "Then when? I mean that. I want a date for when we'll be ready."

I had come out in high school for a lot of reasons, but mostly because I believed the personal was political. I believed in the power of visibility and the obligation to raise one's voice against injustice. The day after I came out, my younger sister found an anonymous note in her mailbox that read, "Tell your fucking faggy sister to go to hell. That's where she belongs." At that moment, everything stopped being theoretical; the personal was all *too* personal. My sister and I ran to the English teacher who was the adviser to the school GSA. She interrupted a meeting of school administrators to hand over the note and demand to know what they were going to do about it. A school assembly was held, the note was read out loud, and the head of the school said, looking out at all the students, "We do not tolerate this. This is not what our community is about." Suddenly, being gay was more important, and even more difficult, than it had been. There were things that could be done, that had to be done.

I went to my first meeting of the year as coadviser to the gay-straight alliance feeling again like the girl who had needed community and comfort and acceptance. There were more than a dozen students at the meeting. Some were my students, others were strangers. The room was full of a tense excitement; you could feel the students' relief in the safety of the meeting, in meeting other people like themselves, in seeing the possibilities of what and who they could be. They needed mirrors. I thought about that writing we weren't allowed to pass out and went back

to my reading list for the year, adding *The Hours* by Michael Cunningham, a novel in which one of the central relationships is between two women who have been partners for 18 years.

The autumn moved on to Homecoming Week, capped off by the junior-senior girls' football game and the fall parents' visiting day on Friday. As an adviser to the junior class, I felt the tension rising between the two classes until, on Thursday afternoon, more than 30 cars in the parking lot were vandalized with shaving cream and motor oil. An all-school assembly was called for Friday before the game.

On Friday, parents' visiting day, I walked into my classroom, arranging my books and waiting for parents to arrive. On my right, I could hear a soccer player and a football player arguing.

"All soccer players are foot fairies," said the football player. I could see his mother cringing as she looked at her hands.

I froze, then said, "You know that kind of language is unacceptable in my classroom."

"Yes," said his mother, weakly. The football player stuttered an apology; I swallowed, then started to teach. The day passed in introductions and awkward pauses, and by the time we got to the assembly, I was exhausted.

I stood with the other teachers on the far side of the gym and listened to a dean talking about the vandalism. "It is not acceptable to destroy people's property. It is not acceptable to write obscenities in the parking lot. It is completely inappropriate to write FAG on a person's car." I heard the distinction: not "unacceptable," "inappropriate." For the second time that day, I felt my stomach churn. I walked out of the gym.

That night, after the homecoming dance, I sat talking to Suzanne, one of my former students. A week ago she had come to find me in the faculty room, asking, "Ms. Katz, when did you know you were…different?"

"I knew when I was 14, but I've had friends who didn't know until they were out of college, and others who felt they knew when they were really young." I looked at her. "Have you been thinking about that stuff?"

Half in tears, she did not meet my eyes as she said, "Yes." Suzanne had spent that night at the dance tentatively dancing with another girl, but had been unable to ignore the stares, the people laughing and pointing. "I thought I could do that here," she said, "but after what happened in the parking lot, I just don't feel safe anymore."

Saturday morning I called Tim, and I told him about what had happened in my classroom, about what Suzanne had said. "I've been thinking about what happened on Friday, and I think I need to come out at school, to the kids. Being silent is hurting me, and if it's hurting me, it must be hurting the kids. They need to know that their words are hurting real people."

Tim paused; I could hear him breathing on the other end of the line. "I won't let you do this alone. I'm going to come out too. We're in this together." That weekend, I couldn't stop thinking about the anonymous words that had shaped my experience of being gay in high school. After striding to the head's office, the gay-straight alliance's adviser had sat me down in an empty classroom. Looking directly in my eyes, she said, "You know you're not going to hell, don't you?" With her words, I felt the shame of being a target lift away.

Monday morning, class meetings were called. I did not know what I wanted to say about the graffiti until I looked at the 11th graders. "When someone uses anonymous and hateful language, because there is no name attached, the entire community is responsible for it. I know that you are better than these words. But what you need to know is that these words hurt. They hurt me as a member of this community, they hurt me as your teacher, and they hurt me as a gay woman. I know you are better than this, and I want better things for you than this language. I don't want to be part of a community where these words are used, and we have to work together now to reject this kind of language. You are going to be leaders, and this is the time to become leaders, to act with honesty and integrity and say that we do not allow this in our community. We do not destroy property, and we do not destroy people.

We are better than this. You are better than this." Next to me, the class president, Emily, began to clap, and the entire class joined in.

That week, at the gay-straight alliance meeting, I said to the kids, "What do you guys think about what happened in the parking lot?" They were silent; I pressed. "Were you surprised? Or was it not a big deal?"

One of the girls looked at me, stonily. "I hear those words so much I don't hear them anymore," she said.

"Do me a favor," I passed out some scrap paper, "and write down the things you hear other people saying about being gay." For a few minutes, the room was silent, and then slowly they began to pass me the pieces of paper.

Faggot.

Dyke.

I'll pay you two girls to have sex if I can watch.

She's gay? I never listened to her anyway.

Across the room, my student Peter was still bent over his paper. I kept going through the pages.

Homo.

Fruit.

You don't belong here, dyke.

That's so gay.

Peter handed me his paper, folded up.

Cocksucker Pole blower Gay freak Fruit Homo Queen Fudge packer Dick licker…

The list kept going. There wasn't room on his page to fit another word.

A week later, the gay alumnus writer visited the school. After many, many discussions—and some student activism—suitable passages had been agreed upon to pass out to the students. In his classroom, Tim had passed out the writing, saying, "When I read this, I know exactly how the character feels. Growing up gay in a time when no one—I mean *no one*—talked about it, I understand his secrecy and his desire for companionship. So it's important to me that we read this, because it's a story you very easily might never hear." His students had listened, respectfully, and then, one by one, in the days afterward, approached him to say how they appreciated his honesty.

In the gay-straight alliance, the writer sat down with the kids. "What are your lives like?" he asked, and their faces were filled with pleasure. So few people wanting an honest answer asked what their lives were really like.

Peter spoke up. "Last year, I was walking down the hallway and these senior guys, for no reason, just looked at me and said, 'Faggot.'" He looked at his hands.

"So what did you do?" asked the writer.

"I just figure that they must be gay too, if they know what to look for." Peter looked up and tentatively smiled. The group began to laugh, slowly, and then, both incredulous and excited, Peter grinned.

Every week, I watched the kids in the gay-straight alliance walk into the meeting and relax. They let go of the masks and guards that even the ones who were out wore; they were giddy and earnest. They began to share their stories with one another—their first visits to gay bookstores, their fears about coming out to their parents, their first dates. They began to share their stories with me. Sometimes Tim and I didn't leave school until 8:30 or 9 at night because the kids didn't want to leave the room, or one another, or sometimes us. I began to recognize the lag and pause of a student who wanted to talk privately, like Victoria, who said, "I need to tell you this story, and I've only told one other person."

Slowly, the story unfolded, of being forced to watch as her boyfriend walked up to another boy, and saying, "I hate you, you faggot," began to beat him. Victoria had been held back as she watched the fists, the scalp splitting open, and the blood running down. Suddenly, the other boys were gone and Victoria and the beaten boy were alone, his split head in her lap, covered in blood. "You have to go to the hospital," she said to him. "I can't go to the hospital. What would I tell them? I can't tell them." She sat holding him all night, and the blood dried, stiff, all through her jeans.

She looked at me. "I never talked about this before without crying," she said, and I held out my arms to her. She grabbed on, and I held her; it was all I could do. I could not forget what she had said, earlier in the meeting: "Words hurt us. Our skin isn't this thick."

In class, we began *The Hours*. "Is everyone in this book gay?" my students protested. "Are these people gay or bisexual? Can't they make up their minds?" The students needed to label the characters, to fit them into boxes. I sighed and tried to talk about contradictions, about fluidity, about identity. Sitting across from me, I watched Gwen and Evan lean toward each other and then toward their books. They were the two who never stopped talking in class, pulling ideas out of each other and the books, swift and sure. Some days I would come into class and see Evan asleep on Gwen's desk; other days, they faced each other, Gwen twisting her hair around her hand until her fingers turned white. In class, a month ago, Evan had looked up from *Mrs. Dalloway* and said, "They are all outsiders. Septimus, and Clarissa, and Sally—they are all outside." How sad he seemed to be saying it.

Now with *The Hours,* Evan and Gwen's eager participation had become ardent. There was hardly a moment when their hands weren't up to say something. One day after class they came up to my desk.

"I have a problem," said Gwen. "Here. See, Clarissa says that she and Sally are married. But people won't let them get married. I don't get it. How can she use that word, when no one will let them do it?"

"OK," I said, "tell me about Clarissa's world. Who are her friends?"

"Richard, and Louis, and Walter, and Mary Krull—"

"And what do they have in common?"

"Well, *they're* all gay too."

"So what's normal? I mean, for Clarissa and Sally, in their world." Gwen's smile became keen. I went on. "So for them, they are married. Everyone sees them that way, and they see themselves that way."

Evan interrupted. "Like when we date people," he said to Gwen. "We don't care whoever we date. But bigger, whole neighborhoods of people like us." He turned to me. "This book, it's everything; it's about everything."

I borrowed a line from *The Hours* that we'd discussed the week before. "It's the book of your life," I said, and I hoped he understood that when I said "your," I meant "my" too.

Spring semester's parents' visiting day crept up. I looked at my syllabus and realized that day's reading would focus on Clarissa and Sally. I thought of the fall, of my student's comments, of Homecoming, of the administrators who had told me that two students were doing poorly in my class because of their discomfort with my coming out. The discussion, with my students' parents watching, would be difficult.

We started class and began to talk about Clarissa and Sally's relationship, about why it worked, about why Clarissa was dissatisfied. Even in front of their parents, my students talked about these relationships without being self-conscious or awkward. The characters were simply people, and being lesbians was just part of who they were. The lives in the book had become real to them, and they could not imagine being dishonest or secretive about those lives.

I watched my students' parents leave the classroom. The only one to come up to my desk was Peter's mother. "I'm going to have to read that book now," she said, and I smiled at her, and then at Peter's quietly pleased face behind her.

When we finished *The Hours*, Evan asked whether he could write a personal response rather than a critical paper as his final project. It was going to be really personal, he warned me. It might not be like a real paper. It wasn't like anything else he'd ever done before; he might fail completely. "Evan," I said, "it'll be OK, I promise."

When Evan handed in the paper, placing it on my desk skittishly, he apologized again. That night, I read the essay: his

moment by a pond, with the only girl he had ever loved, telling her that he likes boys, and knowing nothing would be the same after he had spoken. I wanted to tell him that the book made me remember what it was like to be in love for the first time, that it made me remember moments by water with women I had loved. I wanted to tell him that this book made me believe in love again, that it made me believe that Evan and Gwen, and all my students, would find a way to love another person.

"Did you read it?" Evan asked tensely before class the next day.

"It was beautiful," I told him, and watched him release his breath. Evan had always been not evasive, but elusive, always guarded. That was gone. His smile, for the first time in days, was easy instead of anxious. I handed back the first of the papers I'd graded, including Evan's. I'd paper-clipped an envelope to the back, and, from the corner of my eye, I saw him take the envelope with my note and slip it into his backpack. His paper needed more than the comments in the margins about run-on sentences and word choice. Instead, in the envelope, I wrote to him: *You are going into an uncertain and brilliant world. Find books and cities you love. Find a person to love who will make you happy, who you will love with integrity and bravery. I want these things for you, and I know, in time, you will have them.*

A few days later, I went with my classes to see the movie of *The Hours,* and I watched Evan and Gwen watch me. One of the characters had the name of the partner who had left me almost a year ago. I felt myself cringe as I heard her name, over and over again, but was determined not to let myself show that ache. There were a lot of things I was willing to give to Evan and Gwen, but my sadness wasn't one of them.

I began to go on job interviews, and every time one of my students began a sentence with "Next year..." I felt guilty. On my interviews, I talked about my students, about the gay-straight alliance, about the need to listen to their stories. When the school I'd been dreaming of for months called to offer me a job, I was elated and sad. I thought back over the year, about the students who hung in doorways to ask, "Do you have a minute?" when they needed half an hour, to the three-page letter one of my students wrote, telling me how she had begun to realize she was gay. I thought of the boy whom I had never met before he came up to me at a dance and said, "I think someone's going to tell my dad I'm gay. What do I do?" And I thought of myself at the beginning of the year, quiet, frightened, crying in the bathroom. I thought of the emptiness I had felt when my partner had left, and the loneliness of doing things by myself that I had done for years with someone else. I had needed to fill that emptiness, and I had filled it with my students. They, in return, had reached out to me. Helping them was a way to say thank you to my own teachers in high school, people who I knew believed in me beyond all reasonable understanding. I had known that, if I needed them, they would be there.

The memory of those teachers was never closer than the May night my friend Kate, who worked in admissions, picked me up for dinner, and telling me that she needed to check out some equipment, drove me to the student center. We walked in, and from a corner of the room, 40 of my students shouted in unison, "Surprise!" I looked at the kids gathered against the walls. I saw Tim and the kids from the gay-straight alliance and students from my classes. I saw the kids from the diversity program I advised. Some I knew well, others only from editing their papers or passing in the hallways. I saw Peter and Victoria, Gwen. ("Evan couldn't come," she told me, "but he sent the cake.") One by one, they came up to me and hugged me fiercely. I didn't know what to say except, "Thank you."

"Who put this together?" I asked Kate.

She pointed to Emily, the junior class president, and Brianne, one of my academic advisees.

Emily came over. "Were you surprised?" she asked.

"I don't even know what to say," I told her.

"Everybody's signing a book for you," said Emily, pointing to a cluster of students in a corner. "We wanted you to have something to remember this."

I smiled. "I don't think I could ever forget it."

After the party, Kate and I helped Emily clean up. As we boxed up the leftover cake, I turned to Emily. "I wish I could explain how much this means to me. I feel overwhelmed, but what I keep thinking of is when I was in high school, I had these amazing teachers, and I thought they were the most incredible women in the world. My senior year, one of them—she advised the gay-straight alliance—was leaving my high school, and my best friend and I threw her a surprise party, at the end of the year, with another of our teachers. We wanted to figure out some way to tell her how much we were going to miss her, how important she was to us. I can't explain what it feels like to be on the other side of that."

A week later, a few days before graduation, Emily brought me the scrapbook my students had signed. I could not stop reading it, looking at the pictures of my students laughing, dancing with one another. I loved their happiness. At graduation, I could not stop embracing them all. Minna, a student I had talked through her breakup with her girlfriend, told me, "You're like my mom, here." A student who told me the first day of school that she was stupid in English—it was not her first language—said, "You have no idea how much I learned in your class. Thank you for everything." Katia, a student from my first year who was gay, out, and unremittingly honest about it, said, "I couldn't have done this without you."

Emily walked me back to my car. I thought of what she had given me, and of all of those I had watched get their diplomas, then of not being able to see next year's class in their caps and gowns, and I felt my throat close. On the path in the woods to the car, we stopped to say goodbye. We both began to cry. "Don't go," she said. We hugged, and she walked out of the woods and into the meadow, a girl in a white dress in the sunlight. It should have been an allegory, but it was real.

At home, I took out the scrapbook once more. *If I ever consider being a teacher, I would want to be like you,* wrote Minna. From Katia: *You gave me confidence in the classroom, which I never had.* Gwen's cramped handwriting read, *I have learned more from you than any other teacher and probably any other person, except my parents.* Peter wrote, *You know, you can't tell my other teachers this, but you're my favorite teacher.* Evan had taken the book home after the party; he had written, *There is so much I want to say to you: I want to write how much I will miss you and how important a person you are to so many people. If I could, I would barrage you with a billion adjectives and adverbs in an attempt to explain how significant you are. Thank you for teaching me (I learned much more than English).* Finally, tucked in a corner, was a note from Emily: *Ms. Katz, you told me the story of the teacher you respected so much in high school, and I would just like you to know that from my perspective, you have become her. When I found out you were leaving, I wanted to make sure that you knew how much we cared about you, and how much you have meant to us.*

I don't know how I became the person my students see, but I trust in this transformation. I learned how to be a teacher by listening to my students, by hearing what they needed, and I learned how to be a teacher by every day remembering what my teachers had given to me. I left my first job knowing I could help make my students' lives better, and I couldn't think of them without hearing the stories they had trusted me with. Our truths were as brave and honest as the books we read.

IN THE SWAMP

Cindy Lutenbacher
Assistant professor of English
Morehouse College
Atlanta, Georgia

In November 2002, Morehouse College, historically a college for black men, received a significant amount of media attention when a student took a baseball bat to another student whose glance in the dormitory shower he perceived as a sexual advance. I do not believe Morehouse is any more homophobic than any other college campus; the amount of media focus seemed to me extraordinary. Was it because of the baseball bat? Or because the college is African-American?

I am a white lesbian who has taught English at Morehouse since 1990. Although it is tempting to try to relate some of the experiences of the past few years at Morehouse (for that may be what some would like to hear), I think I have a slightly different story I'd like to try to tell. This one is a story about racism, homophobia, critical thinking, critical living, "engaged pedagogy" (*Teaching to Transgress: Education as the Practice of Freedom* by bell hooks), and how all of those things collide and collude and, I hope, have meaning inside a first-year English composition course, and inside the heart of its teacher.

The story is not a linear one, and the morals within it don't all come at the end. For me, one of the most important morals is that we cannot separate into discrete boxes the many oppressions that inhabit the lives of our students and ourselves. As former Spelman College president Johnnetta Cole used to say, "We are all messed up in each other." For me, this means that I cannot separate the necessity to be my students' ally against the constant tsunami of racism from the necessity for homophobia to end.

As a lesbian, I have a vested interest in seeing homophobia end. Although it may seem perplexing to some, I also believe that as a white person, I have a vested interest in seeing racism end. As the mother of two girls of color, I have a vested interest in seeing racism, sexism, and homophobia end. However, as a teacher, I know I cannot impose my beliefs upon my students. What I can do is to set the stage for critical thinking, for deeper personal and political investigation, for a kind of soul-quest that can open hearts and intelligence to question the roots of our beliefs. For me, the critical piece of setting that stage is that I be at least as willing to live and learn and unearth my own limits as I want my students to be.

When I've presented at conferences about my first-year composition class, I've named the talk "Teacher in the Swamp." What I mean to imply is that I do not believe I can ask my students to be deeply engaged in examining not only the dominant culture but also their own received, unconscious beliefs and values unless I am just as deeply immersed in examining my own received, unconscious beliefs and values. I cannot hope that my students will critically examine homophobia's impact on their lives if I'm not willing to "get down and dirty" with myself and racism, beginning with the mirror and moving through the public sphere of our daily lives. I cannot ask those who are hostile to homosexuality to think about how they may participate in perpetuation of homophobia—and a resultant split in the black community—if I'm not willing to take action against the white privilege that awaits me at every turn.

"We are all messed up in each other." These kinds of profound and critical excavations, reflections, and capacities for change and growth are what I mean by "the swamp," and I know I must be nose-deep in the middle of it—not just because my teacher-self

wants students to be thinking critically, but because I cannot fathom any other path to a future.

Backdrop

About three years ago, in the summer of 2000, I decided to revise my second-semester freshman composition course, English 102. It's not that I was desperate for change; nothing traumatic had happened to make me know it was time for radical revision. I had been teaching English college composition for a decade, and I had been having a glorious time of it, feeling useful, successful, and happy.

But I kept hearing a voice that told me I had not gone far enough, I had not risked enough, and that time was running out the front door. I needed to invite my students into deeper territory, deeper terrains of the soul if I wanted them to write more powerfully—and also live more daringly.

I decided to do away with the usual texts of formal writing, research skills, and argumentation, and to begin with content, with some of the most central and ubiquitous matters that impact our lives personally: racism and sexism. *Begin with content that matters,* I kept hearing, *and the form will follow.* Every step of this process has been, and continues to be, just this way; I hear an idea, follow it, and sit with it, and if it continues to speak, then I try it.

Racism

I knew and believed several things in relation to what it would mean to focus upon racism in a writing course. I believed and still believe that racism affects every person in this country, but that it impacts people of color with much greater concrete, dangerous, and deleterious effects than it does people of whiteness. In my 14 years of teaching at Morehouse, I have not encountered one student for whom racism was not a critical piece of his or her life. Thus, I consider my students to be the experts on understanding how racism works upon their lives.

Reckoning with that reality brought me to another pedagogical precept that I hold dear: "Begin with what the students know, begin with their own lives, start with their own expertise and experience, and honor that knowing." From these ideas came the first assignment of the class, what I've called the "class offering." Each student brings in a piece of writing (quote, article, poem, song, essay, letter, story, speech, etc.) that has mattered to him in his dealing with racism. The students share these offerings with one another in small groups, and then we share some of them with the whole class. This assignment usually takes two or three class periods because the discussions are so rich; we invariably articulate a host of the current incarnations of racism and white supremacy, as well as the historical reflections of slavery, lynching, and other forms of white violence, including the ubiquitous experience of racial profiling.

In an additional attempt to accentuate the experiential, I also show the film *Sankofa* every semester. The film is excruciating and powerful, no matter how many times I see it, and I always watch it with them. We journal-write in response to the film, using guiding questions, such as "What do you believe are the messages in the film?" and "What does the film have to do with your life?" And to provide a safe space for students to take me to task for showing the film, I even offer the optional, leading question, "Is there anything you want to say to me?" To my surprise, most students who choose this question use the opportunity to thank me for showing the film, to explain how they've never had a chance to really learn anything honest about slavery, to express the sense of both horror in the history and pride in their ancestors, or to ask me about my own journey to the beliefs about racism that I hold:

> I'm glad that I was able to experience *Sankofa*. Being an African-American male has caused me to step back and really review my life. Am I doing all that I can to make my ancestors proud of me? Am I keeping their dreams alive? Will I be able to endure this life and achieve all that is set before me? I think that the answers are yes. With so much pride from my ancestors behind me, why

would I fail? I know that they did not suffer in vain, and I'm going to prove that to them.

Sankofa helped me to understand my past and how I should always hold it in a sacred place in my heart because if I forget the struggles of my people, I'm doomed…

When I see injustice happening, am I one to do everything in my power to stop it, or am I someone who would simply ignore it?

The souls of those who were taken from their homeland and brought here to be slaves still speak volumes. I guess their souls will never rest until we, the children of slavery, remember who we are.

Watching a movie like *Sankofa* is very emotional, being an African-American. I wonder how most white people in general react to *Sankofa*? I realize that all people are different and do not share the same opinions. But the white people that I know would state that it was not that bad and it is over. I feel like—no, it is not over. My ancestors were tortured for hundreds of years and to put it in the past and forget about it would be an abomination.

A movie like *Sankofa* is a scream in a room full of people trying to be silent. These movies are necessary so blacks can understand where they have come from, so they can know where to go. White people need to see it to understand, develop empathy, and realize that yes, it was that horrible. People actually went through this and were treated this way. I encourage every white person to try and reverse the role and truly ask themselves how they would feel toward a group of people who did things like this.

The things that students have said in other discussions when they refer back to *Sankofa,* the realities I've come to claim as I learn more and more of history, the vital eloquence I've experienced, from Frederick Douglass to Toni Morrison to my dearest friends—all lead me to a constant encounter with slavery and the past. They lead me to continue showing the film—at Morehouse and in settings with white people.

And they lead me to my own continued encounters with

slavery. To the moment, one hot July night a couple of summers ago, of reading primary accounts of slavery as I held my sleeping youngest child, my child who is African-American, and heard as clear as a wolf's song: "My ancestors did this to your ancestors." Then, later, silently, to the eyes of my students: "My ancestors did this to your ancestors." To the eyes of my friends. My colleagues. My family.

Some white people have tried to avoid any kind of naked encounter with slavery, saying that their ancestors came to this country after the Civil War, so they really don't have anything to face. Or that their ancestors were oppressed too, so they don't really have to claim slavery. But slavery was done in our name and on our behalf, and we continue to gain from it.

If I am to teach young African-American men, I must do so as an ally, and I can only be an ally if I am living—24/7—inside the realities of history and racism and doing everything possible to end it, whether that locus of oppression be in an institution, in the white people around me, or in my own life.

Sankofa opens the door to reclaiming the past, and I try to further that reclamation with what I call "home-town research." Students research the untold histories of racism in their home towns or home states, in order to try to learn something of what their eighth-grade social studies texts omitted. Equally important, I require that they also research the resistance that was mounted, for there's never been an incident of racism to which there was not some form of resistance, even if that resistance was simply to survive. Students have reported that this assignment is both horrifying and deeply satisfying. They say that they learn some things that shock them about the cities that they love, but they are relieved to at least be able to bring them forward and share them with classmates. Furthermore, they see what their forebears have done to resist the madness. In some cases, students have grown to look at their parents and grandparents through new eyes, having learned something of the conditions and times through which they lived.

Sexism

Sankofa offers so many important lessons, but one of the most important and salient is the way that "divide and conquer" worked inside slavery, and it is upon this lesson that I ask the class to move into considering sexism and homophobia. As with racism or any other part of the course, the students represent a range of attitudes, values, and beliefs, from "the man should be the leader and women should be subordinate" to a most sophisticated understanding of the oppression of women. But almost without fail, the students "get it"—that anything that divides African-Americans from one another serves to keep the racist status quo in power. So we begin.

We start with exercises that open up the dialogue, my favorite being "Four Corners," which I've amended to be "Five Corners," in which I post around the room five sheets of paper on which I've written one of the following statements:

- Black women are not really oppressed more than black men are, so I don't really need to be involved.
- Black women need to take charge of their own oppression and not be passive about it.
- Too much fuss is made over the oppression of women, including the oppression of black women.
- The oppression of women will end when men end it, so my responsibility is to do all I can, including challenging my brothers.
- Different genders have different roles in society. I'm comfortable with my role and wish that women would be comfortable with theirs.

The students get up and walk to the posted statement that most closely matches their own feeling, sit down with the others who have chosen that "corner," and discuss why they believe what they do. Each group then reports on the discussion, and the whole class has a chance to respond to one another. From there, we begin to examine the attitudes and beliefs that surface, and I try to be delicate, which is not at all natural to me.

I'm also deeply blessed to have the connection with Men

Stopping Violence (MSV), an organization here in Atlanta focused on ending violence against women, especially domestic violence. Two of their leaders are African-American men who run workshops and six-month groups for men who have committed domestic violence. The two leaders have come to my classes to conduct workshops and allow the students to respond to what they've experienced. They do this without my presence, for MSV believes that it is the responsibility of men to work with men to end sexism and violence against women, just as I believe it is the responsibility of white people to work with white people to end racism and its violence. Then the students write about the workshops, and I'm able to experience it through their eyes:

> The Men Stopping Violence experience is perhaps the most emotionally moving experience that I have ever encountered.... Many males in the world have been poisoned with the belief that a woman must be dominated and abused in order for their manhood to be preserved. It is essential that we as men take a deeper look at our belief system and realize that all that we were taught may not be correct. We should not be afraid to make changes in our mind-set. Instead we should embrace change, for we will all be better people for it.

> Another lesson that I took with me was that change is possible. No matter what happens or what someone does, if they are open and willing to change, then it can happen. I'm very happy to have had this experience.... It makes me think of all the things that I have done and said to offend someone. I am open to change, and I'm ready to start my process in finding myself. Isn't that the point of college?

> I heard one man say, "How could she leave me? She sees that I'm in school trying to better myself, and she still leaves." It amazed me the kind of role that black women are expected to fulfill. Even after being beaten, black women are expected to stand by their man...

Although not all of the responses are so open and favorable, many or most are similar to those of the students above, who see

sexism as the logical consequence of a misogynist dominating culture.

I confess: This part of the course is the most difficult for me. Originally, I thought it would have been otherwise, that the discussions in which I had to face my own accountability for racism would be more difficult and painful. But the truth is just the opposite. When I hear students in places of denial or blaming women or jovially bonding with one another at the expense of women and homosexuals, I find myself so very tired. But I take a breath and think of how exhausting it must be for people of African descent and other people of color to hear us white people live in cheerful oblivion (white privilege) and express layer upon layer of denials of their everyday reality.

I remember a Sunday early in this part of the course in which I had read hundreds of pages of their writings, most of which were filled with avoidance of responsibility for sexism. Each page felt like a blow to my gut. Inside every denial and shift of responsibility, every stereotyping, every blaming of women, I felt the millennia of violence, enslavement, and destruction of women.

The following class meeting, I returned their writings with my brief comments, and we turned to dialogue about the connections between racism and sexism, and about what people of color experience when we white folks deny the things that they know in the depth of the body and soul.

The position of African-American men in relation to the oppression of sexism is one full of contradictions: They are perceived as a larger threat to white male dominance, and are thus presented in the media and other public arenas as generally violent and barbaric. As a friend and mother of African-American boys said, "Black women are just ignored. Black men are ignored *and* targeted." Yet, African-American men, like all men in this society, have been allowed to view women as inferior and to collaborate with their own oppression by buttressing the hierarchy of power and allowing "divide and conquer" to persist.

What I ask of them is that they look at the historic oppression of American women and how the stereotypes that continue to plague African-American women are the ones created in order to serve the power of white men and women. I ask them to consider the ways that they may have served the racist, white powers by not being their sisters' true allies. The assignment is to recall and write about an incident in which an African-American sister was disrespected. Did they intervene? If so, what happened? If not, why not? Here are some of their responses:

> By emulating the master, the male slave believes he is gaining a glimpse of power. [Both] the master and slaves viewed African women only as a means of sexual satisfaction and personal aggrandizement...[and are] the foundation of the problem concerning African-American men "bonding at the expense of the humanity of women," African-American males must bond in the healing of our wounds rather than the creating of new ones. African-American males must bond on the concept that the eradication of these two issues are not mutually exclusive but are dependent upon one another.... African-American males must not expect freedom from racism if they are agents of sexism.

> There is a stepladder in this society that currently values black women at the bottom. If black men don't respect their female counterparts, then who will?

> We black males have not even completely overcome our own internal conflicts, yet think it not hypocrisy to complain about the evils of the white man while tolerating the domestic abuse of our sisters, mothers, lovers, and wives on a scale equally as large. We would rather turn our heads and live in our own collective fantasies than let go of our comfort zone and face the reality that surrounds us. Ironically, though, this abandonment of comfort is the exact same mentality that we want whites to have in dealing with racism from our own perspective.

Homophobia

My first semester of this revised course, I found that something exciting was happening, that we were coming together in ways that were even more profound than I'd hoped. Our standing together inside the "swamp" made for a sense of being allies. About mid-semester, as

we began struggling with sexism and what it means to be united with one's sisters, homophobia entered the class in ways to which I was accustomed—gibes to one another about being "soft" or "Hey, I don't know about you, but I like girls…"

I always challenged the homophobic remarks; I've done that since I began teaching college, for I want the homosexual students in my classes and on campus to know that they are in a safe space. But the challenges could only go so far, because the need some students have to present themselves as heterosexual is fierce. But something began to gnaw at my bones and would not let go.

I knew I needed to come out to them.

I sat with this knowledge for a while. I talked with a friend, a heterosexual African-American woman whose experience of Morehouse is that it is a very homophobic place. She worried that I might be burying my future there, and was I prepared to deal with possible fallout?

I didn't know what the fallout would be, and I still don't. But one reality kept talking to me from the mirror: Because of the color of their skin, my students cannot hide from the line of fire of racism. How can I be a true ally to them if I am hiding from the line of fire in any area of my life? They have to bear the daily flame; how could I do less?

I couldn't hide, couldn't participate in the lies, and so I told them. I told them of my beliefs about being an ally and how that meant to me that I have to stand in the flame. I told them that the courage I see in the ways they are living their everyday lives, the courage that so many of them have in trying to face their own learned demons of sexism, the courage that some of them have in embracing their own homosexuality, and the simple fact that "you are family to me"—all made it necessary for me to come from the shadows and open myself to whatever might come my way by being a lesbian, openly lesbian.

Silence.

I was sweating and shaking from adrenaline, but we went on to talk from there. I let them ask me questions, the usual things about whether I believed that homosexuals were born or made, what I believed about raising my children, and so on. And then, as I'd guessed would happen, over the next several days a number of students came to my office, wrote in their journals, or sent me e-mails in order to come out to me. Some waited until the end of the course. They told me of their own fears of being open, their choices to remain closeted, and of the many students in the classroom who were "frontin'" about their sexual orientation. These experiences (though I guarded their anonymity) opened the door for further discussions in class, including how difficult it must be to be a gay man on campus. The matter returned us to the very powerful political reality of "divide and conquer," and on that basis, we began to see homophobia's deeper claim upon their lives. Anything that serves to divide African-Americans against one another consumes their energy and keeps them less empowered to struggle in a unified and communal way against the racist oppression that all of them face. As one student said, "We black people have been through so much. How could we put that onto a person because of who he loves?"

I asked them to write about their experiences, the personal narratives of homophobia and their responses to the events; I've kept this assigment in ensuing years. For some, this is their first chance to talk about things that had happened to them as gay men; for others, the result is an examination of their involvement in situations where the psychological violence of homophobia was committed; and for some, the discussions touch off a torrent of rejection of homosexuality:

> African-American men have to join together as one whole to fight the bigger issues. This means putting all little social taboos aside. Why should it matter if one guy wears pink while another wears blue? So what, you have more muscles than the next guy. Stop using sports as a fence to hide behind when you talk about what "real men" do. Real men should fight for what is right. Real men should stand against the man who calls him a "nigger" before calling his brother a "punk faggot." Real men stand together in spite of their difference.

My opinion is that the first thing that African-Americans should do is to do away with homosexuality.... African culture does not allow the practice of homosexuality. Homosexuality is something which can never be thought of.... The students should be taught that although they were brought from Africa and are now living in America, they should not do away with their culture.

Similar to racism, homophobia limits the intelligence of humankind. As victims of racism experience discrimination based on their skin color, something they cannot control, individuals who are gay or lesbian are discriminated against due to their genetic makeup. They are viewed by society as being less, when in reality they are just as equal as anyone else. If homosexuals continue to persistently protest, as African-Americans did during the Civil Rights Movement, their voices will be heard, and sooner or later they will be looked upon as human beings...

What is shocking is that the same community who has faced the very same feelings of hatred and bias has now turned a deaf ear to its own people because they have "chosen" to be homosexuals.

Later on, when I found out that my roommate was a homosexual, I was enormously disturbed because of my fear. I recall not talking to him for the first week because I didn't want to come off as "gay." But I am proud to say that I have overcome my fear, my homophobia. I now have a lifetime friend in my roommate. He is the most genuine person that I have ever met. I was able to overcome my fear because I broke down the wall that separated us. I think breaking down that wall is the first step to overcoming homophobia... It seemed hard at first, but looking back, reaching out to my roommate is one of the best choices that I have ever made.

The reason I believe that Morehouse should not really embrace homosexuality is the fact that I think it is morally wrong. I say this because in the Bible it clearly states that men are not supposed to sleep with men and women are not supposed to sleep with women.... On the other hand, as a Christian I believe in loving everybody and caring for one another; the fact that someone is gay does not mean that he or she should be discriminated against.

One of the men (attending the Men Stopping Violence group) admitted that for him attending the class was hard at first because he felt as if men coming together expressing problems and emotions was being weak or a sissy. It is a shame when a man would rather go through the judicial system than open up to another man.... We must stop worrying about what the world is thinking or saying about us, because the world does not care about African-American males. They want us to fight and bicker and kill ourselves.... We must stop viewing gays and homosexuals as weak and start targeting deadbeat dads, criminals, and drug dealers as being weak. We must stop accepting society's views of us and create a new mold. The new African-American man will be strong, responsible, a provider, and a person in tune with his emotions.

The college should not even acknowledge that this issue does exist.

After so many years of suppression and discrimination, we should not have any room to do unto others what was done to us. If no one else can empathize with the homosexual community, we as black Americans should be able. We know what it's like to have to hide, to act a certain way, and to enter through the back door.

Over the years I have been called a lot of things. From sissy, faggot, gay, to gay-ass nigger, I've heard it all. It is hard to hold a straight face, but it is accomplished. I believe it's all about empowerment. Sadly, it comes to the point where you actually get used to it all. Every day I cry inside because of the constant battle I fight, not to be happy, not to be gay, but to be myself.

[*Fall semester*] I know that the Morehouse community will definitely understand that embracing homosexuality will be detrimental to the future success and prosperity of this institution. Morehouse was founded on Christian principles and has traditionally been affiliated with the Baptist Church. It is not time to go against our fundamental beliefs now.

[*Spring semester*] The same United States military that tries to keep black people from reaching high-ranking positions also had a problem with people of homosexual orientation serving their country. The same school system that teaches black people that they can never amount to anything more than blue-collar also

teaches the so-called Christian doctrine that homosexuality is wrong, instead of Jesus' top commandment of "Love thy God with all thy heart, and love they neighbor as yourself." The same media that portrays black people as being thuggish and rugged-out also portrays homosexuals as overly assertive and open. And the same "democratic" government that tries to strip away affirmative action and promotes racial profiling also denies homosexual people marriage privileges and custody to children in court cases. When black men can realize that they are in the same struggle, they will be more willing to embrace a fellow homosexual brother.... Black men have traveled through so much together, including everything from shackles as slaves to the current oppressive behavior of incarceration. As a people, we cannot allow sexual preference to stop our fight for justice and equality.

Some students are deeply threatened by this part of the course and seem to shut down their wonderful minds in considering homosexuality. But for most, the frank conversation and the understanding of the ways that homophobia serves the construction of power in this society unlocks doors and windows to critical thinking that was previously inaccessible.

For all the reasons above and for the sake of the homosexual students at Morehouse, I've chosen to come out to every class since that first. The response is nearly always the same. And my gay brothers always find their way to my office.

Since that decision, I've also come out to nearly every group on campus with which I'm associated: faculty, committees, freshman orientation, a meeting with the president. It's never been easy, but it has always felt necessary. Although I think I'm one of the few people on campus who is open about my affectional orientation, I really don't know what the repercussions will be. Tenure? Job security? Will some rabid homophobe with power try to take my children from me? I tell myself that those are paranoid delusions, but "in the community" we know of too many cases of retribution that have come to people who were open, cases that should be completely bizarre, but unfortunately are not.

Family and Community History

The writing for this course comes throughout the semester in a variety of assignments, but the most successful assignment is a portfolio project titled "Family and Community History." The project is intended to be a claiming of both the past and the present as a way of making an offering to the future, "a gift that you are creating in order to honor the ancestors and to give to the next generation so that they can continue to keep the community alive and healthy." It includes letters to the ancestors, letters to our children and future generations, interviews with family members, hometown research of lost histories and resistance, family trees, artifacts, research into world and national events, journal entries, and other writings that can be contained in a notebook. This project is the place where all the lessons at last come together, where we must stand with one another beneath the blessings and the requirements of those who gave everything.

Dear Ancestor,

You are my motivation and my inspiration.... When I think of all the adversity that you went through just so I could be here, it makes me want to do the best that I can in all of my works. When I am in class and I start to doze off, I think of you. When I try to cut a paper short, I think of you. When I receive a B and know that I could have done a lot better, I think of you. When I am able to sit and converse with whites in peace, I think of you... It is key that you stay in my spirit and mind for the rest of my life.

Dear Ancestors,

I will honor you by getting my education. I owe it to you and to myself.... You died for me to have the right to be educated, so I refuse to be one to dishonor you by falling off educationally.... I plan to raise my children right and stay close to my family also. So many of you were sold away during slave trades and...were stripped of mothers, brothers, fathers, sons, or daughters. So many of us today take for granted our family. It makes no sense at all for this to happen when you paid the price back then....

To My Ancestors,

My wish is to become strong and work as a leader in the community like you did in the Choctaw nation. I thank my ancestors who are native to this land for passing down your love…. To my African ancestors who were brought from West Africa, I thank you for staying strong with so much abuse and harassment. I know the fields where you worked were hot and the work was hard, but you kept your faith and passed on a beautiful generation. To my ancestors who stood up in the civil rights movement, help me to show the burning desire you had for equality and justice. I thank all the ancestors who stood up for what is right and fought for it as well. Please help me become a better man so I can raise up a great nation where if any mouth is hungry, let it be fed; if any man or woman is naked, let him or her be clothed; if any unjust problem remains, let there be a solution. This is what I pray.

Dear Children…

From sit-ins to large protests, there are many ways to show resistance to racism. Throughout history, we have seen these demonstrations by African-Americans time and time again. We have seen these demonstrations in both peaceful manners and violent conditions. From students to elderly, politicians to lay leaders, and slaves to free men, forms of resistance to racism have attempted to "level the playing field" among races…. I hope that you all will have this same dedication to your race. Think about your children. Make it a better day for yourselves and them.

The Family History Project is the place where I believe the course comes together most profoundly for the students. And it's the place of the greatest sorrow and most profound hope for me. By far, the part of the work that leaves us all shaking the most is the interview of family members. Constantly, students report that having to ask the questions opens the door to stories that had not been told and a knowledge they fear they would have lost otherwise. In some cases, it has opened lines of family communication that had been closed. Even the students for whom the family history contains things that are difficult to face report that the *telling* of these stories is freeing and gives them strength. This project leaves no one unchanged.

And that includes me. The interviews and the histories shared bring the students and me into an even closer kinship. To witness the stories and histories that they bring is an event of the soul of galactic proportion. It is not possible for me to encounter the story of Great Aunt Sara, who at 10 years of age had to hide submerged in the swamp and walk two days to Gainesville, Florida, in order to avoid the fate of her older sister and mother, who were lynched for attempting to vote, without my becoming a different person. And there are many stories like this one—a seemingly infinite number of stories of murder of the soul, the constant disrespect and disregard of human dignity—that students and their families have experienced, of heart-shattering heroism, the mothers who worked three jobs, the grandmothers who were there to love beyond measure when young boys were dirtied by stereotyping and false accusations, the fathers who faced the mob, the ancestors who refused to be whipped and then made their way to the Underground Railroad.... I cannot imagine any person truly hearing these stories and not being forever transformed, translated into another being.

Nothing in the stories surprises me. Nothing. It's hearing them from men whom I see as younger brothers that makes the difference.

And that is why I know I must do all that I can to be there in that swamp with Great Aunt Sara and with the students in my classes, if I have any interest in education playing a part in making a world that is worth living in. I must be there for my own sake.

If I truly believe that students at Morehouse are family, then I have no other choice, as a teacher or white person or lesbian or human.

That's the story I'm trying to tell. That's the story I'm trying to live.

Part Three
May–September

NO MORE SILENCE
Randall Furash-Stewart
Amherst, Massachusetts

The summit of happiness is when a person is ready to be what he is.
—Erasmus

I had a dream last night. Every teacher from middle school or high school that I had ever suspected to be gay, lesbian, bisexual, or gender variant was in it. We sat around talking about everyday kinds of things: classroom management, the quality of school lunch, the difficulty of balancing being queer outside of school with being a teacher. I saw the pain they felt in living a double life. I understood, and I forgave them.

Growing up in suburban Maryland, just outside of Washington, D.C., in the 1990s, I was lucky enough to be in a fairly safe place to try on various sexualities and gender identities. I proudly walked through school first as an out lesbian in 10th grade and later as an out, gender-questioning queer by the time I graduated from high school. In my searching for myself, I looked for reflections of the possibilities of what I could be in all my teachers. I was looking for a place where I could fit in my high school community.

Not finding one, several other students and I started a gay-straight alliance. We approached several teachers who we were positive would be supportive, but all of them were too scared to

support us. Suddenly, my school did not seem like such a safe place. We were assigned a sponsor, a guidance counselor who begrudgingly came to our meetings out of obligation. This, while better than nothing, did not help us find the support we were looking for.

That spring, we organized recognition of the National Day of Silence (a day protesting the silence that many queer and questioning youth are forced to feel in schools). I made stickers for all our supporters to wear. That day the halls were filled with students wearing rainbow stickers, but supportive teachers, especially queer teachers, were scarce. That day I learned a very important lesson: It is all right to be queer, but only if you are not an educator. That summer, I took that lesson with me to my job as a camp counselor. I learned to live a double life.

It did not save me. In fact, I found that it did more harm than good. One day a 6-year-old boy came to camp with a skirt in his bag. He confided in me that he wanted to wear it at camp, but he was scared. I encouraged him to wear it and promised that if any kids teased him, I would defend him. It turned out it was actually my fellow counselors who teased him, at our staff meeting that afternoon. Buried deep in my closet, I could not say anything. I swallowed my objections for fear that I would be accused of being unfit to work with children. The camper never again mentioned the skirt. School had taught me well.

I'd seen the same thing happen in my senior year. During choir practice, one of my fellow students commented on something being "so gay," meaning that it was stupid. I spoke up, objecting to his offensive use of a word I held so dear to my identity. He argued that I was being ridiculous. He made a nearby student, who was also queer, cry. Our choir teacher, whom I suspected was queer, just glared at me, as if I had started the whole disruption, but said not a word to the offending student about his language. I felt betrayed by someone I looked to for guidance.

I carried my bitterness about that event with me to college the next year. I was interviewed by someone writing about queer youth in schools. I argued that teachers needed to speak out more and that I was angry with my high school teachers for teaching the queer youth in our school silence. I was driven to go into teaching to end these silences and educate young people to be fully themselves, responsibly, in the world.

My first year of college, I started a job as a teaching assistant in a small special-needs high school program on campus. I was very closeted at my job. I broke out in a cold sweat any time queer issues came up. I was sure to stop homophobic comments when I heard them, but I always panicked when the need arose. Straight coworkers sometimes brought their boyfriends to visit and spend a day working with the kids. I could not even discuss my primary partner or any of my other lovers with my students or coworkers. I was too scared of having to explain myself.

I had mastered living a double life where the personal and professional were completely separate. My last year there, I was out on campus as transgender. I changed the name I went by and most people referred to me by male pronouns. However, while teaching, I kept going by my old name. I even had coworkers who kept the secret with me, calling me one name at work and another name on campus.

Working in public school that year, doing a prepracticum in a social studies class, the need for my double life was reemphasized. The teacher I was working with was doing a unit on social identities. She included sexual orientation in her lesson, and students were very receptive to talking about that issue, as we live in an area where there are many gay and lesbian parents and youth. She also included gender, but as a strictly unchanging biological fact that we are given at birth. A student brought up that some people have sex changes. Everyone giggled and the teacher responded that we were just not going to go there.

When I approached her after class about the lesson, I made the mistake of coming out to her. I was told that she understood that this was a very special issue for me, but she could only push things so far. I accepted that she was right. The school community just was not ready for that silence to be broken.

When I graduated, I changed my name legally and started look-ing for work in schools. Every time I went to a job interview, I sweated over what gender I would be perceived as. Sitting com-fortably in my double life of silent lies, I let interviewers make their own assumptions about my gender. That is how I got my current job as a female. I work as a teacher in a small special-needs middle school program. In spite of my efforts to appear male, I am a woman there. Still, though, I have been pegged as the queer teacher because of my appearance. I am lucky enough to live in an area where being a lesbian teacher, while not easy, is not unheard of. Under this pretense, I have offered support to students who are going through what I went through in middle school.

"Josie" is a student of mine who immediately started dropping hints as soon as I met her. She talked to me about the Indigo Girls and other gay icons that I am all too familiar with. We spoke in this veiled code at first. I told her she was going to be all right by rec-ommending Ani DiFranco albums, never saying the word "queer" or telling her anything about myself aside from the fact that I have seen the Indigo Girls in concert at least 10 times. I even wrote down the Web site of a local queer youth organization for her, but I could not say anything about it out loud. She confronted me one day, asking why I had responded to a poem she showed me with, "You are not alone." I was flustered. I stuttered out something about how I knew people who had gone through the same tough things she was going through. The next day, she brought in a poem about taking responsibility for guiding kids that are going through the same things you went through. I knew she was right, but old habits die hard. I realized I was teaching Josie the same lessons about silence that my teachers had taught me, and it was not OK to repeat that cycle.

Since then I have started talking more openly about queer issues in my classroom. I also have the Syracuse Cultural Workers Peace Calendar in my classroom, which has a picture of Harry Hay kissing his partner in June. I am both scared and excited about the discussions that will open up in my classes.

However, in spite of all this, I am still living the ultimate double life. I still do not mention my primary partner as easily as some coworkers mention their spouses (he is currently my "roommate"). Nevertheless, there is the much larger issue of pronouns. I am unquestionably a queer guy outside of work. Any time I am working with students, though, I am the queer female teacher. It is better than being perceived as straight, but every time a student calls me "she" or "ma'am," I shiver. Many days I am too distracted to be able to devote my full attention to teaching or planning lessons because something very basic to my self-identity, my gender, is not acknowledged at all. I am playing the same game I played in college. Some of my coworkers acknowledge me as a guy outside of work but participate in my lie by calling me "she" at work.

And what am I getting out of all this hiding and secrecy? Maybe some job security, maybe avoiding alienating some students (or parents). However, I am realizing that it is costing me so much more. I am not able to teach my students to be themselves responsibly in the world when I am avoiding doing just that.

Next month, I am starting my medical transition. I will start taking testosterone, which will masculinize many of my features, like my voice and facial hair. My students will inevitably wonder what is going on. I intend to be honest with them. I do not want to continue the cycle of silence and lies by teaching them shame. Luckily, I have my supervisor's support in this, but I think we are in for quite an adventure. Sometimes I have fantasies of transitioning and then going back to a comfortable double life in my comfortable male body. However, I have made the decision to submit my story to this book because I do not want to live my life that way.

I understand now the pressures my queer middle and high school teachers felt. I forgive them, because their silence was part of something much bigger than they were. In homage to my teachers, I will work to make sure I set a proud example to my students for the rest of my teaching career.

TRANSITIONING IN THE SCHOOL SYSTEM

Gayle Roberts, B.Sc., M.Sc.
Science teacher (1969-2002)
Science department head (1990-2002)
Lord Byng Secondary School
Vancouver, Canada

I began teaching more than 30 years ago, in 1969, at Gladstone Secondary School in Vancouver, Canada. Since that time, the public's attitudes toward homosexuality and transsexuality have changed—for the most part, in a very positive way. Until recently intense pressure was put on everyone in society to be "normal." "Normal" basically meant everyone was expected to pass through our school system, become a productive member of society, marry, have children, and not deviate from societal expectations of heterosexuality and appropriate gender role behavior. Teachers for their part were expected to be society's role models and, as such, could not deviate far from the norm, especially in such crucial aspects of their lives as sexuality and gender identity.

My own experiences as a transsexual teacher who successfully transitioned "on the job" in 1996 perhaps indicate that today there is greater acceptance than ever before for individuals who deviate from the norms of yesterday. I base this on my experiences as a child growing up in post-World War II England, then later as a young adult in Canada, and finally as an older adult when I transitioned.

My earliest memory, at about age 5, is of wanting to be a girl. The culture I was born into made it very clear to me that expressing this desire was absolutely unacceptable. I worried what my parents would do to me if they found out. I quickly learned that while it was somewhat socially acceptable for a girl to be a tomboy, the opposite was certainly not the case. I also learned to keep a "stiff upper lip." I was raised to believe that boys don't cry. It is no wonder that I grew up feeling very ashamed of myself for having such feelings. As a method for coping with these feelings, I believed that one day I would be told by doctors that I was really a girl and was the subject of an experiment to see if it were possible for girls to be raised to believe they were boys.

When I was 11 years old my parents emigrated to Canada, where I entered school and eventually university. I have always been interested in the sciences, especially physics and astronomy. This interest led to academic success and eventually a career in teaching—and it also became another method of coping. By immersing myself in academia, I was able to postpone dealing with my gender confusion, which was getting only more painful. By continually keeping my focus on the "outside" I was able to avoid dealing with my "inside." As I matured I developed yet another coping mechanism: I believed my feelings of wishing to be a woman would disappear when I fell in love.

By the time I reached my late 20s I realized that if I were to fall in love and marry, my feelings of wanting to be a woman would just have to go! How I achieved this I don't know; but by brute mental force I stopped those feelings. I fell in love with a wonderful, caring woman. We were best friends for many years. While she was aware of my feelings of childhood and young adulthood, the two of us believed they were now in my past and we could marry and be a normal, loving couple. Little did we know then that what is recognized today as gender dysphoria and gender identity disorder is a chronic condition that usually intensifies with age. With every hope for the future, we married and spent our first three

years as a couple in Singapore, where I taught physics at the United World College of Southeast Asia. Over those three years we explored most of the countries in that part of the world.

In 1983, after completing my three-year contract, we returned to Canada. The Vancouver School Board assigned me to Lord Byng Secondary School, where I taught general science and physics until I retired in 2002. During the late '80s and early '90s, I found it increasingly more difficult to control my ever-intensifying feelings of wanting to be a woman. Fortunately for me, Vancouver had a Gender Identity Clinic. My family physician arranged an appointment for me with one of the clinic's psychiatrists, who recommended that I join what was called the Explorers' Group.

The group consisted of people who, like me, were exploring their own gender issues. In this environment of safety and trust, we were able to explore our innermost feelings. Many of my new friends quickly realized the only way they could achieve the inner peace we all so desperately wished for was to transition. I was a slow learner. I spent several years fighting my inner self. I was afraid of losing everything that was meaningful to me—my wife, my career, and my friends. These fears were not completely unfounded, as I had seen this happen to many of my clinic friends. However, by 1996 I could no longer function. I was three weeks into a new school year when my wife told me she would rather have a live sister than a dead husband. It was then that I realized I had to transition, even if that meant risking everything that was dear to me.

To transition successfully, one needs a plan. At the end of the school year I went to the school administrators and, with them, to the area superintendent, and very openly discussed my gender conflicts. I told them I was suffering from gender dysphoria and that I had a medical condition called gender identity disorder— and to my surprise they were extremely supportive. They told me I was a respected teacher held in high regard by students, parents, and educators alike. They told me that they had never before had to deal with a teacher with my medical condition but that I could count on their support.

So it was no surprise to me that when I applied for sick leave in September I was granted it. Essentially, we agreed that I should take a period of sick leave for my transition and then, when I was ready, I could return to work as a science consultant for the school board until June. Then, in September, I'd go back to active teaching in the classroom. The only thing that the superintendent insisted upon was that I not go back and forth—presenting one day as a man and another as a woman. I assured him that having lived over 50 years as a man and not being comfortable with it, the last thing I would want to do was to go back to being a man.

After four months of transition, I was excited about returning to work. The superintendent and I agreed that it would be best if the staff in the board's office were informed of my medical condition. I have always believed that it is best to be open with people who know you or will interact with you over an extended period of time. By telling the staff, I gave them the opportunity to be comfortable with me and, if they wished, ask questions. I was introduced to everyone in the building. Many of the people I met were colleagues, but many others I had not met before. My first day on the job was wonderful. On my desk in my office was a beautiful bouquet of flowers from my high school principal and a note wishing me success in my new role. Contrary to my fears that I could be placed in some back office counting the proverbial paper clips, I was asked to arrange a district-wide science conference. I was informed that, as part of my new duties, I was to meet with visiting international scientists and science educators.

I knew that the people working in the board offices were required to be civil to me, but I also knew that no one can mandate friendship. So, as I sat in my office wondering whether people would interact with me at a personal level, one of my new colleagues came by and asked if I'd join her for coffee.

During the five months I spent at the board office, I found that I was completely accepted. People asked me to join them for coffee

or lunch or for walks in the neighborhood. As people got to know me they would ask me questions. I never talked about my transition unless requested to do so. One of my most memorable experiences occurred when a colleague gave me a lovely aquamarine ring. She told me she did not wear it now, and as she was going through her jewelry box she thought of me. I wear it every day. For me it was, and still is, a symbol of acceptance in my new role.

As June approached I discussed with the superintendent of human resources where I should teach in September. Basically, I had two choices—one was to return to my old school, and the other was to go to a different school in the district. In the end we decided that I would have the best chance of success in my new role if I returned to my old school, as I would not need to prove to that school community that I was a good teacher. We also knew that no matter how passable I was in my new role, eventually everyone would know that I was the transsexual teacher everyone had been talking about a year earlier. It was just a matter of time before the school community would know of my transition and I'd need to deal with possibly adverse reactions of parents or students.

So it was with a great deal of excitement and trepidation that I returned to my old school in September. My excitement was caused by my wish to see my former colleagues and to return once more to teaching young people. My trepidation was due to my concern about the reaction I would receive from my students. Would I be accepted or seen as some kind of weirdo? I realized that even though the board had given me all the support they could, ultimately my success would be governed by the attitude of my students and by my ability to maintain an appropriate learning environment within my classes.

The first day, in retrospect, was an indicator of things to come. I met my homeroom class, introduced myself as Ms. Roberts, took attendance, collected the usual fees, and then, as was school policy, dismissed the students for the day. None of the students made any untoward comments. They reacted to me as hundreds of students had over the years prior. So far, so good.

The following day, I thought, would be the real test, as it was the first day I would meet the students I would actually be teaching. As it happened, the first class I met that day was senior physics. This class would have at least some students from the junior physics classes I had taught for three weeks the previous school year.

Believing as I do in good planning, I had given some thought to how I should greet this class. Obviously, all the students, whether or not they had had me as a teacher in previous years, knew that I was a transsexual teacher returning to the classroom. (You can not keep that a secret!) I believed I had to acknowledge that at least some of these students knew me in my previous role as a man. At the same time, however, I really did not wish to open up discussion on potential issues around my sexuality or gender identity.

My approach was to say, "I am aware that you are aware of my changed circumstances." I told them how much happier I was as a person. I also told them that I was really pleased to be back in the classroom to teach them, that the curriculum was rather lengthy and I thought it best if we got started on the course. It was my hope that this approach would help any of my former students feel comfortable with me. For the students in my junior physics classes who had not had me as a teacher in previous years, I decided to say nothing to them about my changed "circumstances." As I did with my homeroom class, I simply introduced myself as "Ms. Roberts" and approached the class much as I had done with so many before. The school recognized the possibility that some students might have found my transition difficult, and counselors were available to help them. I was told later that not one student took advantage of that opportunity.

The following days were very much like my first teaching day. The students reacted to me just as they had in the past. It soon became apparent to me that for my students only one thing was really important to them—how well I taught. As is normal in a class, some students interact with their teachers in a more personal way. They will tell you a little about themselves—what their hobbies are, what they enjoy, their goals, aspirations, and frustrations.

I found that many of these students during the first part of the year would come up to me and quietly tell me how brave they thought I was. One student told me she thought I was an inspiration. That was one of the most meaningful comments I ever received from a student. It told me that I was accepted, and just as importantly, that I was a role model with whom some students could identify. I don't believe for a moment that this student had her own issues around gender—rather I believe she saw me as a teacher who had significant personal problems and was able to overcome them and become a much happier person. I believe she realized that she, and others like her, could in a similar way resolve their own unique personal issues.

The next major hurdle I felt I had to overcome was the possibility of negative comments at "Parents Walk-through." This occurs toward the end of September and it gives parents the opportunity to meet their children's teachers. The parents follow their child's timetable, meeting each teacher, who in the space of about 10 minutes tells the parents a little about the course and the manner in which students will be evaluated.

I expected each of my classes would be completely full with the 60 parents of the 30 students I had in each of my classes taking advantage of their opportunity to see the transsexual teacher—or so I thought. Instead, the usual half a dozen to a dozen parents visited my classroom and listened to what I had to say and asked me the usual questions about the curriculum or my approach to evaluation. I was on cloud nine! The parents obviously accepted me.

As one mother was leaving my class for the next one, she asked me if I knew a certain student I had taught a few years earlier. I told her that the name was familiar. She explained that he was her oldest son, who was now at university. We talked a little about her son and I asked her how and what he was doing. Then she told me her daughter was in my physics class and how pleased she was that I had returned to continue teaching physics. As she walked out of my classroom she turned to me and said, "You look very pretty." I was overwhelmed! Here was a parent who managed to tell me, without once bringing up the subject of my gender change, that she knew I used to be a man, that I was an excellent teacher, and that she was totally accepting of me as a woman. I floated on the floor for the rest of the evening.

Later that evening I talked to my principal and asked her if she'd had any comments from parents. She told me that only one parent had discussed me with her, and that was to say that "he looks much better as a woman than he did as a man." My principal smiled as she pointed out that all of the parent's pronouns were wrong but her sentiments were good. A little later, as I walked down the hallway, I became aware that my head was held high and that for the very first time in my life I was proud of who I am. For the first time in my life, I was shame-free!

And so the year went on as it started. That year rolled by and then another five. It seemed so little time passed before I was standing in front of the school staff receiving retirement presents and heartwarming comments. When it came time to thank them, I must confess that all my self-control was swept away as I cried and thanked them for the acceptance they had shown me. I left the school and drove home to my "new sister" of six years who loved, supported, and encouraged me as she lost her husband and gained a sister.

This article is dedicated to my "new sister," my best friend and companion, Edith. During many painful years for both of us, she has encouraged and supported me. Just saying "thank you" seems insufficient. Losing one's husband is not really balanced by gaining a sister. I am truly thankful to her for what she gave of herself.

GOWN TO TOWN: LIFE AFTER BROWN

Tamar Paull
Seventh-grade English teacher
Community Preparatory School
Providence, Rhode Island

The flag was at half-mast when I pulled into the parking lot of my first real job that October morning. Community Prep, a small middle school serving primarily low-income students of color from in and around Providence's inner city, was the perfect place for an idealistic recent college grad to be initiated into the world of education. Not noticing the unusual state of the flag at this early hour, I rushed to my classroom to drink my first cup of coffee and write the night's homework on the board before my seventh graders showed up.

By five minutes to 8 the caffeine had begun its magic and I felt energized and pleased with my plans for the day. It was time to head down to the community room, where I would join the school's 150 students and staff to share announcements, recite a daily pledge promising to take full advantage of every opportunity the day had to offer, and race back upstairs to begin the daunting task of changing young lives. I was fresh out of college, and while I was not exactly certain how to undertake this task, I was quite sure that it could be done.

After a few crucial announcements about the new juice machine and the basketball team's recent victory (undefeated for yet another year!), a fourth grader raised her hand to ask why the flag was broken. I was busy trying to remember which door my class was supposed to use in the event of a fire drill and checking kids off on my attendance sheet just like I had when I'd played teacher in the back of my dad's university classroom, when I heard the principal's explanation. The flag was not broken; it was at half-mast. Apparently a young man had been killed. A body had been found. Something about a scarecrow and iron bars. By the time my principal got to the word "gay," I finally realized what had happened. I felt the familiar hot red discomfort climbing up my neck and cheeks and ran up to my classroom, feeling the coffee rise in my stomach and wishing I hadn't bypassed morning news radio in favor of the oldies. I had exactly one minute to digest the watered-down and patchy version of what would soon enter my vocabulary as "The Matthew Shepard Story" before my students would enter my classroom.

Somehow I stumbled through the morning classes. (Who knows what I taught that first year—something with clearly artic-ulated objectives that I'd be embarrassed to repeat now, I'm sure.) By midday my rage was starting to overwhelm the initial denial: Fresh out of Brown University, I was used to speaking my mind and even being celebrated for such. As a college student, I had come out on a campus and at a time when issues of sexuality were discussed freely and comfortably. Now I found myself working at an inner-city school five miles across the city from Brown, and a world away, with a sizable and vocal population of religiously con-servative families whom I was now obligated to serve and make comfortable.

I stormed into my principal's office and announced that I couldn't stand it any longer: I was just going to come out of the closet. I had to talk to my students honestly about Matthew Shepard's death; I had to make sure they understood, and I couldn't do it without telling them the truth about myself. A carefully closeted gay man, my principal was more than a little concerned by my plan. My boss appealed to my newly developing professional side and convinced

the radical recent college grad in me to take a few deep breaths and spend the weekend thinking through my plans.

By Monday morning my need to come out had not diminished. My 22-year-old maturity, however, had prevailed, and I was now able to sit down with my boss and the entire faculty and staff—whom he had invited to an emergency meeting before school—to rationally explain myself. At a vigil I attended that weekend for Matthew Shepard, a local gay activist and gospel singer sang a rendition of a spiritual proclaiming to Matthew that when he reaches heaven's gates he can rest assured that his death will not be in vain. I took these words to heart, and in fact took them as an imperative. In a school of 150 students, some of whom were learning at home and in church that "God hates fags"—as the Reverend Fred Phelps admonished mourners at Shepard's funeral—I knew I had a responsibility to do something. I carefully explained this to my boss and colleagues. I had to come out, I explained to them, so that our students would think twice before becoming the next to tie a gay kid to a fence, beat him, and leave him for dead. This may seem melodramatic now, but the shock of the event and the growing realization that I wasn't at Brown anymore, Toto, was doing strange things to me.

With surprisingly minimal coaxing, my boss did a 180 and quickly took it upon himself to organize the entire faculty around what I would later refer as the "Ms. Paull Comes Out" episode (Ellen DeGeneres having recently paved the way). Our nine homeroom teachers were on board and the plan was set. The next morning at the appointed hour, every homeroom in the school would have an age-appropriate conversation about Shepard's death. Incorporated in that conversation in the most organic and squirm-proof way possible would be the official outing of yours truly. Realizing that 150 eight- to 14-year-olds were about to find out something that I had been told as a student teacher I would have to conceal my entire professional life made me wonder for a moment if there wasn't some other way to ensure that Matthew's death hadn't been in vain. Maybe I could go to another vigil, or write an anonymous letter to the local paper.

But my pride, both gay and stubborn, propelled me forward. If every other teacher in the school could back me and have a conversation with their students that they had certainly never contemplated before, I—a tried and true lesbian feminist with radical roots and a lefty New York Jewish upbringing—was surely brave enough to face a group of 13-year-olds.

So I dove in. I reminded the students about the flag that had been at half-mast the previous week. I asked if they remembered why. They did. I stalled. I gulped, wishing my cheeks didn't turn red when I was nervous. I told them about the vigil I had attended for Matthew over the weekend, stressing the fact that it was at a church and that many people were there. I pandered. I told them about the gospel singer there and how he had sung that Matthew's death should not be in vain. I paused and asked if they knew what "in vain" meant. They didn't, and I was able to hide beneath my English teacher's hat for a blissful moment while I enlightened them. And then I caught the slightly impatient eye of Hazel, a student whose two mothers were friends and mentors to me; she'd been forced into the accomplice role of helping me stay in the closet during the week, though on the weekends she often knew me as her lesbian moms' baby-dyke friend. So I said it. I think I probably looked at Hazel, telling her what she already knew and letting the rest of my students in on what they probably never expected to hear in school. "As a lesbian…" The rest is a blur. I think I may have blacked out. But when I came to, I saw rainbows.

The terror of that initial moment of coming out was matched with an incredible rush of empowerment and possibility. I could now address the name-calling I'd heard in the hallways; I could teach the book about the gay kid who gets teased on the soccer team; I could have eye-opening conversations with my students, who'd hang on my every word. I could hold my girlfriend's hand on the streets of my small city without worrying about the rumors that would fly if I ran into a student.

Of course, once the initial adrenaline rush of self-disclosure wore off, I realized that my moment of bravery was merely the beginning. A few weeks later the family of one of my seventh graders came in for a routine conference. In what appeared to be a rehearsed moment, they asked their daughter to leave the room. The father looked at the mother, who politely asked why I thought that it was in any way appropriate or necessary to inform their child about my sex life. I did my best to explain myself once again, but my 22-year-old skin was wearing thin, and I burst into tears as soon as they left.

That spring, another student announced sadly that she would not be able to participate in the overnight class trip to a farm in western Massachusetts. When I called her mother to convince her that her daughter should attend the trip, her mother awkwardly explained to me that the family did not consider me an appropriate chaperone for an overnight.

The following year, during a unit on civil rights activists of the 1950s and 1960s, a group of four students called me over to their table. They were reading about three teenage boys who were jailed for civil disobedience and wanted to know whether that meant the boys became gay. I was a bit taken aback, but by then I'd learned to find out what kids are really asking before launching into long-winded explanations of what I wanted them to hear. I asked why they were asking, and they explained to me that their parents had told them if you spent a night in jail, you would turn gay. Knowing their parents, I can't say I was entirely surprised by this opinion, but I was surprised by the question that came next. "Ms. Paull, how did you become gay?"

This was it! The eye-opening dialogue I was hoping to engender when I first came out of the closet. I told them that different people have different opinions on the issue, but personally I thought that I had always been a lesbian. So did that mean I knew I was gay from birth, they wanted to know? I explained that I didn't know anyone who thought about whether they liked boys or girls the minute they were born. "I did," proclaimed Nate. "I liked girls the second I was born." High fives went around the table, and I decided to quit while I was ahead.

Seven years later, I am still teaching at the small, inner-city middle school where I began my career. With new students and families each year, I enter every fall with the sinking realization that coming out once was not enough. If I truly stand by my conviction that as an out teacher I can bring more to my students than I could from behind the proverbial closet door, I have to find the strength to out myself year after year. While I have now developed a pretty sizable bag of tricks, lesson plans, and essay assignments that I can recycle and improve upon each year, I am still honing the Ms. Paull Comes Out episode. Each year it seems to take a different form.

For a few years I lived down the street from my school with my partner. She became an active presence at the school, tutoring students and attending performances. Kids enjoyed her, and for a while I enjoyed the relative privilege of being recognized as an acceptable couple. Coming out during those years became as natural as telling the kids about my chihuahua or my older brother in Chicago.

Last year Providence elected an openly gay and Jewish mayor. I decided to come out the day after Election Day by telling my homeroom how nice it was as a Jewish lesbian to feel represented by my city government. Predominantly students of color, they talked about what it would feel like to have a black or Latino president. I was proud of my students for making that connection, relieved to have come out yet another year, and glad to switch the topic from myself to American politics.

Recently I was counseling a student who was entering the foster care system after having been removed from an abusive home. She confided in me that her mother had not only been physically abusing her, as she had told the authorities, but she did something else too. She would dress up "like a man" and flirt with her daughter, asking her out on dates and commenting on her body. My student looked at me through red and tear-filled eyes and told me that she knew this is not what it meant to be a lesbian because she knew

I was a lesbian and would never do something like that to a child. She knew what her mother had done was wrong but that being a lesbian was not wrong.

All these years later, the flag that was at half-mast has been raised. Hanging in our community room among flags of the more than 50 nations representing our student body is now a rainbow flag. The controversy surrounding the school's bold decision to hang that flag has faded into a distant memory. It hangs in the back of the room, and we don't talk about it very often, but I am proud to see it every morning as I recite the school's pledge with the students: "This day has been given to me, fresh and clear. I can use it or throw it away. I promise that I shall use this day to the fullest, realizing it can never come back again." Every day that I have the strength and support to be the only openly lesbian teacher in my school community is a day I am grateful for. Every student who is learning at home that God hates fags and is learning at school that his lesbian teacher cares about him and isn't half bad is a student I am lucky to have.

There are so many things that presented challenges to me as a first-year teacher that I barely think about anymore. I can now confidently average my grades on an Excel spreadsheet, direct large groups of students in Shakespeare productions, and lead parent discussion groups. Seven years after I first came out, the annual coming out "moment" still makes me a bit queasy and sweaty-palmed. Coming out and staying out can sometimes feel like something of a chore that I appreciate most after it's done. But there is nothing as invigorating as bringing my full, true self to work with me every day. Someday, I am confident, coming out and staying out will become as natural and comfortable as writing on the blackboard while balancing a cup of coffee and keeping the eyes in the back of my head focused on a room full of fabulous seventh graders.

NOBODY CAN TELL ME I SHOULDN'T BE HERE

Mike Russell
English teacher
Benjamin Franklin High School
Philadelphia. Pennsylvania

I grew up in the country in Arkansas; the biggest town within a 75-mile radius had 10,000 people in it. I was baptized in the Church of Christ, which is so Bible-bound it believes that Baptists are liberal sinners who burn in hell because, among other things, they use instrumental music in worship. At the time, I fervently believed in the Church, in the Bible, and in what the authority figures in my life told me.

Every school day, my first-grade teacher led the class in prayer, despite the fact that this was 1978 and doing such a thing had long been declared unconstitutional. This teacher also seemed to delight in being very cruel to many of her students. Back when she taught third grade, she had dragged one poor child into a first-grade room and announced, "This kid's too stupid to learn his lessons. He's going to have to be in first grade for a while." She actually liked me, but nevertheless, I was scared to death of her. For years afterward, if one of my classmates wanted to get a shudder out of us, just saying this teacher's name would work wonders.

The first week of the following year, I was so afraid that second grade would be more of the same that I broke out in hives; it was the only time in my life to date that I've been hospitalized. When I

recovered, I found that my new teacher, Beverly Stevens, was one of the sweetest, most caring people imaginable. Whenever I hear someone talk about the difference a teacher can make, I immediately think of her. She single-handedly made me love school again. She was so dedicated that, many years later, when the Jonesboro school shooting happened, I could easily imagine Beverly in the place of that heroic teacher who sacrificed her life to shield a child. She inspired that much confidence. When I got my Masters in Education, I called her and told her she'd been one of my important inspirations.

From puberty, I'd had crushes on some of the boys at school, never the girls. When I realized this I panicked, refusing to accept that I could be one of *those* people, the kind of person about whom my preacher said AIDS "was a good solution to the problem," the kind of person God hated. I withdrew from my peers and gained a lot of weight. I often tried to pretend that puberty had never happened to me; adolescence felt easier to me if I could put the fact of its existence out of my mind. Living out in the country helped. I could escape into a nearby forest, where I'd be the only person for a mile in any direction and I could shut out the pressures of my life.

Although I hoped that nobody ever had any idea about me, I was a bookworm and a dedicated *Doctor Who* fan, both of which made my masculinity highly suspect in the eyes of my peers. That and my weight gain made me an easy target. I was often teased and ridiculed. Though, to be honest, I must admit that I could frequently be just as rude and inconsiderate to my classmates; I was a teenage boy, after all.

In high school, I made some tentative steps toward accepting myself. I never came out to anyone, but I credit my art teacher, Aline McCracken, with showing me that there were other ways to see the world besides fundamentalism. She never preached or put down religion; she led by example, sharing her viewpoints without imposing them.

My parents were and are good, caring people who sacrificed a great deal for my brothers and me. My mother is an English teacher, and she instilled in me a love of learning and books; for example, when I was 4, every night she read *The Hobbit* to me, a little at a time until she covered the entire book. She defied the common stereotype of evangelical Christians being uncurious people yoked to a blind faith. She believed in asking hard questions. Dad always came across as less questioning, but he was still highly intelligent, an accomplished forester who knows more about trees than I'll ever forget. Nevertheless, they let Leviticus determine their opinions about homosexuality.

By the time I was 17, too much of the Bible seemed contradictory and cruel to me. For example, God repeatedly ordered his chosen people to ethnically cleanse other peoples, to kill women, children, and babies. The Old Testament prescribed stoning to death for everything from being gay to talking back to your parents. It began to dawn on me that either the Bible was wrong or I was evil; my upbringing hadn't included a less literal interpretation.

Eventually, I began to feel that the Bible was wrong. Five years after my baptism, Jesus and I got divorced, so to speak. My parents didn't give me the hard time I was expecting them to. My mom said that I couldn't be forced to come to God, that I had to want to do so, and I've always respected her for saying that. I could tell that my dad agreed with her; he had a way of saying things without saying them.

During that time, I also lost a lot of weight, dropping from 250 pounds to 160. I slowly began to feel more comfortable in my own body. I began to accept that I was attracted to men, though I didn't tell anyone until my freshman year at college. But I also never fabricated any girlfriends or went on dates of any kind.

For years after that, despite coming out, I still internalized the idea that being gay meant I couldn't be a part of mainstream society, that I couldn't be a proper role model. In my college years, my attitude was, "Teaching? Are you kidding? That's what my mom does. I'm not anything like her." Of course, part of growing older

has been finding out all the ways I'm just like my parents and progressing from finding that notion horrifying to accepting it and, sometimes, celebrating it.

But for years, I thought of myself as a permanent rebel, blasting Public Enemy and Yoko Ono from my dorm, growing half a beard, giving a middle finger to the world in general. This attitude evolved thanks to my first serious relationship, with Stephen Parmer, who dragged me kicking and screaming into believing that I could be as good as anyone else, that I didn't need a chip on my shoulder the size of Montana. He nurtured me as well as he could, until his AIDS-related illnesses grew worse, until I had to switch roles and take care of him, until he finally died in 2002.

It was Stephen who first suggested that I could be a good teacher. I didn't believe him at first, but he kept urging the idea, and I finally went back to school to get my Masters of Education from Temple University. I had also begun to think about how people where I had come from were frequently written off as "white trash." In fact, in the school where I attended kindergarten to ninth grade, English classes taught only grammar until the mid '70s. One teacher forced literature into the school despite being told, "These kids aren't going to amount to anything. They don't need that kind of thing." (She's still at that school and is one of the pillars of the town.)

I saw the same attitude she fought against directed toward kids in Philly. The average person on the street tended to think of Philly public school children as unstable, rude, violent, and stupid. I figured that maybe I could help, because I knew what that kind of societal assumption felt like.

I was a substitute teacher and TSS-wraparound while I pursued my degree. I figured that if I could get through subbing, I could handle being a regular teacher. I applied to teach at public schools in Philadelphia, one of the most troubled districts in the country, a far cry from what I had experienced as a student. Philly schools are frequently chaotic, filled with demoralized staff and students who have had to endure often horrific home lives. Some students really do want to learn, but so much class time is spent on discipline problems that kids' skill levels are often years behind what they should be. I had been told all this before, but nothing prepared me for actually experiencing it.

Kids naturally want to know all about their teachers, even their subs. So I frequently encountered questions about my personal life. Did I want children? Was I married? What was my girlfriend's name? Because most of my assignments were short, sometimes I told the truth and sometimes I changed the subject or otherwise avoided answering. I refused to outright lie and invent a heterosexual life. Sometimes, students took the truth well, thanking me for being honest with them and telling me that their mom, aunt, brother, friend, or other loved one was gay or lesbian.

In general, the girls accepted the truth somewhat more readily; the boys were often nervous, some of them half-jokingly saying, "Don't stare at my ass." A few said I shouldn't have told them, that they certainly wouldn't have admitted to such a thing, even if it were true—a few thought I was kidding. One boy asked me if I was going to be on *Jerry Springer*. A few mouthed the bigotry they had heard at churches and mosques, telling me, "God hates you." I quickly learned not to take that kind of talk personally; my kids simply didn't know any better. Of course, that's easy to say—sometimes I did feel demoralized.

I had one truly bad experience as an art prep sub. Usually, I only answered truthfully to high school students, but this one time I came out to seventh- and eighth-grade students in a middle school. They were completely unable to handle it. This particular school was already out of control; almost all teachers on my floor were first-year teachers. And these students became completely unmanageable, often yelling at me, some calling me "faggot." One girl said, "My mom said you ought to be reported."

One eighth-grade boy came out to me; he was pleasantly surprised that someone working at a school would come out. He also

admitted that he was meeting adult men for sex. If I had that time to live over again, I would have cautioned him that such men weren't looking out for what was good for him. But at the time, I felt so drained that I didn't want to start one more argument. This student was very well-behaved, and yet I noticed that his other teachers frequently sent him to the accommodation room. Some teachers didn't bother to disguise their distaste for him. I still feel that I failed him; I just wasn't strong enough then.

A few students were eager for me to teach them how to draw. I gave one girl a few one-on-one lessons during my prep time. I asked her teacher during that period if he minded, and he said, "I don't care if she's in my class or not." His beaten-down, cynical attitude seemed to be typical of that school. The student seemed to appreciate the lesson, though. She almost seemed surprised at having anyone take time out for her.

The next day, after I came out to my students, the principal told me to leave. She claimed that it was because I wasn't adequately controlling my classes, but I knew she was lying. I could have filed a discrimination claim against her, but I just wanted to move on to my next assignment. I was happy to never see that school again.

When I did a semester of student teaching, I really lucked out. My cooperating teacher, Rick Miller, had taught for 31 years and still loved doing it. He hadn't missed a day of work in the past seven years. He had near-total control of the classroom and his students' respect. He had an impressive command of his subject and knew many ways to make it interesting for most of his students. He was a true role model for me, and I will continue to keep him in mind as I progress as a teacher.

Rick, though pro-gay himself, very strongly cautioned me against coming out. He believed that coming out would make my career far more difficult since I would be teaching in a highly homophobic population. He worried that if they knew I was gay, they would just call me a faggot every time I did something they didn't like; I would be known as "that gay teacher." He warned that inner-city culture encourages a rigid, cartoon version of masculinity.

He had good reason to say what he did. From my observations I saw that too many of the student body had never seen their fathers. The boys often learned how to be men from the streets, where anything gay is seen as feminine and weak. And many kids had been sexually assaulted. The mention of anything gay automatically makes some kids remember the awful people who molested them. I didn't know a way around that problem. During that semester, I took Rick's advice, deflecting questions his students had about my personal life.

But staying closeted made me feel like a coward. Rick was right in warning me of the dangers in coming out, but I felt it took too great a toll on my self-respect. Even so, my first semester teaching my own class, I continued to deflect questions about my personal life. However, I'm not the butchest guy in the world, so some students still managed to figure it out on their own, and a few often asked, "Are you gay?"

Stephen grew progressively sicker and died that December; to this day, I feel that he willed himself to live until he saw me started on my career and in a house of my own. He was that selfless. I took a few days off, and when I returned my students naturally demanded to know where I had been. In front of my classes, I said there had been a death in the family. But I did start to tell some individual students the fuller truth. Most of them were sympathetic, wanting to know if I was going to be all right. I had a jeweler interlock our commitment rings and wore them as part of a necklace for a couple of months. Many of my girls thought that was very sweet and sad, and they noticed when I stopped wearing it, one of them saying, "I guess you're not in mourning anymore."

A student offered to set me up with one of her older friends. In a way, her gesture was sweet, except that she was failing my class and had made her offer near the end of the semester, leading me to wonder about her true motives. I declined her offer by saying I wasn't ready to start another relationship yet.

I was out to all the school staff, and they were as supportive

as I could possibly have hoped for. My mentor teacher, Barbara White, made me a plaque with a poem of consolation she had composed herself. She and many other colleagues kept checking in on me to make sure that I was holding up all right. They treated me the same way they would have if I had been straight and my wife had died. It was such a profound contrast to the middle school I had subbed in. I felt part of a group. I felt like I belonged.

Whenever I heard my students say something homophobic, I no longer took it personally, but I felt bad for what such an atmosphere was doing to my kids, regardless of their orientation. Very few children felt safe coming out. However, there had been some exceptions. The year before I arrived at this school, a boy had begun to transition to a girl, and she had been accepted for the most part. It helped that the floor coordinator had gone to every room and explained the legal consequences of harassment. But in the minds of many students, that was an exception. In general, being gay was still not OK.

"Faggot" is so commonly used as an all-purpose insult that many students use it when they don't actually mean to be anti-gay. For example, one day a student barged into my room to gossip with a classmate. I calmly told him, "I'm sorry, but you can't stay here."

He waved his hand dismissively and muttered, "You're a faggot, man." One of my students whispered into his ear. He looked horrified and embarrassed and sputtered, "Oh, I'm sorry, I'm sorry, I didn't mean it," and quickly left. I had to struggle to keep from laughing.

In my English 3 class, one of my students, Jamal (not his real name), delighted in being a class clown. He was never malevolent, but he didn't want to do any of the work either. I found out that he had a part-time job designing and writing Web pages, so I allowed him to turn in his Web work for credit. I would show him how to correct his grammar and usage, and he seemed more interested in applying grammar rules to this real-life context. He ended up squeaking through with a D, though he was easily smart enough to have done A work.

Jamal was late turning in one of these special assignments; he said he had finished the work but had forgotten to bring it. So I gave him my e-mail address and told him to send me his work that night. In Philly, we're often discouraged from giving students our contact information, but I wanted Jamal to meet his deadline. What he turned in was easily worthy of an A. Soon afterward, he started Instant Messaging me, asking me how I was doing, talking about how he couldn't identify with the peers he often hung out with in the halls and in the classroom. His admission was a surprise to me; on the surface, he had seemed to fit in well with some of his peers.

Jamal was one of the students I had told about Stephen's death. Soon afterward, he admitted that he thought he was bisexual. He asked me not to tell anyone and said that I was the only person he had ever told. I was so happy to have been there for him that it automatically made all the crap I had been through before worth it. We continued chatting.

He seemed to have a bit of a crush on me. I didn't want to push the issue, especially if my guess was wrong, so I waited to let him bring up what he was feeling. When he admitted to having a mild crush, I thanked him for the compliment but explained that, of course, as a teacher I couldn't—and didn't—return his feelings. Fortunately, he said he understood, and he impressed me with his insight: He said that he was probably just fixating on me because I was the only gay man he knew.

One day after school, I took Jamal to the local LGBT youth center, a very supportive place that made me wish such spaces had existed when I was a teen. Jamal didn't really take to it, but at least he knows where it is should he need to call on it. He still IMs me from time to time to let me know how he's doing.

In the fall semester of 2003, my second year teaching, I came out to all my students on the first day of school. A summer training session I took recommended that teachers spend part of the

first day presenting a "Me Bag" containing a few items that said something about who we were as people; we would then assign our students to create their own "Me Bag." I chose a few uncontroversial items: books, an example of my artwork, a young coconut. I also included the interlocking commitment rings and a photo of my boyfriend, Andy. Many students took my revelation well. In particular, the girls were fascinated by Andy's picture and by the rings. But many students were pretty shocked, and some of the boys acted nervous when I walked near them.

Two more students have since come out to me. A few are genuinely curious about what gay people are like, and I answer their questions when I can. By midyear, many who were shocked have gotten used to it and now accept me as their teacher. A few still mutter, "You shouldn't have told us that," and wonder how anyone could possibly be gay.

One of the school counselors advised me to go back into the closet next year, because she believed I was making my job more difficult by being out. But many of my colleagues, including the principal, have been very supportive, and when some students have made antigay comments to me, I've been able to get school staff to take the offending student out until he or she could calm down. I've also learned that many antigay comments aren't about me or gays in general at all. One of my students repeatedly made such hateful remarks as "We need a straight teacher and a black teacher," and would accuse me of staring at him. I eventually found out that this tenth-grader couldn't read and was using insults to keep me from finding out. Once I found out and arranged to get him a one-on-one reading tutor three days a week, his homophobic comments ended.

As a teacher, I have to maintain a tough balance. On the one hand, I recognize how difficult many of my students' lives are. This past spring, one of my students was having a rough time because her 27-year-old drug-dealer boyfriend had been shot dead. Even though she was probably better off without him, she still loved him and spent more time in the counselor's office than in my class. I never was able to reach her. Even one of my colleagues, who has been teaching for decades, admitted, "What some of our kids need, we can't give them." On the other hand, if I just feel sorry for them, I'm not doing them any favors.

But I have no regrets about coming out. I've found that the more myself I am in front of my class, the more effective a teacher I can be.

HAPPY VALENTINE'S DAY
Mary Gay Hutcherson
School social worker
James River High School
Chesterfield County, Virginia

On Valentine's Day, 2000, my partner, Yolanda, and I were married at our MCC in Richmond, Virginia, surrounded by about 300 well-wishers. It was a happy occasion, as all weddings should be, but the big difference was that my coworkers were not included in the celebration of my "big day." I had spent a year planning this fabulous event, but I felt I could not share it with the people with whom I spent so much of my time. I had listened in excruciating silence to others in the teachers' lounge talking about their weddings, their engagements, their significant others, while this biggest event of my life was taking place. It was extraordinarily hard— especially for a 10 on the extrovert scale.

I have served as a school social worker for almost two decades, carefully keeping my personal life and my work life separate for fear of being fired or made ineffective at my job. I wondered if teachers and principals would still refer the cases to me, respect my professional opinion, and treat me with respect if they knew who I really was. The pressure was enormous.

I love my work. I have always felt I was really making a difference in the lives of those more marginal students I serve, and that was my mission as a social worker. It has so perfectly suited me in every way, except its homophobia.

*

The wedding was an epiphany in a special, unexpected way. There were so many good vibrations around it and so many negative ones around keeping it secret at work that I decided I would never hide my true self again. Gradually I began to share my lesbian life with coworkers. I put a picture of my partner and me on my desk; I casually shared the wedding experience and even some pictures with my best work friends.

As a result, I felt different. I felt like I have the right to take up space in this world just like anyone else. Doing this made me feel so much happier at work that many people commented on how upbeat I was. I received support through unexpected avenues. For example, as I shared my Christmas family pictures—of Yoli and me with our dogs—with some friends, the school nurse came in and picked up the pictures. She said nothing, but afterward she came to my office to share that her son is gay and she loves him and his partner very much. I felt so much closer to her, and so much more real, than I had ever felt before during the many years we worked together.

A big factor in becoming more open was that I also realized I was close enough to retirement to retire if it became uncomfortable or if I were fired. But the biggest factor was realizing that I have so much emotional support in the world, and I am so lucky to have found the special person to complete my life, that I can handle whatever repercussions come. Free at last!

I was then approached by another gay teacher telling me that some students wanted to start a gay-straight alliance in my high school. She was nervous for the same reasons I had been but equally respectful of these students' right to do this...so we did it. In the process, I came out to everyone involved. This has been quite

liberating, and I haven't had any negative repercussions. I have the support of my principal and my supervisor and the law, to some extent, as the federal Equal Access Act has guaranteed these kids have the opportunity to form clubs like any others that are extracurricular.

So, here I am, 60-something years old, and freer and happier in my work and my personal life than ever before.

GOING BACK TO WHERE I GREW UP GAY

Bethany Petr
Science teacher
Francis Scott Key Middle School (2000–2002)
Paint Branch High School (2002–present)
Silver Spring, Maryland

I work for a school system that "prohibits discrimination on the basis of race, color, national origin, marital status, religion, sex, age, disability, or sexual orientation in employment or in any of its education programs and activities." They offer domestic partner benefits to employees. It's all very promising on a high-falutin' legal level, but "faggot" is still the least-corrected slang thrown at other students in the hallways, and "gay" is used at least a thousand times per day to refer to something that is weak. Students still discuss how "disgusting those fags kissing on MTV" is, and one student will go out of her way to hurt another if it's suggested that the other is a lesbian.

I spent my junior and senior years of high school waiting to go to college so I could find "the gays." I wasn't ashamed of realizing I was a lesbian. I'd already rejected the religious trappings that could have made me feel bad about it. But I believed that you just don't talk about these things. Frankly, as an introvert, you don't talk about much at all. I'd just sit and wait and take solace in the fact that this one really nifty girl that I'd been friends with in middle

school had a button on her backpack with a pink triangle on it, and the back of our student newspaper had an ad for SMYAL (the Sexual Minority Youth Assistance League, an LGBT youth support group in D.C). I'd see these things and know that I'd get my chance to be gay soon.

When I graduated from college, I was given an open contract with the school system, and when I finished my last interview, the staffer asked if I'd like to substitute during the last month of the current school year. One of the last assignments I took happened to be at the high school from which I graduated. I was in for the AP bio teacher, so I got to spend a lot of time in the science office with the faculty who'd taught me when I was a student there. The department head, who'd been my AP physics teacher, took the opportunity to share all kinds of dirt with me about the teachers I had known. One, who had an alcohol problem and whose wife left him, spent months sleeping in that very office. Another was discovered to have been writing a column about the gay leather community. This she shared with great horror. "Can you imagine?"

The next fall my first teaching placement was in a troubled middle school. The kids, for the most part, were pretty tough. My colleagues presented a challenge all their own. My coworkers talked about Jesus a lot. They tried on a daily basis to get me to come to church with them. Toward the end of my first year there, I happened to be in the faculty lounge when a couple of teachers were discussing a student, one of our greatest behavioral challenges, who had finally done something that resulted in his removal from our school for the remainder of the year.

"Thank God that faggot isn't going to mess up my class anymore. I'd like to pummel his ugly little face." Other teachers nodded in consent.

Today, I once again work in the high school that I attended as a student. I tell students not to use the word *faggot* because it makes them sound ignorant. Most of them laugh; only a couple continue to use it. (This represents progress, right?) I watchdog homecoming and the prom to make sure neither discriminates against some poor brave gay students. I know most of them will not attend these events. I didn't either.

I don't talk to many people, not to other adults, anyway. It's hard to relate to people who want to talk about their kids, their boyfriends, their husbands, their straight lives. No one asks me about myself. I don't share any details about my life. Only one staff member even knows I have dogs, and that's only because I keep a picture of them on my desk. No one asks if I'm gay. I'm a walking stereotype, yet only a handful of my colleagues are smart enough to see it.

Every year the social committee collects $20 from us. This is to pay for new baby gifts, wedding gifts, anniversary gifts, basically any celebration of meeting societal norms and expectations. Every year I fail to pay by the deadline. Every year some poor fool in charge of collecting the funds hunts me down. Every year I tell myself I'm going to finally step up and say, "Hey—I'm never going to benefit from this fund. I'm not going to get married if the current government has its way; I'm not planning on having a baby, and there's no way I'm going to accidentally become pregnant. Therefore, I'm not giving you my money." Every year I hand over a check for $20. Introverts don't like confrontation.

Recently, in the office, two teachers were discussing just how gay a particular student was. They laughed and joked and degraded him. I shook my head in disapproval and turned to leave, and one of my more savvy colleagues suggested to them that they were ignorant. It's the small things that keep you going.

Toward the end of this year the students were all abuzz because a student teacher in the social studies department had come out to them. It pleased me that this had impressed, rather than distressed, most of them. What bothered me is that one student described to his friends how he'd gone into the social studies office looking for this student teacher and asked Mr. H., a teacher he regards with great respect, "where the faggot was." This teacher, feigning a limp wrist and feminine lisp, responded that he did not know. They spent several minutes bonding over the "silly faggot" together.

Now, that's the kind of faculty that supports the school message of diversity.

I sent my principal an e-mail last year. It said, "Here is a list of all the high schools in this county that have gay-straight alliances. Why don't we have one?" I got no reply.

So why do I stay in this job, despite the stress that makes me spend nights crying? Well, first of all, the kids could use the influence of a cynical, atheist, feminist, radical queer. There's too much of "the right" at play in the school system. Someone should represent a viable alternative. And second, I can talk to them. They still know how to listen. I don't mean listening and following my instructions; I mean listening to me like I might be saying something worth hearing.

I check the back of the student newspaper every month, but I notice that there's no ad for SMYAL these days. I work for a school system that "prohibits discrimination on the basis of race, color, national origin, marital status, religion, sex, age, disability or sexual orientation in employment or in any of its education programs and activities." I wonder why, with all these trappings of progress, things still aren't any better. I wonder what my students see in this high school that gives them hope that they can have their chance to be gay, and everything will turn out just fine. I wonder, and I worry, and then once in a while I remember that there's me.

DID I MAKE A DIFFERENCE?

Steven Click
Elementary teacher
Barrow (1971-1983) and Fairbanks (1983-1997) public school systems
Barrow and Fairbanks, Alaska

As I sit here writing this piece, now in my mid 50s, I look back over the decades of my life and see what has been and not what might have happened.

I am a product of the 1950s, a time, at least in my perspective, when men were the providers and women were slowly changing their roles in the family. I was raised to finish high school, go to college, get married, have a career, and raise a family. I did all that, in that order, and I look back fondly on many great experiences and adventures in my life. That is not to say that I didn't have my down times, my worries, and my innermost thoughts about who I really was and where I fit into the scheme of things.

Growing up in Southern California in a middle-class family where my dad worked in the aerospace industry and my mom worked in the home, I lived a pretty good childhood. Early on I saw that I wasn't interested in "normal boy things" but would rather create crafts (and sell them to the neighbors), take dance lessons (tap as well as ballroom), roller-skate, and play with girls. In Cub Scouts, I was cast (or did I volunteer?) to be a girl in a skit, but I also fell off my bike and lost a front tooth while trying to impress some girls with my riding skills.

I knew that I wasn't interested in "boy things," like sports,

surfing, cars, trading baseball cards, or later on, talking about exploits with girls. I knew that I was different than other boys but didn't have a name to put with it. It wasn't until I was almost out of high school that I learned the word *homosexual,* and I knew that I wasn't that kind of person. Though when I finally put two and two together, I figured out that my Uncle Bob and (his partner?) Gordon were "those kind" of men. Yep, I had a gay uncle (and no one in the family *ever* talked about it, according to Mom).

So I hid the fact that I had questions and thoughts as to who I really was because I wanted to be like every other guy, to be a regular young man in high school and community college. I dated, figured out how to undo a bra strap, never hugged another guy friend, and was married at 20. We continued our college education, graduated, earned elementary teaching credentials, and moved to Alaska to become teachers in the fall of 1971. We lived, taught, and started a family in a small Eskimo village on the edge of the Arctic Ocean. And after 12 exciting and comfortable years in the bush, we moved to Fairbanks in 1983. I helped raise two great sons, the younger of whom, like his dad, is gay (and, unlike his dad, has been out since he was 17).

I always worked in an elementary school. I knew I didn't have enough patience for middle-school age students, and I think that the older high school kids intimidated me (at least in my younger years). The dozen years in the native village, where I was in the very small minority of "white" people, taught me more about tolerance and acceptance of everyone, their lifestyles, their culture, and the choices they may make in their lives.

In the late 1970s, just after my youngest was born, I accepted the fact that I was at least bisexual (if not a gay man), but I also promised myself that I would be a live-at-home dad until my son was out of high school. From that point on, I led two lives: one, the public one, of being a teacher, husband, and dad, and the other of being a closeted gay man. I lived with the fear that I would be found out and possibly lose my family as well as my job. It was hard work living two lives (some might say "lies").

My life—which included a successful career in teaching, being an educational employee advocate through NEA, a community-service Kiwanis member, supportive father and family member, and an actor in a local community theater at times—continued until year 26 rolled around and I (along with my wife) was given the opportunity for retirement with a "golden handshake" from my school district. I decided that I wanted to take that opportunity but also knew that for her to make the correct decision for herself, she needed to know some personal information I had never shared. I came out to her one evening about three weeks before she needed to let the district know if she was going to take the "handshake." Needless to say, after 29 years of marriage, she was devastated, hurt, and angry.

Within days, everyone in the district knew that I was gay. I could feel their looks, sense the talk behind my back ("Did your hear? Is it really true?") Not one person asked me about my revelation; I might bring up something in a conversation, but even then there was minimal discussion.

Part of me wanted for everyone to know that they had been teaching with a gay man. I told my principal (and friend) about the situation, and he left it up to me as to whether I would give a small announcement at my last staff meeting. I chose not to say anything, as I wanted my wife to have as easy a time at her school as possible. (The next year, as my "news" spread through the community, two parents had their daughters transferred out of her class for fear of contracting HIV.)

I would guess that all teachers ask themselves throughout their careers, "What influence have I had on my students?" I asked myself that almost every day while I was teaching, and many times since retirement. When I saw a former student years later, I would ask them what their memory was of my class. Most answered that I wore some really wild clothes (Hawaiian at 50 below zero, in the

dead of winter, a tuxedo for our Authors Day Celebration) or the cooking that we did in class (escargot when we studied France or dolmas when we learned about Greece). It wasn't until years later that I found out a very important influence I had with at least one student.

Just after moving to Fairbanks, I had the opportunity of working with a most unusual class—one of the "golden" classes of all times. They worked well together, helped one another, were courteous, and basically just wanted to be in school and learn what I was offering. The very quiet leader of the class was a boy who almost always wore a button-down shirt and tie to class (years later, when I asked him about that, he said it was "just a phase"). He earned the lead in the sixth-grade musical and was the peacemaker and the head mediator of the class. I still have the little box with a wizard on the top that he gave me when I was the wizard in a local production of *Once Upon a Mattress*. He was that kind of a kid. He was also one of only two former students who ever asked me to come to a high school graduation.

He and I kept in touch over the years, and I happened to see him the summer after I came out. We had lunch together and I shared my news. He took it quite well, asked some questions; I shared some responses, and after a hug we parted. When I asked him if he or the other kids "knew" or suspected my gay nature back in elementary school, he said that though the term wasn't used, there was some talk. They all knew that I wasn't like the other male teachers—I was more thoughtful, understanding, and not into a macho image.

Later, he e-mailed me asking me some very pointed questions about my "gayness"—When did I suspect? How did I know? How did my sons take the news? Was it normal? I answered, and finally asked him if I was the subject of a paper for one of his college classes. He told me it was something like that but that he couldn't fully explain for a couple more years. Finally, my "gaydar" was activated. It all fell into place: He was reaching out to me because he was questioning his own sexual identity.

I know that I have touched at least one student in a very special way. Of the more than 600 students I've taught, there must have been more than several handfuls of students who are gay, lesbian, bisexual, transgender, or still questioning. I hope that my message of acceptance, tolerance, and equality for all taught them more than their spelling words and times tables.

MS. KEE HAS A WIFE!

Ayana Kee
Elementary school teacher
P.S. 330
Brooklyn, New York

Many people see New York City as a haven of tolerance. But in the five years that I've taught here, I haven't met any female elementary school teachers who were out to their students. I am a second-grade teacher and I am a bisexual, African-American woman. On October 19, 2002, I got married. Since then I've found myself wanting to talk openly about my relationship with my wife. I want my students to know the real me. I'm growing tired of the omissions and the self-censorship. Some days the closet feels cramped.

One Day in May 2003

"Ms. Kee has a wife," said Rashad. I froze.

We were in our classroom getting ready to do math. The children were sitting on our worse-for-wear rug. My back was to them because I was writing the warm-up on the easel.

"Yes, she does. I met her yesterday," he insisted. The sunlight in our classroom suddenly hurt my eyes and the drip, drip of our radiator sounded like metal hitting glass. I finished writing the math warm-up and sat in my chair next to the easel.

I decided not to lie. Ten years of experience has taught me that it is best to be frank with young children. They can detect duplicity as easily as they can smell what's for lunch in our cafeteria. I looked out on the class expectantly. I did not see the shocked stares I expected. I waited for a raised hand and a child to ask the question (or at least for someone to tattle on Rashad). But the children were not looking at me. Four rows of children were sitting cross-legged on the rug, writing the math warm-up in their black and white notebooks.

Correction: Most of the kids were writing, but a few were engaged in the hair-braiding, window-staring, miniscule-scrap-of-paper-turned-into-an-airplane distractions that elementary school teachers see everyday. I shrugged and taught the math lesson.

At lunchtime, I pulled Ms. Johnson aside and related the incident to her. I will never forget the day I came out to Ms. Johnson. We were in the staff lunchroom. (It's really just a small room in the basement, with a full-size refrigerator and a hazardous amount of mold on the ceiling.) Ms. Johnson was carrying on a bawdy conversation with a male teaching assistant. I believe it was about a late-night rendezvous with a lovely lady. I wrote a note mentioning that I had a lovely lady at home and I folded the note twice before sliding it to Ms. Johnson. From that moment on, she was a preaching, teaching mentor for me.

Ms. Johnson had taught almost as long as I'd been alive and was also a pastoral counselor. Perhaps that's how she knew why the kids didn't say anything to me when Rashad spoke about my wife. "It just doesn't fit into their scheme of things, Ayana," she explained. "They ignore what they don't understand."

It fits into Rashad's scheme, though. I first met adorable Rashad, his twin Akeem, his mom Annette, and his mom's partner, Julie, at a Black Pride picnic here in Brooklyn. Annette and Julie have been together a long time, since the boys were toddlers, so the boys have had two moms almost all their lives. My wife got to know them first. Shanté is an artist-activist who is well-known, at least among other young LGBT artists and activists here in New York City. She has been on panels, interviewed for magazines, radio, and television, and filmed in a documentary.

Meanwhile, I've been content to remain in my closet.

I pulled Rashad aside after lunch and asked him to help me keep my private life private. Rashad nodded. He understood the need for privacy. Annette is an out member of the PTA. I found out later that kids teased Rashad because his mom is a lesbian. Perhaps he thought the kids might tease me too. After our little talk, Rashad skipped down the hall to join the rest of the class in the art studio. I stayed on my knees and stared at the wall.

One Day in January 2004

I was teaching the children a fun, Senegalese-inspired dance in preparation for the black history assembly in February. We had rolled up the rug and pushed aside the desks so we could practice in our classroom. I was sitting in my customary chair by the easel and the children were standing in rows.

I took off my wedding ring, put it in my jacket pocket, and buttoned my pocket shut. The ring had hurt my finger as I beat out amateur rhythms on a small drum.

Afua called out from the last row, "Ms. Kee, are you married?"

"Yes," I replied automatically as I tried to remember the next dance step.

"What's your husband's name?" Tony asked from the second row.

I paused. It was a reasonable question. The children had probably met Mrs. Douglas's and Mrs. Friedman's husbands. Mrs. Douglas's husband had been at the school a lot last fall, helping out as his wife's pregnancy progressed. Mrs. Friedman's husband frequently came up to the classroom when he arrived to drive her home at 3:30 P.M. For our writing lessons, teachers were encouraged to talk about their home lives, and most did. Thus, the children were used to hearing all manner of personal details about their teachers. But I wasn't ready to walk the walk.

"That's private," I said.

"Do you have any kids?" Tony tried a different tack.

"Yes. I have 18 children," I replied, smiling. The class exploded into expressions of surprise, disbelief, and wonder.

"And they're all 7 years old," I added.

"I get it," Shamika squealed. "She's talking about us!"

I laughed and the children laughed and then I taught the dance lesson.

Every Day

Many people see New York City as a haven of tolerance. Maybe it is. In the five years that I've taught here, I haven't met any female elementary school teachers who were out to their students. But every day I ask myself: *Is it time for my students to meet the real me?*

SAFE SCHOOLS AND VOICES

Bonnie Beach
Retired teacher
New Trier Township High School
Winnetka, Illinois

It was 2:30 on a beautiful spring afternoon, with a sky that was a knockout blue. I knew the pickets would probably be stationed in front of our school by now, but I didn't know how many there would be or what kind of reception they would get. There was a break in my schedule, and I used the time to go upstairs to the second-floor rotunda, where I would have a panoramic vantage point from which to check things out. I walked up to the rotunda windows and leaned into the overlarge sills. From here I could see it all: the walkways, sidewalks, front lawn, the two-lane street that runs in front of the school, and the quiet, tree-shaded neighborhood that sprawls beyond.

There were the usual gangs of kids spread across the lawn, twos and threes sitting on the concrete walls that served also as benches, and individuals coming and going, as the last period of the day was about to begin. Across the street a man braced against the rear fender of a late-model car caught my eye. He had a large, old-fashioned video camera sitting on his shoulder. The camera was pointed at the near side of the street. I let my gaze follow back along the path of the camera and found a scruffy-looking middle-aged man who held a picket sign in one hand and a handful of flyers in the other. A small group of students standing at the junction between our walkway and the public sidewalk were focused intently on the picket. As I watched, the man approached the group of curious students and extended a flyer toward one of them. Two other men wielding picket signs stood under a tree across the street, talking to each other.

"Three pickets," I thought to myself. "For all the threats this guy made, I would have expected a small army."

He had called me several times. At first he had asked respectfully if he could come and present "the other side" of homosexuality to our health classes. I explained to him that we only invited guest speakers who were connected to our own community, and pointed out that he and the organization he represented were based some 40 miles to the southwest of where our school was located.

"This is a public school," I explained further. "Students are obligated by law to be here. We believe that education is best delivered in a climate where students feel safe and respected. From what you've told me, your message runs counter to what we are trying to teach here. The safety and respect for all of our students, including those who are LGBT, questioning, or those students who have family members or friends who are gay or lesbian, is very important to us. Therefore, you are not welcome here and will not be invited to speak to our classes."

It was then that he told me he was going to contact the principal. I told him that was certainly his right and gave him the phone number. Apparently he got much the same message from our principal and followed up with a letter in which there was the threat of some kind of picketing action. He had called the police, the news media, and our school administration to advise them of today's visit.

I focused on the signs the men were carrying.

HOMOSEXUALITY…AN ABOMINATION AGAINST GOD!
UNFAIR! EDUCATION IS ABOUT TRUTH
STUDENTS NEED TO HEAR THE OTHER SIDE
HOMOSEXUALITY IS SINFUL AND UNNATURAL
STUDENTS MUST KNOW THE TRUTH

Outside, there were several hundred students standing on our walkway or lawns, calling across the street to the two pickets stationed there. A group of 25 or 30 had formed a semicircle in front of the man on the near side of the street. In that group, I recognized several students from my health class. The man with the video camera was frantically panning across the scene. Several students yelled out loudly. The sounds of their voices but not the words drifted up to me through the open rotunda windows. By this time, more students were in possession of flyers. Many looked at them, pointed, talked among themselves, and either dropped them, returned them to the near-side picket, or tossed them into one of our large, outdoor trash barrels.

I saw our principal, Wes Baumann, walk out from under the front portico. Moving toward the nearest group of students, he stopped to talk. There was some laughter and I saw him point his thumb over his shoulder. The group turned and made for the front door. Wes continued to walk among the students, stopping to talk to groups or individuals, motioning for several students to pick up some of the flyers now scattered and blowing over the front lawn.

At the far end of his circuit, Wes turned toward the front door. He stood for a moment listening and looking, then walked quietly back inside.

"You would be proud of what these kids are saying to those men," said Wes, appearing at the window beside me a few minutes later as we continued to watch the action outside. "Most of the kids are disgusted with the fact that those people are out there. They asked if I could just call the police and make them leave. I explained that as long as the pickets stayed off school property, they were perfectly legal. I wonder what that guy with the video camera is doing?"

"Maybe he's making a documentary. Maybe he's just trying to intimidate us. Who knows? What else are the kids saying?"

"A number of students are refuting the statements on the signs and the flyers. I heard kids saying 'We talk about this in our health class. We have heard gay speakers.' One girl told the

214

picketers, 'Gay is OK. My brother is gay.' Another student said, 'We talk about sexual orientation. We do it respectfully. We don't need you.' Their responses are thoughtful and they are asking the picketers good questions. You know what? It's obvious that we've done a lot of good work here already. These fellows chose the wrong school to target."

Wes turned and walked up the hall toward his office. I turned back to the scene on the lawn. Busses were beginning to circle the block and pull up in a long line in front of school. The cameraman was moving around across the street, trying to film between the noisy yellow behemoths. I thought back over my long career at New Trier, this suburban Chicago-area high school. I thought about how this news, so empty of threat now, would once have chilled me. I lost myself to remembering how much had changed.

✽

In 1967 there were few nondiscrimination clauses in employment contracts. There were no harassment prevention policies, and as far as I could see there were no out homosexual teachers in any school I had ever attended, although two of my high school teachers had come out to me when I was in college and had given me advice about being a teacher and a homosexual. "If you are ever threatened," they advised me, "don't run and don't hide. Confront the situation. Count on the good reputation you are making as a principled and skillful teacher to carry you through."

I put their advice to use when the subject of homosexuality and Bonnie Beach raised its scary head during my third year of teaching. I had found a note on the gym floor after one of my classes. I assumed the note had been passed between two female students. The note read, "Beach is a lesbian and you love her. I'm going to tell your parents." I was terrified. My first reaction was to tear the note to shreds and flush it down the nearest toilet. Instead, with a great deal of apprehension, I took the note to our dean of students. He read it. He asked me if I had any idea about which student had written the note, and when I replied, honestly, that I did not, he crumpled it and tossed it into his wastebasket. We talked about other teaching matters, how I liked the Midwest, and after 10 or 15 minutes of small talk he bid me goodbye by saying, "Forget this. Kids say a lot of things about teachers. It's not important."

My overwhelming emotion was relief. The dean had supported me. And he hadn't asked if I was, in fact, a lesbian.

Years passed, and they were good ones for me. I became a successful teacher, coach, and adviser. As a single woman in her 30s whose roommates had all been women, I believed that most of my colleagues assumed I was a lesbian. Being out only by assumption offered me protection from the open disapproval of others and offered others the comfort of not having to "see" and deal with who I really was.

It also allowed me to avoid taking positions on issues that touched too close to home, if I so chose. There were times when a parent intimated his or her discomfort with having a daughter who was involved in athletics, "because, you know, it's not the best thing for a young girl…" In those days I was not eager to follow with "Why is that?" We both understood the inference that many female athletes were lesbians. Worse yet, were those few parents who let me know in ways subtle and not so subtle that they thought I was a lesbian. I didn't pursue that line of thinking either. By and large I continued on in my profession, assuming I was safe in the protection of my dimly lit closet. At the time, it seemed a reasonable trade-off for the life I was living.

The day that every closeted educator dreads came for me during the winter of 1990—a time when I was feeling most gratified with my career and my personal life. I was finishing my last year as president of the teacher's association and my first year as department chair. I had found the love of my life, and we had just moved in together. One afternoon an administrator who was also a good friend came into my office at the close of the school day. She shut my door and pulled a chair over to my desk.

"Bonnie, I've come to tell you what the administrators have

been discussing for the last two hours. A parent called the principal today and said, 'Bonnie Beach is a lesbian. She is involved with a female teacher.' I thought you should know. The rest of the administration and I thought it best for one of us to talk to you about the phone call and our conversation. I volunteered."

I sat stunned. I thought to myself, *Well, here it is. I can lie and deny what the parent said, or I can tell the truth. This kind colleague who has come to talk with me will accept whatever I choose to tell her. If I lie, my partner and I will be at the mercy of anyone who wants to blackmail, intimidate, or terrorize us for the rest of our working lives. That is not the way we want to live. If I tell the truth, we will be free from this moment on.* I was very nervous, but sure of what I was about to do.

I said that what the parent had reported was true, and if it cast the school or my department in a negative light I was willing to resign—as department chair, or as an employee of the district. My friend shook her head and assured me that was not the reason for the visit.

"Both you and Pam are wonderful teachers and you both have earned a great deal of respect at New Trier," she said. "This is just gossip, but malicious gossip just the same. We thought you should know about the phone call and our conversation."

"Do you think it would help if I talked personally with the other administrators and told them what I have just said to you?"

"I think," said my friend, "that if you could do that it would be a fine idea. I don't think it's necessary, but I certainly think it would be the courageous thing to do."

"OK," I replied. After she left I sat quietly for a minute. The sense of my newfound freedom surged inside me. For the first time I was unfettered by my secret, and I felt light, and happy, and scared all at the same time. Then, with some trepidation, I set out for the second floor and the corridor of offices housing our administrators.

Forty-five minutes and five offices later, I opened the door leading to the office of the then-assistant principal, Wes Baumann. I

gave him what was now a very well rehearsed speech about my sexual orientation.

"I guess I've known for a long time that you were a homosexual…a lesbian," he said, clearly uncomfortable with the word. "All my life I've believed that homosexuality is wrong. But I just can't believe that anymore. I'm so sorry for what you're going through, but I'm glad for the opportunity to tell you how I feel. I have tremendous respect for you as a colleague and a friend. Whatever I can do to help you, I will."

As I left Wes's office, I literally ran into the principal. His office had been closed and locked, so I thought he was gone. Now we were standing in the hallway, face to face. This was the conversation I most dreaded. This man was legendary for his aversion to controversy and confrontation. I was feeling as though I had already caused him enough distress today. I delivered a shortened version of my speech.

"This," he said, "will blow over. Hold your head high. Go on about your business, and people will soon find something else to talk about. Have a good weekend, and don't worry."

I walked back down to my office shaking my head. What an amazing day this had turned out to be.

❋

Outside there was a loud noise and commotion. I was yanked from my reverie and wondered how long I had been standing there lost in memory. Some students were yelling, wadding up leaflets, and throwing them at the picketers. The 3:20 bell rang and behind me in the hallway I heard classroom doors opening as students filled the hallways. Athletic teams began to load onto busses. Students scurried down the walkways and out onto the sidewalks.

On his way to an after-school meeting, Wes stopped to check the front lawn once again. He shook his head and muttered, "Amazing. Just amazing. I just can't get over our kids. If we could get all of our teachers and adult staff to take the same kind of responsibility for the climate here we'd be a much better—a much safer school." Without waiting for a reply he patted my shoulder and strode off to his meeting.

This story is dedicated to the people who live in the center of my heart: With love and appreciation to my editor and partner, Pam Liebing. Great thanks and admiration for Hank Bangser, superintendent, New Trier Township High School, and Wes Baumann, retired Principal, New Trier Township High School. Allies of great courage and kind hearts—my companions along the way: Jan Borja, Julie Ann Carroll, Steve and Jo Ham, Michael O'Hare, Darrelyn Marx, Matt Stuczynski, and Bob Ward.

Part Four
Change Agent

THE IMPORTANCE OF DISCOMFORT

Richard Ognibene
Chemistry and physics teacher
Fairport High School
Fairport, New York

"So, Mr. O., what are you doing for Thanksgiving?" she asked innocently on a November Tuesday in 1994. It was the end of sixth-period physics class and the students were huddled around the door waiting for the bell to ring. As is my custom, I asked various students about their Thanksgiving plans. When Priya returned the question, I answered with words that would forever change my life: "David and I are going to my parents' house for dinner."

Like an E.F. Hutton commercial, the room suddenly became very silent as another student asked the obvious follow-up question, "Who is David?" "He's the man I've been dating for the last year," I replied. The bell rang, and as the students filed out the door my stomach churned like Mt. Vesuvius. I was sure I'd be summoned immediately to the principal's office. Yet, amidst the fear and panic, other feelings started bubbling up inside me: relief, freedom, pride, honesty, and excitement. I had finally done it. I had come out to my students. I had not consciously planned on coming out that day. I was just tired: tired of the lies and half-truths, tired of keeping my school life and my home life in separate compartments, tired of contributing to my own oppression.

I have been teaching science since 1986, in three high schools and one community college. I've been out to my colleagues since 1987 and out to my students since 1995. I now have the best job on the planet, teaching at Fairport High School. If you entered our school today you would see a few rainbow stickers on cars in our staff parking lot, you would see signs for our gay-straight alliance, and you would see a principal who routinely chastises students for using homophobic language. You would see a district-wide toler-ance-and-diversity program called Brotherhood-Sisterhood Week. You would see a few brave gay or lesbian couples holding hands in the hallway. And you would see me, an openly gay science teacher who can safely bring his partner to school events.

You might assume that life has always been this good for me and my school, but in fact it has taken many steps to get to this point. Each of those steps seemed impossible at the time. Each step was filled with stress and discomfort. If I have learned anything from my journey, it is that old prejudices do not die easily. As Elisabeth Kubler-Ross noted, there is always denial, anger, and bar-gaining before acceptance. Far too many gay teachers spend their whole lives in the closet because they want to avoid discomfort for themselves or for others; ironically, this tactic just continues the cycle of homophobia, because society needs to go through the dis-comfort to get to acceptance. The discomfort is part of the process.

Step 1: Coming out to myself and my family

My journey as a gay man started in the fall of 1985. I was a gradu-ate student at the University of Rochester. I had finally come to terms with the fact that I was attracted to other men, but I didn't know what to do about it. While reading a student newspaper I stumbled across an ad for the gay-lesbian student group. On a crisp fall evening I walked across the campus to Meliora Hall to attend the meeting; as I approached the building I got scared that someone might recognize me, so I made a U-turn and sprinted back to the chemistry building.

The next week I actually made it to the meeting and met my first gay friends; that night I sat on my balcony, had two glasses of cheap wine, and wondered if my friends and family would still love me. By Thanksgiving I had been dating a fellow graduate student for a month, and I felt ready to come out to my family. I told my siblings, Beth and Chris, late Thanksgiving night; neither of them were particularly surprised. The next day, with my heart racing and voice cracking, I told mom and dad. My parents cried a little, worried about AIDS a lot, and told me that they loved me. For about a year there was some tangible discomfort. Over time, through efforts on all sides, the discomfort disappeared and I was finally able to live honestly with the people I loved most. My family is the rock upon which I have built my life; the reason we are so close is that we were all willing to go through the initial period of discomfort.

Step 2: Surviving in rural America

My journey as a teacher started in September of 1986. I got hired to teach seventh- and eighth-grade science in a rural town 40 miles outside of Rochester. I grew up in suburbia surrounded by highly educated, liberal adults. I had never experienced conservative small-town America. Needless to say, I learned as much as my students did that first year. Initially, my sexual orientation was not an issue; between teaching science, coaching soccer, and attending graduate school, there was little time for dating.

In October of 1987 I attended my first March on Washington. The event transformed my life; being among thousands of gays and lesbians was empowering. I was no longer the oddball—I fit in. The freedom I felt in Washington over the long weekend was astonishing. For three magical days I could be unabashedly gay and proud. I decided that I wanted to live this way all the time.

When I returned to school, I spent the next week coming out to colleagues, one at a time, in excruciating detail. They were uniformly kind, though each gave me some version of the following advice: "It's OK with me, but I wouldn't let too many others know. And heaven forbid the kids should find out." One teacher specifically said, "I don't tell the kids who I have sex with and neither

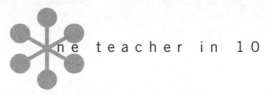

should you." Intellectually I never bought that argument, but I was too young to combat it. Now when people present that argument, I ask them if they wear a wedding ring or have a photo of their spouse on their desk or brag about their children. When they reply yes, I mention that *all* of those simple acts are ways of letting the kids know that you are heterosexual. I also note that sexual orientation is much more than the mechanics of intimacy; it is a spectrum of emotions, feelings, and people in our lives that make us who we are. And if your students can know who you are, why can't my students have that same right?

I survived, but I spent a lot of time each spring looking for a job in a community where I could live a more fully integrated life.

Step 3: Finding the right job and educating the staff

In 1992 I got my lucky break when I was hired by Fairport High School. I had no intention of storming the Bastille for gay rights during my first few years, but several opportunities quickly arose. During my first year at FHS, the Multicultural Diversity Club (MDC) put on a "Diversity Forum" in our auditorium. The speakers included an African-American man, a Latina woman, a woman in a wheelchair, a gay man, and a lesbian. Students walked up the aisles to a microphone at the front of the auditorium to ask questions. As I quietly observed the program, I realized that 90% of the questions were directed at the gay panelists. Clearly the students were thirsting for more information on this topic, information that was noticeably lacking in their curricula.

The following year some of my colleagues wanted to do an in-service training about the elevated suicide risks for gay adolescents and they asked me—untenured me—to be part of it. I thought about it for a few days and realized that I might not have this opportunity again; I said yes.

We wanted the forum to be a faculty meeting so that *everyone* would be there; we had no desire to do an optional workshop where we would be preaching to the converted. Our principal said yes, then no, then yes, then no, then yes…you get the point. There were many heated meetings and much discomfort, but the day of the workshop finally came.

For 45 minutes you could have heard a pin drop. My part of the program was to speak about my personal experiences as a gay student and as a gay teacher. I started full of fear, but my rhythm and confidence picked up as I went along.

Looking back, I realize what a big effect that meeting had on our school culture. The 20% of our staff that was comfortable with gay issues were excited, the 20% that was uncomfortable with gay issues were angry, and the 60% in the middle were exposed to issues that they had never thought of before. It's these people in the middle who eventually became our allies and helped transform the school culture. I still remember a colleague telling me that her brother was dying of AIDS and that our presentation helped her family.

The most surprising part of the presentation was the response of some of my gay and lesbian colleagues. They were uncomfortable because I had exposed the elephant under the rug. Many had been closeted throughout their careers and here was me saying, "I'm gay, I'm a teacher and it's OK to be both." I just kept repeating my mantra: "The discomfort is part of the process."

Step 4: Educating students

Even after coming out, one still has to address homophobia. Once, during chemistry class, I heard a student tell this horribly offensive joke: "What do you call a fag in a wheelchair?" "Roll-AIDS." I was so distraught by that joke and by the prevalence of homophobic put-downs used by adolescents that I wrote an article for our student newspaper in which I effectively came out to the entire school.

Once again there was some discomfort, not to mention a few parent phone calls to one of our assistant principals. The silver lining was the overwhelming support shown by my colleagues and my administrators—support that was at least partially related to the aforementioned faculty training.

Once I came out, I had the energy and courage to be a more creative teacher. The students felt closer to me and became more interested in my subject matter. I remember chaperoning the 1995 Senior Ball. Toward the end of the night, the DJ played "YMCA" by the Village People. I was standing by my date, David, along with the other chaperones. A senior couple, Amy and Jay, approached us and asked us to join them in a dance. We walked out as a couple and joined their circle and had the most spectacular dance I have ever experienced. The memories of all my awful high school and college dances faded away as I danced for the first time with male partner at a school event.

In June I was chosen by the senior class to be their graduation speaker. I addressed the 500 graduates (and 5,000 family members) in the perfect end to a perfect year.

Step 5: Forming a gay-straight alliance

In 1998 two seniors approached me about forming a gay student group. I was a little timid at first, as no nearby schools had a similar group; however, the students' courage inspired me to move forward. Our principal was very supportive but said we'd first have to get clearance from the superintendent. The superintendent was very supportive too, but he needed to make sure the board of education was comfortable with the concept.

It took months of meetings and negotiations to clarify what the group was and what the group was not. The administrators' big fear was that the alliance would be perceived as a club where kids talk about sex.

After a whole lot of stress, the group had its first meeting in March of 1998, but I was not allowed to be adviser. People were worried that the group might be challenged and that I could get hurt in the exchange. I was angry, but in retrospect I know that my district was trying to protect me.

In October of 1999 I officially became cofacilitator of our GSA, which we call the Fairport Rainbow Alliance. The first year we put up signs in the hallway, some of which were defaced. Now we put signs in each homeroom and they last the entire year.

Over the years we've gone from a small group of tentative, quiet kids to a raucous group of proudly out teens. (Even so, we talk about mundane stuff like homework and jobs and family much more than we talk about relationships.) In 2003 we participated in our first Day of Silence, with 50 people participating. I was a little worried about the day, not knowing how students and teachers would respond. But it went off without a hitch. However, discomfort is still part of the process.

Step 6 : Educating staff in other buildings

As a result of my experiences with the Rainbow Alliance, I realized that kids are coming out and dealing with sexual orientation issues at younger ages than ever before. A friend who is a talented elementary teacher suggested we develop a program to broach the issue with elementary and middle-school faculty.

We make a dynamic duo as she is a straight female elementary teacher and I am a gay male secondary teacher. Together we prepared a 20-minute program that included a clip from the video "It's Elementary." We then shared stories about gay kids being harassed by peers and how the harassment is often ignored by teachers.

Over five months we went to six schools. Though we believed our presentation was quite mild, we made some staff very uncomfortable, and multiple times, colleagues told us to soften our presentation.

I can honestly say that these presentations caused me more discomfort than anything I've ever done; they also provided some great results. We gave many teachers the courage to address homophobic bullying and to teach diversity lessons. What once seemed unthinkable suddenly became possible. The discomfort was part of the process.

Step 7: Celebrate progress and plan for the future

At the opening 2001 faculty meeting it was announced that my partner, Matt Fleig, and I had a civil union ceremony in Vermont.

When people cheered I realized just how far my school had come. During the last few years I have helped teachers at other schools start their own GSAs. I have seen a lesbian couple attend our junior prom. I have received e-mails and visits from college students who have recently come out. Seeing the progress makes the struggle worthwhile.

This profession has come so far in the last decade. And yet we have miles to go before we sleep. We need every high school in America to have a GSA. We need curricula that make gays and lesbians visible. Most of all, we need more gay and lesbian teachers, at all grade levels, to come out of the closet. Ambrose Redmoon said, "Courage is not the absence of fear, but rather the judgment that something else is more important than fear." The lives of our gay and lesbian youth must become more important than fear.

Discomfort is part of the process. My challenge to all my gay and lesbian colleagues is this: Put yourself and your school through a little discomfort!

THE HUNTINGTON HIGH PROJECT:
A TEACHER STORY OF SOCIAL ACTION

Irene "Toodie" Ray
Teacher (AP composition, creative writing, TV broadcasting)
Huntington High School
Huntington, West Virginia

It wears a person out. Teaching from a closet is a ridiculous notion; way too much of the best stuff gets buried in there. My dream has always been to teach or work with gay youth. This would, of course, be in an environment where I could be totally out as a lesbian, somewhere my sexual orientation was not an issue. Therefore I could be completely the authentic teacher-person I am.

I've been so tired of semiplaying the "don't ask, don't tell" game. How could I possibly teach kids to be proud of who they are from some dark box? How could I model to gay and straight students that we are all much more alike than we are different? How would they see that I was like their own mothers—always worried about my children (who, by the way, were their classmates and peers), enforcing curfews, expecting high GPAs, attending their activities—*and* I was a lesbian? So I just gave it up; I stopped playing the game. I finally came out at school, especially to students. Too many of them needed me to.

In the state of West Virginia, teachers sign a morals clause; sexual orientation is nowhere near being protected by state law. I can be fired without any reason. Before I came out, I expected that

I'd have to leave the area because even the small-scale feats I'd been doing came with a price: the constant fear that I could lose my job.

Now, despite these very real concerns, an incredible amount has happened at our school, beginning with the formation of a gay-straight alliance and snowballing to a performance about our students' reactions to viewing NBC's *The Matthew Shepard Story*. Suddenly, leaving Huntington High School in West Virginia does not seem as necessary. If one day that morals clause rears its ugly head, and the board of education decides this lesbian teacher does not belong in her classroom, I will go out with much noise.

There were several incidents and situations that led up to the establishment of our GSA and prepared the soil for the school assembly that was the product of Layne Amerikaner's senior project. The first—and most influential for Layne—was also the most positive. A gay student, Justen Deal, sought "refuge" at Huntington High in the winter semester of 2001. He left his home school after years of constant bullying became dangerous. Here he met and became close with Layne and her circle of friends.

The second incident took place in the fall of the next school year, when a despicable crime was committed in our small city. Five young males followed a 28-year-old man from a gay club to a bank parking lot near his apartment, where they savagely beat him, so badly that his friends could not readily identify him. Two of the accused were HHS students. This incident and the way it was handled during the next year and a half caused, to put it mildly, a rift in our school.

This was an especially sensitive subject because one of the students, who had (allegedly) beaten the young man with the butt of a pistol, continued to attended class for the rest of the 2001–2002 school year as he would the next, later wearing an ankle band as part of his "home confinement." He boasted about the gruesome details of the gay-bashing as if he were a hero ridding Huntington's streets of homosexuals. The other student, a star athlete and favored "son," was not charged at all.

Awareness of the mistreatment of gays began to grow among our student body, and just before the holiday break of 2001 Layne and three other students asked me if I would advise a gay-straight alliance for our school. Thirty to 35 students attended the first meeting of Huntington High's GSA in February of 2002.

Later that same school year another school, Boyd County High in bordering Kentucky, also formed a GSA. This school is 20 minutes away by Interstate—but apparently a universe away in mentality—from HHS. Their voyage was not smooth sailing: More than 500 students walked out of school to protest the club's meeting on campus. Local churches organized 2,000 citizens to protest the existence of the club. The situation for the Boyd County GSA grew ugly; sometimes they felt helpless and hopeless—like the whole world was against them.

So our GSA invited them to Huntington for pizza and camaraderie. After the pizza party, I felt grateful for how wonderful my faculty and student body seemed compared to the other school's. I wrote a letter to the population of HHS telling them how heart-wrenching the stories from Boyd County were and how happy I was to be at HHS, where people were more tolerant, open minded, and compassionate—more "21st-century human beings." The letter was printed in the school newspaper. This action had a reciprocal effect—the more thankful I was for their wonderful attitudes, the more wonderful their attitudes became.

A few weeks later the hate group led by the Reverend Fred Phelps, attracted by the Boyd County struggle, descended upon the tristate area to spread their religious message of hate through picket lines and heinous antigay language. In reaction, an antihate rally was held, and my students and I were invited to speak. Huntington High's GSA organized our own "Go Love" rally held in front of City Hall. Both events were successful beyond my expectations. We got heavy and very positive press and support. Parents and community members as well as a few faculty members joined our rally that weekend.

Later, the experiences of Huntington High's GSA and Boyd County's GSA were contrasted in a *New York Times* article. Few people, even those who had earlier participated in the protests in Kentucky, wanted to be associated or identified with the hateful and ignorant homophobic rhetoric that had attracted national news coverage mostly due to the Phelps group. In that light, even the mildest opposition to a handful of high school students and their fearless adviser trying to spread tolerance and acceptance seemed ridiculous. Many people had to question their own homophobic attitudes. Some people recognized that hate is hate in its most extreme form and in its mildest form. These events set the stage for Layne Amerikaner's senior honors project.

Members of Huntington High's Honors Program who stick it out until their senior year must complete an exit project. The project has to be something real, something useful and beneficial to the student and to a community. It requires research of some kind, presentations with visual aides, and documentation, like these projects usually do. But the process must include personal growth, and the final product must reflect a stretch on the part of the student.

When Layne first asked me to mentor her project, she knew she wanted to do something about hate crimes. By the end of her junior year, in June of 2002, she had narrowed her topic down to "something about Matthew Shepard" and using some sort of performance as part of the project. In early 2003 she nailed down exactly what she was going to do: show the NBC movie, *The Matthew Shepard Story,* at school, have students complete a survey about their reactions to the film, and use their comments to create a reader's theater, monologue-like performance. Of course she wanted to perform it for the school. But I knew that completing the project, even without getting class time for the performance, would mean persuading some people at our school to take a few giant steps.

Layne's proposal was approved by Sandy Linn, sponsor of the Honors Program, and then by principal Todd Alexander, who didn't bat an eyelash. First Layne wrote an e-mail asking teachers to take part in her project, and we sent it to the whole faculty via my school e-mail account. While we waited for teachers to respond, she wrote the survey and arranged for the movie to be broadcast over the school's Smart System. A total of 11 teachers agreed to participate in the project by allowing their classes to watch the movie and then complete the survey. However, many more classes than those 11 watched the movie without using the survey. We had made extra copies of the movie, so that if the scheduled broadcast time wasn't right for some teachers, they could play it any time they wanted. As word got out, more and more students were sent to my room for copies of the movie, and students in other classes talked their teachers into tuning in to the scheduled broadcast. *The Matthew Shepard Story* was the buzz of the school, the topic of discussion in classrooms, at lunch tables, in hallways all over the school, and even at dinner tables in homes for almost a week after the official broadcast for Layne's project.

The surveys came in, just under 200 of them. Most of the reactions, on the surveys as in discussions and conversations, were positive or at least curious, or shocked and angered that such a thing had happened. Only a few—at least that I heard of—expressed out-loud antigay sentiments. A handful of kids had real epiphanies: One or two wrote to Layne about how much the movie had affected them, how it had changed their minds about gay people, how after seeing the movie they could no longer understand why they had hated gay people. Others wrote or talked about their own or a friend's or family member's sexual orientation. I answered more questions about homosexuality, hate crimes, the Matthew Shepard incident, and sexuality in general in the three or four days following the movie than I have in the last several years.

The next step was the most challenging for Layne: what to do with those surveys. It is difficult to say how many hours she spent poring over them, trying to find patterns so that she could somehow organize them into a script. She said that even after they were

typed up, she could remember the handwriting the comments had been written in.

Layne's mother is an expert in qualitative research, so no doubt she was able to advise Layne in this next step of her project. Layne finally came up with five categories that she would represent as "characters":

1. Saddened (disheartened by the whole thing; that it can and did happen)
2. Angry (outraged at the two boys who committed the crime, mad at the whole world for being such a rotten place where such things happen)
3. Hateful (hostile, mostly toward gay people)
4. Indifferent (didn't affect me, so I don't care)
5. Unjust (can't believe things like this happen; it isn't right or fair)

Next Layne cast the show. Luckily, she had talented and willing friends. Four of the five students cast had at least some sort of acting experience; all very much wanted to take part in the project. Only one of the cast members was openly gay. As part of the play, Layne decided to read the questions on the survey, and then have the characters respond with answers. Most of the lines were exactly as the students had written them; only a few had been revised for clarity. The script consisted of questions from the survey and her arrangement of the responses.

In addition to writing the script and finding students willing to perform the controversial material in front of several hundred of their peers, Layne got a date for two back-to-back performances approved. We spent three weeks in intense rehearsal, and the show began to come together. Layne and I put together a video that included a beautiful black-and-white photograph of Matthew Shepard, Layne's title and acknowledgments, and the cast list, with soft music in the background. It also included the beginning of the movie, the eerie, slow-motion, sound-distorted scene in which Matthew is beaten with a pistol, tied to a fence, and left to die. We hoped it would provide a powerful intro when projected on the huge screen in our school's auditorium. Once again we e-mailed teachers, this time inviting them to bring their classes to the performance of *The Huntington High Project: A School's Reaction to The Matthew Shepard Story*. All 11 of those classes who had originally participated in Layne's project replied that they were coming as well as several more.

On the evening of final dress rehearsal, one of our two technicians was 30 minutes late; "Hateful" was tired and sounded sleepy but not at all hostile; "Unjust" forgot part of her costume. I told Layne all was perfect; everyone who's done any theater at all knows that a bad dress rehearsal means a wonderful opening. The next morning the cast waited backstage as I prepared to herd the 200 students and teachers we expected to the front and center seats— but they kept coming and coming. Many more teachers than we expected brought their classes to see both performances. We almost filled our auditorium both times.

I was shocked by some of the teachers who attended. Some of them had been accused by students of making homophobic remarks or allowing verbal gay bashing in their classrooms. Students had told me stories of bigotry of various forms—sexism, racism, classism—and now these people were bringing their classes to a performance speaking out against gay bashing and homophobia. I was overwhelmed by what was happening at my school.

Then the house lights dimmed and faded to black, leaving us in nearly pitch-darkness, the only light reflected by the giant white movie screen. The cast took their places. Our video was indeed powerful. It faded; the readers began.

Layne: "What was your initial reaction to seeing what happened to Matthew Shepard at the beginning of the movie?"
Saddened: "Terrible...that doesn't even describe it."
Angry: "Disgusting!"
Hateful: "I said, 'Ha ha, the stupid fag was killed.'"
Indifferent: "I don't really care."
Unjust: "Horrifying."

My kids—well, Layne and *her* kids—were indescribable… extraordinary…glorious…splendid! At times you could practically hear those seeds—the ones Layne had been planting—germinating among 500 high school students; at other moments, showers of tears fell.

Afterward, Sandy Linn (the sponsor of the Honors program), Layne, and I heard compliment after compliment. A number of people said what I too had thought: "You should take that around to other high schools." And it's true; the script is good enough, powerful enough to travel.

It hasn't finished its mission. This little girl from Huntington, West Virginia, this little Layne Amerikaner, with a mind like a river and a heart as big as the moon, made a difference in the lives of many people—a few we know about, but likely many we don't. Where the soil was tilled, she planted seeds, and then she handed beautiful blossoms to her classmates and teachers.

At Huntington High's graduation that year, I heard one of the better student-written graduation speeches of my teaching career; I cried as he talked. Trey Curtis, senior class president of Huntington High's class of 2003, spoke of how important it is to make a difference, to embrace, accept, and create change. He illustrated his point with the National Merit Finalists, the star athletes and musicians, debate winners, the friendships, all the good times, scholarship winners, the experience of losing a beloved classmate during the school year, award winners…and finally he spoke of Layne Amerikaner, who with her senior project had made a real difference in his mind and in the minds of hundreds of people. He called her a hero.

It's funny to me still that the seven of us—Sandy Linn, Nicole Gray, Katherine Mohn, Emanuel Gunn, Philip Pham, Colin Reynolds, Layne Amerikaner, and I—who worked so hard to make *The Huntington High Project: A School's Reaction to The Matthew Shepard Story* come together seem more or less to have just taken this all in stride, like it was something we do every day. We didn't notify the local press; we didn't have enough time to answer all of the audience's questions or discuss the performance with them; we didn't even have a party to celebrate. I am not positive that those six other people all know, all understand what a spectacular, intelligent, brave, important humanitarian thing they did. I hope they have said their own private "hip-hip-hoorays." I hope they know that they have changed potentially hundreds of people they don't even know in ways they will never know, and those people will change others, and so on and so on... It's mind-boggling. All of it began with people willing to take risks.

And Sandy and I are the only ones more than 18 years old. Layne Amerikaner and the other kids are just getting started; they won't be able to stop, not after such a big taste at such an early age. I am honored to have worked with human beings with such courage, humanity, compassion, and grace.

ne teacher in 10

DANCING WITH THE ISSUES
Clarence Brooks
Dance instructor (sixth, seventh, eighth grades)
Bak Middle School of the Arts
West Palm Beach, Florida

A Gay Teacher
When I was asked if I would consider submitting stories about my teaching experiences for possible inclusion in this new book, I was fascinated by the thought of how much has changed in the decade that's passed since the last edition. As a gay African-American male teaching in the South, I can give witness to this. As my stories will show, I am simultaneously a product and an agent of this growth and these changes.

It was the summer of 1998. I was preparing to return home to Seattle from a trip abroad. As a favor to a friend, a teacher at Bak Middle School of the Arts, I agreed to stop over in West Palm Beach, Florida, to interview for a position at the school where she taught. In all honesty, having just ended an 18-year career as a professional dancer, I was not interested in teaching middle school–age youth. But I was duly amazed at the diversity, focus, and talent of the students I taught in the master class.

As my day of interviews came to a close, the principal, assistant principal, and department chair collectively told me that the position was mine if I wanted it. Their only request was that I give them an answer soon, so that if I chose not to accept the offer they'd have enough time to continue interviewing for the position before school started: I felt that that was only fair. But I had another problem. I was worried about being a gay teacher in a public school.

That same year, the Oklahoma legislature was contemplating passing a law that would have made it illegal for lesbian, gay, bisexual, and transgender people to hold teaching positions in that state. I did not relish the thought of packing up all of my belongings, leaving my home and friends in Seattle, traveling across the entire country, and starting a new life, only to get booted out of a job because I was gay. After all, Florida was the birthplace of Anita Bryant's infamous "Save the Children" campaign. To my reasoning, it was quite possible that Florida could follow Oklahoma's lead should this unjust and discriminatory legislation pass.

After several days of mental anguish and mind wrenching, I called the principal and asked her point-blank if she had a problem with me being a gay teacher. I explained to her that I had been out of the closet for roughly eight years and under no circumstances was I about to go back in. I felt that I was out from under the proverbial cloak of shame that denoted the gay closet, and I was out for good. At that time, however, I hadn't even contemplated being out to students. I was mistakenly living under the internalized homophobic impression that my gay sexual orientation (unlike that of my heterosexual colleagues who speak openly about their families) had no place in the workplace and certainly not in the schoolyard.

In my explanation, I told the principal that I would never come out and say, "Hi, I'm Mr. Brooks, and I'm your new gay teacher." But I also assured her that under no circumstances would I conceal my gay identity from a student, parent, or colleague if asked.

I explained to her that I had faced both overt and covert racist bigotry before. Life had taught me that I would face, at best, a modicum of homophobia. If I had my druthers, I would much rather know up front that someone harbored hate toward me rather than risk getting stabbed me in the back by someone I thought was liberal-minded.

I wanted her to save me the time, the energy, the money, and the trouble of making another cross-country move. If she had, or could foretell, any problems with having a gay teacher on faculty, I wanted to know before and not after I had uprooted myself.

I am now enjoying my sixth year as an openly gay teacher in the nation's 14th largest school district, Palm Beach County.

The Faggot Ballet Teacher

In the first months at Bak, during a mandatory lunch duty, I witnessed an eighth-grade male student spill his entire lunch on the cafeteria floor. When I saw that he made no effort to pick up any of the mess, I approached him and asked him to get the broom from the cafeteria manager. Oddly, he ignored me and then turned his back to me.

Since our student body was by and large very well mannered, focused, and disciplined, this behavior seemed out of the ordinary. After my third, more forceful request, he physically challenged my authority by standing up—towering over me—and looking down at me. At this point, I threatened him with a visit to the assistant principal and a referral. After a brief pause, he backed down and retrieved a broom.

I was shaken by the experience. Why had he ignored my request to clean up his mess? Why had he physically challenged me? Was it an issue of race? As he left, I saw that he had been seated with quite a diverse group of his peers. Clearly, race was the not the issue.

When he returned with the broom the answer became all too clear. As he cleaned his mess I heard him say, "I didn't know if I was supposed to back down from the faggot ballet teacher or not."

I was shaken. For the rest of the day that statement echoed through my head.

The pain came with the realization that I had not come out to any students. This young man and his classmates had determined that I was a "faggot" anyway: I was a male teaching dance, therefore I had to be gay. But that was not the end of the internal fight going on in my head. Because I was perceived as a "faggot," I could be ignored, or even worse, physically and verbally challenged. The fact that I was a teacher and that I was an adult was of little consequence to this young man.

Now I was shocked. He had absolutely no respect for me as a teacher, as an adult, or even as a fellow human being. If he and his peers had no respect for these identities, how would a student who was perceived to be LGBT fare?

It took me a few days to recover. But I did so with full dignity and grace, determined to make changes. I was not going to let this ever happen to me again. I also decided to champion the cause of protection for real or perceived LGBT youth. I joined my local GLSEN chapter and Equality Florida, began collaborating with PFLAG, and started my volunteer relationship with Compass, Palm Beach County's LGBT community services center.

Failing School District

In the fall of 1998, GLSEN National surveyed the largest school districts in the nation to analyze LGBT youth attitudes about their school environment. Palm Beach County, *my* district, received a failing grade.

I had been teaching only a few months when the results of this survey were made public. Here was the opportunity for change that I was seeking. I vowed to improve this grade.

I drafted a letter and sent it out to the superintendent of schools and all seven members of the district. Introducing myself as a new gay African-American employee, I invited them to call upon me as a resource available to them to earn a passing grade and make our schools a safer place regardless of real or perceived sexual orientation, gender identity, or gender expression.

The one response I received from the school board was a message from my principal. She received a call from one school board member asking for a definition of the term "heterosexism" that I had used in my letter. That was the extent of their reaching out to me as a resource or agent of change. My principal merely asked that I keep her informed about any other such actions I was planning so that she would not be surprised in the future.

Teaching the Children of Homophobes

It was 2001, and the School District of Palm Beach County had just refused to add "sexual orientation" to the discrimination policy, although they had agreed to add this language to the harassment policy. GLSEN Palm Beach had won a partial victory on behalf of all public school children regardless of real or perceived sexual orientation, gender identity, and gender expression.

The final public discussion prior to the vote was quite contentious. Homophobic individuals and organizations came in by the busload to voice their antigay bigotry. I was not present at the meeting, but the following day as I walked into my musical theater class, I heard the bigoted echoes of this homophobia.

One of my students, in a voice intentionally above a whisper, echoed her parent's homophobic sentiments. Ostensibly, she was talking to a girlfriend, but it was obvious that I was the intended audience of this hate.

In true Christian character, I turned the other cheek. I taught class, being sure to give her the same kind of constructive criticisms I offer to all of my students. I was the teacher and she was the student. She and her homophobic parents depended on me to help educate my misguided charge. As I taught, I steadied myself by humming Rogers and Hammerstein's immortal lyrics from *South Pacific*:

> "You have to be taught to hate and fear before you are 6, or 7, or 8.
> You have to be carefully taught."

"That's So Gay"

With the school board's decision to add "sexual orientation" to the harassment policy, I decided to conduct an unscientific survey of homophobic comments that could be defined as harassment. I found three four-minute windows of time per week to research this topic.

At various times before, during, and after school, I would stand quietly and inconspicuously in a crowded and well-traveled corridor as the unsuspecting student body passed me by. Just as a wildlife conservationist would camouflage himself to observe animals in the wild, I was careful not to draw attention to myself as I unceremoniously tallied how many times I heard homophobic comments such as "faggot," "that's so gay," and other such terminology.

I was surprised by my findings. Over a period of four weeks, I heard these terms spoken roughly 17 times per week. Considering the fact that Bak is a magnet school of the arts, with diversity and individuality as the bedrock of the school culture, this was an astounding discovery.

Today when I hear such derogatory comments, I am quick to address them directly and to make it a teachable moment. My general lesson is to make the student(s) aware that the remarks—no matter how innocently they were intended—are indeed derogatory and hurtful to me and to countless others within earshot who are or who have LGBT family members, relatives, and friends.

After asking the students' art major, I name a few famous LGBT individuals whose record of achievement in that field has left an indelible mark on our lives, culture, and history. Before telling them that school board policy prohibits such abuse, I assist the student(s) in finding other more appropriate words for what they are trying to express. I also ask for their assistance in ridding our campus of such demeaning phrases by enlisting them to educate their peers.

Coming Out in the Schoolyard

October 11 is National Coming Out Day. Just as I had come out to my family and friends several years ago, I determined that I was going to come out in an "appropriate" and absolute manner. "Appropriate" would, of course, be self-defined. After all, being both an artist and a teacher requires thinking out-of-the-box.

One of my prime methods of LGBT activism was to write editorials in response to articles I had read. One such article I read was in *Dance Magazine,* an international dance publication. The article,

written by a retired ballerina turned clinical psychologist and advice columnist, dealt positively with the fact that many local dance studios had LGBT youth participating in their programs and needed to be aware of this population. The article listed GLSEN and PFLAG (among others) as resources that directors and faculty of dance studios should contact as resources for more information about issues that concern LGBT youth.

For two decades, I had read this and other national and international dance periodicals. Never had I come across an article written with such openness, respect, and advocacy for LGBT youth. I wrote the author to thank her. She in turn asked if I would agree to have our subsequent e-mail exchanges copied into an editorial for a future edition. I drafted my part of our correspondences acknowledging the fact that I was a gay, African-American dance instructor, listing my full name and place of employment. I knew full well that most of my past and present students, as well as most of the local dance studios, would see this editorial.

The reaction was something I could not have planned. Some enterprising student brought a copy to school, enlarged it, and then distributed copies around campus. I had honestly forgotten about the editorial until one of my assistant principals called me into his office to tell me that he was dealing with a "situation." Evidently, one student had called home to tell his or her homophobic parent. This parent called the area superintendent to alert her to the fact that an "openly homosexual person" was teaching at their school.

Her response was purportedly that I, as an American citizen with the right to free speech, was entitled to write the article. I had done so during my own time and without the use of school facilities or supplies. Although my union, the Classroom Teachers Association, has coverage for LGBT teachers, I was so glad that I had previously come out to the entire school board.

I received no personal flack for coming out in *Dance Magazine*. The students who were caught making copies were reprimanded for using school property for noncurricular activities. Unfortunately, the topic of sexual orientation was skirted. No matter. Even though I did not have a public forum to discuss this "situation," the article and I were now the talk of the campus. In fact, three non-LGBT parents thanked me for writing the editorial. When I walked the hallways, students turned to watch me pass proudly and gracefully by. Students were quick to learn not to say "that's so gay" within earshot of me.

Being a Mentor

My campus has roughly 1,350 students, so the number of students who greet me by name on a daily basis amazes me. I often tell people that I have nearly 200 children, the number of students in the dance department. But six years of teaching have taught me that I "teach" anyone who knows my name or reputation.

A few years ago one of my colleagues took a call intended for me from a recently graduated high school student. During their brief conversation, this young lady explained that although she was never a student at Bak and had never met me in person, she was calling from college to thank me for being out and openly gay.

She wanted to thank me for being there, somewhere out there, visible. This message touched my straight colleague as deeply as it touched me. I never learned this young lady's name, but she taught me the good that it does to publicly acknowledge all diversity, my own as well as others. By my interpretation, the mere fact that I was another gay person in a universe of heterosexist hegemony kept her sane. My being openly out let her know that there were others like her out there in the world, living gracefully and contributing proudly.

Each and every group has its distinguishing characteristics and histories, but the coming-out process is something that distinguishes the LGBT experience from other oppressed populations. At times these histories and characteristics run parallel to that of other minority groups.

I am visibly an African-American. I cannot hide my skin color. My homosexuality might not be so visible; I might have the option to remain in my closet and pretend to be straight. Nevertheless, I

can state from my experience as a double minority that neither identity has more baggage than the other. Unfortunately, all oppressions are equal, and they cause harm to everyone—the intended victims, the bystanders, and yes, the perpetrators.

I believe we should openly acknowledge our identity or identities. If we lived in a perfect society, a society that accepted, tolerated, and respected everyone regardless of real or perceived characteristics, I might feel differently. But we do not live in such a utopian or democratic world; we are still building toward it. Until that time when we reach this goal, it is important to note the vast contributions that LGBT individuals, among others, have contributed to our universe.

SOMETIMES YOU HAVE TO RISK THE DARKNESS TO SEE THE LIGHT

Laura Persichilli
English teacher
Smithtown High School
Smithtown, New York

"Watch out, man, that's the lesbian teacher," the small teenage boy said with trepidation. I turned and looked at the table of rambunctious boys and considered approaching them to question the comment. They settled down, trying not to look me in the eye.

As I watched my class of 11th graders sitting quietly in the library receiving a lesson, I pondered how to react to these unknown boys. I decided that, although the comment had unnerved and angered me at first, it wasn't really negative—it was simply the truth.

Later that day, after the hallways cleared and the buses were dismissed, I thought back to a time when I wasn't so comfortable in my own skin. Years before, while teaching English in another Long Island public high school, I was careful, cautious, fearful. I never even considered coming out because of the possible repercussions. Would I be harassed by students, parents, school administration, my own colleagues? Would I lose my job? There were clearly too many risks, and I was not about to challenge the

heterosexism that has kept so many gay teachers in a closet nailed shut by homophobia.

So on I went, teaching and living a lie. Then one day it fell apart, and I learned a lesson that has changed me forever.

It was September of 1997, and my new class of 10th graders was entering my classroom. They were quiet and nervous—it was the first day of school, and they were new to the building. Each of them sat down and waited for me to speak, except for one. She bounded into the room, getting everyone's attention. She was loud, rude, abrasive.

I knew she would immediately try to undermine my authority. I began to address this new group of students, and much to my surprise, after only a few minutes, she settled down and seemed to be listening. I wondered what I had said that got her attention.

As time passed, Crystal continued to make her presence known as she entered the room. She insulted her classmates on a daily basis, although most were too afraid of her to say anything. There were times that I expected a fight to break out, but the verbal confrontations never came to blows. Students feared her or pitied her, but they all quickly learned to ignore her. Still, as soon as I began to speak, Crystal would stop the antics.

At the end of the first grading period, Crystal announced to the class that this was the first time that she had ever passed English. "You rock, Ms. P.!" she said with a smile. Of course, she followed that up with a five-minute tirade about how every other teacher in the district was an "incompetent asshole."

All I could say was, "I'm proud of you, Crystal, but please don't speak that way about others." I wanted to reward her success, but it was so difficult to compliment such rude behavior. I worried that the rest of my class would think me weak. I changed the subject, but Crystal's face was still swollen with pride, perhaps for the first time in her academic life.

The year went on without incident in my class, but I soon discovered that Crystal was not doing as well in her other classes. Other teachers constantly sent her to the assistant principal. She wasn't well liked by anyone, but as the school's star soccer player she knew when to draw the line and the administration knew how far to go with disciplinary measures. It made me sad, but I decided that my incredibly unique teaching style must be the reason for her success. The year ended, and Crystal passed English. She thanked me, gave me a high five, and left for summer vacation.

The next school year began and I moved on to a new group of eager tenth graders. As I stood outside my classroom door during the change of classes, I often spotted Crystal creating a scene. She was wilder than ever, but she always stopped to wave to me in the midst of her chaotic behavior. Her teachers dreaded every minute they spent with her and often asked me how I could even speak to her. I ignored them. I began to worry about her. She seemed unusually thin and less muscular than I remembered. Her soccer jersey hung loosely from her frail body. Something wasn't right.

As time passed, I busied myself with new ways to teach *Lord of the Flies* and *Of Mice and Men.* I spent endless hours grading essays and torturing myself with the paperwork that makes you wonder why you went into teaching. But as soon as I stood before my classes, I remembered how important my work was. Absorbed in complimenting myself for my service to such a noble profession, I forgot about Crystal, and it was weeks before I noticed her absence. When I questioned her English teacher, I learned that Crystal was in a drug rehabilitation program. While most of the school was relieved over her absence, I was shocked and saddened by the news. I naively assumed that an athlete like Crystal would never get mixed up in drugs.

It was about six weeks later when I realized how my "gaydar" had failed me. Although closeted myself while at school, I always had a sense of which students I believed might be gay. Many of them struggled in school and had problems at home, but I wasn't about to put my career on the line by broaching the subject with them. Crystal was not on that list. She spoke often of her "boyfriend" who lived in Florida. I never thought to question if he really existed. Why would she lie? It's funny how your own twisted

sense of reality can keep you from seeing things clearly. After all, I was not exactly the model of truth.

Crystal returned to school with a new look. Her long curly hair was now shaved so short that you could see her scalp. Her designer flared jeans and short, tight T-shirts were replaced with baggy khakis and men's button-down shirts. She passed me in the hall several times but didn't seem to notice me. She was louder than ever. She would shout random comments down the hall at no one in particular. I wanted to stop her so many times and ask how she was doing since her return from rehab, but my sudden fear of her newfound expression of sexual orientation kept me from looking her in the eye. What if she always knew about me?

Talk of Crystal's return subsided rather quickly. My colleagues speculated about the drug use, but no one mentioned the fact that she might be a lesbian. That was the one comfort of heterosexism—everyone must be straight, so there was no need to discuss otherwise. As wrong as it was, it worked for me.

Spring arrived, adolescent hormones raged, and I continued to consider myself teacher extraordinaire. Then tragedy struck, shattering my tremendously undeserved ego trip. The principal called an emergency faculty meeting after school. We were informed that Crystal had died the night before from a drug overdose. She had been missing for a few days and was found at the home of a friend that she met at the rehab program. They were shooting heroin, and the police suspected that it might be suicide. The friend was being questioned.

I sat there for what seemed like hours after the meeting ended. I was dizzy, nauseous, and unable to get out of my chair. Somehow, I got myself down the hall to the English office, where there was always someone who had the inside story because they played tennis or golf with the principal. My breathing was just returning to normal when I heard one of my colleagues, for whom I'd had great respect, say with disgust, "I heard she was a lesbian. No wonder she killed herself."

The rest of my story is simple. In June I left teaching and moved to California. I felt as though I had betrayed Crystal and all those other gay students who might have benefited from my honesty. It took about six months for me to realize that I had run away like a wild rabbit being chased by the neighborhood dog. The long months of tears, depression, and reflection led me right back to the scene of the crime. I returned to Long Island and landed a job teaching English in Smithtown. I knew that the classroom was where I belonged.

Within three months of landing my brand-new nontenured teaching position, I went head-first into a battle with the district to start a gay-straight alliance. I was responding to a request by students who seemed to recognize immediately that I was gay. While I was still testing the waters and not quite ready to wave my rainbow flag, I knew that I had been given the gift of a fresh start, and I wasn't about to blow it this time.

These amazingly courageous students spoke to me about the uncorrected physical and verbal harassment suffered by gay students. They had researched other GSAs across the nation and were determined to make their school a safer place. They were smart, savvy, and willing to launch an attack on the opposition. I never flinched. I never thought about losing my job. I simply did what I knew in my heart was the right thing to do.

It took nearly one year to get the GSA approved. We argued with the high school administration, we went head-to-head with the superintendent, we went to Board of Education meetings and pleaded, and we discovered that heterosexism and homophobia is alive and thriving beyond what any of us had imagined. We solicited the help of incredible organizations such as Long Island Gay and Lesbian Youth (LIGALY), Parents, Families, and Friends of Lesbians and Gays (PFLAG), and the Gay, Lesbian, and Straight Education Network (GLSEN). We learned important lessons about politics, and were shocked and appalled by the true colors of many individuals. However, we also were warmed by the support of those who were brave enough to risk criticism from others.

Now tenured, I am about to enter my fourth year of teaching in Smithtown. Our GSA has had two successful, albeit not

entirely easy, years of service to the school community. We have displayed rainbow-splashed posters, administered a school climate survey, conducted workshops for both students and faculty on antigay remarks, handed out "safe space" stickers to teachers and staff, and commemorated both National Coming Out Day and the Day of Silence. We are still learning, exploring, and testing the waters. We are risk-takers and initiators of long-needed change. We are, despite the beliefs of many, both gay and straight, standing together in a united front against discrimination and in search of equality.

I still think about Crystal and the lessons that she will never know that she taught me. I don't live my life with regret now. I live it with a sense of empowerment and wonder.

"Watch out, man, that's the lesbian teacher."
You bet.

ONE MORE PERSON TO LOVE THEM

Mike Record
Language arts department chair
Broward County Public Schools
Fort Lauderdale, Florida

They insist it's a choice we make. They insist we can simply choose another way to be. But those of us who have tried to hide who we are and those of us who have lied to ourselves and others know you can't deny your true nature. For a few years when I was younger I lived a lie and forced myself down a different path. But the sense of misery at an unfulfilled destiny led me to admit the truth: No matter how hard I try to redirect my natural urges, I was born to be a teacher.

Being gay and therefore "one teacher in 10" has, for me, meant being an advocate for lesbian, gay, bisexual, and transgender students. To the consternation of my straight colleagues, being an advocate for LGBT students has also meant being a role model. These teachers think that they don't announce their sexual orientation to the class—so why should anyone? Heterosexual privilege has a significant power to blind people to the reality in front of them. They don't understand in how many ways they announce their sexual orientation to the class every day.

I made a decision in college that I wasn't going to work anywhere that didn't tolerate my living honestly. If that meant I wasn't going to teach, then I wouldn't teach. That might be why

I gave up Future Educators of America as a sophomore in college to take a leadership role in the gay and lesbian student union.

But, when I graduated in 1994, the classroom called me back, and I become a seventh-grade teacher. I am surprised to report that it turned out that being gay and being a teacher has not been difficult to reconcile in the nation's fifth-largest school district. Quite honestly, when I started out, it didn't occur to me that my two identities would need to be reconciled, but they did. As I talked to veteran teachers, I started hearing stories of those who avoided talking about their personal lives, used false pronouns, or lied outright to prevent colleagues finding out they were gay. "It's about classroom management," someone told me once. "I can't be an effective disciplinarian if kids don't respect me because rumors are flying around the school. And if anyone at school knows, everyone at school knows." I wasn't going to hide like that, but I desperately wanted to be an outstanding teacher. I had a problem that needed a solution.

In search of the "solution" to my "problem," I stalked the teacher supply store obsessively and searched the Education section of the local bookstore daily. That's when I found *One Teacher in 10*. Back in those days, the idea of a gay teacher was not as common as it is today. For me, then, *One Teacher in 10* had come out just in time. I devoured it.

The last page of *One Teacher in 10* listed information about contacting local chapters of GLSEN. GLSEN, I thought, would be a way to meet a husband. The Gay, Lesbian, and Straight Education Network sounded to me like a party circuit for single teachers. So I enthusiastically headed into gay Fort Lauderdale. As a first-year teacher, I would be the belle of the ball.

GLSEN, it turned out, was some kind of advocacy thing; no husband material in the room that night. As I ruminated on my disappointment, I was distracted by someone talking about the position of LGBT students in the local school system. It had never even occurred to me that there was such a thing as a gay student.

How could it not have? Seventh grade suddenly deluged my

consciousness. I was no longer at the Floridian Restaurant; I was at Coral Springs Middle School and later Taravella High School—hating myself and terrified that someone would find out what I really was. My entire adolescence was nothing more than a morass of sorrow at the realization that the horrible word "faggot" symbolized both the verbal violence I received and the strange set of feelings I encountered the first time my gym class met in a locker room. Where I went to school, kids got beaten up for having the wrong brand of jeans, let alone the wrong sexual orientation. How could GLSEN not be about the students?

Over the next five years, I gave an extraordinary amount of time to GLSEN. I cannot describe my experience with this movement as anything other than life-changing. What it turned out to be about, more than anything, was giving people a sense of their own power—which is at worst a cliché and at best a mantra.

The first test of my mettle as a GLSEN member was the *Miami Herald* reporter who interviewed me at a joint meeting of GLSEN and the Gay and Lesbian Youth Group of Fort Lauderdale—one of the first functions I attended as a middle school teacher. Not only were there newspaper reporters there, but two school board members had shown up at GLSEN's invitation to hear the youth talk about what their school days were like.

Their stories were sad. They fell into one of three categories: (1) hiding who I am; (2) honest about who I am and tormented by peers; and (3) I dropped out months ago.

When the *Miami Herald* asked me if I was willing to be credited with the quotes I gave during the interview, what choice did I have? In the face of all this inequity and suffering, was I going to perpetuate the problem by hiding? Newspapers throughout the next four years identified me as Mike Record, an openly gay middle school teacher. As much as I regretted the pigeonholing, the appendage to my name has been something of a blessing in disguise. When I interrupt the use of the word "faggot" in my class, I invariably have a student comment, "Oh, yeah, you were the one in the paper for being gay." Suddenly I am out without having to

come out. Then I have to talk about the fact that my identity, and the work I do in the community in the name of fairness, should not be the reason they stop using the word "faggot." They should stop using the word "faggot" because it's not a nice word. It's wrong to put someone down because of who they are.

As simple as that assertion is, many people just don't get it. In my own community, there is a contingent of people who will go on record as saying that LGBT kids *should* be harassed and discriminated against. To interrupt the harassment and discrimination, these folks argue, would be to validate a lifestyle that is dangerous and unacceptable. GLSEN Greater Fort Lauderdale made a teacher training video with the Broward County Public Schools' Office of Diversity and Cultural Outreach. The simple message of the video was that every student deserves a safe and welcoming classroom, regardless of sexual orientation or gender identity. However, one school board member told us that teachers called his office and complained that they were asked to watch it. They found it inconsistent with their religious practices.

Sadly, much of the opposition to the safe schools work GLSEN does is based on so-called religious principle. During a GLSEN issue campaign, our most vociferous opponent was Reclaiming America for Christ. This organization works to train local Christian activists to win school board seats and inject "Christian" principles into public education. It always shocked me that the general public was not alarmed that, despite everything we know about multiculturalism, this group was seeking to undo the separation of church and state.

GLSEN has brought me face-to-face with people at their worst, but it has also exposed me to people at their best. One of the most rewarding experiences in my life was sitting in the office of State Senator Skip Campbell with three Broward County youth. We had traveled eight hours in a cramped rental car to lobby for the Dignity for All Students Act—which would make all Florida schools responsible for protecting all students from bullying and harassment. It would mandate that schools track incidents and create policies that ensure the appropriate response when an incident occurs. Of Florida's 64 school districts, only four currently have a policy that extends protections to all students, including LGBT kids.

Three students and I formed a lobbying team and headed into the capitol building. Joey, David, and Crystal were juniors and seniors in Broward high schools. They witnessed on a daily basis how pervasive antigay slurs are and they wanted to do something about it. This is what brought them to GLSEN Greater Fort Lauderdale. These young people were intimidated to be in the state capitol, in the office of a legislator, but they did it because there was a problem in their schools no one was doing anything about. It was during that visit that Senator Campbell agreed to be the bill's first sponsor. Suddenly, how a bill becomes a law was no longer a *Schoolhouse Rock* cartoon; it had come to life in front of us.

I'm proud of the work I have done on behalf of GLSEN. Everything I have done on GLSEN's behalf has made schools safer places, increased the number of students to whom educational opportunities were available, helped my colleagues be better teachers, or reminded citizens in our democracy about their own power to change whatever is wrong. I am not going to hide these activities. My school district has a character-education curriculum. They probably didn't know what they bargained for when they decided to teach traits like citizenship, honesty, and tolerance in *my* district.

Most good teachers get letters from students telling them about the impact they've had. The most powerful notes I've received from students have been related to my taking a stand on antigay bias. To these students, it is inevitable that antigay bullying will occur in classrooms. It is inevitable that teachers either let it go on or suffer rumors that they themselves are gay. Further, in these students' minds, any open challenge about a teacher's sexual orientation will be met with the "That has nothing to do with why we're here today, so let's get back to learning English" speech. To witness a teacher look a student in the eye and with an unwavering voice say, "Yes, actually, I am gay, and I'm probably not the

only gay person you know," is shocking to them. But the shock wears away as they listen to the rest of the speech. "Everyone in our class is welcome here. I am going to make this classroom a safe place for each of you, no matter what makes you different. That's why we don't use put-downs in this class."

As I look back on my own journey, I realize now that I was lucky enough to have a mentor whose career has paralleled mine in such a way that I have been able to learn from her in high school, college, and graduate school. One day, after she got her doctorate and I was starting graduate school, I asked her for advice about being a classroom teacher. She said that things had changed so much in the short time she had been out of the classroom that she felt ill-equipped to advise me. After a moment, though, she corrected herself. "Love them. That's the one thing I can tell you that will help you in every situation. Nowadays, one more person to love them—in some cases the only person to love them—is the difference between them making it through school or not."

This felt right when I heard it. I come with a love of language, literature, and learning in general. My goal is to pass that on to my students. So love is already there. Slowly, we are getting to where we need to be. While it's easy to lose hope, the situation is clearly better now than it was when *One Teacher in 10* was published, not only for us as a nation but also for the tentative young teacher who first picked that book up 10 years ago. Someday, when bureaucrats say "Leave no child behind," they're actually going to mean it. That's the day I'm working toward.

THE BEST WAY OUT WAS THROUGH

Sheridan Gold

Special day-class teacher, alternative education
Marin County Community School
San Rafael, California

Sometimes when you are holding a secret, you use so much energy trying to hide the secret that the hiding keeps you prisoner in your own mind. You can't say certain things, you always have to censor what you do say, and you are always going back and forth in deciding what to say, depending on who you are talking to.

When I first started teaching, this is how it was with my students. My students were in alternative education, i.e. expelled youth and kids locked up in Juvenile Hall. Just as the community was extremely intolerant toward these kids, so were my students intolerant of anyone who was different from them. They were the most homophobic students I had ever run into.

Every morning I would hand out newspapers, and we would discuss the current events of the day. However, every morning before I handed out newspapers, I would scan them to see if there were any articles about gays in the military, gay marriage, or even gay-bashings. If there were any of these stories, I'd choose not to pass out the newspapers, and we'd go to the next activity. This way I could have some kind of control over the conversations—and to my delight, no student ever questioned why we weren't reading the newspaper on any given day.

The years passed by and I was somewhat comfortable in the closet. The kids got the message that I was not open to discussing anything gay-related, and the subject rarely came up as a class discussion. However, there'd always be the whispering, the gossip about their lesbian teacher, and the questions followed by laughter about such things as the meaning of the rainbow or what my husband's name was. "What does the rainbow mean, Ms. G.?" "I don't know, other than what comes out in nature after the rain," I would reply, my heart racing and my breath becoming shorter. "Are you married, Ms. G.?" "No," I would reply sternly, even though I was in a 20-year relationship. My stern reply gave them the message I was absolutely not into sharing my personal life with them.

Then Matthew Shepard was murdered and my life changed forever. I was stunned. I knew I could no longer be comfortable in my silence. My students needed to see a real live lesbian, somebody who was happy and healthy.

It wasn't easy, coming out. I didn't accomplish it in the snap of a finger. What my students thought of me was terribly important: I wanted to be accepted and liked and respected. But what kept playing over and over and over in my mind was that if Matthew Shepard could go through what he went through, I certainly could come out and say, "Here I am, I am gay, and I am happy."

During the time of Matthew's murder, I had been teaching for five years. I was in a Masters program creating an in-service to help make schools safer for LGBTQ youth. The tragedy reminded my professors and me just how important that in-service was. Matthew's murder brought home the importance of my work to a much higher level— not only for potential victims but especially for potential gay-bashers. Matthew's murderers were recently out of high school. I taught high school, and my colleagues taught high school, and we were all responsible in some way for the choices our students made. It was our responsibility to create a safe learning environment, free of name-calling and violence. If I could impact these teachers to stop the homophobic slurs, the bullying, the laughter, the gossip, perhaps I could turn all the horror into something positive.

I started my in-service with an original monologue about my life growing up as a youngster surrounded by homophobia. I start out as a very joyous, smart, and lively girl and end up a taunted, terrorized dropout. There's not a dry eye in the audience at the end of the 20-minute performance. It's my hook, and the teachers grab on. From there, the teachers are open to receiving statistical information about gay youth and those perceived to be gay and they are stunned at what they hear. We all leave the four-hour in-service changed people.

Although in seeing the impact of this work on other teachers I grew stronger, I was still guarded. On the first day of school in my ninth year of teaching, one of my students asked me a question that set me free.

"Hello everyone," I said. "Welcome to the first day of school."

Before I could continue, a returning student raised his hand and asked, "Ms. G., aren't you going to tell everyone your secret?"

"What secret?" I asked innocently, knowing full well where my student was going with his question.

"You know, Ms. G.," he continued, "your secret."

"Oh!" I exclaimed. "You mean when I was a kid I had a pet rat I let out every Saturday morning and let her run under my covers and snuggle up while I read?" The students shrieked and squirmed.

"No, Ms. G. Your secret. You know, your secret?"

"Oh," I exclaimed. "You mean that I am Jewish?"

"No, Ms. G.," he said as a smile spread slowly across his face. "That you are gay."

I looked at my student and said with a laugh, "That's no secret. Everybody knows I'm gay. Do you have any concerns about that or is there anything else I can help you with?" He became mute and shook his head. We moved seamlessly along to the next subject.

I am out of my prison of silence.

A MILESTONE FOR LIBERATION
Takashi Sugiyama
Home economics and health teacher
M Private High School
Saitama Prefecture, Japan

It has already been five years since I quit teaching at a private high school in Saitama, Japan. As I reflect on that experience, I see how my journey to that school—and to where I am now—began long ago.

My High School Days
I realized my gayness when I was 17 years old, a second-year high school student. I noticed that I was attracted to a boy, T., and my gaze followed him everywhere. The main topic that boys talked about at school was girls; for example, a guy had dated someone, or a guy had sex with someone—"someone" who was, of course, a girl. That was always the worst moment for me. T. was heterosexual and liked to talk about girls. I liked him very much. He didn't have the same kind of feelings as me, however, and neither did many other boys. The rigid rule of sexual love being only between a man and a woman was oppressive. I feared that my sense of feeling would be buried or destroyed by this strong heterosexual environment. I thought I'd never be able to reveal my feelings.

I was quite shocked when I discovered my sexuality. Although I had been aware that I was different from other boys around me, I didn't realize I was gay because I hadn't learned anything about different sexualities at school and I had no information about gays and homosexuality. I was alone. At middle school and high school, students and teachers told me, "You're like a woman." In high school I was called *okama,* or "homo." It hurt, but I couldn't talk back to them.

Some of the teachers and students in my high school class also made fun of gays. A boy said, "I met a male molester on the train last week." I couldn't stand the idea that people thought all gays were like that molester. I could not accept myself as gay. I sought out "normal" gay people, but I could not find ordinary gay people in this heterosexual society.

All I learned at school was that being gay was wrong or sick. Eventually, however, I started asking myself questions about why people use talk of homosexuality only to amuse others and why we don't learn about sexuality, including gay issues, formally at school.

After Finishing High School

I entered a university in Tokyo, majoring in education. It was my dream to become a teacher. I also hoped my gayness would be cured. Just after I started university, I joined a *konpa,* a group of male students from one university who meet a group of female students from a different university with the goal of meeting a romantic friend or lover. However, the more I participated in it, the more consciously I knew that I differed from the others. I felt oppressed. Moreover, realizing that I was gay influenced me enormously in my dream of becoming a teacher because I had the idea that a teacher must be flawless, and thus heterosexual. I thought I would not be morally qualified to be a teacher if I could not change my gayness.

I had nobody to talk it over with. I was frightened. I stopped attending classes and shut myself up in my house. I felt like I couldn't go anywhere.

Finally, I approached a gay organization. It became one of the most important things in my life. I made friends with other gay people of my age. I learned that being gay is normal. I was very

happy, especially when I found a boyfriend. Finally, I had a positive image of myself and gained self-confidence.

Encounters With Sei-Kyo-Kyo and Naohide Yamamoto

I sought out an educational program that would have parameters to protest homophobia and could teach about all kinds of sexuality. Almost every school uses a guidebook created by MEXT (the Ministry of Education, Culture, Sports, Science, and Technology) for sex education. It doesn't touch on homosexuality at all. Then I heard about a group of teachers who belonged to Sei-Kyo-Kyo, a private organization that supports research and education on human sexuality and gender bias. They were educating students about homosexuality. Founded in 1982, Sei-Kyo-Kyo provides workshops and teaching materials that help teachers to help students make choices about their sexuality and social lives that are informed by scientific fact and human rights. Since 2001 it has published research articles, lesson plans, and other resources for educators in its journal, *Sexuality*.

I met Naohide Yamamoto, the president of Sei-Kyo-Kyo, in 1995 when the Fuchu Youth House incident became a court case. Young members of Occur, a national gay rights organization, were refused the use of a public educational institution, and in response Occur sued the Tokyo Metropolitan Government. Mr. Yamamoto testified before the court for the justification of gay rights. He pointed out that it is necessary to include gay issues in education and that the decision of the Tokyo Metropolitan Board of Education lacked credibility from the viewpoint of human rights; Occur won the case.

Mr. Yamamoto was an inspiration to me. When he asked me to be a board member of Sei-Kyo-Kyo, I was hesitant because I was still a university student, but I did become a member and engaged in educational research. I visited many schools and met various teachers who actively carried out education on gay issues. Moreover, I met a group of gay and lesbian teachers who have included gay sexuality in their curricula. It was the first such group established in Japan.

I think gay teachers should come out in order to point out problems in education and to introduce different viewpoints about sexual diversity that are missing in sexuality education. But because of persistent heterosexism and homophobic conditions in Japan, nobody wants to come out as a gay teacher. Even teachers in the Sei-Kyo-Kyo circle did not want to reveal their names because of the fear of revealing their gayness publicly.

With Mr. Yamamoto's support, I came out at Sei-Kyo-Kyo and became the chair of gay and lesbian issues. It was Mr. Yamamoto who introduced a teaching job to me in the 1997 academic year. One day he said, "Sugiyama-san, why don't you teach at J High School? That will make your dream come true, won't it?" I went to the school and took an exam and had an interview. Later I learned that my sexuality became a topic of discussion. Some teachers supported me, saying, "It's no problem that he's gay. We should evaluate his personality, his teaching skills, and his ideas for the position." I also knew that Yamamoto recommended me strongly, saying that I am a good person and that I have a firm viewpoint on sexuality education.

I got the job.

A Rookie High School Teacher

From April 1998 until March 1999 I taught home economics and health at M High School and was an assistant classroom teacher for second-year students. This high school was exceptional in many ways, and working there changed my expectations as a teacher. Unlike most Japanese public schools, students at M High School called their teachers "Mr." or "Ms." with their surnames instead of the traditional and much more formal way of referring to teachers as *sensei* with their surnames. In many schools, students rise and bow at the beginning of classes following a teacher's or head student's call; this emphasizes the authority of teachers and the hierarchy at school. M High School didn't use this ritual, which indicates clearly that both teachers and students were considered equal human beings.

But there was a downside to the informal atmosphere. During the cleanup period, no students showed up, so the classroom teacher and I always had to clean our classroom. (In the Japanese school system, except at university, students are expected to clean the entire school.) Many students said they were free to decide whether or not they would attend homeroom sessions and their classes. Although there were 40 students registered for the class, at first there were typically only five or six students in the morning homeroom session and only two or three students in the math class. If 20 students attended a class, it was evaluated as "excellent." Over time, I came to have 30 students consistently in my classes.

In my school, teachers were able to make lesson plans freely on their own. I was able to cover more topics in my sex education lessons in one year than most teachers cover in 10. In Japanese public schools it is usually very difficult for teachers to include their own ideas in sex education courses due to governmental guidelines, which they are expected to follow. I organized my lessons around three key points: "The Structure of Human Bodies," "What Is Love?," and "Society and Sexual Diversity." In the second section I introduced gay issues. I used a love letter—written by a boy who fell in love with a same-sex classmate—as an introduction, and I asked the question, "Who you think wrote this letter?" I continued, "I know him. He's a teacher now."

"I don't know who he is," a student said.

"This person is *me*."

I had come out. I felt all of my students looking at me. I then talked about the difficulty of being gay. I hoped that they would understand being gay as a familiar and normal existence.

I was glad about my coming-out. Students gradually accepted the fact that I was gay and naturally connected with me. I was very happy that I could talk freely with students about myself and even about my then-boyfriend, who lived in Osaka. I told them that the long-distance relationship was hard. When I went to the Kansai area once a month to prepare my application for graduate school, some students said, "Sugiyama-san, you'll get to see your boyfriend, won't you?"

After my coming-out, a student handed me a letter and said, "Sugiyama-san, please read this," and ran away. It was filled with her struggles, experiences, and sufferings as a lesbian. I could feel her pain through her writing. Some other students secretly came to my office to talk with me. I helped them as much as I could, and I became more confident about myself.

Closeted Teachers

My position as a gay teacher who came out publicly is an extreme rarity in Japan. I soon noticed there were three other gay teachers at the school. One of them revealed his orientation to me; eventually two others revealed came out to me secretly, or we ran into one another in Tokyo's Shinjuku Ni-chome district, where many gay bars are located. We started getting together secretly and going to Shinjuku Ni-chome to socialize.

However, none of the three ever came out at school. In fact, they sometimes tried to avoid meeting me at school because they feared people would suspect they were gay if they were seen being friendly to me.

One evening one of the closeted teachers called me on my cell phone and said, "Sugiyama-san, I'm at a gay bar in Shinjuku Ni-chome, and I ran into one of your students here. He's sitting with an *oji-san*." (*Oji-san* literally means an uncle or a middle-age man, but in the right context it is widely understood to be a man who sexually exploits teenagers.) He continued, "We pretended that we didn't know each other."

I talked with the closeted teachers about this student, who was in my homeroom. I was shocked that he'd elected to go to a gay bar with an *oji-san*. I was even more shocked when one of the teachers said, "We have to do it," by which he meant that a young gay person must be invited by an *oji-san* to experience gay sex for the first time.

I was very angry with their attitude. Did they take it for granted that a young gay man's first sexual experience would be that he gets molested by an older man, and that we as gay people have no other choices? Why would a gay teacher say something like that without thinking about his student's feelings? Then I remembered

that a researcher had said that closeted gay teachers intentionally keep their distance from gay students.

After that I gradually distanced myself from the closeted teachers. I realized that gay teachers would not necessarily be on my side. It was extremely difficult for me to share my thoughts and work with them for the good of our students. They did not face their own situations, were narrow-minded, and were not working to establish better conditions for gay youth. A year later I resigned from the school to enter graduate school.

Despite these bizarre experiences I generally built very good relationships with teachers, students, and parents. I hid nothing and faced the students seriously and honestly, and I think this won their hearts. I also think my course made an impression on students. It was very significant for me to have examined human sexuality by supervising classes and conducting lessons. Teaching school as a gay person was a great encouragement for me.

Where I Am Now

Through my experiences, accepting myself as gay, establishing friendships with other gay youth, having a boyfriend, and teaching sex education at school, I arrived at a positive gay lifestyle. Gay issues are not visible in sex education in Japan. Education is based on heterosexuality. Although many people say, "We are very tolerant of homosexuality in Japan," in practice homosexuality is thoroughly ignored rather than tolerated. Gay issues are not clearly included in governmental education guidelines, so most schools and teachers do not render them seriously as a topic in their courses. Students, however, learn about gay issues outside of classes through friends, teachers, and the media, which usually contains negative and humiliating portrayals.

I am confident in stating my position in favor of inclusive sex education, especially because I do not want other gay students to experience adolescent loneliness in high school as I did. Nowadays, I work for Sei-Kyo-Kyo as chairman of the gay and lesbian issues section, basically as a volunteer. I give lectures at schools or at meetings and write essays for books and magazines, as well as modeling lessons for curricula. In Japan, sex education that includes gay sexuality is gradually spreading. For example, gay issues were introduced in a home economics textbook for high schools in 2003.

I sometimes wonder what the three closeted teachers I worked with are doing now. I look forward to a time when they can act naturally and live ordinarily as gay teachers in public. That day will be a milestone for liberation in the country's educational system.

The author truly appreciates the advice from Keiko Ofuji in writing this essay.

IT'S BETTER TO LEAD
THAN TO FOLLOW

Bart Birdsall
Media specialist
Greco Middle School
Temple Terrace, Florida

If someone had told me six years ago that I would become one of the "leaders" in the Tampa Bay LGBT community, I probably would have laughed in that person's face. I've always viewed myself as a follower.

As the "baby" in my family, I have always had people taking care of me. My earliest memory is of my sister holding my hand on the way to first grade. I followed. I did not lead.

In the 1980s and '90s I was busy partying both in Europe and the United States at schools and universities. Surrounded by liberal Europeans and out to my family and friends, I felt no reason to fight for my rights. "Being gay is not my whole life," I once told a friend.

I was content to let others lead the way. I followed.

Then my sister died, and the bottom fell out of my life. I wanted to die. Needing a change in life, I discontinued my literature and language studies and enrolled in my school's college of education.

Suddenly, after years of being out to everyone, I found myself going back into the closet. *How "out" can I be as a teacher?* I asked myself. Professors, other students, and, later, GLSEN Tampa members could not help me with that answer.

I realized I had to create my own answer to that question. I decided even having to keep my mouth shut about my life was unjust. Having to keep quiet made me angry. I suppose this realization was the first time discrimination slapped me in the face.

Step by step, I came back out. I told teachers at my school. I became cochair of GLSEN Tampa and joined the Safe Schools Coalition of Hillsborough County. At the request of the Safe Schools Coalition, I called school board members to set up appointments to discuss the harassment of and discrimination against LGBT youth. I can still remember my nervousness at calling my "bosses" and asking for an appointment. Eventually, I met with every school board member. We took students with us to tell their stories. Each meeting made me braver. When I found the administration prevented a student from forming a GSA, I spoke with the assistant principal in charge of clubs. When I could not get her to agree to allow the GSA, I went above her head to the assistant superintendent. As a result of meeting with the assistant principal, the school allowed the GSA to form.

In addition, the principal placed me on the school district's Antibullying Committee. On the committee I have lobbied hard for and achieved the inclusion of "sexual orientation" and "gender identity" as protected classes in the sexual harassment policy.

After much difficulty, I will perform a teacher training on LGBT issue in the upcoming school year. Throughout my activist work in the schools, I have made a couple of enemies but many more friends. I realized that helping make schools safer for LGBT youth would empower both students and teachers of the future to take a stand. I didn't want even one more person feeling it was necessary to "shut up" about his or her life.

I selfishly went into this volunteer work to find answers, to find job protection for myself. I looked for a leader to give me answers, but I had to find my own: not to be afraid, to do the right thing, and to do what I believe in.

On a personal note, I grew up believing that when people found out who the true Bart was, they would reject me, hate me, and be disgusted. Since I've come out and become an activist, I have found

more people liking—even loving—me than ever before. And when I see the courage of LGBT youth starting gay-straight alliances at their schools, I think, "This is why I continue to work on this issue!" To see the youth starting to take over the leadership is thrilling.

What is strange is feeling that leading is even better than following. Following is full of questions and fear. Leading is full of answers and empowerment.

WHERE I'M FROM

Jan M. Goodman
Teacher
King Middle School
Berkeley, California

I'm not from TV
Where families stay together,
Mothers kiss their children goodbye
And give them a lunch as they go to school
I am from my secret place
Where mothers hurt you and then they leave
Without worrying about your school lunch, or a kiss.

I'm not from the world of Christmas
Where families wake up to rooms of presents
And sing carols at midnight mass.
I am from my hidden Jewish self
Whose traditions died with my grandparents
Until I cooked matzo ball soup at age 25.

I am not from the world of fairy tales
Where princesses wait for princes
Or transform frogs into handsome husbands.
I am from real life
Where classmates tease and hurt
And there are many ways to live and love.

I am not from ancestors who "founded" this country.
I am from dislocation,
From grandparents who escaped persecution in Europe
To seek American streets lined with gold
And made a life for themselves, despite anti-Semitism.
I am from sights, tastes, and advice
"Always wear clean underwear in case you're in an accident"
"Girls can't play baseball"
"Be who you are" but "Do you have to dress *that* way?"

I am from fitting in and being shut out
From schools where teachers and students looked like me,
and spoke my language
But did not understand my pain
Where there was always enough food, but few vacations
Where policemen pulled over the cars of darker-skinned people
And let me pass by
Yet people yelled "*dyke*" when I held my lover's hand.

I am from a world of contradictions
Where I must sort through confusion
To finally arrive at
Where
I
Am
From

I wrote "Where I'm From" during the second week of my
English–American history class at King Middle School in Berkeley,
California. To begin the school year, the eighth graders and I
explored our racial, cultural, and family identities through brain-
storming, discussion, and writing of "Where I'm From" poems (an
exercise from *Reading, Writing and Rising Up: Teaching About
Social Justice and the Power of the Written Word* by Linda
Christensen). Mine was carefully crafted to express the fact that

lesbianism was central to my view of myself but not the totality of my existence. I needed my students to know that I too have struggled through pain and confusion to become the person I am today. By coming out as a lesbian, a Jew, an abused child, and an antiracist white woman, I gave my students permission to be who they are, acknowledge privilege, and receive respect for all parts of themselves. This set the tone for the entire school year.

Next year will be my 30th as an educator. I've worked as a teacher from preschool to adult education, an elementary school principal, a consultant, mentor, curriculum developer, researcher, and writer, in progressive and conservative communities, on the east and west coasts of the United States, in the public and private sectors. In every setting, my lesbian identity and pride has been an integral part of my public persona.

As I look back on three decades, there have been challenging, frightening, heartbreaking, humorous, and joyous moments. It's never been easy. I came out and began my teaching career in the early 1970s, when lesbians were invisible in society and a shameful element of the feminist movement. My family and friends needed considerable education to become, ultimately, supportive. There were times when I was the only lesbian administrator in a conservative school district or the only gay teacher in a school. In defense I developed what I call the "Supreme Court Syndrome." I reasoned that I would have to be twice as good as a heterosexual teacher (or administrator) in order to protect myself from anyone who would attempt to challenge my competency on the basis of my sexual orientation. If I were an exemplary teacher, then I could survive any challenge to my right to teach, even up to the highest court.

The "Supreme Court Syndrome" has given me the strength to fight back in a myriad of situations where I've been targeted by homophobia. Despite the challenges, I don't regret a single time that I came out to students, teachers, parents, guardians, community members, or the media. I don't see myself as a heroine; I just did what I had to do when it had to be done. I took advantage of teachable moments and created them when they didn't exist. I

refused to cut out a part of my heart-soul-identity and store it in a closet. In doing this, I became a role model and supportive resource for children of all sexual orientations, kids from gay-parented families, LGBT staff members, and other people whose lives I touched, professionally and personally. As I reflect on this three-decade journey as an educator, there are many lessons to share.

Lesson 1: Take risks to move out of your comfort zone. Understandably, the biggest factor that keeps us from coming out is fear, both real and imagined. Every time I identify as a lesbian, I open myself up to struggle and possible repercussions. However, most often, I have found unexpected support.

I remember my first year as a principal in a conservative school district south of Oakland, California. As I set up my office, I unpacked the photograph of my lover and moved it to several places in the room, eventually choosing to display it strategically on my desk, facing me. Visitors would have to go behind my chair to see it. On Mondays, when discussions among the staff inevitably centered on husbands, wives, or church sermons, I was unusually reticent. After I had gained the respect of the community, I opened up to colleagues, many staff members, and some parents—and I put the photograph in a more prominent place. Later that year the school secretary told me, "I never knew a lesbian until you came to school. I always thought lesbians were sinful people, but you are wonderful. Now I'm confused, but I think that's a good thing." In June, I was interviewed by a television reporter during the Gay Freedom Day Parade. The caption read JAN GOODMAN, LESBIAN EDU-CATOR. The next morning, the custodian greeted me, "Hey! I saw you on channel 4 last night. I was real proud of you!" I can still remember the unexpected hug that followed.

During my first year as principal in Berkeley, I arrived at school one morning and was greeted by two concerned staff members. "We need you to see some disturbing graffiti," they said. "We'll go with you." As we approached the back of the school, I looked at the wall facing the playground and saw, spray-painted in large, black letters, THE PRINCIPAL IS A FAG! I first felt a great deal of fear for my own safety. The elementary school students and teachers would arrive in 15 minutes; I had to think quickly to decide how to deal with the situation.

I was extremely vulnerable and uncomfortable. My first instinct was to remove the problem, to protect myself. I spoke with the custodian, who sympathetically awaited my instructions. "Please find some paint to cover the words," I said, but then hesitated. "On second thought, cover the wall with butcher paper. This is a hate crime, and I'm going to report it." I wrote a note to the teachers about the graffiti so they would know why the wall was covered. Then, I went into my office and dialed the Berkeley Police Department. Later in the day, when the students were all in their classrooms, the police arrived to photograph the message. Throughout the day, I was approached by supportive and nurturing staff members, parents, and guardians, and I received many warm embraces. I had moved out of my comfort zone to confront homophobia head-on, and this felt good to me.

Lesson 2: Remember that you are not alone. It is incredibly alienating to feel that that burden of reeducation is solely on our shoulders; however, that is rarely the case. There are many heterosexual people who are anxious to support LGBTQ colleagues but don't know what to do; they need our assistance to figure out what steps to take. As an out lesbian, I open myself up to new allies in the fight against homophobia.

In my first year at middle school, I planned a social living class with Patty, a teacher who was also new at King. We agreed to include a range of social justice issues and created a one-week model on same-gender relationships. Although the topic was relatively unfamiliar to Patty, she was eager to be a model of a heterosexual woman who confronted antigay stereotypes even though these misconceptions were not directed at her. Patty's willingness to take on the curriculum defied the common middle school stereotype that anyone

who talks respectfully about LGBT people must be gay herself.

Presently, I work closely with Victoria, an eighth grade humanities teacher. Married, with a daughter in our school, Victoria is my number 1 ally at King and a good friend. Last year, our school had a Day of Silence, when all LGBT people and allies did not speak. Rather than remain silent, Victoria came into my classroom and told my students why it is important for her, and all heterosexuals, to stand in solidarity with gay people in our struggles for equality. She also gave the same message to all of her classes. When we designed a project on "Unsung Heroes," Victoria helped find LGBT people to include in the students' research choices; she also consistently shares current events that connect to gay issues and writings by LGBT youth.

Lesson 3: Take advantage of teachable moments. There are countless times when I reflect back on a situation and think, "If only I'd..." These teachable moments are opportunities to confront and address homophobia, make a commitment to recognize and respond to it, and then share my strategies with colleagues. As a preschool teacher, I discovered that homophobia is learned at an early age. One day, I was approached by a group of 3- and 4-year-olds, who appealed to me, "Jan, please help us! We're playing Sleeping Beauty, and we don't have anyone to be the prince and wake her up. We asked every single boy at school and they all said no! Can you be the Prince?"

"I can't be the prince," I replied. "I'm a woman and a prince is a man. But I can be the princess and wake up Sleeping Beauty!"

"*No way!*" the girls insisted. "A princess can't kiss Sleeping Beauty. Now, what are we going to do?" The girls huddled in a corner of the room to solve the problem. After a few moments, they came to me and said, "We decided that it's OK for you to wake up Sleeping Beauty. It doesn't have to be a prince!"

Teachable moments occur every day, during class discussions, staff meetings, parent or guardian conferences, in hallways, PE locker rooms, on the playground, with our children, and in the community. Whenever I hear a student use the word *faggot*, I now find it easy to intervene and say, "That offends me." The other day I approached a group of students who were shouting "That's so gay!" to one another. Their response was, "It's not an insult." I then asked them to name a time when they said "That's so gay" to describe something positive that had happened. "I can't think of one," the students replied, and then added, "Oh...now I get it. Sorry." Teachable moments occur every day; don't pass them up.

Lesson 4: It's about safety, not morality. Keep in mind that students of all sexual orientations can not learn in school environments where homophobia, racism, or other forms of oppression are tolerated. Every educator would agree that safe schools respect the rights of all students. Contrary to the beliefs of fundamentalists, the issue only becomes a "moral" one when schools fail to protect students who are misunderstood, ostracized, and harassed by others. It is a moral issue when an at-risk population is systematically excluded from representation and resources in the educational system.

To emphasize the issue of safety, I worked with the Associate Superintendent for Curriculum and Instruction to bring the exhibit "Love Makes A Family" to our school district. The exhibit (available from Family Diversity Projects, www.familydiv.org) features photographs of families with LGBT parents and interviews with the members of each family, at elementary and adult reading levels. For a month, the photographs were set up in various schools throughout the district, and principals were asked to send all classes to tour the exhibit. I conducted a workshop for principal-teacher teams from each school to help them respond sensitively to the exhibit. There was some resistance: Not all classes attended; a teacher brought her kindergartners to the exhibit but did not mention the word *gay*; some teachers refused to take their students; homophobic responses to the exhibit were not always confronted. However, thousands of students in grades K–12 learned that there are many ways to live and love, and children from gay-parented families found validation in the photos and stories. If that's not safety, what is?

Lesson 5: When you're out, you can become a resource and role model for others. As a visible lesbian in the school system, I have become an unofficial contact person for students, teachers, administrators, and parents who are dealing with sexual orientation issues within and beyond the classroom. In our middle school, students are more likely to take the risk to come out as gay, lesbian, bisexual, or transgender because they know that there are positive, supportive role models on-site; I am honored to be one of them.

I often get calls from teachers who have come out, or administrators who want to support a gay teacher, parent, or guardian but are unsure of what steps to take. In our district, principals may face resistance from a small but vocal group of parents who request a class change for their child after a teacher comes out. I help administrators recognize their responsibility to enforce our district's nondiscrimination policy—which includes sexual orientation—and our commitment to include LGBT issues as part of the curriculum. Therefore, any classroom in Berkeley should address these issues, so moving a child from one class to another will not make a difference. These interventions are never a burden; they are a step to change the cycle of oppression that makes schools unsafe for all students, and in some cases they save lives.

Lesson 6: Turn anger into action. In a homophobic world I am assaulted by negative messages that injure a core element of my identity. I have been told that LGBT people are unfit to teach children, that family diversity discussions should not include gay-parented families, that homosexuality is a moral issue and should be omitted from the sex education curriculum. This makes me justifiably angry, but if I let my anger disempower me, I become immobilized.

During my early years as a principal, I worked with a teacher who had applied for my job and resented the fact that she did not get it. She became increasingly confrontational at staff meetings and consistently challenged my authority. When I responded calmly and continued to treat her with respect, she planned the ultimate act of revenge. During the spring Open House, she circulated a false rumor among staff and parents that I was having an affair with a female teacher at the school. When this divisive lie reached my office by the end of the evening, I was enraged. For a moment I was consumed by anger, unable to fight back.

After quite a while I calmed down and found my pride; it had been obscured by the rage and hurt. I called Essie, a heterosexual ally and principal who was friends with my accuser; she agreed to advise the teacher to stop the rumor. "I'll talk to her, and don't you worry, she will stop," she reassured me, but that wasn't enough.

Although I trusted Essie to keep her word, I made an appointment with Ron, the personnel director, the following morning. "I need you to know that last night, Mrs. C. told a number of parents and staff that I am a 'lesbian agitator from San Francisco' and am having an affair with a female teacher on our staff."

Ron delicately inquired, "Is it true?"

"That is not the point," I replied. "But I will answer your question. The rumor is only partly true. I am a lesbian—many people in the school already know that I am gay—and I am active politically in the gay community. However, I am not an agitator, I do not live in San Francisco, and I am not having an affair with a staff member. With all due respect, what are you going to do about it?"

"As long as you're not having an affair," he said, "there's nothing to worry about."

I felt my anger rise again, and struggled to remain calm. "Ron," I emphasized, "First of all, it is your responsibility to stop sexual harassment in this district. This teacher's goal is to jeopardize my job as principal. I need you to know that if you don't intervene and Mrs. C. succeeds, I will not be fired or told to discretely leave the district; I will publicly and loudly fight for my right to stay. I also want to point out that just a few years ago, the male principal of Elm School married a female teacher who worked for him at his site for many years. Was that a problem for the district?"

Ron looked at me, recognizing the district's double standard and his responsibility as a personnel director. "OK, Jan. You're right," he conceded. "I'll take care of this." As I rose to leave the

office, Ron awkwardly put his hand on my shoulder and said, "I've never had a—a—situation like this before, but I'll deal with it."

I'm not sure what occurred, but the rumors stopped and Mrs. C. discreetly retired that summer. My anger had turned into action; the district was forced to look at inequities in its policies; and I emerged from the situation with a newfound pride.

Lesson 7: Some battles are not worth fighting. It's important to choose your issues; otherwise you will burn out as an activist. When I was a principal in Berkeley, our PTA sponsored a workshop about how to address sexual orientation issues at the elementary school level. The library was overflowing with concerned staff members, parents, and guardians, including several deeply religious teachers who attended church in the school community. Most everyone wanted to find strategies to confront homophobia or create an inclusive curriculum. At the end of the workshop, I expressed how wonderful it felt, as a principal and as a lesbian, to see so many staff and community members at the event. The night was a high point in my career; unfortunately, it was followed by a low point.

On the day after the workshop, it was time for my weekly lunch date with a struggling student. He came to my office and said that his grandma told him that he couldn't have lunch with me anymore because I was gay, and that the preacher at church says that being gay is a sin. That same day, his grandma put a beautiful card in my mailbox with a message that God could show me the right way. In it were a variety of Bible quotes about homosexual sex. I was deeply saddened, particularly because the child would lose a source of significant support. At the same time, I realized that there was nothing that I could say or do to change his grandma's opinion of me. I had to let go of it. The lesson: It is important to save your energy for the fights that can be won.

Lesson 8: Struggle against all forms of oppression in schools. In many ways, my oppression as a lesbian has given me the strength and empathy to fight against all forms of injustice in schools. In my commitment to make schools safe for students, staff, and community members of all sexual orientations, I find it impossible to ignore that many students and adults, including those who are LGBT, are marginalized, disrespected, misunderstood, and disempowered, mirroring the inequities in our larger society. From the first week's "Where I'm From" poem to the last day of school, my students know that I will work for fairness and equity for all people, including children. I consciously teach my students that LGBT people have made significant contributions to U.S. history, and at the same time that our country was built on the backs of enslaved Africans, dislocated indigenous people, and poor immigrants from Europe and Latin America. When we study the First Amendment as part of a unit on the U.S. Constitution, we read a news article about Karl Debro, a heterosexual teacher who taught about homophobia, was reprimanded by his school district, and won over $1 million in a lawsuit. During the same unit, we look at racial profiling in light of the 14th Amendment and hypothesize as to why no one on Death Row is affluent. My students see me as a teacher, also a lesbian, who looks at all inequities in our society and believes, as we say in our Passover seder, "No one is free if any person is oppressed." Because of this belief, I gain many allies, both teenagers and adults.

Lesson 9: If you respect students, they will be more likely to respect you. Although it is often a challenge, I work hard to create a democratic classroom, where all students have a voice and there is room for discussion and disagreement. I am open to respectful criticism, rarely raise my voice, use inclusive language, and am an advocate for students' rights. I let students know who I am and how I feel. In short, my students know that I respect them, and usually this is what I ultimately receive in return.

During the middle school social living class, half of the curriculum focused on sex education. The question was not whether I would come out to the 90 students during the unit, it was how and when. The issue was particularly compelling because so many

teenagers struggle with sexual identity during middle school, when homophobia is at its peak. Patty and I had planned a week to focus on lesbian, gay, bisexual, and transgender identities. We had several videos, some readings from gay youth, and a culminating panel from the local Gay and Lesbian Speakers' Bureau.

After a brief introduction to the unit, I asked my students, "How many of you know someone who is lesbian, gay, bisexual, or transgender?" About half to two thirds of the students raised their hands. "Actually, all of you know someone who is gay," I said calmly. "Your social living teacher is a lesbian." In two of the three classes, students responded with silence, surprise, and some respectful questions. However, my second period's spirited response remains vivid in my mind.

"You're a lesbo," one young man shouted as he fell off his chair. "You don't look like a lesbo. You don't act like a lesbo." A number of students erupted with laughter.

"The word is 'lesbian,'" I corrected, in a friendly and calm manner. "And how does a lesbian look or act?"

"Well, you're nice," he replied, "and you don't dress like a—"

Tameka, a leader in the class, waved her hand in the air. "I got something to say. I don't think it's our business to know if you're a lesbian. That's a private thing. Besides, it's against the Bible. It's unnatural. It's not normal."

"You're right that it's not the norm," I responded. "About 10% of the population is gay or lesbian. That's one out of every 10 people. So…in a class of 30 students, three could grow up to be gay." When a chorus of "Not me" followed, I remained focused.

"You each have to decide whether you will treat 10% of the population with respect, or whether you'll prejudge them in a negative way," I continued. "I'm telling you that I'm a lesbian because I know we care about one another. I also know how important it is for you to feel safe in the world, and I want you to think about whether or not you make the world safer for others."

When the gay speakers arrived at the end of the week, I warned them that my second period class might be disrespectful. However,

I discovered that my coming-out had challenged my students to examine their personal beliefs and actions. As two men and two women sat down, Tameka approached me. "This is your day," she said. "You just sit down in the back of the room and listen to the speakers. I'll take care of the class." Tameka sat in the director's chair with the class participation clipboard and warned the students, "These people deserve your respect. That means no talking during the presentation and no fooling around either," she added, snatching an umbrella that was waved in the air. "If you do, I'm sending you out."

With Tameka in charge, I relaxed and studied my transformed class. They listened respectfully. Their questions were thoughtful and empathetic. "Did you know you were gay in middle school? How did the kids treat you?" "Were you ever physically hurt? Did anyone defend you?" The panel was impressed. So was I.

Lesson 10: Keep up the struggle. In a few weeks, the school year will begin again. My lover will meet her fourth- and fifth-grade students and plan an appropriate time to share her family with them. Our son will start high school and will figure out whether it is safe to let new friends know that his moms are lesbians. Our daughter will leave for college, her first year on her own. My eighth-grade class will write "Where I'm From" poems, and I'll share mine.

As I open the classroom door for my 30th year, I will join LGBTQ educators and our allies as we work to transform a world full of injustice. The task is formidable. It takes courage, perseverance, and commitment. It is impossible to estimate how many attitudes we will change, how many lives we will save. But I know that schools will be safer and more respectful places because of our influence. And isn't that what education is about?

LIVING WITH THE POSSIBILITIES

Ruth Kupfer
English and reading teacher
Lincoln High School
Lincoln, Nebraska

Ten years ago when I wrote the essay "You Can't Tell Him I'm Not" for *One Teacher in 10,* I was excited to have the opportunity to tell a story about a pivotal moment in my teaching life. I had been propelled into disclosing my sexual orientation to my school's administrators when I reported that a student was sexually harassing me. As I wrote about that upsetting treatment and the way it affected me in my classroom, I began to realize that I was also empowered by the outcome of the experience. Finding the courage to speak up in that situation opened the door to a new sense of freedom and purpose in my career as a public school teacher.

Even so, I had a difficult decision to make when it came time for me to decide whether to use my real name or a pseudonym on my submission to *One Teacher in 10.* On one hand, it *was* a story about coming out to my administrators. But my ultimate decision to use a pen name came out of the fear that, without job protection language written into my teaching contract, it was still a possibility that someone would want to rid my district of a teacher who spoke out about her sexual orientation.

In the decade that has passed since then, I have moved from being guarded and apprehensive, weighing my every word and action, to the way I find myself now—unflappable and eminently

288

mindful of my responsibilities to my students and to myself as a lesbian teacher. Finally—now that I am 50!—my lesbian identity is synthesized into the whole of who I am, and I feel completely at ease in the classroom and in my school every day, whether references to sexual orientation arise or not. I wouldn't think of using a pen name for any of my writings now.

The next time I outed myself came when I made two presentations at the National Council of Teachers of English (NCTE) national convention. Each was about what it has meant to me to be a lesbian teacher. These speeches came about as an outgrowth of my Masters work in curriculum and instruction, for which my final project was to write about the intersection of my teacher and lesbian identities. I chose this project deliberately in order to continue the personal development I started when I wrote for *One Teacher in 10*.

Through writing my narrative project and making those presentations at NCTE, I explored the juncture of my professional and sexual identities from several angles. I investigated what it means for me to work with students who are straight as well as those who are questioning or openly gay or lesbian, and in the process I examined the implications of my position as a teacher who was working through the stages of a personal lesbian identity. Taking that story to a national audience at the conventions and in publication represented a risk I was ready to take on a journey from which turning back was no longer an option.

As it has turned out, that journey contained a series of experiences and circumstances that have brought me to this self-assured stage in my identity. Of these, one notable factor in my growth has been the climate at my school—one in which difference is valued and nurtured. If these qualities were not prevalent in my work setting, I am sure that it would be much more difficult to feel as safe as I do about being openly lesbian.

My school is a public high school serving close to 2,000 students in Lincoln, Nebraska's capital city, and the kids who attend it

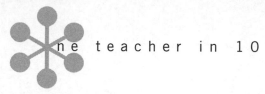

represent all racial and socioeconomic groups. We also have many students who have emigrated from other countries and are English-language learners, and like many schools our kids often identify with various social subgroups, like the goths or jocks or preps. There seems to be a place for everyone to fit in there, no matter what their background is or how they identify themselves. Our school's educational goals include preparing students to live and work with others who are different and teaching them to value those differences. These expectations help create an environment in which a person's sexual orientation is one of many characteristics that define her or him.

I would like to say that everyone at my school—staff and students—is gay-positive, but I can't. There are still some staff members who believe that anything having to do with lesbian, gay, bisexual, and transgender concerns—whether curriculum or policy-related—represents an immoral influence that doesn't belong in public schools. A couple of years ago a teacher at my school wrote a letter to our principal protesting the school's sanctioning of the now-traditional Pride Prom event in the spring. Pride Prom is a yearly highlight of the activities of the Gay-Bisexual-Transgender-Straight Alliance (GLBTSA) groups in each of the six high schools in Lincoln. They come together at a dance at which everyone can feel welcomed, regardless of how they identify or who they bring as a date. One of the posters advertising the event contained a picture of two men in tuxedos, one behind the other with his arms around his partner, and the teacher wrote in his letter that he felt this was an inappropriate image to have posted in our hallways. He continued, saying that the Pride Prom was a dangerous event because it sanctioned same-sex sexual activity, and that in doing so it would promote the spread of HIV. To reinforce his point, he attached statistics from an Internet site about the numbers of HIV infections and deaths from AIDS.

The other club sponsors and I also received copies of the letter, and when I read mine I was furious. It took me about 10 seconds to stomp to the principal's office to demand that he let that teacher know in no uncertain terms that Pride Prom would go on as scheduled and that his notions about HIV and AIDS—as well as LGBT youth—were riddled with dangerous misconceptions. The principal listened carefully to my concerns; we talked about the best approach to the teacher's homophobic response; and he incorporated my suggestions into the conversation he had with the letter-writer. Not one poster came down, and the dance was a roaring success.

Our GLBTSA was founded in 1992—the first to be formed in the Lincoln area. Since then it has evolved into a club that from year to year has 70-plus members. It has enabled LGBT and straight ally students to develop powerful voices that are heard all over the school. With projects ranging from bringing panels of the AIDS Project Names Quilt to school to working against the passage of the state law restricting marriage laws, students have been able to create a compelling understanding about what it means to be gay and what the civil rights of LGBT people are. As a result, no one who goes to our school believes for long that no one they know is lesbian or gay, and an expectation that their lesbian and gay friends be treated with respect soon becomes clear among most of the school's social groups.

As one of the cosponsors of the GLBTSA, I have had the opportunity to engage in amazing conversations with students as they develop the language and the insight they need to become leaders in the young queer movement. Having grown up in an era in which they were able to easily see real lesbians and gay men on TV, read readily available queer-themed novels, and study gay and lesbian history in school, they have been able to express their own orientations in ways that are much more authentic and healthy than my generation was allowed. Interestingly, they have been as much my role models as I have been theirs: They give me a sense of how to be adventurous and inquisitive, and I show them that lesbians do grow up and become vocal, productive community members.

Of course, those changes in the larger cultural climate in the last 40 years have played a part in creating a more comfortable personal

space for me as well. Today I find myself talking with my straight colleagues about queer TV programming and queer rights issues as well as about the joys of life with my partner, Mary, and our typical trials with being homeowners—conversations that make me feel accepted as an equal, and that were unimaginable when I started teaching in 1976. Just a couple of weeks ago, a straight teacher in my department, my friend Joanna, told us to watch a new show she loved, which features five gay men who improve a straight man's appearance and apartment. We took her advice, and *Queer Eye for the Straight Guy* quickly became one of our favorites.

This collegial acceptance has been crucial for me in sustaining my confidence as a teacher-leader. The backing of ally teachers was manifest this past year when a concern was raised about the use of the term "queer" in the title of our GLBTSA's newsletter, which the club members named "Queer Times." The newsletter is delivered via the mailboxes of teachers who are expected to distribute them to club members in their classes, and a couple of teachers peeked at the contents and discovered this title. They refused to distribute the newsletters and raised strong concerns about the term with our principal, who in turn brought the issue to the Principal's Advisory Council.

Another GLBTSA sponsor and I were invited to that meeting to address questions about the use of the term *queer,* and we explained how it has been transformed from its pejorative connotation to one that is inclusive of the wide range of diversity present within the LGBT community. We gave examples of ways the term is used by universities to name courses, by journalists in mainstream publications, and especially by those who are part of the young LGBT movement to express the limitless arena of self-expression they explore.

One teacher in the meeting suggested that students would not be able to discern the difference between derogatory and positive uses of *queer.* Two of my straight colleagues in the English department spoke up to say that they were confident that their standards for behavior would enable students to distinguish the difference, and they defended the club members' use of the word. That these individuals didn't defer to me or the other sponsor (a gay man) to address the concern meant not only that they had done their homework thinking about LGBT issues, but it also suggested that they saw these issues as ones about which they *should* educate themselves.

Even more crucial than the support of straight colleagues is the bonds I have created with other queer teachers. The strongest of these has been with my friend David who teaches at another high school in Lincoln and sponsors the GLBTSA there. The conversations we have about the pitfalls as well as rewards of being queer teachers help me create ways to perceive and approach my work as well as inspire my courage. But more important, they remind me that this is a journey that I undertake together with many other creative and loving people.

These valuable bonds have led me into yet another stage in my identity development, one in which my focus is on actively helping others better understand their responsibilities to LGBT students. So for the past few years David and I have been making presentations to other educators about the importance of making schools safe for LGBT students. Together we have assembled information that we use for these workshops, including facts about the status of LGBT youth in schools, legal responsibilities of educators to ensure a safe environment, and ways that classrooms and hallways can be made welcoming to LGBT students. We also tell pieces of our own stories: David recounts growing up with teasing and harassment from classmates; I tell about how the invisibility of LGBT people and issues during the late 1950s and '60s prevented me from understanding and expressing my sexual orientation.

The comments that workshop participants make during and after our presentations make me feel that the workshops we are leading are enabling other educators to recognize ways in which they can support LGBT students and parents—and to think hard about their personal beliefs and classroom practices. Additionally, I know it is good for me to keep telling my own stories about growing up lesbian and being a lesbian teacher,

because it reminds me of the ways my growth has been fostered.

It has been essential for me to have family members who support and push me. My longtime partner, Mary, continually weighs risks with me and urges me to embark on the paths that need to be traveled for the sake of LGBT kids, even if doing so could be somehow perilous. Our goddaughter is a young Latina college student with whom we talk at length about the racism and discrimination present in her experiences. Her unflinching ability to speak up to those who are biased toward her is a constant inspiration for me. Both women provide me with perspectives that help me to understand what I need to do and how I should do it, as well as always assuring me a safe and loving home in which I can revitalize my energies for this work.

When I think about the life I've been able to build as an openly lesbian teacher here in Lincoln, Nebraska—a city of only 250,000 people in the Midwest—I become amazed. But then I remind myself that it's all the result of intensive efforts—my own and those of valued friends and family—and that if it's possible to be an activist lesbian teacher here, it's possible all over this country. I just took that first step, and kept moving, and found that the rewards always overshadowed the risks.

ABOUT THE CONTRIBUTORS

Tarah Ausburn currently teaches high school English at South Pointe Charter High School in Phoenix, Arizona. She spends her free time dodging her students who have snuck into the city's queer nightlife, frolicking in an estrogen-laced household of four womyn and their cats, and creating slogans that could one day be another bumper sticker for her car.

Bonnie Beach was a teacher, coach, and department head at New Trier Township High School for 35 years. She is retired and—with her partner, Pam—does consultation work in educational diversity. They live in Estes Park, Colorado.

Bart Birdsall has been a middle school teacher for seven years. For five years he taught language arts and reading. Currently he is a media specialist. He lives with his partner, Tim Garren, in Tampa, Florida.

Clarence Brooks, after 18 years as a professional dancer, is enjoying his sixth year as a dance instructor at Bak Middle School of the Arts in West Palm Beach, Florida, where he teaches ballet, modern, and jazz dance to sixth-, seventh-, and eighth-graders.

Steven Click retired from teaching in 1997 and moved to the central coast of California to live with his architect partner, Dana. Steve is working on his artistic talents, volunteers in a few LGBTQ groups, and is sometimes a "guest teacher" (substitute) in the local schools.

Kathleen Crawford has taught both middle and high school in a variety of content areas for over 19 years, in public and Catholic schools. She is currently teaching math at Highland Middle School, with an eye on future writing, consulting, and training opportunities. Kat and her partner, Cindi, live in Louisville, Kentucky, with three teenagers, Ellie, Anna, and Joe.

Brian Davis has survived nine years as a middle school teacher. He enjoys blending language arts and social studies into a seamless whole for eighth graders in San Francisco, where he lives with his husband (the law be damned!) and two overweight cats. He is actively involved in Marriage Equality California (MECA) and urges his students to get involved in whatever issue they care about and to fight hard until they win.

Mike Fishback teaches language arts and social studies at the Park School of Baltimore and cosponsors its middle-school gay-straight alliance. He is a 2001 graduate of Yale University, where he majored in political science.

Joel M. Freedman (jmfreedman145@yahoo.com) currently coordinates drama and teaches English literature and composition classes at King/Drew Magnet High School in Los Angeles. A former actor and director, he has been married 20 years to Mike Player, the founder of the improv sketch comedy group the Gay Mafia.

Michael Fridgen, a graduate of the University of Minnesota, Duluth, is the music specialist at Pinecrest Elementary in Hastings, Minnesota. After school he operates a small studio of private voice and piano students.

Randall Furash-Stewart has been in love with teaching ever since his first job when he was 15 as a peer health educator at the Washington, DC nonprofit Advocates for Youth. He graduated from Hampshire College in Amherst, Massachusetts.

Sheridan Gold has been teaching at-risk youth for the last 12 years. She also presents workshops to educators about breaking teacher silence around homophobia. She recently married her partner of 26 years, Dianna; they live in Sonoma County, California.

Jan M. Goodman has worked as an educator for 30 years, most recently at King Middle School in Berkeley, California. In addition to teaching, she coordinates beginning and veteran teacher support for Berkeley Unified and works for the Berkeley Federation of Teachers. She is the founder of the Lesbian, Gay, Bisexual, Transgender, and Allied Issues in Education Network for the Association for Supervision and Curriculum Development (ASCD). Jan lives in Oakland, California with her partner, Maggie, and their two children, Ali and Niki.

Julia Haines, MM, CMT, educator, music therapist, multi-instrumentalist, and composer, has designed and implemented music therapy programs over the past 20 years. She works at Stratford Friends School, a Quaker school for students with learning differences, and shares her life with her beloved, Rosanne, in Philadelphia, Pennsylvania.

Mary Gay Hutcherson, LCSW, has been a school social worker for 18 years. She is currently retired and living with her partner, Yolanda Farnum, and their four Pomeranians in Chesterfield, Virginia, where they are activists for gay rights and social justice. She is the organizer of Virginia Rainbow Rivers and the editor of Richmond Lesbian Feminists Newsletter Online, and she was the leader of the Marriage Equality Action that received press coverage nationwide.

Chip James has been a school social worker for 15 years. He is a consultant for CANDLE (Community Awareness Network for a Drug-free Life and Environment) and the American Psychological Association, providing professional development on LGBTQ

youth issues. He is cofacilitator for TRUST, a psychoeducational support group for LGBTQ teens, and he has a psychotherapy practice in Nyack, New York, where he lives.

Elizabeth Katz teaches in the English department at Phillips Exeter Academy in Exeter, New Hampshire, where she lives in a dorm and is an adviser to the gay-straight alliance. She has been teaching for three years and has worked with GSAs since she was in high school.

Ayana Kee loves teaching, writing, and dancing. She received her BA from Duke University in 1994 and her MS from the University of Oregon in 1998. Ayana began teaching in elementary schools in 1994. In addition, she enjoys working with other teachers and is an instructor for education courses at a local college. She lives with her wife, Shanti Smalls, in Brooklyn, New York.

Judee King was a second-generation San Franciscan who credited her love of writing to growing up in this enchanting city of Golden Gates and cable cars that climb to the stars. Judee worked in the field of education for 26 years—doing everything from facilitating programs for at-risk teens to directing after-school programs—until she succumbed to breast cancer in 2004. She is survived by her loving girlfriend, Dani.

Ruth Kupfer has taught English and reading in public secondary schools for 28 years. She is also currently serving as a cosponsor of the Gay-Lesbian-Bisexual-Transgender-Straight Alliance, which is in its 12th year at her high school. Ruth and her partner, Mary, make their home in Lincoln, Nebraska.

Anafaith Lubliner has been a theater and music teacher for four years. She is also an an actress, writer, vocalist-songwriter, and wild improvisational singer who takes any word from the audience and creates a song on the spot. She lives with her gorgeous drummer-juggler partner, Katrine Spang-Hanssen, in San Francisco. For more information about her music and antics go to anafaith.com.

Cindy Lutenbacher has been a teacher for 18 years. She is currently an assistant professor of English at Morehouse College, where she has taught since 1990. She lives in Atlanta, Georgia, with her two daughters.

Patricia Lyons has been a teacher of religion and ethics for five years. She lives with her partner, Karen, in Alexandria, Virginia.

Jannette Manuel has been a teacher for four years. She is currently teaching family and consumer science courses in the Seattle School District in Seattle, Washington. She is originally from the Philippines and has lived in Seattle for 15 years.

Patricia Nicolari is currently an administrator for the Ansonia High School Alternative Education Program in Ansonia, Connecticut; previously she taught health and physical education in grades K–12 over the past 22 years. She has been on the GLSEN CT Board for the past six years and is actively involved in professional development for faculty in Connecticut schools regarding LGBT issues. She was named 2004 Teacher of the Year in Ansonia.

Richard Ognibene has been a teacher for 18 years. He currently teaches chemistry and physics for Fairport High School. He lives with his partner, Matt Fleig, in Rochester, New York.

Tamar Paull comes from a long line of wonderful teachers. She discovered the treasure of Community Prep School as a student teacher eight years ago and has been teaching English there ever since. She lives in Providence, Rhode Island.

Laura Persichilli has been teaching English for nine years, currently at Smithtown High School in Smithtown, New York. She is president of the Long Island Gay-Straight Educators Association and a member of the Long Island Coalition for Same-Sex Marriage. Laura lives in Riverhead, New York, with her partner.

ne teacher in 10

Bethany Petr has been a teacher for four years. She is a science and computer science teacher in Montgomery County. She lives with her partner, Emily, in Columbia, Maryland.

Irene "Toodie" Ray has taught in public schools for more than 20 years; she is also a codirector of Marshall University's site of the National Writing Project. She has two grown children, Ian and Morgan, and lives with her partner of 10 years, Donna.

Michael J. Record is a native of Fort Lauderdale. For six years, he has taught seventh-grade language arts for Broward County Public Schools, the nation's fifth-largest school system.

Gayle Roberts is an MTF transsexual who transitioned "on the job" in 1996. She was a high school physics and general science teacher for 33 years and a science department head for the past 12 years. She taught in Vancouver, Canada, and at the United World College of Southeast Asia in Singapore. She holds a B.Sc., an M.Sc., and a diploma in teaching. Gayle retired in June 2002 and now lives with her "new sister," Edith, and her mother-in-law just outside Vancouver.

Mike Russell has been a teacher for two years. His students have informed him that he is "so hype" for not dismissing them from the classroom before the scheduled time. In Philadelphia, Pennsylvania, he is currently working on a novel tentatively titled *Storming Arkansas,* is painting his walls to resemble the time tunnels in *Doctor Who,* and is vainly ordering his three spoiled Siamese cats to stop throwing up on the carpet. Against all known laws of the universe, his wonderful man, Andy Matthews, continues to put up with him.

Takashi Sugiyama is a Ph.D. candidate at Yokohama National University and a researcher and lecturer for Sei-Kyo-Kyo, the Council for Education and Study on Human Sexuality in Japan. He taught at a private high school in Saitama Prefecture and was the principle editor of a book titled *Homosexuality and Other Sexuality: How to Teach About Human Rights and Living Together* (Kodomo-no-mirai Publishing, 2002).

Malana Summers has been a middle-school instructor for 24 years. She currently teaches eighth-grade language arts and social science. She lives in Atwater, California, with her partner, Kim, and Tweety, a precocious cockatiel.

Steve Trujillo is a 27-year veteran of public school teaching and counseling. A native Californian, he has been writing for years of the incredible journey of California public education and its metamorphosis.

Roberto Wheaton has been teaching for 20 years and is currently teaching high school science in Southern California, working on his graduate degree, and running marathons.

Josephine Allison Wilson is in her third part-time year of her Ph.D. in gender at the London School of Economics (LSE) Gender Institute. Prior to that, she completed a Masters degree in (just to be original) gender and a Bachelors degree in psychology and philosophy at the LSE. She is also a dancer, drummer, and story-teller who performs regularly in London, where she lives.

Dan Woog is the openly gay head soccer coach at Staples High School in Westport, Connecticut. He is also a writer. His most recent book is *Jocks 2: Coming Out to Play.*

ABOUT THE EDITOR

Kevin Jennings is the founder and executive director of GLSEN (www.GLSEN.org), the Gay, Lesbian, and Straight Education Network, a national education organization working to make schools places where young people learn to value and respect everyone, regardless of sexual orientation or gender identity. The second edition of *One Teacher in Ten* is his fifth book. He lives in New York with his partner, Jeffrey Davis.